# Speak Swahili, Dammit!

## By James Penhaligon

*TPL*

*Trevelyan Publishers Ltd*

*Falmouth, Cornwall, UK*

*Trevelyanpublish@aol.com*

# Speak Swahili, Dammit!

## By James Penhaligon

First Published in hardcover and as an eBook by **United Writers Publications Ltd**, in August 2010.

Paperback published in December 2012 by **Trevelyan Publishers Ltd**, Falmouth, Cornwall

eBook published in January 2013 by **Trevelyan Publishers Ltd**, Falmouth, Cornwall

British Library Cataloguing in Publication Data: A catalogue record for this book is available from the British Library.

**Website http://www.jamespenhaligon.co.uk**

## Dedication

This book is dedicated to Ingrid, my dear wife and long-term companion, and to friends, relatives and East African compatriots, departed or still living, in Africa, and everywhere they have blown. May they, and we, always remember Africa in all its spectacular beauty, and return often to drink of her blessed waters.

### 'I could not put this book down!'

Beautifully written, takes reader on unique journey into childhood in Africa, the bush, eccentric characters, wild animals...heartbreak, excitement, humour, compassion. Characters extremely well portrayed... author's love of Africa and animals shines through...this book reminds me of Gerald Durrell's writing at its best. An excellent job of bringing a magical time in Africa back to life ... deserves its place amongst the top shelf of African memoirs.'

### 'Paradise lost'.

Wonderful story about life in East Africa, long gone but fondly remembered ... entertaining, funny, sad, a unique boyhood, filled with unusual experience and adventure. Deep love of *watu* (African people), and Africa shines through. Nostalgic.will appeal to armchair travellers and anyone interested in life beyond the village green. Highly recommended!'

### 'Don't read it on the train!'

Do not read on the train, because if you are like me you will laugh out loud and people will think you strange. Like all the other reviewers, I *really* enjoyed it. I have never been to Tanzania, but the author really brings it to life. Highly recommended.

### 'A Must for Africa-lovers!'

I laughed, I cried, I stayed up until 2 a.m. to finish this book. I hope there's a sequel in the pipeline. It's a fascinating narrative of life in 'darkest' Africa.

### 'Better than the reading-list!'

I was given a reading list by a travel company before a trip to Tanzania. This book wasn't on it, but is by far the most enjoyable book I have read...not just 'local memoir'...so well written, provides wonderful insight into the mind of a growing boy...happens to be set in Tanzania...opens window into race relations & culture of colonial and post-colonial period without preaching. Skillful weaving of Swahili makes me want to learn - it sounds so musical.

## *'Outstanding Book!'*

Just finished reading it, in tears.... An outstanding book, well-written...distinctive style, great cogency and economy of words. Thoroughly recommend to any reader, whether or not they know Africa or Tanganyika/Tanzania.

## *'Fall Out Of Chair!'*

This was a great read, and I learned a bit of Swahili vocabulary while reading it. There are some laugh-so-hard-I-fell-out-of-the-chair moments and the author's writing style has a great flow to it.

## *'A Rite Of Passage!'*

A book that everyone, of all ages, will enjoy. However you approach it, no matter your age or gender, you'll connect with the author.... Neither place nor time is important, it's the story! Well and seamlessly written... holds one's interest from the very beginning. I cannot wait for more from James Penhaligon's pen.

# Foreword

Memory is strange. It's said that there is no such thing as history – only biography, the way a person recalls an event. Others may remember the same thing differently. Fifty-odd years is a long time. Enough to forget and warp much. This book is based on my personal recall of events. Big things, like my father's death, the leopard that hitched a ride on the constabulary motorbike, my failure to conquer Mount Meru, or the events surrounding *Uhuru,* or independence for Tanganyika territory, are accurate enough. Smaller, day-to-day, happenings draw on memory with a varying level of accuracy, glued together by some necessary invention.

This book is as faithful as possible to the ambiance and mood of the places, times and people it portrays. It has not been passed through 'ye olde school of perfect English', for such a 'cleansing' would detract from, not improve the story. This is a memoir about a remote place and time in Africa, not an English county village. Characters of many nationalities, tribes and tongues, only a small number of who spoke English at all, people it. And, like anywhere else, even the English language developed its own local idiosyncrasies and slang.

People's names, and some of their details, have been altered to protect their privacy.

# *James Penhaligon*

James Penhaligon is a medical doctor and semi-retired consultant psychiatrist in Cornwall. Born to Cornish parents, and raised deep in the bush in Tanganyika, later to emerge as Tanzania, he remains a fluent Swahili speaker, and has never been able to escape his early influences, or the gaze it gave him on life. Despite having left Africa, and carving himself a successful career, James has always had a fascinating East African story waiting to be told, and now he has written it.

James lives with his wife and a rebellious Boxer, who denies he's a dog, in a house overlooking the sea in Falmouth, Cornwall. They travel to East Africa frequently.

# One

It's 1966. I'm fifteen and a half years old, and in just a few minutes we're leaving Geita forever. It's five in the morning. The sun won't come up till half past six. I'm sitting on my suitcase in the lounge of our wooden bungalow. I'm heartbroken. The Land Rover will be here soon, Fritz the old driver keen to get on the road. Gretchen is coming too, to see us off. I'm so much in love with her, I don't know how I'm going to say goodbye at the railway station in Mwanza. I'm sure I'll never see her again. I ache deep inside. Maybe I'll die of heartbreak. I rather hope so. It's pitch-dark outside, and the only sound is the creaking of crickets.

Mum and Becky are still packing, finding space to force last minute things into their luggage. I'm thinking how our lives were changed by this place, how we came to this point. Outside, an *njiwa*-bird or ring-necked African dove, makes a plaintiff call. They're supposed to be sleeping. I wonder if this one knows we're leaving. It's the end of a lifetime for me. It was here, always here, my life took wings.

Fleeting, unsequenced wisps of memory breach the void. Green and white striped tablecloth, black front door, warm cosy bed, disgusting kiss on cheek. Adults talking about you like you aren't there. Need to compete with big sister. Trivia. Bigger things take time. The world is a mystery; my place and role baffle me. Where am I? Who am I? Where am I going? Where do I come from? Answers don't come. Big sister Becky tells me I came from Mum's belly button. Mum says I'm her and Dad's son. Not sun in the sky, but a boy-child.

I will shine one day, bright as a star. Mum knows, because a fortune-teller told her when she was thirteen. At a fair in Johannesburg she went in the tent with the signs of the Zodiac. For sixpence, her fortune was told. The old lady studied her palm and said five things: You will marry a man from far away across the sea, but he will be already close. You will be separated by war. You will have five children. One will be a great disappointment. One will shine like a star. She married Dad, who came from far-away Cornwall, but was 'close' because he was her second cousin. They were separated for five years by war. She had five children. I'm the one who'll shine. She's sure. She doesn't say who's the disappointment.

I have entered the world at a time of great difficulty and struggle. It was the worst, but I'd like to hope the best, day of Mum and Dad's lives.

Many things end with fire. I start with it. Roaring flames consume our wooden house. Only blackened foundations, ash and half-burnt timbers remain. That's the night I'm born. 1951, the Zulu town Nongoma, capital of Kwazulu, later seat of King Zwelethini Zulu, and his uncle, Paramount Chief Gatsha Buthelezi, whose surname means Blunt. In 1951 it isn't as exalted. It has the only mission hospital for miles. We live nearby in Hluhluwe, or 'Who The Hell Are We', as Dad first reads it from the map. Now known for a game reserve. Mum and Dad run a concrete-block and corrugated-iron trading store. Sugar, soap, tea and cornmeal for tribal Zulus. Tragedy brought them here.

After rejoining the Royal Navy at the outbreak of war in 1939 as 'A-1 fit', Dad is discharged in January '46 with leaking heart valves, epilepsy, and health grading 'E'. He's thirty-seven, and we all pay a high price for his patriotism.

With intractable seizures, Dad languishes most of 1946 in Tara Epilepsy Hospital in Johannesburg. They're very poor. No income, except a five-pound a month Royal Navy 'disability' pension, and four children to support. Bertrand is sixteen, Fraser thirteen, Rose three, and Becky nearly two. When Mum goes to visit Dad in hospital she has to choose – raisin bun for tuppence, then walk three miles, or bus-fare and hunger. After discharge from hospital Dad is very weak. He's offered, and accepts, a job where Mum can help him. Hence 'Nongoma' is stated as place of birth in my passport.

That blazing night the family takes another dive over the poverty cliff. Almost nothing is left. Not Dad's Purdy shotgun, nor his hard-saved box of silver coins. Not the paltry savings of copper coins in a jar. This, when found, is a rounded lump of yellow metal. Nobody's clothes, not even those carefully collected for me, are saved.

One very special thing, Dad's *DSM*, or Distinguished Service

Medal, awarded to him for his gallantry during the sinking of *HMS Turtle* by the Luftwaffe in 1942, was kept in a metal box under a bed, and survives, with only one ridged edge slightly melted. It's a prized possession, one of only two things of Dad's I have. The other's his broken wind-up watch, which he wore on the sinking ship.

'Those that have little shall have less', Dad says with gallows humour. It's the bottom. Can't have less now.

How the fire starts they have no clue, though rumour circulates that Mr Stevens, the landlord, torches the building for insurance. He goes on to become a wealthy businessman. He advises Dad not to renew his home insurance, because the house and shop contents are 'covered'. They aren't. Everything is lost.

Neighbours accommodate us, clothes are donated, and sympathy and largesse from Zulu and European is heart-warming. There the saga of Zululand ends. After the fire, Dad travels to Johannesburg. Waiting for a haircut, he reads the daily Star newspaper. On the second page is a headline: 'Murder In The Bush'. How can he know those four words are a signpost to the rest of his, and all our, lives?

A Mrs Williams, wife of a Welsh gold miner in Geita, somewhere in Tanganyika Territory, has been shot.

The unfortunate lady and an African driver are taking a week's gold production from the mine to a town called Mwanza, eighty miles through tsetse-fly infested swamp and jungle.

The killer, a German miner called Stroessner, actually dines with the Williams family the previous evening. They drink into the early hours, apparently not unusual in the bush. He discusses the shopping trip MrsWilliams is making with the gold transport next day. Asks her to visit the travel agent in Mwanza for him. Get a flight timetable to Germany. Mwanza to Nairobi with East African Airways, Lufthansa onwards. He's already given notice, after yet another row with the mine manager.

Stroessner's got a drink problem, and often goes late to work. Now he's desperate to get out of this *scheisshaus* place. Jump before he's pushed. Leaving the Williams' home at four in the morning, he drives out on the bush-road to Mwanza, hides his Land Rover in a thicket ten miles from the mine, and uses a shovel to dig a shallow grave.

He's prepared a story for the driver. He's broken down, and his vehicle is round the corner. Please come and help. He checks his *Mauser* 0.22 bolt-action rifle, and lies in wait. With the gold from the transport Land Rover, he'll have a secure future. He'll work out how to get it to Germany.

The transport drives up, and he waves. They recognize him and stop. He asks the driver to accompany him, and then shoots him in the head. Mrs Williams is still in her seat when he shoots her through the windscreen.

Stroessner drags her body to the dead driver, and rolls both into the two-foot deep trench he's dug. He douses them in petrol, and throws a match. They burn only partially. Not enough petrol.

At five am, with the first rays of equatorial sun topping the tree line, he covers the charred corpses with a few inches of soil. He disguises the site with twigs and grass, drives the gold Land Rover off the road, and hides it. With six bars of gold bullion in his vehicle, he goes back to the mine. By six he's in bed. It's been a long night's work.

Stroessner feels unwell later that morning. Guilt, hangover, or both. He goes to the mine doctor, who admits him to the house, which serves as *Mzungu*, or European, hospital. British Tanganyika is racially segregated. Stroessner's stomach pains may be caused by a peptic ulcer, the doctor says. Common with heavy drinkers. Rest and antacids are prescribed.

Hours pass. The driver and MrsWilliams fail to return from Mwanza. Her husband is worried. He wants to drive out and look for his wife. The manager orders him not to. Can't have a bush-novice out there alone. 'Bloody lions, for Chrissakes!'

Next morning a radiotelephone call to Mwanza bank establishes that neither the couple, nor the gold, have arrived. A search party is recruited. Ten miles from the mine, they discover Land Rover tracks into a thicket. Here is the missing vehicle, minus occupants and gold, bullet hole in windscreen. It is unmistakably blood and brain tissue on the front seat. The search continues.

A shout is heard from a tracker. Half-cremated remains are found, driver's arm and lady's leg protruding grotesquely from the loose ground. The bodies have contracted, first through burning, then rigor mortis. That's why they come up.

In Geita suspicion turns on Stroessner. There are only three Land Rovers on the mine. One is the doomed transport, and one belongs to the mine manager, who's been up most of the night drinking in the company of several boozers. The third is Stroessner's. Sherlock Holmes isn't required. Before the manager and mine police-chief, Mr Higginson, reach Stroessner's hospital room, there's a sharp retort.

The room stinks of cordite. There's blood, shards of bone and gloops of dripping brain on the walls. The bastard's shot himself in the mouth. Beside his bed are a written confession, and a hand-drawn map of where he hid the gold. Buried on the golf course, next to the ninth fairway, not fifty yards from the club bar. They recover it.

What is Stroessner's point? Why kill two innocent people to steal gold you'll never even cash in? Nobody knows. Williams goes mad. He and the children are sent home to Wales. They need three police escorts to stop him jumping from the train to Dar es Salaam. He's never heard of in Tanganyika again.

Dad, like others reading the paper in August '51, is shocked by the murders. He doesn't know how intimately what happened on that lonely bush road in the hours before dawn will be connected to our futures, and his own death.

By a strange twist of fate, two months after reading that paper, Dad applies for a post advertised in a Durban paper. It's a ropeway manager's job on a mine in Tanganyika. He doesn't know where Geita is, and he's forgotten the bush murders. If appointed, he'll run a system of cable-borne carts transporting gold-bearing ore from a shaft in the bush to the mill at the mine. A medical examination before appointment isn't required. The interview in Johannesburg is brief. He's hired.

Meantime, against medical advice, Dad takes a short contract as relief skipper on a trawler in Walvis Bay, the South African enclave in South West Africa. We live in Swakopmund, a picturesque town on the sea a little north. Until 1916, when it became a UN mandate of South Africa, South West, or *Südwest*, was a German colony, and Swakopmund resembled a village on the Rhine. Dad goes fishing, and Mum looks after Becky, two, and me. Three months old, during a rare rainstorm, I am christened in the Lutheran Church.

There are scarcities in Swakop, and eggs are a luxury. A kind, over-involved and ancient Prussian landlady, who speaks only German, goes to great lengths to procure eggs *'für die kinder'*, for which Mum feels she must show exaggerated gratitude. Foreigners expect that. Becky, who can speak Zulu, is a favourite of the *Frau*, and within weeks also speaks German.

One day, frustrated by all the attention I'm attracting, Becky angrily declares that *gani*, Zulu for baby, hold him big – thinks he's important, and, for all she cares, can *hamba*, Zulu for go, *von wo ehr gekommen ist*, German for where he came from.

One day Mum takes us to a little park. There an elderly German war veteran is playing a violin. People give him coppers. He has a peg leg. Shot off in a long-forgotten campaign. 'Poor old man,' Mum says to Becky, on whom the comment has lasting effect.

That Sunday in church, at the end of a prayer, everyone says 'Amen'. Becky mumbles incoherently. When the next prayer ends Mum listens carefully. 'Pah-ole-man,' Becky shouts. 'Poor old man,' is what she means. She just can't forget him. Everyone laughs. It does sound a bit like Amen. Later, when asked why she feels so sorry for the fiddler, she explains 'one leg on, one leg off, and one stick-on.'

I'm three months old, born in one country, christened in another. It's an omen. Soon we'll be moving even further afield.

Dad is enthused about his new job. The mine belongs to the *Rhodesia-Katanga Gold Mining Company Limited*, registered head-office Chelsea, London. Because of Geita's remoteness, Dad escapes a medical examination, which he'll doubtless fail. Difficult enough recruiting staff to the bush without subjecting them to physicals. He works at Walvis until the end of December 1951.

We return briefly to Johannesburg, and then travel by train to Durban. There we embark the liner *Rhodesia Castle* for the ten-day voyage north up the Indian Ocean to Dar-es-Salaam. Here we board the locomotive-drawn train to Mwanza on Lake Victoria.

We're going to Geita. We know little about it, except it's deep in the bush. Won't be that bad, Dad assures Mum. Rent-free house, good wages. Soon they'll save enough to go home to

Cornwall, buy the small farm Dad's always dreamed of. At long last their luck is changing.

'Isn't Geita the place you told me about, the one in the paper, where that poor Welsh lady and her driver were murdered?' Mum asks.

'Scrub me with barnacles,' Dad exclaims, 'you're absolutely right!' He has a wealth of lovely naval expressions. Mum feels a surge of foreboding. Better not tell him. He's so desperate to improve our lot.

Years later Mum recalls the rigours of the first journey to Geita, and how little they knew. In the local Sukuma dialect the place-name means 'Valley of Death'. Ominous.

There's only one industry in a region of thousands of square miles: the mine. Fewer than two percent of the African population in the district work for money. Most live from subsistence farming, fishing and hunting. Others are limited to being *wa-omba*, or those who beg, because they are *wasikini*, poor people.

Geita is eighty miles southwest of the ramshackle and torpid lakeside town of Mwanza, on the hintermost end of the railway line from the Indian Ocean.

The train journey begins at Dar es Salaam. Mum and Dad have bottom bunks, Becky and me top ones. The story of the journey becomes a family legend. Dad is amused that the Africans call the locomotive *gari-moshi*, smoking car. The narrow-gauge line heads north and west, away from the coast, into wild, hot country.

For two days and nights it struggles and wheezes over ravines, across plains, up forested hills, through valleys of stark aridness, and surprising oasis-like patches of verdant green.

Stops are few, stations rudimentary. Wild animals abound, great herds of elephants loping lazily across the plains, prides of recumbent lions suspiciously eyeing the train, eland and wildebeest grazing beside small pools, endlessly and futilely flicking ears and tails at obstinate black flies.

Hippos show dark snouts and bulging eyes above fetid water in muddy places. Repetitive scenes and unremitting heat. Occasional signs of humanity. Sudden clearings appear, clustered with *makuti*-thatched mud huts. Small children run naked, laughing and waving, scrawny chickens scratch dusty ground, elders sit impassively, wildebeest-tail fly-whisks in hand. They've seen the *gari-moshi* many times.

The engine struggles on, coughing and groaning uphill, wheezing over and over in rhythm, but ever more slowly, *'I think I can, I think I can'*, exuberant going down, *'I knew I could, I said I could.'* Mean speed is thirty miles an hour. Walking pace approaching hill summits, galloping down.

Bigger stations like Dodoma materialise out of the shimmering heat. Sweat-streaked Europeans appear as pale ghosts among the *watu*. Some command porters in skins and rags. Others wave tiredly at their compatriots in the train. It's appallingly hot.

Forty-eight hours from Dar the locomotive, tiredly drawing six carriages, trundles across the last stretch to Lake Victoria. Proximity to the lake is declared in stunning geology. Great smooth, cheese-coloured boulders grow like outlandish mushrooms, some big as a car, others taller than a house. After so long in the super-heated dryness of the interior, nearness to a great expanse of cool water brings welcome movements of air, carrying exotic perfume. Heady essences of drying fish, cool water, rotting lilies and water-hyacinth, spices, wood smoke, hemp, mangoes and guava are all on the cooling breeze greeting the train.

There's ten minutes of chaos at Mwanza station, when overheated passengers trundle luggage and greet suntanned, sweating, strangers. To reach Geita there's a bone-crushing ride in a Land Rover to come. Only eighty miles from town, but it will take over five hours.

The African driver is waiting at the station. He's tall, slim and handsome, late middle aged and smartly dressed in a khaki safari suit. He has a neatly trimmed pencil-line moustache. Dad spots him. 'Safari suit and thin moustache,' the assistant manager wrote in his telegram. This driver is to become a source of mystique and humour. He doesn't fit any pattern – he's unique.

'Hello, I am Fritz,' he says, detaching himself from a knot of people. 'You are ze family Penhaligon, yes?' Mum and Dad are amazed. This black man speaks English with a strong *German* accent. There will be time to find out why. Right now it's just good to be off the sweltering train, though it's hot enough here too. We've been travelling a long time. Becky's complaining, and I've got a temperature. Time to get to Geita.

In 1951, few roads in Mwanza are tarred, and the others are only barely graded within the town boundaries. As the road curves beyond the ramshackle outer-shops, it becomes a neglected, forgotten route. Potholes are everywhere, some three feet wide. We haven't seen anything as rough as this in Zululand or South West Africa. Elephant grass and thorn bushes grow in the middle. The bush closes in. On the best stretches our maximum speed is a bone-jarring thirty-five miles an hour, which means not changing beyond third gear. Where the potholes are bigger or deeper, or where the middle growth exceeds three feet, we barely make twenty. Washaways from floods have cut gulleys or *dongas*. The driver slows to five miles an hour and engages four wheel drive.

Like an old traction engine, the Land Rover judders and growls, and crabs its way obliquely, sometimes side-on, down a steep slope, across an uneven bottom, and up again.

Fifteen hard miles later we reach a lagoon of Lake Victoria. Rotting wooden jetty, a queue of vehicles waiting for the diesel-engined ferry. When the rusting relic isn't broken down, it plies across in daylight hours a dozen times. The load limit is two five-ton lorries and five cars, or ten cars if there are no lorries. There are four lorries in front, so we wait. Eventually we'll know the routine. We'll learn to rise early for Mwanza, to beat the hauliers. That, or wait for the second or third crossing. No fun, sitting for hours by that sweltering, fetid bank.

Loading and offloading, the laconic crew is singularly unrushed. We learn a new word. *Badaai* means 'later', but Dad says it hasn't quite the same sense of urgency as *manana* in Spanish, or *dreckly* in Cornwall. It takes half an hour to cross. On the other side, Mum sees a five-foot snake swimming lazily between the jetty piers. Fritz says it's a water cobra.

Now the road is worse. We plunge into a tunnel of wild green, along a narrow track hacked from invading bush. The sky disappears above the tree canopy. Insects buzz, birds screech, the Land Rover snarls, down, up, round, precariously listing to left, right, front or back.

Ten miles, and an hour from the ferry, we reach the 'Tsetse belt'. Tsetses can read, Dad says. There's a painted wooden sign nailed to a tree beside the road. It declares:

YOU ARE ENTERING TSETSE BELT. CLOSE
WINDOWS.
HM GOVERNMENT, TANGANYIKA TERRITORY.

The windows are hurriedly closed. Mum covers my face. The temperature soars. The tsetses attack. Fat, angry flies, four times bigger than a housefly. Always angry. One gets in, mocking the closed windows. It bites Dad, and the pain is worse than a bee-sting. His cheek swells an angry red. We'll grow to loathe these demon-flies.

Four miles of unventilated heat later, a sign says:

YOU ARE LEAVING TSETSE BELT. OPEN WINDOWS.
HM GOVERNMENT, TANGANYIKA TERRITORY.

We open them, and receive a fresh-air asphyxiation-reversal. These 'educated' tsetses know when to call off the assault. They are confined to narrow strips. A 'riverine' species, they live close to water, trees and shade. They can't tolerate direct sunshine, are unable to cross open ground. This is used to control them in some parts. Infested areas are cut into parcels by removing vegetation. It restricts them to smaller and smaller zones, disrupting breeding and feeding. In some areas it achieves extinction of the pest. In 1951, and for many years after, this isn't done near Geita.

'Your accent,' Dad says to Fritz, 'is it German?'

'Ja, yes, Ich *wahr*, I mean I *vos*, in der *Schutztruppe* before.' This explains everything. Dad hasn't a clue what the *Schutztruppe* is. Sounds like shooting and troops, or doing something unpleasant on troops. He forces himself not to laugh. Fritz is an earnest and serious man.

'When?' Dad asks.

'In der vore.' Fritz isn't exactly talkative. The war, so he was a soldier.

'Last war?' Dad says.

'Nein, der forst vun.' I will learn a great deal about this war. World War I in Tanganyika, the British led by a succession of incompetent generals, the Germans by the legendary *Oberstleutnant*, or Lieutenant-Colonel, later *Generalmajor*, Paul von Lettow Vorbeck. Three and a half decades after its end, the legacy of the campaign still lies heavily on the country, despite a second world war having come and gone. By Fritz's tone it's clear the conversation is ended. The ex *Schutztruppe askari* is no small-talk man.

More miles and hours we later we emerge from the bush onto a huge plain fringed by rock-strewn hills, on whose slopes gnarled dwarf trees desperately cling. Mum says it's lunar. On the flat ground, herbivores graze on sparse, dry grass, and drink from small, muddy, watercourses. When the monsoon floods erupt, they overflow and merge, and half the plain turns to chocolate-mousse. In the dry season the water evaporates, leaving vast expanses of slate-coloured sludge. In bad years even that dries to dust, and blows away on the hot, *djinn*-driven wind.

The local *watu* say evil *djinns* appear as dust devils, Fritz informs Dad, breaking his silence. First thing he's said in an hour. Judging by appearance, this is no place to spend a night. Skulls and bones of wildebeest, kudu, Thomson's gazelle and eland litter the landscape. It's a gigantic open-air ossuary.

This is the gateway to Geita. What will we find out here, cut off from civilisation? The open space narrows, the trees close in again, and then the Rover begins to painfully climb a very steep hill. When we finally reach the brow, we're overlooking Geita mine to the west.

# Two

While Becky and I sleep, Mum and Dad are hot, eaten alive by *dudus*, a Swahili word for any insect, and they're exhausted. With great relief they collapse into bed. In the morning, after the sleep of exhaustion, they emerge into glaring sunshine to survey their new home and surroundings. This will be the crucible of all our futures.

Compound Hill has breathtaking panoramic views of the dense-green forested valley, with small hillocks rising in the medium distance, and faraway blue peaks piercing the horizon. So much for nature. Man is here. The mineshaft bores unsentimentally into the hillside. Like in a movie, the background sets the scene, but actors inhabit the foreground.

The 'camp', or residential area, has three parallel roads running downhill, a quarter mile apart, joining 'Top' and 'Bottom' roads. Top Road connects the camp to the mine workings, mill, head office, mine store and engineering and carpentry works. It terminates at Barrat Stores, the corrugated wood-and-iron, Indian-run, and only, shop. The other way leads to large wooden houses for the chief engineer, doctor, chief assayer, and, finally, most exalted, the general manager, whose house is at the end, and biggest of all.

Bottom Road peters out into a footpath ending in dense bush at one end, and Lone Cone Club at the other. The club is named for the shape of the hill behind. An upside-down, thin, symmetrical ice-cream cone, with arid, treeless sides, so steep I never hear of anyone ever climbing it.

From the club the road runs a quarter of a mile to a tiny, church-like building all on its own. The mortuary. It continues past the church, the kindergarten school, and the 'African' hospital. From there it becomes the route to the *'boma'*, four miles away. Here is located the nearest government police station, or *Boma*, in the middle of a mud-hut village. This encroaches onto *Boma Duka*, a dozen Indian shops crowded into a long concrete and corrugated iron building, with a shared verandah piled high with merchandise. This place will have magical and magnetic power over Becky and I.

The roads connecting Top and Bottom road are half a mile

long, with ten widely spaced wooden houses either side. The houses grow sequentially bigger up the hill, the whole camp top-heavy.

All Geita roads are stone and dirt, and have to be frequently graded by a pre-war bulldozer, when they can get it to start. To prevent washaway by tropical rain deluge during the monsoons, there are three-foot deep ditches on the sides. Where roads cross, steel pipes the width of forty-four gallon oildrums carry floodwater under the intersections. Usually these are dry, and frequently the chosen abode of pythons, which like shade, but, it's said, they really *can* swim when push comes to flood.

Our house is at the base of the hill. We're minor miners, Dad says. There are two bedrooms, so Becky and I share. It's a pretty little wooden place, raised on four foot stilts because of monsoon *gharikas* or floods, and, more importantly, to prevent termites eating it. These voracious little white ants have no preference when it comes to food. The stilts are soaked and regularly repainted with tar-like insecticide, so pungently effective that even termites can't leg, or stomach, the climb.

The houses have electricity from a wood-burning generator at the workshop. Water comes from a concrete reservoir near the summit of Compound Hill. This is fed by a pipeline running four miles from a dam, which in turn takes water from Lake Victoria, ten miles further away.

We don't need heating. Water for bathing is warmed in forty-four gallon diesel drums on concrete bases, under which fires are lit in the early evening. There's only tepid water by day, and it can't be drunk from the tap. It isn't only luke-warm, but carries bilharzia, typhoid, cholera and countless nasties. It has to be boiled, passed through a slow ceramic filter, then bottled and cooled in the fridge.

Cooking is done in cast-iron *Belling* wood stoves, black and identical in all the houses. Like much of the equipment, they were bought and shipped as a job lot from England in 1926.

Windows are left open. Wire mesh fly screens keep insects out. Geita is a torpid, sweltering place. Its so bereft of man-made sound that the buzzing of bees or the fluttering moth wings are a clamour. Everywhere teems with insects, and there's a constant background of scratching, fluttering, and crawling.

For long minutes the throaty cooing call of the *njiwa* bird permeates the bush. In the cool of evening other noises begin. Frogs croak in throaty chorus in hidden pools, crickets screech in rising crescendo, wild dogs bark. Sometimes the insane giggles of a *fisi* or hyena, or the thunderous roar of a prowling lion, drowns out other sound.

We arrive in Geita a day before I'm six months old. My memory is blank, but won't be for long. Though lost to recollection, these early months and years will shape me deeply, and I shall never escape their influence.

Dad takes up managing the ropeway. He presides over a double system of steel-wire cables which run, supported on pylons, to and from the mine in Geita, and a series of mine shafts seventeen miles away at Ridge Eight, known to us as 'Rijate'. It's impressive. Every two hundred yards the cables are supported on huge steel tripods, which stride away like alien beacons into the heat-shimmered distance. On those cables, hanging on lop-sided arms, run car-sized, rusty red 'buckets'.

The outlandish contraptions trundle squeakily on rusty bearings in close Indian-file between their distant destination and the tipping station, where labourers wait to turn them over and discharge ore. From there a busy smoke-belching front-loader takes huge bites to the mill for crushing.

Becky is two and a half when she first sees the system. 'Swing-ang, swing-ang, daddy bucket, daddy bucket,' she yells in awe and delight. Any suspended thing becomes 'swing-ang', which Dad discovers when Becky spots him naked in the bathroom.

They give Dad a Land Rover. It's old and rattly in 1951, but she seizes my young heart. She's an open olive-green, canvas-topped, short-wheelbase petrol version, registered MZ 202, for Mwanza. The old girl will be around for the next fifteen years.

The *waSukuma* and *waGallua* people in Geita are fascinating. Apart from those working for the mine, who have shabby and disintegrating European clothes, both male and female go topless, and generally wear short loincloths, or *kanzus*, round their waists.

Both tribes have a love of bodily adornment, including many copper and elephant-hair bangles and anklets, and tribal scarring on the face. Many have pierced ears, through which they insert larger and larger, heavier and heavier, devices, in Geita graduating to shiny store-bought bronze or silver coloured padlocks, a European addition to their culture, to stretch their earlobes as long as two feet. The Galluas of both sexes, too, like to knock out their front teeth, considering the large gap *maridadi*, or pretty, and 'better for kissing'.

Mum laughs about Dad's 'fresh Geita milk'. He craves a glass of fresh milk, is fed-up with canned and powdered imitations. In sign language, he explains what he wants to a passing Gallua. That it's a liquid, he demonstrates by running the outside tap. That it's white, he shows by pointing at the white-painted house-wall. At last the bemused tribesman beams. An hour later he returns with a bucket of frothy white milk. Dad's delighted, and pays him twenty cents. It's so nice, he thinks, to have milk straight from a cow, even if the bearer doesn't look too hygienic. Heating will take care of that.

Mum boils the milk on the range cooker. She lets it cool, and then pours him a big glass. He drinks greedily. It tastes shockingly unpleasant. He's drunk half when he begins to feel queasy. He's violently sick. The 'milk' is powdered *mahogo*, or cassava, mixed with water. The tribesman hasn't been dishonest. The *Mzungu* asked for white liquid, and that's what he brought.

When are my own memories first formed? I can't remember. Some 'early' recall has to be from later recount, confused with memory. Unable to discriminate between experience and legend, I 'remember' some things I never experience. With time, direct and vicariously gained memories are stored together, blend into a continuum.

In humans and sentient animals, vicarious, or second-hand, learning and memory serve a vital evolutionary purpose. Without it, each individual would have to personally take every possible risk, know no danger not directly experienced. Vicarious learning, plus individual experience, is education. It starts at birth. It's difficult to separate some of my direct and indirect memories, but at least the stage is fixed. Geita doesn't change, our house remains the same, and Dad only ever works on the ropeway. If I fail to remember at two, there will be plenty of time to learn.

I have one clear memory from very early. The *bundi msitu* bird, or African forest-owl, always is. Geita wouldn't be Geita without it. Its sonorous, haunted call comes at night from where the bush encroaches our garden. I never find where it hides, though it calls to me, just me, every time I'm alone in the darkness of my bedroom. It's a message I try to understand. What is it? Pleading, or warning? Owls don't go 'tu-whit-tu-whoo'. It's neither a superficial sound, nor easily imitated. It resonates a deep and mystical mood, of ancient wisdom in the wild, and the eternal soul of the bush. I feel it in my heart and stomach, and even in my bones.

Sometimes, after the *bundi-msitu* has gone to sleep, from much further away, much, much further, comes that spine-chilling, half-giggling, almost human, sometimes jolly, sometimes alarmed, maniacal, racket from those creatures I'll get to know, hate, love, fear and dread, the *fisi*, or hyena.

Dad drives about in rattly old MZ 202, fixing or doing all day in the blazing bush. We're close to the equator. Mum works as a clerk in the mine store, where every nut, bolt, fan belt or cog for running the enterprise is ordered, kept, recorded and issued.

My older brothers, who have been in boarding school in South Africa, follow us to Geita three months later. They fly, landing on the way in Southern and Northern Rhodesia, then Nairobi in Kenya, from where they get a small charter-plane to Geita. Much quicker than our journey. The eldest, Bertrand, turns sixteen within weeks, and leaves for England to join the Royal Navy. Fraser, fourteen, will follow, but has to wait two years.

Fraser has informal school lessons from Mr Hessler, Mum's colleague at the mine store who, like Dr Weiss, is a German-Jewish survivor of Auschwitz. It's a strange concept: two survivors from Auschwitz having a chat, as one does. 'Tell you what,' one says, 'here's a plan - why don't we bugger off and live deep in the snake-infested, disease-ridden, sweltering bush in Tanganyika?'

There's someone else I should mention. My sister Rose is five, left behind in an institution in Cape Town. 'Deaf, dumb and mentally retarded'. I don't know she exists 'till I'm twelve.

One day Dad and Fraser come home with a living nightmare

for Mum. She retells it for years.

Dad drives to Nungwe bay, fifteen miles away, Fraser and a friend riding on the open back. They have shotguns for wild ducks. There aren't any, though the Nungwe sky is often crowded with them.

On the way back Fraser sees a huge male lion come out the bush behind the Land Rover. Dad hasn't seen him. *Simba* keeps pace behind, the Rover doing less than twenty on the bumpy road. Fraser tries to alert Dad. He shouts, yells, and beats on the cab-roof. The engine's too loud. *Simba's* gaining. Fraser bangs frantically on the roof. Dad laughs. Boys will be boys. Anything to make them happy.

The road's a little easier. Dad puts his foot down. The Land Rover speeds up. So does *Simba*. He breaks into what looks a gentle lope. The apparent slowness of his stride is deceptive. The gap closes. There's something about the hunch of his shoulders and angle of his head. He's just five yards away, preparing to spring. *Simba* wants Fraser and his friend for lunch.

Fraser's shotgun is loaded in case he sees wild duck on the way. Birdshot. He can see deep into the open pink cavity of *Simba's* mouth. He senses his moist, warm breath. Suddenly Dad sees the danger in his mirror. He jabs the accelerator to the floor. The Rover surges, Fraser falls against the cab-roof, and the shotgun goes off. *Simba's* face is peppered with birdshot. He swerves into the bush in blinded agony. The Rover plunges on, the lion is gone.

Fraser fervently tries to convince himself the shot was accidental. That reflex, not thought, pulled the trigger. But he saw the shot hit the lion's eyes. He must have been blinded. What will happen to him? 'You had no choice,' Dad says, 'him or you.' For the rest of his life Fraser worries about the poor *Simba's* eyes. Was he completely blinded? Make him helpless prey for that most vicious of enemies, *fisi* the hyena.

Mum tries not to think what may have happened, and tightens her control over Becky, who's prone to wander off, alone. This place is full of danger. Wild animals, poisonous snakes, scorpions and, for all Mum knows, cannibals.

Becky and I are given into the daytime care of a strictly instructed *ayah*. These are wives, girlfriends and daughters of

African mineworkers, who supplement income by caring for European, Indian and Chinese children. The daily ritual is to be collected by *ayah* at seven am, and taken to a central point.

There are two big trees standing in a clearing half a mile from the camp, where several *ayahs* congregate to while away the heat of day. One is a giant acacia, the other the 'mother and father of a baobab', as the mine manager remarks. Baobabs really do look as if they're growing upside-down. The branches are like enormous inverted roots.

The acacia provides welcome shade. I'm carried there strapped onto my *ayah*'s back with a blanket, African style. Becky, two years older, walks, and never has that experience. We're home by six, exhausted and ready for bed.

Of my early playmates, Lutoli is the closest. Like me, he was born in '51, though nobody recorded the day or month. His father was killed before he was born, trying to defend a goat from a marauding lion. His mother lives on a *shamba*, or farm, between Geita and *Boma Duka*, and augments her income as *ayah* for a Singa-Singa family. Singa-Singa is what the *watu* call all Sikhs. When very young I think they are performers, who serenade for a living. Turban must be stage-costume. Never hear one perform.

This Singa-Singa family is nervous, and don't allow the *ayah* to take their child outdoors. Each morning on the way to work his mother leaves Lutoli at a cousin's shack. This extraordinarily fat lady brings him to the upside-down baobab tree to commune with other *ayahs*. One is mine, Amina, pronounced *Ah-mean-ah*. I meet Lutoli. By the time we can walk, run and talk we're inseparable.

Mum and Dad make friends easily in Geita. One day they're having a 'sundowner' with a surveyor. His name is Andy Sparks, and he's in Geita on short-term contract. Dad gets on with him, because he was also in the navy, which he refers to as 'the Andrew'. Mum finds that amusing. The conversation, which follows, is one they never forget.

'Nice house,' Mum says.

'Yeah, nice,' he replies, 'but they won't give it to anyone to live full-time.'

'Why not?' Dad asks.

'The wives.'

'The wives?' Mum asks, intrigued.

'Too spooky.'

'What?'

'They say it's too spooky.'

'Why do they say that?' Mum asks.

'You don't know? I've only been here a month, and I know.'

'Know what?'

'Dick, you're sitting in Stroessner's chair,' says Andy.

'What?' says Mum.

'D'you mean. . ?' says Dad.

'This is the Williams' house. You're sitting in the chair bloody Stroessner sat in the night he killed Mrs Williams and the driver. Surely you know the story?'

Read about it,' Dad says. He examines the chair. It's an ordinary wooden lounging chair with big cushions. Same as in our house. They're *maninga* wood, made by the Chinese carpenters. Rough, but adequate. He remembers. Stroessner sat here, right here. He was drinking with his intended victim and her husband, while the children slept down the passage. All the time he knew, was making plans: soon he'd be lying in wait for his hostess on the lonely road to Mwanza. How could anyone be so cold blooded? It's a strange feeling. Mum has pins and needles all over. They could at least have got rid of the chair.

'Horrible,' Mum says.

'Awful, wasn't it?' Andy Sparks says.

'Cruel,' Mum says.

Dad thinks about poor Mrs Williams. One night he has a terrible nightmare. He's walking down a dirt road, all overhung with dense vegetation. There's a Land Rover up ahead, he can just see the back end – it's parked half-in, half-out the bush. The engine's running. He's also running, because he knows someone's going to be killed. He's going to be too late, no matter how fast he runs.

He's approaching the Land Rover. Getting very close. His breathing is laboured, because he's come a long way. A shot rings out, an ear-piercing whiplash in the eerie silence before dawn. He's too late. He wakes up shivering.

Mum's superstitious. Poor Mrs Williams won't go away. First

Dad reads about her. Then we come here, where it happened. Then the house, the chair. . . Now Dad has a nightmare.

'We should visit her grave,' Mum says at breakfast.

'And?'

'Put some flowers there, pay our respects. . .'

'But we didn't know her,' Dad says.

'Just let's do it,' Mum says. 'Perhaps she's a soul in torment. Maybe paying our respects will help to give her peace.'

'Okay,' says Dad, 'I know when I'm beaten.'

Two days later Mum picks a huge bunch of flowers in the garden. The place is a horticulturalist's dream. Bougainvillea, hibiscus, golden shower, azaleas, all grow wild. A riot of colour. Dad comes home half an hour early. They drive out along Bottom Road, past the African hospital, onto the *boma* Road, then off on a spur to Samina, where the cemetery is. It's seventeen hot, bumpy, pot-holed miles, with midges and tsetse flies for company. Must be a stream nearby, Dad says.

They're standing by the grave. It's only been eight months, but already the jungle's reclaiming it. There are small bushes and creepers growing on the turned soil, and the wooden cross is already half-eaten by termites. Their little transparent bodies scuttle about in the holes they've made. A stone's been ordered months ago. Mrs Williams' parents sent money from Wales. They're slow workers at *Lakeside Monumental Masons* in Mwanza. Somewhere invisibly near at hand an *njiwa*-bird makes a plaintiff cry. Hoo,who-hoo. It's spooky here, even in daylight.

Mum feels a cold shiver down her back. Mrs Williams wasn't ready to die, she tells Dad. 'Superstitious nonsense,' Dad says. They put the flowers in a vase, leave it on the grave.

'Where did they bury the poor driver?' Mum asks.

'His family buried his body on their farm,' Dad says.

When a child learns to speak it's usually with one person, its mother. Only later, as fathers testify, does the child talk to others. I am too young for that. And, for most waking hours, I'm with people who speak only Swahili. Because there are two speechless babies, the *ayahs* are at pains to teach us. My first words are in Swahili, which becomes my natural, if not 'native', tongue. Being constantly with Lutoli polishes my fluency. Soon we're talking continually, to the great delight of the fawning *ayahs.*

Swahili is a colourful and beautiful language. Its name is derived from the Arabic word *'sawahil'*, or 'coastal plane'. It's the *lingua franca* of the coast, but the slave, and other, trade carried it far in to the hinterland, to the peoples of Lake Victoria, and throughout the regions of Tanganyika, Uganda, Rwanda, Burundi, Kenya, Congo, Nyasaland, and the north of Mozambique.

My Swahili germinates and puts down roots. It doesn't remotely resemble the crude 'Kitchen Swahili' of the Europeans, or *Wazungu*. Judging by the *ayahs'* glee when I use rude words and phrases, the ladies are pathologically crude. I don't mind. It's funny. By two and a half I am swearing profusely. It causes hilarity in the *ayahs* and their menfolk, but degrees of confused anger among the *Wazungu*, depending how much they cotton on. I gain the crudest, rudest and most colourful of invectives.

Swahili holds a special premium for vulgarity. I discover there's no shame in saying things. What *is* shameful is bad actions, cruelty, meanness, plotting, snubbing guests, or being unpleasant on footpaths. Kindness, hospitality, generosity and reliability are esteemed. Coarse language doesn't debase social position or reduce affection. *Au contraire*, humour is the greatest delight, the funniest tales or jokes are filthy, the dirtiest speakers most esteemed.

Everyone competes in ribaldry. Profound and specific indelicacy is used with laughing abandon. Coarse and expletive repartee and joust is endemic. The *watu,* or people, speak unadulterated truth. If asked what he or she is thinking, out comes every lewd and bawdy thought, pride and honour intact. Not even the young are spared broadsides of profanity. There's no discrimination by age.

To enliven matters, Swahili evolved slowly, borrowing from Arabic during the slave trade, German, English, Portuguese and many 'local' languages, including Luo and Kikuyu from Kenya, Buganda from Uganda, Masai, Gallua, wa-Arusha, Nyamwezi, Chagga, Haya, Nyakyusa, and many others in Tanganyika, and, especially around Geita, the Sukuma language. The list is not exhaustive. There results from this a collection of swearwords and insults surpassing in quality all competition by an order of magnitude. The *watu* enjoy and celebrate this achievement gaily, excitedly, and with not a nebula of guilt or self-reproach.

I engage in colourful swearing all day, with phrases and words, which would, if she understood, cause Mum to hyperventilate. My contribution to discourse earns me a reputation among the *watu* as like-minded, and the foulest-mouthed three-year-old they know. They adore me, and delight to hear me use my slick vocabulary against *Wazungu* masters, who, unaware they are being abused, titter politely to hear a small white boy talk 'like a native.'

'You have the face of a *samaki*,' I say in Swahili to Mum's lady guest, who's drinking tea in the garden. Fish-face. I'm smiling angelically, because it's my script. The *Mzungu* smiles back. My audience, the *watu*, giggles helplessly.

'Jimmy's so fluent,' the *Mzungu* lady says to Mum. I know it's a compliment, even if I don't follow the English.

'*Mkundu yako na nuka,*' I say. Your anus stinks. I put on a serious expression. You wouldn't swear looking serious. The *watu* convulse, trying but failing to keep straight faces. The *Mzungu* lady smiles again. A little strained now. She senses, but is not sure, she is being grievously insulted by a three-year-old.

'Although I can't say why,' she confides in Mum, 'I sometimes feel Jimmy doesn't like me.'

'I'm sure you're wrong,' Mum says, but she looks worried. The *Mzungu* hastens to change the subject.

'It's amazing how well he speaks African.' Mum nods. She's blushing red. She's concluded I'm saying unsavoury things, but she doesn't know what.

I learn to spit. Not artless de-gobbing. This is high science. Not just an expulsive ejecting sound with pursed lips and tongue. I draw my lips back in a forced grimace, make a sucking 'tsch' against my upper front teeth. Through an impossible-to-explain mechanism, a drop of saliva ejects at high velocity. With time, my accuracy increases. Most *watu* can hit a moving fly at six paces. Soon I'm pretty sharp myself.

I learn to blow my nose Swahili-style. This is a public act and, if you're accomplished, a spectator sport. One nostril is closed with a thumb. The head is projected slightly forward. Big blow out open nostril, ejecting *makamasi*, or snot. Doing well means making distance. Repeat other side. Wipe fingers on *majani*, grass. I'm getting good at this.

'Handkerchief,' Mum says. Won't a chief be upset?

Dad tells me my origin. 'We were sitting here having a drink in the early evening, and saw a gang of monkeys on they-there hill,' he says in his Cornish way.

*'Fanya nini?'* I ask. What you do?

'Well, Mummy wanted another baby, and we didn't have one, so. . .'

'Stop it Daddy,' Mum says, but he just grins.

'I took my big knife. I like *Nyanis*, monkeys, so I ran up the hill and cornered one in front of a big tree.'

*'Fanya nini?'* I ask again. What you do? Mum clicks her tongue. She knows what Dad's going to say. Said the same to Bertrand in Transvaal, years ago.

'I caught him, cut off his tail, and brought him home. Mummy shaved him for me.' Mum smiles. What can she do?

'And that shaved monkey, Jimboy, is you!'

*'Nyani?'* I ask in amazement. I'm a monkey?

'Yes, but don't tell anyone, or they'll send you back up they-there hill.' Here begins a long-standing idea: I'm a de-tailed and shaven monkey in a human family.

There's a walk-in cupboard between the bedrooms in our house. It has no window, and it's pitch-dark inside when the door's closed. Cockroaches. Big, black monsters that scuttle for cover when we enter. Becky and I call them cockdies. Mum and Dad don't use physical punishment when we're naughty. They don't need it.

We're terrified of being locked in the cockdie room. It's an effective threat, because even though I don't speak much English, the word 'cockdie' brings me to heel. They only ever put me there for half a minute, but terror of cockdies in darkness is powerful stuff.

*'Dudu mbaya,'* I say to Becky, *'mimi ogopa.'* Bad insects, I'm frightened. Dad and Mum overhear me. They crease up laughing.

'What are we raising?' Dad asks Mum. 'He's a savage, but he *can* put those Swahili words together!'

Honest swappings of casual profanities with the *watu* are

everyday by the time I'm three. One day I sit alone on a big stone near our house. Along comes a freshly washed and dressed young man. He's going out for the evening. I recognize him as the chief engineer's cook. He stops to greet me. 'Jimu,' he says, '*Jambo.*' Hello.

I reply '*Una kwenda wapi?*' Where are you going?

'*Kutembeya,*' he says. For a walk. He explains he's out '*ku tafuta kuma*'. To look for a vagina. He spits a long way through his teeth. I wish him speed and success in his quest, and he continues down the path, giggling. I block my nostril and blow my nose at a tree. I am reaching longer and longer distances.

I learn to threaten *watu*. '*Hi hospitali,*' I say, brandishing one fist. This means hospital. '*Hi Samina,*' I follow, showing the other. This is Samina. The bush graveyard. Works well on small *totos*. They don't know what a *Mzungu*, or white person, can do. Even a little one like me. '*Nta zika ko ziara,*' I say. I'll bury you in your grave. A useful insult is to tell someone they're mad. '*Kwenda Dodoma*' is shorthand. Go to Dodoma. Central Tanganyika, the only mental asylum in the country. '*Kitchwa na penduka,*' I add for completeness. Your head is turning around. Insults like these are lightly given, laughingly received.

Meantime I notice strange things. Some people have a very fat leg. So swollen, the space between shin and foot is completely filled. Only toenails protrude at the bottom, like the elephant feet they turn into wastepaper baskets.

I don't know how many are affected among the *watu*, but enough to suggest they're a different tribe. Not like other people. The sight, so shocking at first, becomes mundane. Here or there someone has a fat leg. This is 'elephantiasis'. *Filariasis* is the zoological term. A tropical parasitic worm blocks the lymphatic ducts and causes grotesque swelling of the limb. I don't see any *mutu* with two elephant-legs.

'*Madudu,*' an *ayah* says. Bugs. '*Ngonjwa ya madudu mbaya.*' Sickness of the bad bugs.

Some people have scarred and pitted faces. Mostly Africans, but some Indians too. Smallpox before mass immunisation. Kills millions, leaves many more scarred.

I'm four. Dad comes home with his stalwart Nyasa assistant, Wait, and takes two *Whitecap* beers from the fridge. Wait sits on the floor, Dad on an armchair. Dad offers Wait a chair, but he refuses. Having a beer with a white man is one thing, sitting on a *Mzungu* chair is another. They speak about the ropeway, Dad in rudimentary Swahili, Wait in broken English.

I amble in from the garden, sit down. I love Wait. He's tall, light skinned, with finely chiseled features I later recognise as Nyasa. He always wears *Wellington* boots, regardless of the heat. Some of the *Wazungu* call him 'Boots'. It's clear he dotes on Dad. I listen to them a long time. Mum and Becky are in the kitchen. Dad fetches more beer. Wait drinks from the bottle. Doesn't want a glass.

'Time for bed,' Dad says, pointing at me. I don't understand. My English is as poor as my Swahili is good. Dad sees my incomprehension.

'Wait,' he says, addressing the Nyasa, 'tell him to go to bed.'

'Jimu,' Wait says, *'baba na sema kwenda kulala.'*

*'Siwezi,'* I say defiantly. It's posh Swahili talk. Shorthand, one word meaning 'I will refuse,' or 'I won't.' Before learning this I have to use lots of words. That's kitchen-Swahili. I'm slicker than that.

Wait translates. 'He is saying. . . No.'

'I'll give him a hiding,' Dad says.

*'Baba na sema...,'* Wait says. Father says... And he explains.

*'Ntakimbia,'* I respond sophisticatedly. I will run away. Shorthand again. One word saying it all.

'He says he will away run.'

'Mummy,' Dad yells, and Mum comes. 'Get this kid to bed before I lay into him.' He's choking on his beer.

In bed that night Dad asks Mum 'What kind of monkey are we raising? Jim doesn't speak English. He's a native, and a cheeky one.'

Just up the road a furnace burns night and day, and its hunger for fuel changes our lives.

# Three

Strange how everyday changes have impacts greater than we'd ever imagine. We wouldn't dream the mine's use of wild timber for electricity generation will lead to meeting our best childhood friends. Or the object of my long and deep infatuation.

In Geita they use native forest timber as fuel to generate electricity. Cut at random in the bush, it's loaded on lorries and trucked to the mine. The lorries pass over a weighbridge both ways. After drying in the open, it's burnt in the furnace at 'Engineering Works' on Top Road.

The heat boils water to power a huge steam engine which drives the generator. It looks and sounds like a locomotive without wheels. Not surprising, as it's made from scrap salvaged from Singida railway yard. For a long time they can't get enough timber to feed the hungry furnace. Then a solution arrives. There's an old Sukuma saying: 'make a plate full, and a hungry man will come.' Geita's timber problem is a stranger's opportunity.

In 1952 a former *Afrika Korps* Officer called Eugen Blüger comes to Geita, with a contract to provide timber. We get to know his background well. Geita's like group therapy for the displaced and dispossessed. Everyone is expected to reveal his or her life story. In the *Korps* Eugen held the rank of *Hauptmann*. He's first cousin to Otto Müeller, a German former naval officer who runs a farm called Lotanga across a narrow lagoon from Mwanza.

Eugen acquires a fleet of four *Bedford* five-ton tipper lorries, and hires twenty tribesmen to cut and load wood. It's a lucrative business. His wife and two children arrive, and the family moves into a vacant house. The children will be best friends to Becky and me, and play a big part in our lives. Gretchen will be my first love, but we're too young now.

In no time, the Blügers become an active and well-liked part of Geita society. 'Acceptable Kraut,' says Mr Snel. The war and its repercussions are still big in the people's lives, and even little Geita can't escape that.

During the retreat of the *Afrika Korps* after the battle of El Alamein, Eugen's tank hits a landmine, and he and two *kameraden* are reduced to walking across the North African desert. They stumble into an American ambush, and Eugen's legs are riddled with heavy machine-gun bullets. It evokes ghoulish interest in Geita, particularly among the children. It's whispered fragments of lead still break through his skin eight years on.

Like other expatriates, Eugen enjoys a drink at the club. There is, in the early nineteen-fifties, residual tension between Germans and those who fought them in the war, but there's sufficient, if grudging, respect for this one, who fought bravely for his country, was wounded, works hard for his family, and behaves as a gentleman. The British and South Africans who served in the war make Eugen welcome, and engage him in friendly conversation, limited only by his poor English and guttural accent.

Eugen is strikingly handsome, a tall, slim, aristocratic man in his early forties. There's a framed photograph of him and another soldier, both dressed in the khaki uniform of the *Africa Korps*, hanging in the lounge of his house. Becky and I admire it when we visit. The other soldier in the photograph, smiling broadly, with his peaked cap at a jaunty angle, is *Feldmarschall*, or Field Marshall, Erwin Rommel. This is a heroic picture, and Eugen, not Rommel, our hero.

Late in 1955, when I'm four, the mine suffers yet another power failure, and the decision is made to change the ancient steam-driven generator for a newer, more reliable, model. The replacement is purchased and shipped to Geita, and four burly English South African engineers arrive from Johannesburg to install it.

On the second night they go to the club. They're annoyed to see Eugen, a German, there. They remember fighting on the losing side at Tobruk. There they were disgraced for surrendering to a numerically inferior German force. To be fair, they didn't know they outnumbered the besiegers. Still, they hate all Germans. Exactly what takes place, or how it starts, is unclear. What I know I hear later.

One of the South Africans calls Eugen a 'Nazi bastard' and punches him. Several people present report that all four launch a vicious and ugly attack. He's knocked to the floor, and kicked.

Astonishingly, though later expressing shock and disgust, nobody intervenes. Its unfortunate Dad isn't there, because he wouldn't have stood for it.

Eugen is badly beaten up. One of his lower legs, where the femur was weakened by bullets, is fractured. When they stop kicking him, he's taken to hospital, which in Geita means that house-with-beds, the death-place of the murderer Stroessner, with visits by Dr Weiss, the German Jewish doctor, who, like Mr Hessler, who works with Mum at the mine store, is a survivor of Auschwitz. Many of his relatives perished in the Nazi gas chambers, but he takes the Hippocratic oath seriously, and doesn't discriminate against anyone, not even Germans.

When I'm older, I hear people talk of how Richard, or 'Dick' Penhaligon, a Cornishman who fought the Germans and saw comrades killed, 'nursed an enemy back to health'. Mum explains Dad's attitude by quoting him. 'If I was a German, I'd try to be a good one. I think Eugen's a good one.'

Dad thinks all Germans love *advocaat*, made of raw eggs, brandy and Demerara sugar. Why, I don't know. From the day Eugen is carried to hospital, and for the next three weeks, Dad has a special routine. He drives home in MZ 202 after work, and dashes to the kitchen.

He breaks eggs into a bowl, adds milk and Demerara sugar, pours in a hefty measure of brandy, shakes it up in a big beer bottle, puts a top on, then roars off down the road to see Eugen. Sometimes I go with him, and once Gretchen, Eugen's eight-year-old daughter, comes too. Even at this age I'm fascinated by her sky-blue eyes, pretty face and long blonde hair. I have hopeful thoughts. If, like her dad, she gets into a fight, I'll save her, and then she'll love me.

To others, Eugen wincingly says he hates raw eggs, has never tasted *advocaat* before, and hopes never to do so again. But, he says, he can't rebut the kindness of the Cornishman, whose accent makes it impossible for him, with fledgling English, to understand. So he puts on a grateful expression and drinks, only to have the glass refilled.

Eugen pretends to understand Dad, and Dad him. In truth, no real communication happens, except that both men become deeply fond of one another.

Mum accompanies Dad sometimes. She recounts a conversation between the men. 'How is your wife?' Dad asks, passing a glass of advocaat to Eugen, propped up in his bed.

'Mein life, it is bad, ja!' Eugen says.

'How is that?' Dad asks.

'Zat ist brokken mein leg,' he replies, pointing at his plaster cast.

When Eugen is recovered, three months after the assault, he takes his wife, Gretchen and Dieter, to visit cousin Otto Müller at Lotanga. He sings the praises of the *'Britischer seeman'* who had been so kind.

'A sailor?' Otto asks. 'A good one I think,' Eugen responds. 'Will you introduce me to this. . , Dick?'

*'Jawohl, der* Dick,' Eugen replies.

'I need a good sailor to fetch my boat, Lotanga, from Uganda,' Otto says.

Otto Müller is a German Tanganyikan of the old school. Eugen tells Dad about him, and his story is recounted many times at the bar in Lone Cone Club, in case anyone should forget. He was born in 1905 on the farm his pioneering Bavarian grandfather established on the shore of Lake Victoria.

The farm is Lotanga, a *Muanza* word Otto says means 'looking at the water'. He grew up there, went to primary school at a mission in Mwanza. When he was nine, his father, hailing from an old military family in Prussia, sent him 'home' to Germany to continue his education.

Prussia was alien. Otto hated the cold, disliked the people, and longed for the friendly colours, smells and faces of Africa. He only came home for short holidays in sixteen years. Eventually he graduated in agriculture and mechanical engineering. At twenty-five he returned for good, fresh-faced Bavarian bride at his side, to assume management of Lotanga farm, and the five year old Lotanga ferry service his father established in his absence. It was 1930.

Eugen tells Dad about Otto over a beer on our verandah. I listen intently. The talk of war and submarines mesmerises me. Maybe I should be a submariner. When Otto returns to Lotanga after the war, things have changed since he went to Germany. So much happened here in Africa while he was away. In 1914

World War One broke out. Who'd think one Serbian gunman on a side street in Sarajevo would cause such pandemonium?

At four I'm more obsessed with soldiers and war than I am even with Gretchen. I have little space for anything else. German, Japanese and British soldiers and war-machines crowd my imagination. Dad has difficulty convincing me I've not only missed the First World War, but the second too. I'm cross because he won't start a third. What about U-boats, I ask. At the bottom of the sea, he says. Isn't that where they're supposed to be?

So what about the First World War here, in Tanganyika? The year after the declaration of war in 1914, the British colonial army in Kenya prepares to invade *Deutsch Ost Afrika*. The gallant resistance of the German-led *Schutztruppe*, comprising German officers and native *askaris* under the command of their legendary leader, Paul von Lettow Vorbeck, will deny the vastly superior invaders their predicted rapid victory, and divert hundreds of thousands of much-needed British and empire troops away from the western front in France.

The British are neither up against Dervishes in the Sudan, nor pursuing someone like the crazed *Mahdi*, and his hordes of camel-riding tribesmen. They're facing the most cunning, wiliest enemy they would ever encounter, supported by well-drilled, dedicated, fearlessly brave *askaris*.

Vorbeck writes of his strategy in his book, *My Reminiscences of East Africa*. He knows at the outset he can't win against such a numerically superior enemy, with so much *matériel* of war, but he can, and will, cause them much nuisance, forcing them to deploy masses of troops and equipment against him, robbing the allies of much-needed resources for the European war theatre.

Vorbeck's army is the *Schutztruppe* the driver Fritz mentions on that first road-trip to Geita. In a brilliant guerrilla campaign, they strike in unexpected places, and then disappear like phantoms, to re-group, and attack elsewhere, sometimes hundreds of miles away.

Cut off from re-supply from Germany, Vorbeck infuriates and humbles the British by ambushing convoys at will, even rearming his *askaris* with captured British weapons. Lacking every type of heavy weaponry, he organises the salvage of the

4.2 inch guns from the German light cruiser *Königsberg*, after she's cornered and sunk in the Rufiji delta by Royal Navy Monitor-gunboats in July 1915. With the huge guns on improvised carriages, the *Shutztruppe* engage the shocked and startled British forces in long-range artillery duels. Worse, Vorbeck has recruited the scuttled *Königsberg's* gunnery crews, who train the askaris to an alarming proficiency in artillery.

This is supposed to be a walkover against a small, isolated, ill-equipped colonial force, not a real war. To crown it, Vorbeck leaves infuriating 'thank you my generous English friends' messages nailed to trees. A gentleman.

'If he's ever captured,' General Aitken angrily declares, 'I'll lose no time stringing the devil up, boots and all, from the nearest tree'. A foreigner, running rings round the imperial army. Not on, old fruit, simply not on. Not when the troops Vorbeck is drawing into this crazy bush run-around are so needed on the Western Front. He'll have to teach this impudent man respect. He doesn't ponder how a hanged man will show respect.

In the end, it's events in Europe, not Africa, which determine the fate of *Deutsch Ost Africa*. Vorbeck doesn't limit his campaign to the German colony, but exports it to the unprepared British and Portuguese in Mozambique and Rhodesia. The armistice comes when he's on the march in Northern Rhodesia. He gets the news just after capturing another British fort, where he's planning further raids. It comes with a captured British dispatch rider.

At first the *Generalmajor* thinks Germany's won. Then he's ordered by Berlin to surrender his East African forces to the British, to whom he's so long given the slip. He agrees, only on condition he surrenders personally, but his 'undefeated' *askaris* don't, and keep their weapons. The *watu* still love him for that. Vorbeck's campaign will be remembered as the greatest, most successful guerrilla campaign in history.

In 1946, twenty-eight years after his limited surrender to the British at Mbala, Vorbeck is living destitute in Berlin. When told, Field Marshall Jan Smuts is appalled, and, with Montgomery, arranges a modest British military pension for their tricky old enemy. Who says there isn't chivalry?

Vorbeck becomes my hero when I'm four. Oh how I wish for

him to come back and lead another jungle campaign, with me in it. At least the jungle's still here, not at the bottom of the sea like the U-boats.

Otto tells Dad that Vorbeck's Tanganyika story doesn't end there. He returns to visit Tanganyika in 1953. He arrives in Dar on the SS Rhodesia Castle. It's too early for me – I'm only 2 then. Otto says Vorbeck climbs down the gangplank onto the wharf, where he spies a ragged gathering of *wazee*, or elderly men. He realises at once they are his old *Schutztruppe askaris*, come to greet him. At first they don't recognize their old commander, or *Obersti*. He's 83 years old. He's changed with age, for it's been forty-five long years.

'Did you serve in the *Schutztruppe?*' he asks a great-grandfather in a ragged *kanzu*, or gown.

'*Lazima,*' the old man croaks. Of course. 'And I am here to greet our *Obersti.*'

'*Jina lako?*' Vorbeck asks him. What is you name?

'Wilhelm,' replies the elder. A good German name.

'*Jina Lako?*' he asks in return. Your name?

'*Pumbafu,*' roars Vorbeck, embracing the old bag of bones. Fool. 'Don't you recognise your old *Obersti?*' The *mzee* falls to the ground and hugs Vorbeck's legs.

After the 1918 armistice, the renamed Tanganyika Territory, this huge former German slice of the continent they called *Deutsch Ost Afrika,* is joined to Uganda Protectorate and Kenya Colony, as the third part of British-ruled East Africa. All this happens while Otto languishes in Germany, receiving between 1913 and 1918 only two letters from his parents in Lotanga.

No point writing, they say, when they know, as Germans in East Africa, they are cut off and isolated from home by the Royal and allied Australian, American and Japanese navies, which have destroyed or captured all German shipping east of Suez.

There's a brief but notable maritime exception, the raider-cruiser *Emden* and her indomitable *Korvettenkapitän* von Müller and crew, who wreak havoc with British shipping in the Indian Ocean, famously shelling a sleeping Madras by night, and eluding a huge fleet of hunters from four navies, until her luck finally runs out and she's destroyed by *HMAS Sydney* in the battle of the Cocos Islands in November 1914. Closer to home, the imperial light cruiser *Königsberg*, named by the *watu* during pre-war visits to Dar es Salaam as *manowari ya bomba tatu*, or man-of-war of three chimneys, is forced to seek shelter in the Rufiji delta, and finally scuttle herself.

For the duration of the war, there's little mail between Germany and her East African outpost. In the last weeks of the war an attempt is made to re-supply the *schutztruppe* by air, using a *zeppelin*. Somewhere over Egypt the British intercept her radio signals to Berlin, and cunningly send her a message, in German, that the war is over. The tricked and hapless *zeppelin kapitän* turns his unwieldy airship back towards the fatherland.

The Tanganyika twenty-five-year-old Otto returns to in 1930 is already adjusted to British rule. German East Africans are pragmatic. They accept the new name for their country, and a King in London instead of a Kaiser in Berlin. 'Zey are both *scheiss*,' Otto says, 'so vot iss der difference?' The old colonists continue as before, intrepid workers, imaginative, tireless developers, and successful entrepreneurs.

Between 1930 and 1938, Otto and his wife settle into running the farm and ferry service to Mwanza, had two daughters, and replace his parents as doyens of the budding Müller Empire. In 1939, overwhelmed by what he later calls misplaced patriotism, he flies to Germany on the second last civilian flight for five years, to join his country's struggle against France, England and the 'Bolsheviks'. Same month Dad goes home to rejoin the Royal navy. Strange, two white men from Africa going to join opposing sides in a European war.

Otto is sent to the *Kriegsmarine*, the German navy, and due to his engineering qualification becomes second engineer on a destroyer. He doesn't like to talk about the war. When he knows and trusts Dad, he opens up to him, who as a fellow-sailor he considers a comrade.

He is a veteran of both the Baltic and North Atlantic. He is only a few miles from *Bismarck* when she sinks *HMS Hood*, causing the loss of more than twelve hundred British lives. He is glad Dad is transferred off Hood before that. From 1942 to 1945 Otto serves as Chief Engineer on U-boats, mainly in the Mediterranean, and sees carnage on an awful scale. He lives day to day, never knowing when his last hour would come.

At this time Otto begins to reappraise the Nazis. They come to power on a wave of patriotism, promises of employment, and national rejection of the ruinous terms of the 'perfidious' treaty of Versailles. With time, they reveal themselves as something much more sinister. Paranoid bigots promote their warped ideology, cadres rule over things of which they are ignorant, brutality enforces 'loyalty' and compliance, humanity is debased.

Otto is in a war he's committed to fight, but no longer feels right is on his side. He receives the Iron Cross for bravery in action, but writes *'Gott ist nicht mit uns'* in his diary. God is not with us. It's all so hollow, wasteful, and barbarous. He pines for the sunsets and peace of his real home.

When Admiral Doenitz surrenders all German combat forces in April 1945, Otto is at sea in a U-boat. The crew only hears the news when they surface to charge batteries off the coast near St Nazaire in France. After six months forced labour in an American POW camp, being irritatingly called 'Fritz' by the guards, Otto escapes back to Tanganyika, his wife and daughters, Lotanga and the Mwanza ferry service. He picks up his pre-war life, and begins to energetically expand and improve the business.

Dad says men like Otto are living demonstrations, that even here, in the remotest corner of equatorial Africa, enterprise and industry is possible. I will, in my early years, be much influenced by the presence of such men.

In 1954 Otto decides the twenty-foot motorboat of Lotanga Ferries is too small and antiquated for a forward-looking service. True, the British raise that German freighter, the *Graf von Gotzën*, which the Germans scuttle on Lake Tanganyika after losing the war in 1918, and restore her to service as the *MV Liemba*. Is it theft to take over someone else's ship, even if it's been sunk? Anyway, Otto is a modern man, with modern ideas. He has the entrepreneurial frontier spirit so renowned in Tanganyika.

After consultations with boat builders in Port Bell, Kampala, Otto orders a new super-ferry, to be called *Lotanga* after his home and business. The new boat has an important assignment with Dad, though he doesn't know it. I'll also come to know her well.

*Lotanga* is fifty foot long. Otto is proud of her. She's traditionally built by *'Warabu'* or Arab craftsmen. Her hull is constructed of generous African hardwood ribs, assembled on a huge keelson. These are planked with inch-thick carved and joined *matunda* wood, hewn from the forest, sawn and matured for two years. The planks are fixed to the ribs by two-inch dowels of even harder wood, and, in traditional Lake Victoria style, smeared with *shamamu,* made with lime, animal fat and *dawa,* traditional poison from the forest, guaranteed to repulse invasion of the wood by insect or related life.

When the hull is complete, six months after *Lotanga* is first ordered, the engine arrives from Germany. It's made by Daimler Benz in Stuttgart. A five litre, passively aspirated marine diesel, it's a six cylinder monster. With it come gearbox, propshaft, propeller, fuel tank and remote control assembly.

Two German engine-fitters arrive under separate cover, and commence fitting out the engine and drive. After completing their job, and disgracing themselves with local prostitutes, they go home, and the *Warabu* carpenters resume work, their task to build the deck and wheelhouse, with access hatch to engine, prop-shaft, fuel tank and bilge.

The planks for the deck are *maninga,* dark-rose coloured and fragrant timber which assumes, after sanding, the appearance of antique joinery. They're a foot wide, two inches thick, and the length of the beam where they are laid. The result is artistic, strong and ageless.

With the deck in place, construction begins on the wheelhouse, strategically placed above the engine, to which the controls are inserted, using the skills of a mixed African-Italian electrician-cum-gambler-cum-pimp in Port Bell, who, when sober or not suffering the effects of *'bhangi'* or cannabis, is the best boat-control *fundi* on Lake Victoria.

The wheelhouse, resplendent and varnished, *shamamu* being too crude for that, is complete. Then come the thwart seats, or pews. There are twelve, the longest in the middle, the others progressively shorter towards bow and stern. They're of solid handcrafted *Iroko,* three inches thick and eighteen wide, supported on and bolted to legs of blackened angle iron in 'L' shapes, a centimetre thick, six inches square. The longest seat is twelve foot, enough for eight passengers. The shortest is six foot and will seat four. The mean passenger-per-pew equation is six, so *Lotanga* will carry seventy-two passengers, a great increase on the eighteen of the old boat.

In May '54 *Lotanga*, rich timber-coloured of hull, glistening with *shamamu*, with a green stripe below deck and painted thwarts, is ready for launching. The wheelhouse, in glass and brightly varnished *iroko*, stands proudly astern, and the shining steel propshaft, three inches in diameter, emerges aft to meet the eighteen inch wide, four-bladed, bronze propellor, housed in a gap in the massively built rudder-stem. Behind that is the rudder, six inches thick, four foot long and five foot high. *Lotanga* is a noble sight.

Otto stares appreciatively at his new vessel. It's taken eighteen hard and frustrating months to build. He's had many problems in that time.

The German engine supplier dispatches the wrong gearbox couplings, and takes two months to send the right ones. The Schwabian engine fitters are arrested mid-job for refusing to pay for the services of those harbour prostitutes, while drunk on Nubian gin distilled by a one-eyed Kikuyu harbour labourer. The *Warabu* carpenters put down tools when told by a wandering Ishmaili prophet that the *shamamu* they are applying to the hull contains pork fat, which is *'haram'*, or forbidden, not only to eat, but even to touch. Wrong nails are supplied by Patel, the hardware merchant, and he tries to rectify that by sending others even more wrong.

The paint isn't right. *'Verdamte* house paint,' Otto curses. Won't last a week in water. A Chinese 'chemist' at a Kampala branch of timber exporters suggests to Alefu, the boatyard headman, that he 'marinise' the paint by adding sulphuric acid. It's done, and results in a hundred litres of stinking brown sludge. Otto has to be restrained from attacking a cowering Alefu.

There are other problems. One by one he solves them. Anyone who weathers force ten gales in the Bay of Biscay in a steel cigar tube is equipped for adversity.

Now Otto has a new problem. How to get *Lotanga*, the boat, to Lotanga, her future berth, four hundred miles across the open waters of Lake Victoria? Otto is a former *Kriegsmarine* engineer, not a sailor or navigator. He's never taken a rudder in hand with intent. Never bothered with stars, other than viewing them as a pretty backdrop to courting his *freundin* on a summer evening by a lake in Swebia, bottle of Riesling in ice bucket on the side.

He's pondering the dilemma when cousin Eugen, hobbling on injured leg, comes to visit. 'Introduce me to *der Britischer seemann*,' Otto tells Eugen. 'Maybe he will fetch *Lotanga*.' Dad meets Otto with Eugen at Lone Cone Club. The three men get on well, and drink 'a herd' of *Whitecap* lager while sharing stories of the war.

Otto's account of U-boat life fascinates Dad. He's been on British ships, which try, sometimes with success, to destroy submerged U-boats with depth charges. He's thought how brave the crews are, cowering in long metal tubes deep under the water, waiting for charges to explode and crush them, powerless to do anything, just living in hope the enemy above will lose sonar contact. When oil and wreckage float to the surface, meaning a hit, he is distressed for the sailors who are dying so horribly. Otto is the first German submariner he's met. There aren't many who survive. Dad feels a camaraderie beyond nationality or language.

Otto is equally keen to hear of Dad's experiences in the Royal Navy. He listens intently about *HMS Hood*, how Dad is transferred off her just weeks before she is sunk by Bismarck. He's intrigued about Dad's next ship, the fleet escort corvette *HMS Turtle*, her sinking by *Dornier* bombers off Grimsby in 1942, the Captain's determination to go down with his ship, how Dad saves him and a boy-seaman, and survives with five others out of a crew of sixty-eight.

He remembers losing his close friend who grew up with him in Mwanza. A *Dornier* pilot. Shot down somewhere close to the north English coast in 1942. Not far from where Dad's ship is sunk – by *Dorniers*. This subject is best avoided. Otto admires Dad's Distinguished Service Medal, or DSM. *'Das ist ein Britischer Eiserne Kreuz,'* he says, holding it close to read the lettering. Iron Cross. He has a German one.

By the time evening draws on, and the blood-red African sky plunges towards the horizon, sending crimson shafts of light and shadow across the polished bar top, Dad and Otto have forged a mutual liking and regard which will last till Dad's death, and for many years cause Otto to talk of 'der Cornish sailor vot I luffed'.

Before they leave the club, Otto tells Dad why he's come to Geita. 'Ritchie, *mein freund,*' he says, alcohol and camaraderie breaking down remaining boundaries, 'I vant you to go to Port Bell, Kampala, for me, *und* brink back mine boten.'

'What?' Dad says.

'Hiss boot,' Eugen says, slapping Otto on the back, 'ze big vun vot is builded *für* das ferry.'

'You what?' Dad asks, trying to work out what they're saying.

'Let us take vun bottle visky und go to Eugen's house,' Otto suggests, 'zere ve talk more, yes?' He burps, immensely pleased with his *Englisch*.

By the time Dad staggers home, humming *Lilli Marlene*, which his drunken Teutonic friends have loudly sung, he's agreed to ask for a week off work, go to Port Bell, and collect Lotanga. He even has a crew in mind.

'I'm fetching a boat,' he tells Mum, who's never seen him so inebriated, then he falls asleep, fully clothed, in an armchair. Mum covers him with a blanket, and leaves him. He's had difficulty sleeping ever since the head injury in 1945. She won't wake him now.


Three weeks later, Dad boards an East African Airways *DC3*, or *Dakota*, en route from Mwanza to Nairobi, and from there on to Entebbe Airport in Uganda. With him is his Nyasa assistant, Wait, and Umali, the servant he engaged in Geita. I'm bitterly disappointed he won't take me. So what if I'm only four, I want to go. From Entebbe they hitch a lift with a Scots government official, who kindly drives them all the way to Port Bell. A year later, purely by coincidence, the Scot is transferred to the Geita area as *DC*, or District Commissioner.

At Port Bell they are met by the head boat builder, Alefu. Dad can't believe how old and wizened the Arab craftsman is. His face has the look of old leather, and he's completely toothless. He wears a filthy *kanzu* over his thin body, and a red fez on his head. Yet his eyes, grass green, are much alive, as is his razor-sharp tongue. He speaks bad English.

'Ze best dhow in za lake,' he proclaims, 'I builded it!' German and Arab accents are surprisingly similar, Dad thinks. *Lotanga* is bigger than he expected. The timbers are finely worked, and to the knowing it's apparent each plank has been individually shaped and carved to fit in place, each wooden dowel inserted and driven in by hand, the caulking done so carefully as to be almost invisible. The joinery is, indeed, so detailed and perfect, it causes Dad to wonder how such a thing is possible in such primitive conditions, with such old-fashioned tools. The hull has the shine of mature *iroko* and *shamamu*, which is only seen on Arabian vessels. The *maninga* deck, dark rose coloured, contrasts strikingly with the gleaming hull. The wheelhouse is graceful and generous.

'You like?' Alefu asks, seeing Dad's amazement, sidling up and smiling toothlessly.

'I like,' Dad says, admiration for the old man growing. There are twenty *Warabu* workers standing around, watching the reaction of Dad and his crew to their work of so long. Alefu decides to introduce them.

As he calls their names, each man steps forward and bows his head. Dad says he's never experienced such a formal occasion before, including his decoration with the Distinguished Service Medal. After the last grinning man has gone back to watching, Alefu instructs a woman, who may be a daughter, but just as easily a junior wife, *'tuletee kahawa'*, bring us coffee. From now on Mum has to get used to Dad requesting coffee in Swahili, and adding that he needs more *bibis,* or wives, to bring it.

An hour later Dad, Wait and Umali motor out of Port Bell, Uganda Protectorate, en route for Lotanga, near Mwanza in Tanganyika Territory. I will hear the story of that voyage many times. The best account is from Umali, our servant, who achieves my highest esteem and affection as mentor and friend. His version of the voyage is colourful, not through untruth or embroidery, but perception.

Umali is a tribesman from a small hamlet near Geita.

Although he learnt the skills necessary to be employed by the 'Wazungu', or Europeans, he retains the magical and colourful thinking of his people, and is a deeply entertaining, if superstitious, storyteller. I leave the story of the voyage to him, but something happens at home a week after Dad brings Lotanga to Tanganyika for Otto Müller, and I must digress.

It's late at night, and we're all asleep. Mum hears a sound from somewhere in the house and nudges Dad awake. 'There's someone in the house,' she whispers. Dad sits up and listens. Sure enough, he hears a bang, then a curse in German. Footsteps. Someone is walking round the lounge, crashing into furniture.

Dad leaps out of bed and dashes to the bedroom door. He opens it deftly and flicks the light switch on the other side. A most curious sight encounters him. Caught in the bright light, holding an upside-down bottle of whisky in one hand, and pouring it into a glass, is Otto Müller, clearly the worse for wear already.

Dick,' he proclaims, 'I am zo hippy you to see!'

'Otto,' Dad breathes, relieved but amazed.

'I vos brink you vun drink, but ziss *verdamte* glass IST licking der viskey,' says Otto, staring perplexedly at his now completely empty bottle. Dad sees the problem at once. Our housebreaking visitor has felt his way into the kitchen in the dark, and found a glass to pour his whisky in. Only it isn't a glass. It's Mum's pie funnel, for holding up pastry on pies. It's got holes both ends. He has poured the whole bottle of Johnny Walker through the pie funnel, all over the lounge floor. When he realises the gravity of the loss, Otto bursts into tears.

'*Mein* bottle ist empty,' he wails in genuine grief.

Dad gives him his sincere condolences. Luckily, he finds a bottle left over from Christmas, and the men console each other. It takes Mum weeks to rid the house of the reek of whisky.

# Four

Umali is a villainous raconteur and opportunist. He always seems old to me, but never, in all the years, ages more. He's of the Sukuma tribe, those who settled locally in antiquity. The word *Sukuma* means 'let us abide in the north'. I decide I must be Sukuma too. Umali's in his forties when he comes to us as cook and kitchen help. He's slightly built, thin to the point of emaciation. He has a cap of short snow-white hair, and a wrinkled, hairless face.

Unlike many of his tribesmen, he has no ear-piercings, tribal scars or bracelets. He is cantankerous and irascible, but possessed of a satanic sense of humour. He claims he's an accomplished *pishi* or chef, having worked in Mwanza for an Italian family for three years, and Indians for six. He's a *fundi*, or expert, he proclaims, in Italian and Indian cuisine.

So thin, so small, so bent, so dark, so white-haired, Umali gives the distinct impression, Mum says, of an irreputable, unreliable and untrustworthy garden gnome. But, she stresses, there's an enchanting twinkle in his eye. He has a mischievous, captivating grin, with big white teeth glinting in the wrinkled darkness of his face. Except for one tooth, which is missing. Umali is an *mpengu*, or gap-tooth-person. This is the raw beauty of Swahili – it's got wonderful, punchy, descriptive words, even for things like missing gnashers.

From my earliest recall, Umali is my *rafiki*, or friend. He loves my intransigent refusal to take orders from elders, my preference for 'African food' cooked outside, my fluent, poetic, swearing. To me, Umali is sent by a higher power, to encourage wilfulness, disobedience, profanity and non-conformity. And to ensure my Swahili vocabularly, including profanities, grows each day.

Umali becomes for me, not just lovable rogue, but wise and obturate elder of the bush, teacher, protector, story-teller, advisor, comfort, source of humour, not to mention cook, baker and boss of house and garden servant, the diminutive, dull-witted, but immensely strong Tembo, or elephant.

By the time I'm five I've secured Umali as my closest confidante, teacher and friend. It will be many years before I turn to anyone else. This friendship will shape my life. From it I learn to value my elders. They have more to offer than younger people. *Hekima, usawa, uvumilivu* come to mind. Wisdom, balance, patience. A balanced view and, yes, *kukomaa ucheshi,* mature humour.

I confide a great secret in Umali. I tell him I am going to marry Gretchen.

'The *Geremani* girl with white hair?' he asks. I nod. 'Five years is too young,' he laughs, 'but if you want her, you must never give up. Myself, I prefer someone fatter, and much darker.'

I can't defend Umali from one sad thing: he is a rogue of great stature. While he knows little of Islam, and has never left the environs of the Lake Victoria coast, he pretends to be *Hadji,* one who has made the great pilgrimage to Mecca. His tribe, late converts to Islam, are much impressed, which opens a most gleefully exploited commercial opportunity for Umali.

Many of the local *watu* are Muslims. Illiterate in this wild place, far from Mecca and other holy sites, isolated in the bush, they practise very simple Islam. Their food has to be *'hal-al'.*

There's a nearby settlement of *Ishmaelis,* or followers of the prophet Ishmael, who butcher cattle, sheep and goats. Due to tuberculosis in the livestock, expatriates are wary of eating local meat, though fillet steak, well cooked, is 'okay'. Pork, *haram,* and forbidden to Muslims, comes from the Müller family at Lotanga, and frozen mutton and lamb twice a month on a small *Caspair* charter plane from Kenya.

Chickens, or *kukus,* aren't sold by the *Ishmaelis,* but even they must be slaughtered according to *Sharia* law. This involves a prayer invoking the blessings of Allah, and killing by cutting the throat to let the *'haram'* blood drain away.

Umali promotes and advertises his skill and authority to perform Islamic *makuku* executions for a fee, based on him being a *Hadji,* who has made the pilgrimage to Mecca. To us he admits he's never been further than Mwanza. I learn not to always trust a religious man.

From infancy, I see headless *kukus* run amok in the garden, until, after a few crimson-spurting seconds, they collapse, quiver, and lie still, their smaller feathers wafting in the breeze. *Sumuni* is the charge per *kuku*. Fifty East African cents, or half a shilling. Forty *kukus* meet their maker to earn their killer a pound.

Surprisingly, Umali's claims about being a *fundi* in cooking Italian and Indian food are not so far-fetched. The dishes he prepares are excellent, Italian, Indian or even English.

Umali's an innovator in cooking and baking. Because he never speaks English, the names he gives his creations are never quite right. Bread rolls, baked in the Belling range, are *sconzie*, or scones. Our *sconzie* are the finest, freshest, most wonderful-smelling, crispy, delicious rolls. Umali makes a dozen a day. His names for Italian dishes will lead me into many future and futile arguments. *Spangetti, Ravinoni, Fetevini, Bologniss.....*

*Rosti* is his ubiquitous word for meat, whether fowl, mutton or beef, cooked in the range. It's not easy, because it's wood-fired and needs continual log feeding. Umali loves to complain. I love his cursing and un-Islamic swearing as he chops wood. His profanity to inanimate wood or oven is both natural and hilarious. Here he invites an iron stove-door, which has burnt him, to have wanton sex with a lump of wood. Now he calls a too slow roasting chicken *malaya*, a prostitute. The insults and suggestions never affect my appetite.

Umali's wife, my *ayah* Amina, arrives after him at Geita. They have a tempestuous relationship. He's devoted to her, lusts after her, and believes she's a goddess among women. Our first memory of Amina, who becomes our *ayah*, is of the unforgettable *finya*, or 'pinch'. Amina's *finyas* are excruciating. If we challenge, or fail to respect her, out of sight of our parents, she *finya's* us.

The action involves firmly grabbing a fold of skin between thumb and index finger, squeezing, then deftly twisting outwards or, in medical parlance, in external rotation of the hand. The pain is exquisite.

There's an incident with Amina, which Dad notices. She causes one of us to cry. There's a fuss. He threatens her. She doesn't understand. He doesn't clock her bawdy riposte. She survives.

Amina has two large, rabbit-like teeth in front, and no others. She's a real *mpengu*, of many gap-teeth. She's thin and dark, like Umali. She has livid scars on her cheeks and forehead, her arms and neck. During a long and passionate affair with Nubian gin, drinking leagues above a reasonable quota, she engages in vicious no-holds-barred fights with other *wanawake*, or women, and even men. Becky and I have discovered domestic disruption through alcohol intoxication. We'll see much more in Geita.

Sometimes Amina turns her drunken rage on Umali. By the time I'm six it's a regular experience to open the back door to a wide-eyed, terrified, Umali, who gasps for sanctuary, lest he expire from the attentions of his wife. We let him into the kitchen, slam and bolt the door just in time to stop an axe or panga-wielding, wildly enervated, red-eyed Amina making his worst fears come true. Umali, cowering in the kitchen, says, *'yeye majinga.'* She's an idiot. *'Uso kama samaki!'* he adds. Face like a fish. Safe to say with a locked door and a *Wazungu* family in front of it.

Then Amina's sober again. Umali beams with happiness, his near escape forgotten, and regains the bounce in his step. She cooks for him on a fire outside their quarters, lavishes affection on him, and she seems, to the uninformed, a model wife. Umali, like his tribesmen unafraid of talking about such things to children, tells us *'jigi-jigi na rudi.'* Sexual intercourse is back. Until next time. Like those spiders where the female eats her mate after sex. It seems like love for a while. . . It doesn't strike me as strange or unusual that I, four years old, should be discussing an adult man's sex-life with him.

Despite her proclivity to overindulgence and violence, Amina is, paradoxically, a kind and worthy woman. She keeps a close rein on Becky and me, and we know how far we can go. As we grow older, the *finyas* peter out and stop. Amina turns to persuasion, and finds it works better. She's kind to us, thoughtful and humorous. She has the loudest, most raucous laugh. Her spitting accuracy is Olympic gold-class.

In Tanganyika, as in many parts of sub-Saharan Africa, the *watu* eat a variety of insects. In Geita one is very popular. We call them 'flying ants', although the scientific name is *Pseudocanthotermes*.

After heavy rain, as often as four times a year, they emerge en-masse from the ground. They're an inch long, a third in width, white, soft-bodied, plump creatures, with flimsy, transparent wings when they come out. They take to the air in huge swarms, and flutter about in what seems a meaningless frenzy, but to them is the mating ritual. After only a brief career as sexual aviator, they lose their wings and fall to earth, mounds of crawling food.

When they fall the *watu*, using pots and baskets, run around gathering them. The wispy, tissue-thin wings not already shed are plucked off. Heaving potfuls are cooked on fires.

Becky and I have no culinary inhibitions. We love the taste and texture of pot-roasted flying ants. They're buttery and salty, and have the texture of crunchy peanut butter. A mouthful is six to eight at a time. They add deliciousness to *ugali* or stiff maize porridge.

Mum remonstrates with Amina and Umali when she sees us eat flying ants. It's her fault, she says. She should never have let us spend so much time with the servants. She allowed it against her better judgement, and what she gets is us eating insects. She tells Umali ants are off our menu. He pretends to agree. Becky and I become the keenest gatherers of the fluttering bonanza. Mum gives up. Like Napoleon, she chooses battles she can win. She never tells Dad. The thought will make him ill, she says.

He would be ill too, if he looked at some of the other food. The *watu* love eating, but don't restrict their diet like the *Wazungu*. The furry lower legs of goats or sheep, roasted on a fire until the hair's burnt off, are delicious to gnaw on. Fish heads, complete with eyes and tiny brain, go well with *ugali*, as do huge, chewy, sheep's eyes. I spit a small hard bit out when I eat an eye. Someone tells me it's a lens, whatever that is. Intestines, barely cooked in boiling water, and dipped in a homemade chilli sauce - great to tear 'tween hand and teeth.

Every town has its memorable street-characters. The bearded one-eyed tramp scaring small children, the loud vegetable hawker, the threatening beggar, the over-aged prostitute pounding a well-worn beat. Geita has Mlozi. He's between twenty and thirty, people think. According to his late mother, he was born in the year of the 'great rain'. This pins it down nicely. The monsoons bring big rains every year. Maybe her roof leaked, or water ran under her door. Who knows? Something to do with rain. Mlozi's age is approximate.

He sits on a huge *mwamba* or flat granite rock at the end of Top Road, next to the turn-off up Compound Hill. *Mwambas* like this are the sort of places where chiefs stand to talk to their tribe. They're sacred, so Mlozi must think he's important. He's there every day, from sunrise till after sunset. He sleeps somewhere in the compound, although nobody knows where. Somebody's sheltering and feeding him, because Mlozi does nothing except sit and talk to himself, yet, though filthy and odoriferous, he looks in good health.

He wears strips of cloth. Not just old rags, like many *watu*, but purposefully torn ribbons of fabric, of every colour. Where he gets it, nobody knows. He wears a moochi made of strips of green, red, orange and blue cloth, all knotted together, only just preserving his modesty. Sometimes. There are torn coloured ribbons plaited into his thick, overgrown, hair and wispy beard. More round his forehead and neck. He is truly Ribbon-Man.

He has *mifupa*, or bones. At least a dozen are tied round each ankle on thin rawhide cords. They're dry, make a rattling sound when he moves. Lutoli says they're only chicken bones, so they don't really count in *ishara*, or omen, terms. Real *mchawis* or witchdoctors have bones from scarier animals, like *fisis* or hyenas, or even lions. Some even from people... Such *mchawis* have powerful magic, not Mlozi.

He talks to himself constantly. A whispering commentary, which sounds like two different voices, one male, the other female, giving different views about mundane things. I find it strange, because everyone can see the sun's up, the birds are in the sky, *watu* are walking past, and the hills are all around. Say something I don't know, I think, as Lutoli and I stand and listen.

Sometimes the strange man reads my thoughts, leaps to his feet, and violently shakes a *Kimbo* tin, that universal measure-of-all things. *Kimbo* is canned lard, and the empty tins are very popular. His one is full of stones, producing a very loud rattle. '*Kwenda wewe!*' he shouts. Go you. Don't come here, return home! His eyes bulge like a frog's; veins stand out on his neck. The *Kimbo*-rattle alone is enough to stampede us.

Yet we find Ribbon Man irresistibly magnetic. It becomes a game of dare. How long will we stay before we run? Dread, fear, delicious panic. Beats boredom.

As time passes, we flee less quickly. This drives him to ever louder stone-in-the-tin and ankle-chicken-bone rattling and shouting. Lutoli says Mlozi's possessed by a *jinni* or *djinn*. Bad spirit or demon. His fat aunt told him. Amina says he's just mad. Umali reserves judgement.

We go past Mlozi often. The road's perfect for our *garis*, or homemade cars. We make them out of steel wire from the mine-store dump. There's long pieces, in lengths and coils, discarded there. First we make two wheels. They're circles of wire, with a middle loop forming an axle. Then we make little wire loops to attach the mid-part of the axle to a long stick. On top of the stick we attach a wire steering wheel.

When they're finished, we walk about pushing the contraptions in front. It's amazing how well they work. Turning the steering wheel immediately turns the wheels. Over time, we make better and better models. Technology marches on. Top Road's the best place to drive *garis*. It's smoother than all the other roads. That's why we see Mlozi so often. A couple of times he scares us so badly we run off without our beloved *garis*.

There's an open-air dump on the ground beside the engineering works. There are all kinds of discarded rusting iron things there. Most interesting are the 'war helmets'. Hundreds of them. They're World War II British army helmets. They're so old, and have been exposed to the elements so long, that none of them have any webbing or straps left. Some have neat round holes in one side, and some have two holes on opposite sides. Lots of people on the mine take un-holed ones home, to use as water-basins for their dogs or chickens. Umali tells me how they came to be here.

After the war, an enterprising Arab, or *Mwarabu*, buys them from wandering Dervishes who finds them on battlefields in the North African desert. He puts them on a *dhow* and brings them south to Dar es Salaam, where a *Mzungu* from Geita mine buys them for underground use by African mineworkers. The bullet holes ignite the *watu*'s superstitions, and they refuse to wear them. Rejected a second time, they are dumped beside the engineering workshop.

The place where we find these helmets, and many other things, is, to Lutoli and me, an Aladdin's cave. We spend many happy hours hunting through this treasure trove. Lutoli cuts an interesting profile, barefoot, dressed in rags, carrying a spoked motorcycle wheel, and sporting a rusted, two-holed British army tin hat covering his eyes and half his face.

At home I discover the *wasikini*. *Masikini* is a poor person. *Wa* is a plural prefix in this case, though plurals have varying rules in Swahili. In Geita *wasikini* don't only lack goods and money, but also have visible and pity-provoking physical defects. It seems *wasikini* always have a crippled leg, shrivelled hand or cast eye. They're invariably thin and emaciated, and have a skin disorder.

With these attributes, the *wasikini* are qualified to beg from the *Wazungu*. Only they have the right, they believe, and, though other, healthier, *watu* may try, there's an informal, but very efficient, *wasikini* trade union, which will go to great trouble to stop them.

Stories abound of this or that 'normal' *mutu*, gaining a pair of old trousers or cup of sugar by begging at *Mzungu* doors, is ambushed, assaulted and robbed by several cast-eyed, withered-legged and psoriatic *wasikini* on the footpath. They always know. Mum says it's bush telegraph, but I don't understand. There are 'telegraph poles' sticking into the sky in Mwanza, so maybe it's to do with the sky. Sky-talk, pole to pole. But here there are only leafy trees, no poles.

The *wasikini* call one at a time. Knock on door, open it, *masikini* outside, leaning on withered leg, eyeing me through good eye, cast eye staring blindly over my head. '*Masikini,*' he or she says in a special voice, as if it isn't evident.

Said this way, the word doesn't just mean 'poor person'. It's a whole sentence, which says 'I'm a poor, pitiable poor, person, look how unlucky and miserable I am, feel pity, Oh Great One, and lessen my suffering with generosity.' It's accompanied by a most carefully cultivated, heart-rending sob. The world is just too cruel.

'*Jambo,*' I say. Hello. It's a brash response to a thespian masterpiece.

'*Jambo Bwana mkubwa,*' he or she answers, still whining. Hello big Master. I like this. Nobody else says I'm big.

'How are you?' I ask, knowing the answer.

'Bad, Master, very bad.' These actors should be on the stage. Mum comes to the door. She takes pity, gets distressed by the *wasikini*'s tales of woe, which are slickly adapted according to audience response. The *wasikini* discover the loss of a young infant presses Mum's pity-button best, and now all *wasikini* at our door have been preceded to the grave by their cherubic, well loved *watotos*.

Mum tries to ease their pain by giving generously. The recipient shifts to business-mode, examines the spoils efficiently. 'This has a hole,' he or she might proclaim, or 'Is this all the sugar you can spare?' When satisfied, or realising there's no more today, the *masikini* prepares for next time. He or she morphs to mystic and sorcerer. The cast eye is fixed. The other glazes over. 'Good luck will be yours, God will help you, and the fortunes will favour you,' the *masikini* says, with the air of he who decides. It adds superstitious fear. You'll be nice next time.

Mum's a *masikini* goldmine, Umali complains, 'I wanted that jug and blanket.' Mum hunts around, finds something else for him. Between the *wasikini* and Umali, it's an expensive thing.

One day when I'm four, Becky falls out the big tree in the front garden. I don't have a clue what she's doing up there. At least when boys climb a tree it's for proper reasons. Someone runs and tells Dad. He arrives so quick it's like a miracle.

I've just come out of the house to see why Becky's screaming, when MZ202 careers into the dirt driveway in a cloud of dust, scattering small stones. I'm taken by surprise, and Dad misses me by inches. If not for Becky's screams and the bright blood pouring from her left ear, he'd rebuke me for nearly being hit. He gathers her up, puts her on the passenger seat, orders me off the driveway and roars off to the hospital.

Becky's injury isn't as serious as it looks. A small stick's penetrated her eardrum and burst a blood vessel. She isn't going to miss the opportunity to get everything she can. Dad has to take her to Barrat's store on the way back from Dr Weiss. She returns to the house, turban-like bandage on her head, and a huge packet of sweets in her hand. She gives me a few, but not many.

A few days later Dad takes me along for the ride when he calls on a big shot on Top Road. He stops MZ202 outside the big shot's house, pulls up the handbrake and tells me to wait. He's barely gone when I decide to give the handbrake a try. I take it in both hands and try to push it down. It won't budge. There's a spring-loaded black button on the end. I try pressing it in, then pushing the lever down. It gives way with a sudden jolt.

The Land Rover begins, ever so slowly, to run downhill. It gathers speed. Then Dad's running beside it, yelling. He manages to yank open the door and jump in my side, frantically reaching over me to grab the handbrake. We're going faster, nearing a thirty-foot precipice, when he manages to do it. MZ202 slows and skids to a halt, back wheels locked, front wheels inches from the edge.

'Don't ever do that again!' Dad exclaims when he stops puffing.

*'Nini?'* I say. What?

Dad tells Mum. 'First he gets in my way in the driveway, then he tries to go over a cliff in the Land Rover,' he says. 'Has Jimboy got a death wish?'

# Five

In July 1956 we travel to Europe. For me it's the first of many trips to the 'old country'. Dad's contract includes two weeks' annual leave in East Africa, and three months abroad after two years. He's been asked to combine his long leave with buying advanced winding engines for the ropeway. These are manufactured in Munich, Germany, and he has to go there to discuss details with the manufacturer.

I turn five at the beginning of the month, and am so excited by the prospect of going on a big aeroplane that I hardly sleep the last two nights. I've longingly watched the Caspair mail-plane fly overhead most weeks when it comes to Geita from Nairobi in Kenya. It's a single engine Cessna, and lands on the grass runway a mile beyond the club. I've never been in a plane. Dad says we're flying in a *DC4 Argonaut*, a very big aeroplane. The anticipation is almost more than I can bear.

We drive by Land Rover to Mwanza, where we catch our old friend the *gari moshi* to Dar. Forty-eight hours of jolting, blazing daytime heat and dust, welcome nighttime coolness, soot in the eye looking out the window.

Sometimes the hissing locomotive does it out of pure spite. 'Take that, take that, take that!' it wheezes jubilantly when I recoil to rub smarting eyes. Wild game, African villages, sweltering water-stops at desolate, seedy stations like Tabora and Dodoma.

Other stations are even more forsaken, where, though there's hardly any evidence of the hand of man on the countryside, scraggly, half naked hawkers fight to get to our windows, screeching the virtues of proffered animal carvings, patterned *kanzus* or loincloths, bananas, mangoes and oranges. At each stop another tribe. Who cares? The only thing, which matters to me, is the big plane, and soon we'll be on it.

In Dar I have to wait two more whole days. There's been a delay. Plane needs a spare part, somewhere called Benghazi, Dad says. We book into the *Inn By The Sea*. It's a small collection of round huts and rusty iron roofs, just above the high-tide mark on the beach. The huts are bedrooms. There's one big one with bath and toilets.

Becky and I are only interested in the sea. The beach is on the side of the sheltered harbour entrance. There are no natural waves here, but when a ship goes in or out, the wake sends mountains of water rolling our way. Mum makes us wear a water-safety-thing she's constructed. It's a jacket-cum-armband, of stitched canvas, filled with hundreds of bottle corks. Got them from the club. It goes all the way from my neck to my bellybutton, and as far as my elbows each side. Wearing it I feel as stiff as a tree. When the ship's-wake rollers come, I jump up and down, because I can't bend.

One morning I find a thing of stunning beauty on the beach. It's at the high water mark, where driftwood is piled high by the receding tide. It's a car's steering wheel. I have no idea how it got there, but am immediately smitten.

It's a spoked, chromed wheel, with a big bright-red boss in the middle. A logarithmic improvement on the wire steering wheels we play with in Geita. Not that I understand logarithms. I run up and down the beach, steering my imaginary car, making engine and gear changing sounds. I get encouraging shouts from *Warabu* fishermen. *'Upesi, upesi!'* they enjoin, laughing. Faster, faster!

I persuade Mum and Dad to ask the hotel manager to look after my steering wheel while we're away in England, so I can collect it on our way back. Only when he's agreed do I relax. The manager tells Mum and Dad I've spent too much time with natives, because European kids don't get attached to garbage. Have to watch it, or I'll be speaking Swahili in preference to English. Mum and Dad laugh. It's too late for Jimboy, who's careering about the beach, steering with the wheel, shouting Swahili abuse at other imagined drivers, to the delight of several applauding *Warabu* fishermen.

The delayed Argonaut's even bigger than I imagined. I spot it when we emerge from the concrete airport building onto the tarmac. It stands sideways-on, with an iron staircase going up from the ground, so long I think of Jack and his beanstalk, which Mum has read to me lots of times in her attempts to improve my English. Only it doesn't end in cloud, like the illustration. Instead, it leads to an open door in the huge, gleaming silver fuselage, which suddenly looks, to me, far too big. *BOAC* is emblazoned in huge letters above a row of square windows. British Overseas Airways Corporation.

The behemoth's wing is so long it almost touches the terminal building. The shadow it casts is as dark as the sky is bright. Slung under it, side by side, are two engines, each as big as Dad's Land Rover. The propeller blades are like gargantuan art-statements, pointing at sky, ground, building, and me. Suddenly I realise this thing cannot fly.

I stop walking and announce to my family that, though I'm very grateful for Dad's kind intentions in taking us to Europe, I personally have now had enough holiday, I've got a lovely steering wheel, this aeroplane definitely can't fly, and I'll appreciate being taken back to Geita immediately. It's in Swahili, but they get the gist.

'*Hakuna barabara ju,*' I add for completeness. There's no road up there. Umali says so. Flying is impossible, even though he's seen the small planes at Geita *kiwanja ya ndedge*, landing place of the bird, or aerodrome. Sorcery or trickery, one or the other. He's a strange Muslim.

'Of course it flies,' Dad says, putting an encouraging hand on my shoulder and squeezing, 'it'll be alright Jimboy, really.' I look up and see his confident smile. He looks relaxed. Who am I to believe, him or my instinct?

'It's okay,' Mum says, also smiling. She doesn't look frightened.

'Don't be silly Jim,' Becky says. She's holding Mum's hand. She doesn't look as sure as she sounds. She's very loyal to Dad. Are they in cahoots? Or is cahoot a small cigar?

'This plane flies every single day,' Dad says, bending down to make eye contact. He puts his hand on my other shoulder. 'There's nothing to worry about, Jimboy, really.' He kisses my cheek, stares me in the eye. 'Would I lie to you?'

'*Sijui,*' I say. Don't know. I'm searching his eyes for signs of dishonesty. I don't see any. '*Njema,*' I say after a long pause. Fine. There is no option. Dad looks at Mum, who nods, and then he gives me a soggy toffee.

We're strapped into our seats. I have to admit they are nice, comfortable seats. There are clean white covers on the back tops. To stop *Brylcreem* staining the seats, Dad says. Why do men put greasy stuff on their hair? Before Dad can answer, there's a retort from an engine exhaust.

One by one the four *Rolls Royce Merlin* engines cough, splutter, then roar into life, and the huge propeller blades disappear into a whir. I'm amazed I can see through them. The tarmac, for example, or the windblown *mutu* waving two red ping-pong bats. I *know* the propellors are turning, so why is he telling me?

In turn the engines roar louder and louder, reaching a crescendo, shaking the huge plane like a leaf, before cutting back to guttural grumbling. Testing, Dad says. Doesn't sound good. Testing for what? Even the pilot doesn't know if this thing can fly. My misgivings grow. Before I can tell Dad I'd like to reconsider, the four engines bellow together, too loud for talking. The monster begins to roll.

After a long time we turn onto the runway and stop. The engines thunder again, then things outside begin to zoom by, faster and faster. It's a race to nowhere. Suddenly the angle changes, and the ground leaves us. Up and up, everything below smaller and smaller. Patchwork. Cloud. White cotton wool wafting across the windows. Sun breaks through. Cotton wool below now. Blue sky, bright sunlight on shiny wing, and Toyland way down there. I fall asleep cuddled into Dad. They laugh. At last I've worn myself out.

The *BOAC* route to England is by five doglegs in a general northerly direction, each four to six hours long. My memories are patchy. First stop Nairobi, Kenya Colony. Evening, getting dark. Small bus to airport hotel. Early morning, board again, fly to Khartoum, Sudan. Waiting in steaming terminal for someone important, 'running late'. Finally comes. Hot and bothered, fat and bald, white safari suit, speaks French. Stinks of *mavi*, or poo. Mum says it's 'garlic'. Lick what? Of course it's *mavi*.

Next stop Benghazi, Libya. Overnight again. Hot, smelly room in strange hotel. Incense, Mum says. Walk in bazaar. Arab men sucking smoke up tubes from big bottle, making gurgling noise. Hubble-bubble, Dad says. Smells like a bonfire. Shifty grey-bearded character in *dishdash* offers six camels for Becky. Blonde girls, premium prices. Dark hair, only four camels.

By this calculation, Gretchen is worth more than Becky. I

agree. I tell Dad it's better we sell Becky than Gretchen, even if we get less camels. 'You say price Meester,' the shifty man says when Dad doesn't haggle. 'I good man, I look her good,' he pleads as we walk away. We remind Becky of the Arab who looked-her-good for years. And Dad reminds me I was ready to sell my sister.

To make up, I tell Becky that, when she marries, I wish her husband looks-her-good. We leave at midday. Rome. Evening. Stay in lovely room with balcony overlooking the Tiber. Lots of little boats. Last leg to London. Arrive early afternoon.

Most of our leave is in Cornwall. I meet granny, Dad's mum, for the first and only time. Strange old lady. Very thin, one eye looking sideways. A white *masikini*. Squint, Mum says. Not her fault, so don't stare. I never meet Dad's father, Edgar. He died before I was born. Houses in Cornwall are small, poky. Gardens tiny, wet, mushy, slippery. It never stops raining. It's misty too. They call it 'mizzle'.

Germany. We stay in a small hotel in Munich, where Dad is seeing people about ropeway engines. Two things are clear. One is whatever we see or do, it's offered *'mit musik'*. Applies to buying a jewellery box for Mum, clock for Dad, doll for Becky, and toy car for me.

The Germans have decided to put music into, or adjacent to, everything. They still believe their wartime propaganda about England being *'ein land ohne musik'*, a country without music, Dad says, and they're teaching us. Indeed, we are asked, when Dad books a table for dinner, if we want it *'mit musik'*. For a fee in *schillings*, the restaurant manager puts a record on. Will the other diners object, I wonder. They don't. Dad pays, and we are serenaded with gusto by Germans singing to Um-pa-pah music.

Dad goes off somewhere about the ropeway engines, and Mum takes Becky and me for a walk. It's eleven years after the end of the war, but much of Munich is still scarred and broken. It was the 'carpet bombing' of 1945, Mum says. Why bomb a carpet? Many ruins are boarded off. Construction is everywhere, great cranes dissecting the skyline. We come to a place where the pavement runs beside a park hit by a big bomb.

On one side is a massive crater. At the bottom, standing axle deep in muddy water, is a child's pram. The metal parts are rust-red, but the blue and white striped canopy still looks new. We can see inside. There's a piece of blanket, green with mildew, but with patches of red and white pattern still visible. Half in, half out of the pram is a doll, its head turned to one side, glass eyes staring. Mum says the pram was for the doll. Becky and I think it's too big. The doll was in the pram when the bomb struck. Held by a baby.

I have a nightmare about the pram. Pretty lady, like Mum, pushing pram with baby clutching doll. Whistling sound, louder and louder. I saw a film once about the London blitz. Bombs whistle as they fall. Bang. *Ka-boom*, pretty lady blown apart. Baby, pram, flying high in air. Pram lands on wheels, doll half in – half out. Blood all over. Isn't that what happens? There's always blood if you're hurt.

'Can I see General Vorbeck?' I ask Dad. After all, we're in Germany, and I'd like to ask him to come back and start a new war, with me as an *askari*.

'Out of the question,' says Dad, who's busy looking at a brochure, in German, of steel cables.

We go home by mail-ship. Board *MS Windsor Castle* at King George V docks in London. First port of call, Gibraltar. Stop at Barcelona, Genoa, and Port Said, Egypt. We enter the Suez Canal. At the southern end is the sweltering and dusty town of Suez. We continue south into the Indian Ocean, to Mombasa, Zanzibar, and, finally, Dar es Salaam. I see too many things to remember, eat lots of ice cream and swim in the ship's salt-water pool.

The rolling waves look like beaten copper at dusk, with the plunging sun turning everything golden. Then it's daylight, and the water is blue or green. I never tire of staring at the hypnotic, restless sea. Blue, golden, green. Never the same. Soapy suds froth in the ship's wake and there's bleached-white on the tops of breaking waves. They call them 'white horses', though I can't see an equine connection. Big people have odd notions.

In Dar I haven't forgotten my beach-found steering wheel. The manager at the *Inn By The Sea* has kept it safe, and I'm joyously reunited with it. He says it belonged to an American car. Chevrolet.

The *gari-moshi,* wheezes across the familiar countryside. It's a comfort to be back where the land isn't uniform peppermint-green, marshmallow-soft and wet, where the sky is wide and blue, not closed and grey, where rain, when it briefly comes, is sudden, flooding and oh-so quenching, and doesn't gently weep in wind-driven icy misery all day long. That's how I will remember our trip to *Ulaya*, or Europe. That, a water-filled bomb-crater, a pram and a doll.

Now it's Mwanza, Land Rover, home, steered all the way by me, with my shiny Chevrolet wheel. '*Der kind* iss liking der veel,' Fritz remarks, surprising Dad by talking. Geita, at long, long last. The big aeroplane to England did fly, I have to admit, but I like it not one bit. It isn't how it should be. Too big, too heavy, too noisy. I'm amazed we survived, that we're back, still alive. Never again, I promise myself. The ship was altogether better.

Strange how quickly life returns to normal after a long time away. Within days our epic journey to England and Germany, and all the places en-route, are distant history. It's just like old times when I go with Umali to Barrat Stores. We're walking along Top Road when we see a big group of *watu* standing near the turnoff up Compound Hill. It's where Mzlozi, *djinn* or *jinni*-possessed ribbon-man, hangs around on his flat rock or *mwamba*. We join the crowd, who're in jolly mood and much-entertained.

Mlozi's predicting the future. He's got even more colourful ribbons and stripes on his hair, forehead and neck. He's more animated than we've ever seen him. He's jumping from foot to foot on his *mwamba*, making the dry chicken *mifupa*, or bones, sound like galloping hooves, at the same time rattling his *Kimbo* tin and stones. His knotted ribbon moochi is loose, and we can see his *mboro*, or willy. If it were only Lutoli and I here, we'd be running for safety by now. Umali senses my anxiety, takes my hand in his. '*Pole*, Jimu,' he whispers. Pohl-eh. Be restful, Jimu. The surety of his hand calms my fears. With Umali, no *djinn* or *jinni* can get me.

'The world will end, all will die in months three!' Mlozi shrieks. He rattles louder. Several *watu* giggle. 'A long snake will bite you while you sleep at night.' More giggling. Entertainment like this is rare.

'Whose snake?' a woman asks. More *watu* giggle. Mlozi's ill-fitting moochi has been noticed for what it doesn't hide.

A laughing young man in a mine-helmet and very shredded shirt takes the stage. 'Is it the snake of your pants?' The crowd erupts in merriment. One fat *mama* falls over she laughs so hard. Her *kikapu*, or basket, bursts open and oranges roll down the hill. This is Geita cabaret. Even Umali and I are laughing. We haven't thought of an *mboro* as a pants-snake before. Is it a pants-adder?

'Just mine, just mine,' Mlozi mutters, suddenly deflated, stopping in mid-dance, sitting down on his rock, returning to his soft, rhythmic muttering monologue. Just mine, just mine. Is he saying his *mboro* is going to bite while people sleep? That's funny. . . but he looks sad. He begins to mumble descriptions of the sky, the hills, and the trees. Why does he do that? Can't he see we've got eyes too? It's difficult to hear him after his yelling. It seems he's talking to someone invisible, answering questions. I wonder why he shakes his *Kimbo*-tin-and-stone-rattle.

The *watu* begin to drift off. Umali says Ribbon-Man is mad, like Amina says. He doesn't believe in *djinns* or *jinnis*. He's a *Hadji* after all. As we walk away, I see Mlozi's crying. There are tears on his face. I haven't felt pity before. I do now.

I didn't see Gretchen arrive. She's pretty in denim dungarees and floral shirt. She's sad. 'Vy zey they make fun uff him?' she asks.

'Dunno,' I say.

# Six

They come with a soft, high-pitched drone, in the torpid air of night. The female anopheline mosquito seeks a blood meal, and the unknowing donor is human. While drinking, she unknowingly injects a terrible parasite. Plasmodium *Vivax, Ovale, Malariae or Falciparum* are the agents of malaria. It's endemic in sub and equatorial Africa. The fly-screens on the windows give false security. The mosquitos get in, and navigate up the concentration gradient of exhaled carbon dioxide, to find unprotected skin to pierce with hair-thin, needle-sharp, proboscis. Then they drink.

Dad complains of a headache in the morning, and by afternoon develops high fever. For the first time in almost five years in Geita he comes home early from work. He's been used to poor health since the war. He takes tablets for epilepsy, and can't exert himself too much because his heart won't keep up. Rheumatic fever after the loss of *HMS Turtle* off Grimsby, and four hours in the North Sea, is the cause.

Dad works on, refusing to go off sick, often when he should. He's been unwell ever since the war. 'Don't say anything to anyone, Mummy,' he says when she pleads. 'They'll fire me, then just what shall we do?'

Today's different. He can hardly walk. Mum sees him get out of the Land Rover, and knows something's wrong. She opens the door and helps him to the bedroom. He lies down. Becky and I have been playing in the garden, her with a doll, and me with my Chevrolet steering wheel and a rusty army helmet on my head. We watch Dad stagger to the house.

'Daddy needs to rest,' Mum says when we try to see him. We have lost interest in our games. We sit in the lounge and watch Mum walk from the bedroom to the kitchen and back. She takes him a drink.

'Is Daddy alright?' Becky asks.

'He'll be fine,' Mum says, voice strained. After an hour she decides to call the doctor. 'Stay here and be good,' she says as she goes. The doctor's house is half a mile up the hill. Mum can't drive, so she walks. There are no telephones, apart from the radiotelephone at head office.

We wait a long time. We don't hear any sound from the bedroom, and are afraid to check. Finally there's a crunch of tyres on gravel, and Dr Weiss's car is outside. Mum hurries up the steps, through the lounge to the bedroom. Dr Weiss follows.

Josef Weiss. German Jew, doctor, Auschwitz survivor. He comes to Tanganyika, of all places, in 1948, looking for a new life. Mother, father, two brothers, a sister, all perish. He meets his wife in a resettlement camp in 1945. She's a survivor from Treblinka. In 1957 he's a portly sixty, with thin grey hair, round steel rimmed spectacles, and, despite life experience, a wicked, even warped sense of humour.

Josef tells Dad two things when they meet in '51. Dad is, he proclaims, the 'spitting image' of Edward, Duke of Windsor. Come to think of it, he isn't wrong. When Dad meets Marina, Josef's wife, she gasps and says, 'You iss der double uff zat luffly man.' The second thing Josef tells Dad is that he shouldn't have taken a job in such a disease-ridden place as Geita, given his poor health. Dad pleads with him, says it's his only chance to support his family. Josef, against his better judgement, relents. He lives to regret it.

Now Josef shuffles past Becky and me, winking as he goes. Last time we saw him he made hand-signals of giving an injection, and we ran away screaming. He laughed to bust his gut, the sadist. He enters the bedroom. We strain to hear the voices.

'It vood be best,' we hear Josef say. No humour. Serious.

'Must I?' Dad answers, sounding very tired.

'Best do as Josef says,' Mum says. The door opens. Dad comes out in a dressing gown, leaning on Josef, who looks grave. 'I'm going to hospital,' Dad says, 'be good, you two. Jimboy, you're the man here when I'm away, look after your Mum and Becky.' He gives me a wink, but it's pain in his eyes. He stumbles to Josef's car, like a very old man. Josef closes the door. They drive off slowly.

Mum tells us about the next hours. Dad is gravely ill. Josef says it's malaria, but that's not all. His scarred and damaged heart valves, from the rheumatic fever after the sinking of *HMS Turtle*, are an ideal site for bacteria to grow. They've thrived, and he has bacterial endocarditis. 'Emboli' or little bits from the infective growths shoot off in all directions, causing small, bright pink blemishes on his skin. Josef knows the signs.

Dad becomes conscious and looks at Mum's face, leaning close to hear his voice. 'Bring me seven beers,' he says. Josef is close. Why *seven* beers?

'Do it,' he says, 'geef him vot he asks.' Mum goes to the club, comes back with a bottle of *Whitecap*. She feeds some to him with a teaspoon. He sucks greedily, like a small infant. Suddenly there is a quiver through his whole body. His pupils begin to dilate.

'Becky and Jim!' he says, and his breathing begins to take a strange rhythm. Mum, sitting at the head of his bed, holds him tight.

'Please Ritchie, darling baby, please don't leave me,' she sobs. He stops breathing. She holds him even closer. After a long time Josef coughs.

'He vill not suffer now,' he says.

He can *not* be dead. Not Dad. He just *can't* be. It's a mistake. A lie. Blackmail. They don't need to do this. There are two women standing ten yards away. One is saying, 'He's dead, Jim,' and the other is Mum, wiping her eyes with a hankie. *Apana*, no!

'He's gone to be with God,' the woman says. 'He's happy now.'

'God?' I say, 'happy?'

'Yes, God Jimboy,' Mum sobs, reaching for me. She hugs me, I feel her stomach heave.

'He'll be alright,' the woman says, bending down and putting her arms around me. I pull away. Becky is there. I haven't noticed her. I was playing with a Dinky-car on the ground, driving it up a little road I'd made. What is happening? What do they mean? *Dead?* They're fibbing. . .

'Daddy's dead,' Becky cries.

'What?' I say.

'He's gone, Jimboy,' Mum says, choking.

'Where's he gone?' I say. He's in hospital. It isn't far. I'll go see him. He's alive. He can't be dead.

'Daddy's gone to be with God,' Mum says, trying to suppress her sobs. This is getting serious. They're all saying Daddy is dead. I begin to panic. What if they're right? They can't be.

Maybe I should try a different tack. Surely that will show they are making a mistake.

'Why?' I say.

'Nobody knows why,' the woman says. She's Mary O'Rourke and I suddenly hate her.

'But why should Daddy be dead?' I say, my voice a thin whine.

'God decides,' the horrid woman says.

'I love you,' Mum whispers. Becky sobs. Her face is white, her eyes red. They've known an hour, were terrified to tell me because I'm 'highly strung', and they don't know what I'll do. Vomit. That's what I want to do. They can't all be acting. Something's happened to Daddy. While I was playing with my stupid toys, God's attacked him. He won't get away with it. No! He's my Daddy, not God's. He can't have him. I don't care if he did create the world.

*Wesley-Richards* is an old London firm of gunsmiths. They're posh and expensive. I know, because Dad paid a hundred guineas for his gun, had to go to the gunsmiths in London for a 'fitting' when it was ordered, and a 'sighting' when it was ready.

The rifle's a *375 Magnum*, one of the biggest, most powerful guns in 1957. The calibre makes it an 'elephant gun' in African terms, though Dad doesn't shoot elephants. He buys it because he loves guns. He wants to shoot targets, and maybe defend us from charging rhinos or marauding lions.

I'm four when he first takes me shooting. I'm too small to hold a rifle. Dad kneels on the ground and aims at a tin can. He tells me to pull the trigger. I ask what he means in Swahili. Exasperated, he takes my hand and places my finger on the trigger. I clock him and pull as hard as I can. The gun bellows, the tin leaps brokenly into the air, I shriek in fright, and black smoke belches from the barrel. It smells like a firecracker. I'm shivering. Mum admonishes Dad.

'Make him a man, get him used to loud noise,' he says. He wets the corner of his handkerchief and wipes soot from my cheek. Now my face smells of pipe tobacco. I will always associate that saliva-and-tobacco smell with him. I calm down. Mum returns to her seat on the picnic blanket.

Dad shows me how he loads the gun. He opens it by pulling

the knobbly bit upwards and back. He says it's the bolt. A shiny hollow he calls the breech appears. He drops a huge bullet in, and closes the breech again by reversing the bolt. Up to five bullets go into a metal box he calls a magazine, clipped underneath. How can it be a magazine? Mum reads those. Old ones from England, with pretty ladies on. Pulling the bolt back after firing ejects an empty bullet-case or 'cartridge', and inserts a new one.

Suddenly I'm not frightened anymore. It's very loud, true, but I'm not hurt, am I? I pull the trigger again. Another tin jumps skywards. Dad works the bolt. I fire. Again. And again. This is fun! Eventually, despite jumping at every retort, even Mum is grinning. She tells me I am a *fundi* at shooting. Swahili for expert.

Dad takes me shooting many more times in the next year and a half. When he dies, I know exactly how the *Wesley-Richards* is operated.

'He can't be dead,' I say again, still refusing to believe.

'Now, look, Jim,' says Mary O'Rourke, 'it's no good going on like this. . .' Mary is Mum's friend, but I'd kill her if I could. She's long popped in for a cup of tea, and constantly smokes. I won't forget her brand of cigarettes, because they're very popular in East Africa. *Sportsman Filters*. Product of Kenya.

By five, I'm infatuated with smoking. Lutoli, other African friends and I pick up cigarette butts thrown away by big *Wazungu*, and smoke them. No amount of coughing or spluttering puts us off. We want to be big people. I don't know my smoking is noticed. But it is, I discover. Everyone knows Jimmy's a smoker. Mary O'Rourke is holding a full packet of *Sportsman Filters*, in her hand. A red and white packet. Her lips move, and as if from a distance I hear her say, 'You can have these, Jimmy. . .'

What? Is this woman trying to buy Dad with cigarettes? Is she crazy? Has she helped God to kill Dad? Something stirs deep down. Anger. I look at Mum's pale face, Becky's red eyes. I know what to do. Take action. Fight this. I know how to work Dad's gun. I know where it is, the bullets too. *Piga risasi ko Mungu!* Shoot God! That'll change things.... I'm running towards the house. My cheeks are wet, and I can't see through my tears. It's a hot day, but the air is cool on my face. My heart bangs wildly, like it wants to escape. They don't have a clue what I'm going to do. Mum says I want to be alone. I'll show them. I'm not giving up on Dad.

I get to the bedroom. The gun's in the wardrobe, behind the clothes. I know, because Umali told me where Dad keeps his *bunduki*. I pull it out. It's heavy, and the barrel hits me painfully on the head. I ignore my pain and lay the rifle on the bed.

The bullets are in a shoebox, under Dad's side. Bullets are called *risasi* here. I take three, stuff them in my shorts' pocket. I heft the gun on my shoulder, holding the butt with both hands. Down the passage to the back door. I don't want to be seen, or they'll stop me.

Down the kitchen steps, across the back yard, into the elephant grass. Need cover. It's taller than me. I disappear. Now.... I drop the back end of the gun on the ground, barrel pointing up. God is there. Holding the stock between my knees, I take the bolt in both hands and pull it like Dad used to do. It's stiff. Try again. Moves a little. Massive effort. Snap. Up. Pull back. Slides open with ease. Reach in pocket for *risasi*. Slot into shiny breech. Push bolt forward, down. Easy. Notches into recess by itself. Ready. I reach for the trigger. Hope my aim is good. Have to hit God. See how he likes it.....

Mum and Becky will speak about that gunshot for years. A *375 magnum* is one hell of a gun. The explosion of its cartridge is like a small bomb going off. A cracking, whipping, fierce bang. In Geita it shatters the stillness of midday, and bounces off surrounding hills. Cacophony. It echoes and re-echoes for several seconds.

Mum has heard the sound of that discharge many times. She has recoiled in terror at its venom. She freezes.

'Jim's got the gun,' she shouts at Becky and Mary when the echo stills. 'Oh God, he's got the gun and he's shooting!'

'*Hupo!*' Umali yells, gesticulating as he runs down the steps. There! He points at the grass, where a tendril of smoke coils into the air.

They start running. It's only thirty yards. I'm pulling open the breech, fumbling for another bullet. God may not be killed by one shot. Another may do it. I'm sobbing, angry, determined.

*'Mimi itabidi kumuua!'* I shout. I'll kill him!

Umali reaches me first. I am still trying to load when he scoops me up, sending the gun clattering onto the ground. He holds me tight. I struggle. My face is wet with tears. I try to lever myself from his chest. He's too strong. Suddenly I notice his face is also wet with tears, his eyes red and swollen.

'*Pole*, Jimu,' he says, '*Pole mtoto.*' Sorry Jim, sorry child.

'I'll kill God,' I sob.

*'Ana jua,'* Umali whispers as I stop struggling. He knows.

'He knows?'

*'Lazima.'* Of course. He's walking now, carrying me back to Mum and Becky, and dreadful Mary O'Rourke.

'I'll get the gun,' I hear Mary say. Then Mum is holding me, and we are all crying.

'What were you doing?' Mum asks.

'Shooting that *Mungu*,' I say. I'm exhausted. The running, the crying, the shock. I'm asleep almost before Mum puts me where I want to be. Dad's side of the bed.

I wake in the dark. The crickets are screeching. Far away a single hyena giggles. There's moonlight outside. Mum is talking with someone in the lounge. There's a man's voice. A gravelly low tone. I don't know who it is. The gun has to go. Mum agrees.

Something stirs in my chest. We're going to starve! Mum always says Dad's the breadwinner. I think it's bread he wins, loaves of it, in a curious food game. Then she explains it means all food, and 'winning' is another word for earning.

Did Daddy die because he didn't eat enough? Starvation's the only thing that can kill you, isn't it? If only everyone would realise that, nobody would ever have to die. What's *wrong* with people? Anyway, Dad has gone to be with God. Oh hell, if I've killed God, Dad's all-alone up there. A bit late now. But food. . . *I* will have to win it, or Becky and Mum will also die. I hold my breath. I can hear the man's voice. Something about 'little Jim'. They haven't heard me getting up.

I climb through the window. It's six feet from the ground this side, the house being on a slope. The other side's ten foot. Shorter stilts here. There's a patch of sandy ground below. In the pale moonlight it looks a long way down. My throat still aches from crying, and I've a pain in my side where the gun jerked. No time now. I can't let us starve. I drop silently to the ground, the impact buckling my legs. Sprawled out, knees and hands skinned. I try to ignore the pain, not cry out.

At the far edge of the garden are some untended yards between us and the neighbour. Elephant grass, a few thorn bushes, an anthill. Beyond, the Hewitts have a vegetable garden. The moon slips behind a cloud, everything goes black. I feel my way through the grass. My hands and knees are stinging. I choke on a sob.

I reach the garden. I've been here before. Then it was light. I grope my way to where the carrots grow in rows. By feel alone, I begin to pluck them. I make a pile. Then potatoes. More difficult. They won't come up when I pull the leaves. I feel for a stick. Dig at the ground, scooping away soil with my other hand.

In a nearby tree my invisible old friend the *bundi-msitu* bird, that most spooky of African owls, hoots. What's he trying to tell me? A hyena giggles shrilly, not so far away. I shiver. The crickets are silent. Are they frightened, like me? The moon slides back round the edge of the cloud. Light again. Good. I can see what I am doing. Bad, I can also be seen. The Hewitt's house is quiet. There is only one light on. They don't know.

I have enough potatoes and carrots. I take my shirt and lay it on the ground. I put my haul on it and tie it in a bundle. Time to go.

I haven't thought this through. I'll never reach the window. I'll have to go in a door. Back door is best. Straight into the kitchen. The voices still come from the lounge. I open the back door and collide with Mum. I drop my bundle, and the carrots and potatoes spill on the floor.

'Jim, what've you done, where've you been?' Mum demands, shocked to see me shirtless, muddy, bleeding from hands and knees.

'I want. . .' I begin, but my voice breaks.

'What's this?' Mary O'Rourke says, bending to pick up my vegetables. The carrots are inch-long, the potatoes marble sized.

'To get food for you,' I finish, ''cos Daddy's gone.'

'Darling,' Mum gasps between sobs, 'we won't starve, I promise.'

Next day she apologises to the Hewitts for my piracy. They understand. My foray has a result. When their vegetables are ripe, they give us lots.

Later that night I wake up shivering, as if covered in ice. I'm in bed with Mum and Becky. We cry ourselves to sleep. My throat aches and I shiver so violently my teeth chatter. Mum turns the light on. I'm bathed in sweat; my skin is hot to the touch.

Within hours of the fever I'm a coma. I have seizures. Dr Weiss says it's cerebral malaria, that it's 'bad', that there's little chance I'll get over this. He gives Mum a sedative. They say three seizures with cerebral malaria, and you die. I have five. They say malarial coma of more than three days is fatal. Mine lasts five days. If, by miracle, I survive the coma and seizures, there'll be brain damage. I can't disprove that. Am I brain damaged? Who knows? Can I blame life's failures on *Plasmodium Falciparum* and its anopheline carrier? Don't know.

Dad's funeral is during the worst of my illness. Mum talks about it so many times it feels I was there. On that grim day Mum doesn't know if she's going to lose me too. It's a dreadful time for her. The grave has been blasted out of the granite, which is too hard to dig. The rough wooden coffin has rope handles. It's carried by white men, while a knot of *mwanaume*, or men, Dad worked with stand at a respectful distance. Wait's face is streaked with tears. Anand Singh, the Singa-Singa who will replace Dad on the ropeway, is visibly traumatised.

Dr Weiss stands beside Mum, supporting her. It's like a dream. Last time she was here with Dad, he was still alive, and they came to pay their respects to poor Mrs Williams. Mum had a bad feeling then.

The murdered woman has, in death, strangely impinged on Dad's life. He read about her murder in Johannesburg. Took a job here, not realising it's the same place. He sat unknowingly in her killer's chair, in her house, here in Geita. The open grave, waiting to swallow Dad, is right beside Mrs Williams. It doesn't seem real. What chance all this is coincidence? Is Mrs Williams satisfied now, or does she want more? Terror for me grips her. Mum's upbringing among the deeply superstitious Pedis in the Transvaal has affected her deeply.

The priest from Mwanza is talking. His voice seems to come from far away. A time to put away childish things. A time to gather stones together, a time to cast them asunder. . . a time for war, a time for peace, a time to live, a time to die. . . Insects buzz, perspiration itches. Committing departed brother to the earth, in the certain knowledge of resurrection. Coffin is lowering on ropes. *Mwanaume* are allowed to do this. Mum takes the first handful of soil from a shovel proffered by a tearful Wait. She lets it fall through her fingers into the grave. It resonates on the lid. What a Dreadful thing to be doing, she thinks. Mary O'Rourke hugs her.

The priest starts to sing. A strong baritone. Other voices join. *Nearer my God to thee.* . . More handfuls of earth are dropping. Led by tear-stricken Wait, the *mwanaume* take up shovels. Earth and rock cascade. The last bit of coffin-lid is covered.

Mum can't stay. She doesn't want to go, but there may be a new tragedy at home. As they drive away they hear the *mwanaume* singing as they fill the grave. It's a sad sound. An old German hymn, from the days of *Deutsch Ost Afrika*. It's called *Gott is die liebe*, or God is love. They're singing in Swahili.


*Mungu ni pendo, apenda watu.*
*Mungu ni pendo, anipenda.*
*Sikilizeni furaha yangu,*
*Mungu ni penda, anipenda.*


God is Love, loves his people.
God is love, he loves.
Listen my friends,
God is Love, he loves you.


*Mungu* loves you so much, he sticks you in the ground.

At home Mum finds Umali and Amina surprised and overjoyed because, after five long days and nights, I open my eyes and ask for *maji baridi*.

'He wants cold water,' Umali laughs delightedly. Amina's doing a little jig. Mum calls Dr Weiss, who declares a miracle.

'I haff niffer seen anysing like it!'

77

Now is time to grieve our crushing loss. It's a huge, dark weight on our chests. We feel dead inside. Daddy's not going to come back, and no amount of crying or denial changes that.

I'm sitting up drinking an ice-cold Pepsi, when Mum tells me I've got a visitor. It's Gretchen. She's eight, and a big girl now. She's pretty, with long blonde hair, light blue eyes and even white teeth. She smiles a lot. She's visited every day I've been sick, and just sat by my bed. Mum thinks it's very sweet.

One day before I wake up Gretchen says to Mum 'Jim vonte die, like hiss vader, vill he?' She's crying, and still has a strong German accent when she's upset.

Now we three cry all day, and, cuddled together in one bed, all night. Will this agony never end?

Dad didn't like life insurance. Said nobody should benefit from someone's death. He had a point. But Mum is left in the Tanganyika bush with two young children, and two hundred pounds sterling in the world. All that stands between us and the 'poor house', she says, is that two hundred pounds. And the tenuous goodwill of Geita Gold Mine. I will test that to the extreme.

# Seven

I've never thought about death till now. I turn five in July 1956, Dad dies the next February. I'm kept from the realities, never see his body or attend his funeral. I only see his grave months after he dies, when my eldest brother Bertrand drives us there.

They put him in the mortuary near the club. They keep him there two days, while the Chinese carpenters make a coffin, and a grave is blasted from the granite of Samina graveyard. The mortuary or *kifo nyumba* looks like a tiny church. It's twenty foot by ten, and has slit-windows high up to stop peeping.

*Kifo nyumba*, literally 'dead-house' is two hundred yards downhill from our garden, and its red tin roof is visible from there. It stands in a small clearing, surrounded by gravel, beyond which wild trees and bushes grow. A footpath leads round the clearing to the door on the far side. Lutoli says the *Wazungu* take bodies there in darkness. He refers to Europeans like I'm not one.

After Dad is dead and buried some weeks, *kifo nyumba* becomes pressingly important to me. I am morbidly fascinated. *Mzogas*. Dead bodies. What are they like? Why don't they move? Do they really smell as bad as they say? How long till they become a 'skelington'? Do 'skelingtons' get up and dance? Seen dancing 'skelingtons' in a cartoon. Not becoming for Dad's 'skelington' to be dancing. That would look happy. Can't dance in a coffin, can you?

Two things happen to exacerbate my curiosity about death and *kifo nyumba*. First is Tembo's puppy, second the passing of Mr Valari (senior).

Tembo is a semi mute, miniature Gallua tribesman. He's four foot six tall, hardly more than my height at six. He's intellectually challenged, an outcast from his tribe. He works for us from the outset, and lives in an outbuilding in our garden. He has no friends, but is slavishly devoted to Mum, who's been very kind to him. It is she who named him *'Tembo'* or 'elephant', and not as a joke. He's small, but prodigiously strong. He has shoulders and arms like a weightlifter, and can lift rocks his own size. He works tirelessly and uncomplainingly. I never know

Tembo well, because he rarely speaks, and briefly then.

I don't know where Tembo gets his puppy. It's a curious little dog. Black and almost hairless, it has a fat tummy, and a pencil-thin tail. It never looks healthy. Even as a tiny puppy with half open eyes, it lies languidly in the heat, and doesn't chase its tail or play. It has an aura of impending death, and an awful smell on its breath. Something is wrong. At only six, I sense another call from that terrible servant of God the visiting preacher talked about. Angel of death. Not like nice angels. A murdering one.

I come into possession of a glass syringe and needle. I find it in the grounds of the African hospital, litter from a spilled dustbin. I think how unwell Tembo's puppy is, and decide to help. I will give it an injection, like Dr Weiss. What does he inject? Water. Obvious. What else goes through a needle? I'll fill the syringe, and inject Tembo's puppy. It will fix him, whatever's wrong.

Tembo, surprisingly, doesn't countenance my cunning plan. In his limited way he says I shouldn't. I look at his puppy lying listlessly, and decide I have to, Tembo or no. I fill the syringe, a five millilitre one, with tap water, put the needle on, and await my chance. At midday Tembo disappears into his quarters. I strike.

The puppy doesn't even wince when I plunge the needle into his thin buttock. He squirms weakly when I press the plunger to force water in. It's over. I flee the scene, my good deed done. He is my first patient. I never imagine one day I will become a doctor, move to England, specialise, and lecture to post-graduates.

I don't know exactly why the puppy dies that afternoon. Was it going to anyway? Has my injection done it? Tembo finds him lying dead, and brings his *mzoga*, or corpse, accusingly to me. I haven't expected my patient to die, at least not so soon.

I'm stunned and sobered. Mixed feelings. On one hand I'm horrified, and devastated for Tembo and his puppy. On the other, there's a dawning realisation. If, indeed, I killed the puppy, that makes me less than powerless regarding death.

When Dad died I had nothing to do with it. I neither saved nor killed him. I was only told it had happened. I was totally and completely powerless in its presence. It seems death is an independent, overwhelming and insurmountable force, over which I have no control or influence. Only God has. Which is why shooting him is the best thing.

But this is different. Whether causative or failing-to-treat-successfully, I'm instrumental, involved, in a death. Horrible, but exciting. A glimmer into a power I needed when Dad died. With it, I can reverse his death.

I help poor Tembo dig a grave. He lowers the sad little *mzoga* and covers it with soil. I fashion a cross from two sticks and one of Dad's pipe cleaners. The little mound and cross is all that remains. It is not the end of the matter. I've found an opportunity to research a question, which has haunted me: how long till an *mzoga* is a skelington? I'll revisit Tembo's puppy.

Mr Valari (senior) is in his sixties. I'm not sure why he's in Geita, because he doesn't work. He lives with his son, Mr Valari (junior), and his wife and children. They're Italian. His son is an electrician.

It's shortly after I turn six, five months after Dad's death, a month after Tembo's puppy, that the news breaks. Mr Valari (senior) is dead. I don't know what he looks like alive, because he's a recluse who seldom ventures beyond his son's wood-built house. Now he's joined the legion of the dead. This time I'll not be sidelined and denied the knowledge. On the day he dies, I resolve to peep into *kifo nyumba*. I'm determined to see a human *mzoga*. It's research.

From the age of two I've been trying to make things from wood and nails. By six I'm an accomplished wood-*fundi*. In Geita, it seems, everyone's a *fundi*, or expert, at something. I find some discarded planks and begin to build a ladder. It's so poor, Tembo, uninvited, comes to my aid. He neither asks, nor seems interested, what it's for. It's five or six feet high, with a step every foot. Interestingly, it's later used by Mum to reach ripe pawpaws in our garden, and is still around ten years later.

It's still the day of Mr Valari (senior)'s expiry. Before nightfall I drag the ladder through the elephant grass next to the road, and hide it in the bushes next to *kifo nyumba*. When they put Mr Valari (senior) there, I'll climb up to the slit windows. Then I'll see how a dead person looks.

I don't know if they'll put him there that day or the next

morning. Either way, I am resolute. Maybe, even, my newfound power around death and dying, which I've found with Tembo's puppy, will enable me to bring Mr Valari (senior) back to life. If I can do that, I'll find out more about my power. Using that, I'll get Dad out of his grave at Samina. Isn't that what happened in the Bible? Jesus came back. Someone else must have been involved. Anyone who can bring a dead person to life must at least have killed a puppy.

Next day, when I'm sure Mr Valari (senior)'s *mzoga* must be in *kifo nyumba*, I creep there under cover of the bushes and elephant grass. It's around noon. Most people are sheltering from the sun.

My ladder is heavy, and I struggle to place it against the wall. Nobody can see me from the road. The only moving thing is a *mwewe* bird, or hawk, a miniature black shape soaring high in the sun-scorched sky. He's like a small black crucifix against the pale blue. I wonder if he can see me. With the ladder in place, I begin to climb.

The top of the ladder is just under the sill of a slit widow. It's very wobbly. I reach the window and look in. For a few seconds I see nothing but darkness. Outside it's fierce sunlight. Inside it's gloom. Slowly my eyes accustom. Shading them with one hand, I begin to make out shapes. I hear loud buzzing.

There are two shelves along the opposite wall. On the bottom one there's a long white parcel. An *mzoga!* At one end it's partially unwrapped. His head. Someone's been here to look, and left without re-covering his face. The buzzing's coming from there. It's fate. I'm supposed to see him. As I stare, a fat black fly noisily rises from behind the cloth. They're *loud*, these big flies!

Suddenly this doesn't seem such a good idea. He's there, all right. It's definitiely him. His pinched dead face is peering out of the cover. What shocks me is he looks alive. Not as I imagined a dead person.

There's a yellow waxiness about his thin face, but nothing, to my mind, pronouncing death. I expect a sign. Swelling, bruising, blood. . . Tembo's puppy wasn't bruised or bleeding. Just swollen around his tummy.

Surely people, being more, well, *human*, should have more

outward evidence? Mr Valari (senior) doesn't. I've never seen the old man close up, but he looks very much like his son, Mr Valari (junior). Both are thin, rangy men. Like rope, I think. I don't know if they closed his eyes after he died, but they're wide open now, and staring when I peer through the high window.

His eyes are focused on me. There's a resigned grimace on his face. He sees me, accuses me of killing him. Not fair. I haven't injected *him* with water. I am innocent. I feel my power evaporate. I can't bring anyone back to life. Just then the hovering fly lands on his eye.

How I don't break a leg I don't know. It's not recoil at his staring eyes, or even the flies. True, the ladder wobbles, but I don't fall. It strikes me I can't revitalise the *mzoga*. Then my concentration lapses. The ladder moves backwards in slow motion. I'm free falling, clinging to my ladder. I thump into a thornbush. I'm knocked breathless. I lie gasping. The pain starts slowly. My chest, my back, everywhere. I've bruised my ribs, and am scratched all over by vicious thorns.

As I fall Mum and Tembo run up. He tells her where I've gone. She's alarmed to see me in the thornbush. She sees the ladder and knows what I've been up to. 'Shame,' she says, 'you shouldn't be looking in there....' Tembo gives me another of his accusing looks. His eyes say this is connected to his puppy. They help me up and carry my ladder home. Josef Weiss puts iodine on my scratches.

'You vant to be ze Frankenstein, yes?' he laughs, hugely pleased at his wit. No, I don't want to be one of those horrid tinned sausages from Barrat Stores.

If I can't bring people back to life, there's something wrong with what I know about death. Skelingtons. . . they're the key. Becky says they're *skeletons*. I don't believe her. It's from the 'skelingtons' I'll get magic to raise Dad from his grave. I'll dig up Tembo's puppy.

Tembo, for all his quiet ways and untrammelled views on life, has made a shrine. He's planted flowers, and is often seen in the evening sitting on a stone, staring quietly. When I dig up the *ziara*, or grave, I can leave no trace. Tembo will look accusingly at me again. No matter, I have to see if the puppy is now a skelington. Or is that really a skeleton? English, or *Kiingereza*, isn't easy.

Before I can dig, a surprise comes from Europe. My brother Bertrand has heard of Dad's death while serving as able seaman on *HMS Ark Royal*, an aircraft carrier in the Mediterranean. He's seventeen years my senior, twenty-two years old. It takes time to arrange compassionate leave, then he flies via Cairo and Dar-es-Salaam to Mwanza, where he catches a lift on a timber lorry.

He arrives early one evening at our front door. Mum lets him in, and there's a tearful family reunion, made of bereavement and loss, and joining of survivors, or whatever happens at such times. I don't feel connected. I neither know nor recognise the tall, gaunt young man in white tropical naval uniform. He left to join the navy when I was one. I haven't seen him since.

Bertrand is feted and treated like a celebrity. It's not every day they see a young sailor here. They queue to buy him beers at the club, and Mum has to help him home several times. Big people are strange. They seem very strong, being able to enjoy themselves so much when someone has died.

Bertrand takes time out from the club to borrow a Land Rover and drive us the seventeen miles to the cemetery at Samina. The road has tall grass and bushes growing in the middle, and potholes the size of dustbins. The going's slow and hot. When, after two hours, we near Samina, we're assailed by midges, tiny flies which zoom down our noses and into our eyes. Big flies at *kifo nyumba*, small ones here. Why?

I'm standing by the grave, which I've never seen before. It's horrible. How can Dad be here, under the ground? Mum said they buried him, but somehow I didn't expect this. The disturbed earth and stone are not yet covered by thornbush and elephant grass, as the other, older graves are. There's another exception. Mr Valari (senior)'s grave is even fresher and starker than Dad's. God is mocking me. Here they both are, Dad and Mr Valari (senior), and there's absolutely nothing I can do. I feel unpleasantly that day I've killed Tembo's puppy and Mr Valari (senior). I've no clue how to bring Mr Valari, Dad, or even the puppy, back to life. Did I somehow kill Dad too? I was angry with him sometimes. Painted in fading black on Dad's cross is:

*RICHARD PENHALIGON 1909-1957*

*Darling Husband, Father & Hero*
*'Home is the Sailor'*

I see, when Mum points it out, that Dad's buried next to Mrs Williams, who was murdered by Stroessner before we came to Geita. Mum says Dad read about it in a newspaper while waiting for a haircut in Johannesburg. Her grave, alone in that cemetery, has a stone. Cursive letters are carved on it:

*SANDRA WILLIAMS 1922-1950*
*Dearly Beloved Wife, Devoted Mother*
*Cruelly taken from us*

Mrs Williams reached out long ago to Dad, in a newspaper article about her murder. Now she's drawn him from so far away, to lie beside her forever. That's what Mum says to Bertrand. Strangely, I understand every word. In English. Why would this unknown lady do such a thing? In the heat, I feel a tingle of dread running up my spine. To compound it, a three-inch scorpion, tail held scimitar-high, stalks across the top of the gravestone towards a slowly moving centipede, oblivious of the danger. Life and death go on.

Midges invade mouths, noses and eyes. They drive away all thought. We keep our visit brief. We set off back to Geita. How can I ever make dead people alive? I'm desperate.

Bertrand's handsome, toothy and lanky. It's funny to think I've got such a big brother. I'm sorry when he goes.

I return to my plan to dig up Tembo's puppy. Surely, when I discover how long it takes to turn into a skeleton, which I now accept is the right word, because Gretchen says so, I'll be wiser about death. I'll re-visit the concept, and find how to go to Samina and bring Dad back.

A golden opportunity arrives. Tembo goes away. Although eschewed by his tribe for his small size and diminutive wit, they send him a message that his mother has died. Another death. This time an African woman in a village called Biharlomoulo, sixty miles from Geita. I wonder if they put her in another *kifo nyumba*, and if her eyes are open. It's a sign. Death keeps signalling. The message is clear: dig up the puppy's *mzoga* and

85

see if he's a skeleton yet.

One evening during Tembo's absence I carry out my grisly plan. I take the spade and dig up the puppy. It's still wrapped in the red and white dishcloth I stole from Mum. She's been looking for it everywhere. The earth-stained parcel stinks even worse than the *machula*'s bucket. It makes me choke. Determined to discover the truth, I persevere and unwrap it. He is partly 'skeletised', or is that skeletonised? Some bones are exposed. Some parts still furry. His face is dried out like a mummy, giving him an appearance of an older, wiser being. Everywhere there are fat earthworms, sliding about, unaware and uncaring to be pulled from the earth. What does this teach me? I put the little parcel back in the ground, smoothe the soil so Tembo won't know.

I ponder for days, without resolving the problem or answering the question. But the thought of finding out about death, skeletonisation and resurrection never goes. I retain a morbid fascination for death and dying. It colours my growing up, and gives different meanings to many things, not least religion. Jesus was resurrected, and before that brought the walrus, or was it Lazarus, back from the dead, didn't he?

# Eight

The legend of *Lotanga*'s voyage from Port Bell, Uganda, to Lotanga, Tanganyika, is told and retold in Geita for years. Umali's the first to tell me, when I'm able to understand Swahili. That's when I'm two. I hear the story from Wait at four, and Dad tells me snippets when I'm five. My English is so poor, I don't take much in. The tale of the voyage is clearly important. After Dad dies in 1957, Mum frequently mentions the epic voyage, and other adults make comments about 'your father's narrow escape on the lake.'

By six, I want to know the whole story, from beginning to end, in sequence and detail. I need to own it because it's part of Dad. I ask Umali, not only as my most trusted historian, but also as Dad's companion on the trip, to tell me.

We're in a circle with Amina and Umali around a fire by the servant's quarters. Supported on three big stones, a pot of *mboga*, or vegetables, with a lump of fatty goat-flesh floating in it, is boiling furiously, smelling delicious. A little distance away Tembo whittles a piece of wood with a knife blade. He likes to be part, yet outside, gatherings like this. Amina will see he gets a generous helping of the *chakula* when it's ready.

The moon is full, the bush illuminated in yellow light. The crickets are still. It's an extraordinarily quiet evening. The light from the fire flickers on Umali's face. He adopts a distant, philosophical look. Amina watches him closely. When he's like this, he's in the mood to tell a great story. Even Tembo notices, and stops whittling. Umali, as always, speaks in Lake Swahili. He gives his account in dramatic style, voice rising and falling, speeding up and slowing, with long pauses for effect, and to make the listeners long for what's next.

'Lake Victoria is very big,' he begins, holding out his arms. 'From Port Bell to Lotanga is two hundred and fifty miles as the great black *kunguru-bird* flies.' The crow. 'But there are many shallow places, and islands, some with people, some without. To make this journey you have to go here and there, weave your own course, or road, to avoid many dangers.' He lets the silence hang.

'Crocodiles as big as three or four men, great floating logs, ready to puncture a boat. Bad people, *mwizis*, thieves who board at night to *chinja* you, cut your throat, steal your money.' He whistles between his teeth, and spits. 'There are more dangers than you can imagine.'

'We left Port Bell, your father, the Nyasa Wait, and me, as the sun went down in the west, and the moon rose on the other side. Your father was brave to set out so late. I would have waited for morning, but who was I to tell the *Bwana*?' Umali shakes his head. 'Your father was a courageous and clever man.' He sticks out an arm, straight at shoulder level, with index finger pointing into the dark. The light and shadow from the flickering fire play across his face and illuminate his eyes.

'We headed south. The engine went *pap-pap-pap*, bubbles came from the water at the back, and smoke went from the big pipe on top. Your father stood at the wheel. He had a pipe in his mouth. He looked happy. He said he always loved boats.'

'As we travelled, the moon went behind a small cloud. It didn't come out again. The cloud must have joined its bigger, fatter brothers. For some time we didn't see the moon, or enjoy its light. We motored on. In the darkness it was impossible to see anything. Your father the *Bwana* was the only one who knew where we were going. He wasn't worried. He had that gold and glass thing he said was a *'compasi'*. I didn't understand how he could trust that little thing in the dark.' Umali looks wistful.

'It grew black, like I never saw. There was no moon. Even the stars were gone. It had been a hot, very hot day. I had the feeling I get before the rain. A pain in my right knee, I just knew. . .' Umali rubs his knee as if feeling the pain. 'The wind started gently. A cool, welcome breeze after the heat. Your father was at the wheel, and the Nyasa Wait and I made tea on a primus. Your father was grateful. Know what he did?' Umali shakes his head and smiles. His eyes glint.

'He was a great man, the *Bwana*. He took out a silver flask from his pocket. The one your mother keeps on the sideboard. It had whisky. He called it *Scotchie*. Like petrol. It burns, I know because I tried it before.' Umali grins wickedly. Dad said his whisky disappeared quicker than he drank it. 'He poured it into our tea, just a little. It tasted wonderful. It strengthened the tea and sugar. Like drinking the *maji ya Mungu*.' God's water.

Umali smacks his lips. He turns to Amina, who, like me, is enthralled. 'You have never made *chai* like that one for me, sweet one of my longing.' She slaps him on the shoulder. He laughs delightedly.

'We enjoyed that tea,' Umali resumes at length, grin making way to stern expression, 'but by then that baby wind, that cooling breeze we so appreciated, began to blow harder and harder, colder and colder, no longer pleasant. Then the fattened clouds, far above and unseen in the darkness, burst above our heads, with thunder like the roar of *Shetani*, the devil, and lightning came to split the sky to the water, and made such light it was brighter than day!'

'A storm?' I say.

'Not just a storm, the worst I've seen, and it happened then, at the exact time when I, who had never before been on a boat, apart from a *mtumbui* hollowed from a single tree, at Nungwe Bay, went my first time on the great water.'

Umali looks at Amina quizzically. *'Chakula tiari?'* Is the food ready?

'It can wait,' she replies in Swahili, 'I want to hear the ending.' She's heard it many times before. That's the beauty of old fashioned story telling around a fire. Excitement and newness never diminish.

'Now I began to feel fear,' Umali says, taking Amina's cue, his eyes closing to express his feeling. 'I felt an unpleasantness inside, here, in my chest.' He pounds his thin ribs.

'My heart began to say it was not happy with this boat, this water, this thunder, this lightning, those waves, which rocked us like the high branches of a mango tree when boys throw stones to release fruit. I began to think this, my first time on the great water, is a mistake, and if I was not so frightened I would *kunya* over the side to relieve my groaning bowels.'

Umali breathes deeply. His nostrils flare, and he opens his eyes. He spits three yards through his top teeth. A great spitter. Only Amina is better.

'Your father stayed at the wheel, his pipe clenched in his teeth, and he turned the wheel left, right, left again. But the boat was like a dry leaf in storm water. It went where the water said, and no man could control it. By now the waves were higher than the deck, and broke over it, trying to drive us down into the black water. The tops of waves came away in the wind, which shrieked with the voice of *Shetani* himself, and shot like small stones from a catapult, to hit me and the Nyasa with painful force.'

Umali opens his arms, his eyes wide. It must have been terrible, I think, to hear the very voice of the devil! He continues.

'We thought we had come early to our end. I even beseeched *Allah*, if he would only let me live through this storm, I would blind one eye and break one leg, and become a *masikini*, a poor man.' Amina chuckles.

'I'd like to see you a *masikini*,' she laughs.

Umali pouts.

'What happened then?' I ask. Umali is still here, and Dad didn't drown, nor Wait.

'Your father somehow kept the boat facing the wind and waves. The engine went *pap-bwaaf-pap-bwaaf*, as the back heaved in and out of the water and the propeller turned, now in the water, now in the air. . .' Umali draws an open hand across his face to illustrate panic. 'Then *Mungu* gave us a death sentence. Maybe it was *Shetani*, I don't know.' God or the devil, one or the other.

'What happened, *Mzee*, old one?' Amina says, adding to the tension. The pot's boiling furiously on the fire. She leans forward and deftly lifts it and places it on the ground. 'Tell us what then became of you.'

'It was then the engine died,' Umali sighs, '*Ari Kufwa. . .* it left us completely without control.' He turns his face to the moonlit sky. The firelight illuminates his features, craggy and mysterious, his eyes reflecting deep distress.

I follow where he's looking. High in the sky a cloud drifts in the direction of the lake, revealing a full moon. I remember, Umali said *Ramadan* ended yesterday evening, with the first sighting of the full moon.

'*Ari kufwa?*' Amina says, emphasising the words. It died? She knows the story. But the expression of wonder, or asking for confirmation by the audience, is integral to story telling.

'*Kabisa!*' Umali shakes his head. It died completely. His expression says, 'Where was my God when this happened?' He lets silence hang a long time.

'Your father knew it was big trouble – *mbaya, hatari.*' Bad things, danger. Umali purses his lips. 'It was then he showed me and the Nyasa he was truly a man of the big sea. . .'

'What did he do?' I ask, my heart beating with tension.

'The boat turned sideways on to the wind and waves, and the water struck at us in fury, waves taller than a Masai cattle-herder breaking over the deck, submerging the seats, while the big wind pushed the boat leaning on its side so we had to grasp the handrails with all our strength, not to be hurled into that shrieking, *Shetani*-inspired blackness. We hung there, in fear and in hopelessness. But your father didn't panic. He struggled uphill out of the wheelhouse, carrying a coil of rope and three blankets, which were for us to cover ourselves at night. He bought them at the *Boma Duka.*'

'*Blanketi?*' Amina asks dutifully, one huge tooth shining in the firelight. She stirs the pot of *mboga* cooling on the ground, replaces the lid. She makes that sucking 'tch' sound and spits fully ten feet. I'll never be able to match her.

'*Blanketi,*' Umali confirms. 'I thought he was mad. What could we do with them? Did he want us to sleep while the deck heaved and bucked like a drunken rhinoceros trying to copulate? With water up to our knees?' Amina laughs and slaps her thigh. A drunken rhino trying to do *jigi-jigi* is quite a picture.

'But our *Mzungu* had a plan. He gave the blankets to the Nyasa and me, and told us to make knots in the corners. We obeyed, for there was nothing else to do. While we struggled to tie the knots in the wet blankets, he cut the rope in pieces. With these he joined one knotted blanket corner to another. After several minutes fumbling, because of the wet and the dark, the three blankets were finally tied together, corner to corner. Then he fastened long lengths of rope to the corners of the whole. He told us to help him, and we carried the blanket-and-rope-thing to the back of the boat. He secured the ropes to the bollards used for tying up the boat, and threw the blankets into the raging water.'

'What for?' I ask, intrigued.

'Your father said it was a 'sea anchor', and I was amazed what happened. The ropes went tight, and the boat began to turn, bringing the point to face the anger of the storm. The bucking and rolling reduced, just like that.' Umali snaps his fingers.

'The trouble was not over. We didn't know how long before the water tore the blankets away. We no longer feared we would sink, but we were still in a mad storm, without an engine.' Umali shook his head and smiled. 'Do you know what amazed me most of all?'+

'No,' I say.

'The *Bwana* kept his pipe in his mouth the whole time.'

'*Bwana* loved that pipe,' Amina murmurs softly, looking sad, placing her hand on my knee, 'he was a good *Mzungu*.'

'The waves stopped swamping the deck, but the *Bwana* said Lotanga had taken water. We took up a hatch, and shone a torch. There was water, as deep as the height of Tembo.' He inclines his chin at Tembo, who, to hear better, has moved closer to, but not into, the circle round the fire. Tembo grins sheepishly. He enjoys stories. He's stopped whittling.

'I had to go down with a bucket, fill it, and pass it up to the Nyasa, who emptied it over the side. It was hard work, and slow. The boat wasn't bucking like an injured gazelle now, but it still moved this way and that, and I fell many times, hurting my shoulder and my head against the sides, which, in the blackness, I could not see. At first the water was above my waist.'

'He was in trouble,' Amina laughs, tapping my knee, 'who knows, but you may never have seen your Umali again.'

'That is true,' Umali says gravely. 'I was down there a very long time, perhaps an hour. . .'

'Then?' I ask.

'The storm ceased. Just like that!' He snaps his fingers. 'It seemed to go on a long, long time. But the whole thing started and finished in two hours. *Bwana* checked on his watch.' Umali smiles.

'We had covered only twenty miles from Port Bell. Now the lightning and thunder stopped. The scream of the wind died, and the moon came out from hiding, to light up the world like day.' Umali shakes his head in wonderment. 'I heard several fishermen coming home in dugouts lost their lives that night. The lake, it can be evil, a playing place for *Shetani*, where he destroys people and takes them down to hell. It's not always as it looks, a peaceful glittering thing of beauty.'

'Now we were on a vast flat plate of water, shining in the moonlight, and the air was still, like we had died and gone somewhere else. We were still in trouble. We had no engine, we were just sitting there, wondering what to do.'

'*Fanya nini?*' I ask. What did you do?

'*Bwana* said there was a loss of diesel to the engine. He took his torch, still sucking his pipe, and went down to the engine underneath the wheelhouse. After a few minutes he came out and said he'd fixed the problem. A fuel pipe had come off and he'd put it back. He turned the key. For a few seconds the starter motor made a sound, *whee-whee-whee-whee*, and smoke came from the chimney. Then, like a great buffalo, which wakes from sleeping, *garum-garum*, the engine began to roar, and *pap-pap-pap*, the propeller began again to stir the water. We were so happy. I even hugged the Nyasa, in spite of his ugliness.' Amina giggles and pokes him in the ribs.

'The Nyasa is better-looking than you, you wrinkled, dried out fish,' she laughs.

'*Hau,* I am again insulted,' he quips, making his best sad face. He continues. 'The rest of the journey was easy. It took three more days to get to Mwanza and Lotanga. On the way we saw fishermen in dugout *mtumbuis*, islands with people and islands without people. In the shallows close to Musoma we saw house-sized hippopotami lying with their snouts just above the water, watching us with evil eyes. In one place there were crocodiles, great reptiles as long as three men, or four of Tembo.'

He inclines his head at Tembo, who grins hugely. Unlike Umali and Amina, he has good, white teeth. When he smiles there's more than a hint of the *fisi*, or hyena, about him.

'Eventually we arrived at Lotanga, and *Bwana* Müller, the Geremani, was very happy to see us. He had heard of the sudden storm in the north of the lake, and feared we, and his beautiful boat, were lost to the evil *djinn* of the waters.'

What a great man Dad was! I can see how much Umali admired him. Dad sailed many oceans in different vessels. *Lotanga* and her crew must have been very different. Yet he coped, and won Umali's admiration. It fills me with pride. But why, oh why can't he be here with me now? I feel tears running down my cheek, and I sniff loudly.

Amina notices, as she always does. She puts her arm around me, draws me to her. *'Baba iko ndani, toto, hawezi ku acha,'* she whispers. Your father is inside, child, he'll never leave. I wipe my tears on her *kanzu.* It's used to it.

*'Tu-ile,'* Amina says at last. It's time to eat. She lifts a buttock on the log she's sitting on, and lets out a loud *jamba.* It sounds like a trumpet. We laugh. Amina farts with aplomb. She upturns the still-steaming *ugali* onto a huge iron platter, then pulls the dish of *mboga* and fatty goat close. We reach out as one, take handfuls of *ugali,* roll it in one practised hand, and make deep dents with a thumb. Then we scoop it into the *mboga.* It's delicious.

Just then Lutoli appears. It's amazing how he senses there's freshly cooked *chakula* in the offing. I move up on my log. He sits next to me and reaches into the *ugali* pot. He isn't shy. Nor am I. Umali and Amina regard us with obvious affection. To them we are their children. I feel happy. These *watu* are my family. I'm a bit guilty about Mum, but decide you can have two families.

After eating till our stomachs are full, we drink *chai.* It's tea, brewed, together with milk, and lots of sugar, in a pot. If the *watu* can afford a tin of condensed sweetened milk, that's a very good day. The *chai* is stewed, the pot left to simmer with the ingredients in. It's the only way to make tea.

# Nine

Long, hot days. Nothing stirs. No sound. Everything alive sleeps. The *leguaan* in his hole, hyena in the fastness of his hide, leopard in the branch of canopied tree, python in overgrown ditch or *donga*, frog under leaf at water's-edge. Pet dogs skulk from sun's furnace under houses, *watu* hide in windowless mud huts.

Every breathing thing tries to live out the day. Even insects avoid the heat. In the distance objects shimmer, like through a bonfire. They dance, change shape, change again. How can a hunter aim if the object moves like this? This is why they don't hunt in the day. *Jua kali.* The sun is angry. The laconic greeting of a *mutu* to another if they chance to pass. '*Kali sana,*' is the response. Very angry. No one looks up. Can't say 'Good day' if it isn't. Too blurry hot.

I'm lying on my back in tall grass. Life's suddenly very quiet. At least it's cooler here. Somewhere invisibly close by an *njiwa*-bird breaks the silence with a tired and throaty ooh-oor-oor. The sound of torpid midday bush. Even the *njiwa* is tired. It falls silent again. African siesta-time.

High in the wide, shimmering, aching, sky are small drifting black shapes. *Mwewe,* the hawk. They, alone, move on this canvas. Soaring on thermals from sun-blasted ground, they float far and effortless over hill and bush, wings fixed, deep-set yellow eyes searching. *Mwewe* see miles, swoop from nowhere to carry off prey their own weight. Rabbits, baby sheep or goats, puppies and kittens, have met sudden nemesis in sharp talon and beak. Beautiful but deadly, I think, awed by the aerial display.

It's more than awe. There's continuity here, a never-ending expectancy that tomorrow, like today, at precisely. . . what is the time? I look fleetingly at the sun, but have to close my eyes. Everything goes red, like blood. You can't see the sun more than a second. It's high, near the top of the world. A *mwewe*-bird is directly between me and it. A small black silhouette framed in white heat. It's *saa sita.* Time six, or six o'clock.

Swahili time-keeping is six hours behind English. Six o'clock is twelve midday. Sensible. To the *watu* the sun comes up at twelve, goes down at twelve. Back to my musing. I expect that, precisely at *saa sita*, or midday, tomorrow, as today, in this sun-scorched place, absolutely nothing will happen. It's boring, but comforting. Yet I wish I had something to do.

I don't know where Lutoli is today. Sometimes his fat aunt sends him on errands which seem to last all day.

A dog, that'd be nice. A reliable friend to share these quiet moments. If, that is, I can coax him out from under the house. Some people with dogs can't. Most hounds round here won't brave the heat of day.

Feral, or wild dogs are all over Geita. Product of uncontrolled breeding between all the diverse kinds of domestic dogs brought here by expatriates, mixed with African wild dogs attracted by the smells of man and easy food from his garbage. The half-breeds and quarter-breeds breed again and again, until Wild Dog, Alsatian, Boxer, Afghan, French Poodle, Rhodesian Ridgeback, Pointer, Corgi and Bloodhound are all represented in what becomes known as *Shenzi*, or 'rubbish', dogs.

In 1955 Mrs Snel imports two pedigree *Dachshund*, or sausage dog, puppies from Germany. Brother and sister. She names the boy Fritzie, and the girl Mitzie. The German breeder hasn't bred morals into his little dogs. Fritzie grows to be an unbounded canine philanderer, and Mitzie a whore. First they practise incest, producing six more *Dachshunds* of equal immorality, and then they turn to low-life, or *Shenzis*, for good measure. Soon Mitzie gives birth to six low-slung *Shenzis*, while Fritzie fathers a dozen more.

A sea change in the genetic makeup of Geita *Shenzis* takes place. Short-legged *Shenzi* breeds with short legged *Shenzi*, then they breed again. The mixing genes fancy each other, and, from the epicentre in Geita, ever-shorter legs and longer bodies spread out to the district like ripples in a pond. Out of this epi-phenomenom, in 1957, on a *shamba* ten miles from the camp, Sandy is born.

Sandy is ten weeks old when a wandering Gallua offers her for two shillings. She's a furry, hand-made, teddy bear. She's low to the ground, and has the hanging ears of a *Dachshund*. There are seams running up her legs, and down the middle of her belly, like she's been stitched in a factory.

We fall in love instantly. Mum gives in easily. Truth is even she can't resist the little *Shenzi* who licks our faces the moment she's close enough. Mum insists she do a lap-test before agreeing to buy her. She has to prove she's old enough to be separated from her mother. She puts a saucer of milk on the ground, and Becky and I watch with bated breath. The little fur-ball stumbles on short legs to the saucer. When she gets there she sits down and stares at us in turn. Finally she's staring intently into my eyes.

'Drink, girl,' I say. Her deep brown eyes don't blink. 'Drink,' I urge. She turns to the saucer and puts her mouth to the milk. A tiny pink tongue begins to lap. Becky and I applaud. Mum goes inside and comes back with two shillings. Sandy has joined our little family.

Meantime, there are other matters in mind. I'd like to use the word 'venerable' when talking about Puncture-Car, though I never know if the old car was a distinguished or expensive model. I notice the discarded car when I'm three, Mum says, and fascination for the rotting wreck never leaves me. I still don't know what make she was, or the year she was built. Nobody says whom she belonged to, or why the owner pushed her off the side of the road a quarter mile from the club.

She's from the nineteen thirties, or forties at the latest. She was once black, but now she's a patchwork of black and red rust. She has massive mudguards back and front, with a running board between. There are two doors, making her a coupé. Her bonnet's long, and opens on both sides, hinged to a chromed part down the centre. There's a two-inch deep pool of rusty rainwater on her floor, and she reeks of oxidising iron, a sharp, acrid mustiness.

Her seats are cracked brown leather, green in creases where algae thrive. Her steering wheel is huge. It has chromed, but rusty spokes, and a big black boss in the middle. Nothing like as pretty as my *Chevrolet* wheel.

Her gear lever has no top, and is unmovably seized. The pedals are flat on the floor, submerged in red-brown water, with rotting leaves floating on it. There are round dials in the dashboard, which remind me of the *Grundig* radio in our lounge. Her tyres are not only flat, but have largely disintegrated, leaving black lumps of gloopy rubber, with shiny green stuff growing in between, and hanging about the rusting spoked wheels like eccentric strings of pearls.

Never mind her state. Never mind there's a small tree growing through her boot, forcing the lid open and buckling one side. Never mind the smell of rust, the vines and creepers, which envelop her windscreen and interlace the wipers. Puncture Car's blurry magnificent.

Before he dies, Dad humours me by stopping MZ 202 every time we pass where the abandoned car lies. He lets me look and admire her many times. After he's gone, Mum tries many things to console me. She knows how angry I am with God, and everybody. One day, seven months after Dad dies, she speaks to Mr Snel, the manager, about Puncture Car, and me and he decides to tow her home to our garden so I can see and play with her every day.

He takes his Land Rover down to her, secures a chain, and drags her, screeching in complaint and trailing branches and leaves, to our garden. It's a great day, and I'm bursting with excitement.

Lutoli's also driving, using my shiny *Chevrolet* steering wheel, which I've cherished ever since I found it on the beach in Dar-es-Salaam. It's only now, since I've got a whole car, I can let anyone else play with it. Three of Lutoli's *rafikis*, tribal friends, stand on the running board on the left. Perched on my right are Becky, Gretchen, and her brother Dieti. Gretchen seems as excited by the old car as me. Sitting on the boot are two more *totos*, and another is perched on the bonnet. For a reason I can't discern, I've insisted everyone wears one of those rusty World War II British army helmets. Gretchen's blonde hair and her chin are about all we can see of her.

With all passengers aboard, or clinging on, I announce 'we're off'. We make a great roar of engine noise, grating gearbox, hooter and collisions with small objects, and the side passengers rock the car. Mum tells us we'll wake the dead. I file the idea away for later. Maybe noise is the secret I've ignored for resurrection. We aren't loud enough to wake our hidden, secret passenger. He sleeps through the cacophony.

His Latin name is *Dendroaspis Polyepsis*, but everyone calls him black mamba. He's been given many pseudonyms, but most chilling is 'widow-maker'. He belongs to the genus *Elapidae*, and has fixed fangs, unlike many lesser cousins. He can grow to great lengths, and examples eight feet long are not rare. Such specimens have a diameter of up to two and a half inches.

The black mamba's a shy, unassuming reptile. He's known to be timid, and avoid contact unless cornered. Then, in a desperate attempt to escape, he will try to get away, and, in passing, make several lightning-quick bites. His poison is an extremely potent neurotoxin. Tiny amounts are enough to paralyse the muscles of the throat and respiration. Death, which is said to be quick and agonising, is by asphyxiation.

I don't know this the day Puncture Car comes home. I also don't know mambas are deaf. Explains why he doesn't hear the racket. Doesn't explain why he doesn't feel vibrations, because mambas should have sensors for that.

The others have tired of playing and gone off, leaving only Lutoli and I. We take off our helmets, because we can't see properly with them on. We survey our limousine. I'm in the passenger seat with my Chevrolet wheel, Lutoli's in the driving seat. He pretends to work the gears. Puncture Car's lovely. I reach and press the knob on the glove box. It falls open.

The mamba's awake. The pupils of his hooded eyes are dilated in the twilight of evening. His head is black and coffin-shaped, and I'm drawn to his slit-like reptilian mouth. A long forked tongue darts in and out. I see only part of him in the glove box, for the back's missing. The scaled brown body extends into the engine compartment. The inside of his mouth is coal-black.

I don't know how long we stare at each other. There is something strangely hypnotic in the eyes of a mamba. My arm dangles over the glove box. Time is frozen. An urge to leave the car rises in my breast. Have to do it gently, quickly. I draw my arm back slowly, and even more slowly reach for the door handle. It's stuck. I've put my Chevrolet wheel down the side of my seat. Lutoli has stopped playing driver. His eyes are wide. I hold my breath and shove the door with my shoulder. It creaks open. Then I'm out, running, screaming. Lutoli's almost as quick. He's only a yard behind.

'*Nyoka!*' I shout hoarsely when I spot Umali peeling potatoes on the steps.

'Snake, where?'

'In the car!' Lutoli and I yell hysterically.

'Snake in car!' Umali bellows in Swahili as he runs, a panga magically in his hand.

I learn there is nothing that galvanises the docile and peaceable *watu* more than the word *nyoka*. Where they come from, or how they get there so quick I don't know. Suddenly there are four, then eight, then more, all bearing pangas, sticks or rocks. The wild-eyed mob, led by a manically energised Umali, gets to the car. And stops.

*'Wapi?'* Umali breathes, nostrils flaring, panga raised high, where?

'There!' I shout. I point to the glove box. It's empty. He must have retreated backwards into the engine compartment. Before Umali can comment, there's a commotion amongst the *watu* behind, and I see them yelling, cursing, and striking at something on the ground.

Then I see him. He's made a dash for safety and dropped out of the engine. He's quick, but they're quicker. He's fully seven foot, but as I watch he's chopped into pieces only inches long. It's over in seconds, and his head, forked tongue still darting in and out of his mouth, spins, attached to a six inch piece of body, to lie twitching in the dust next to my bare foot.

*Wazungu* adults don't swear in front of children. But they do swear at the *watu*. The victims of their invective don't understand the words, but they know when they're being abused. Always keen to add to their own repertoire, they use English swearwords blindly, without understanding, but with even greater flair and venom than their teachers. A large boulder mashes the snake's head into the dirt.

*'Blurryfuckenblackbastar!'* screams the thrower. He's clearly a good English-learner, but hasn't a clue what he means.

*'Blurrystupidbitch!'* shouts another, vigorously trampling the mangled remains. Like them, I don't understand the words, but they seem right. In time I'll incorporate them in my vocabulary. This is vicarious learning with a twist.

With much shoulder slapping and congratulations, the *watu* disappear as magically as they came, back into the elephant grass and thorn trees surrounding our garden. Umali, Lutoli and I stare at the remains of the mamba. Some bits are still twitching.

I discover two things that day: the *watu* hate snakes, and there really is a bush telegraph, with or without poles. I retrieve my beloved Chevrolet steering wheel. I don't know why, but I've got a feeling it's got magic, and that's why the mamba didn't bite me. Later I tell Umali, and he agrees. 'Some things are *hirizi*,' he says. A charm against evil. Everyone knows *nyokas* are in cahoots with *Shetani*, the evil one. You need charms.

Funny how things come in twos or threes. The Puncture Car mamba saga is only a month ago, when I decide to conduct an experiment with a coir rope, an old wicker chair, and a branch high on a tree in our front garden.

Lutoli joins me. He's an ever-smiling, game little chap, and we have been hanging around forever. We've learnt Swahili together, in the company of *ayahs* under the baobab tree. He's proud of his well-spoken *Mzungu* friend.

'If we throw this stick, with the rope on one end, over that branch,' I say, 'we can bring it back down and tie it onto a chair.'

'*Sababu?*' he asks. Why?

'Sit in the chair and pull ourselves up,' I say.

'*Ndio,*' he beams. We take turns throwing the stick, but our arms and muscles are not man enough. Tembo arrives and asks what we're trying to do. We explain. He doesn't say anything, just takes the wood and rope from Lutoli, and hurls it high into the sky. It flies past the jutting branch, and falls down the other side. He lets out rope, and brings the stick down. We thank him, but he just shrugs his shoulders and walks away.

I fetch Mum's beloved wicker chair from the verandah. It's one of those with close woven reed, and it has armrests with holes. Lutoli and I thread the rope through the armrests, and tie it back on itself three feet above the chair. Now it's time to winch ourselves up. On this occasion, as it's my idea, Lutoli votes I go first.

It isn't possible to pull myself up in the chair. My weight pulls the rope too tight round the branch. I find that by hauling on the rope, and lifting myself out of the seat, I can raise the chair a foot at a time. By increments, I labour up the side of the tree, the ground moving further and further away. In later years, I note the branch is only thirty feet up, but it's higher at six.

After much effort I arrive under the branch. There's something not quite right with the rope. It's been looped over the top, not wound around it. The rope is brown coir, not green. Now it's coiled three times round the branch, and it's green. Grass green. Then I see the head. It's smaller than the black mamba's, but a similar shape, and its eyes are red and staring unblinkingly into mine.

My face is eighteen inches from a green mamba. I release the rope very slowly. My heart beats so hard I think it might burst. The snake doesn't move. I go down, foot by foot. When I am halfway to the ground I yell, for the second time in four weeks. *'Nyoka, nyoka!'*

By the time the chair's legs meet the ground there is a *mêlée* of axe, panga, stick and stone-bearing men and women, and a teenager who fits a pebble to a long sling. He hurls his sling round and round, then dispatches the stone at the snake on the branch. It hits him, or frightens him, for, rapidly uncoiling, he falls heavily to the ground in a tight bundle of convulsing green. He's dispatched just like his black cousin. Congratulations ring out, backs are slapped, and the *watu* go whence they came, leaving Lutoli and I speechless.

'Snakes are bad,' he says.

*'Ndio,'* I say. Yes.

'Shall we try again?' he asks.

*'Lazima,'* say I. Of course. The next few hoists up the tree are fun, and uneventful, though Lutoli and I get blisters on our hands, and a telling-off from Mum when she comes home to find Lutoli dangling high in her only, much-loved, wicker chair.

About this time Geita is treated to one of its comedies. Major William Bigginsbottom, late of the British Army in India, latterly of Bexhill-on-Sea, in his sixties and unmarried, has kept in touch with several wartime colleagues.

Coming from an aristocratic and wealthy family 'at home', the Major has spent the years since VJ day in 1945 travelling old haunts, looking up old comrades. Higginson's is one of the addresses he's kept, and he finally makes his way to Geita to re-acquaint himself with his old Colonel.

He arrives, this colonial relic, in an open Land Rover driven by a faithful but aged Gurkha from his Indonesian campaign, sporting a sunburned red face, six inch twirled grey moustache, pith helmet and smartly tailored, if sweaty, short khaki safari suit, plus polished army boots and white socks. He actually carries a swagger stick.

Higgs is delighted to see him, and the Major is not fazed by the mixed-race marriage of his old friend. They settle into fond reminiscences of the Burma campaign, and invite Kaizer, who fought in the Kabaw valley, to join their evenings.

In the spirit of camaraderie and past adventure, they drink enormous toasts to one another, and eternal calumny to Japs, Nazis and communists. Higgs, Maria and Bigginsbottom drink from glasses, Kaizer straight from the bottle. Like Wait.

One afternoon the Major goes outside to the little fenced shower enclosure. He's forgotten to take the latchkey to regain the verandah. One of Maria's young female cousins is helping around the house.

'Wewe,' the Major shouts from outside, naked from the waist-up, towel around his waist. He pronounces it way-way. It means 'you'. From the verandah only his top half is visible. To the young girl, there's a naked old man out there.

'Mimi?' she asks, shocked. Me? What does he want in his state of undress? He smiles appeasingly. He wants to be let in. The message is misconstrued. She's affronted. 'Mimi, apana!' she says, me-no! She turns and flees into the house. The amorous major and shy kijana tale spreads like bushfire.

Lutoli and I decide to establish our own republic when we're six. The Wazungu are too repressive. Andrew Miller, a Yorkshire boy, son of Mum's friend Mary, wants to take part. We set out up the hill above Top Road one morning, supplies of food and drink in a kikapu, or woven basket. We carry it in turns.

I'm on a mission. I'm angry, I don't respect the posh-speaking, dishonest Wazungu. They're wenwe's. Not Swahili. Just 'when we were in Kent', or 'when we had a mansion in Surrey', or 'when we were in Devon'. That's how all the big Wazungu wakoloni, or colonials, start all their stories. They sit on barstools at the club, drink locally brewed beer, smoke local cigarettes, breathe local air, go home to a local house, eat local food, and sleep in a locally built bed. They get their wages because of local gold, and use local *watu* to dig it. But they only talk about 'home', and *'wenwe'*. They tell everyone who'll listen how wonderful it was in Brighton, Devon, Somerset and Canterbury.

Geita, Tanganyika? They denigrate it with gusto. The worst thing ever. Just look at the *watu*. . . they're animals. These *wenwe's* don't think so, they know. Anyway, 'it's far too hot, old bean.' Wipe streaming brow with handkerchief, take long draught of cold *Whitecap*.

Yet they stay, these unredeemed habitual moaners, contract after contract. They always return after visiting their wonderful 'home'. There's no pleasing them. They'll complain, and hate, as long as they breathe. It's enough to make me ashamed of my white skin. Lutoli is right. Our own republic is what we need. I'm not sure about Andrew.

The hillside above the houses on Top Road is densely wooded. We wind our way upwards between the trees. It's much further than we expect. After over an hour, we emerge onto the rounded summit. There are trees here, but not so densely packed. I find a flat and shady space under a large acacia. The sun's very hot. We beat the elephant-grass flat with sticks. Lutoli gathers dead branches, and makes a barricade.

With solemn ceremony, we declare the eternal independence of our Republic of Kichoncho. The word means nothing. It just comes to us. It must be fate. We feast on dry *ugali* and water. The cuisine isn't up to much. But the view of the mine and camp is panoramic, and independence is liberating.

'One day all Tanganyika will be free,' Lutoli says. I stare at him curiously. He's a strikingly handsome chap, always smiling, with deep dimples and brilliant white teeth. There are more than looks. Pride. Refusal to be suppressed. I feel a surge of affection for him. 'The *Wazungu* will go,' he adds, grinning.

*'Mimi?'* I ask. Me?

'No, Jimu, you will stay.' He pauses, then says *'Wewe ni yetu.'* You are ours. He strikes his chest with a closed fist. Good enough for me. I can stay when the *Wazungu* leave. It will never really happen, so I don't have to think about Mum and Becky.

'What's he saying?' Andrew asks. His Swahili is rudimentary, and he's deeply suspicious.

'Says there'll be *uhuru* one day, and Europeans will leave.' Andrew cuts his eyes dangerously at Lutoli. They'll never be friends.

'No we won't,' he says. Lutoli shrugs. He doesn't like Andrew.

Lutoli and I visit our home country often, without Andrew. We agree he's a bad *Mzungu*, and therefore banned. We choose a two-president solution to the question of government. That's the entire population, which is fair. We paint a national flag onto a square-foot piece of hardboard, then nail it to a stick. It's a bright red star on black. Becky's Christmas-present paints.

We decide on a set of rules by way of a constitution. It will be handed verbally down through the generations, as neither of us is a writer. Donning oversized rusty WWII British army helmets, we stand at attention, salute our republic, and recite our constitution. The rules are simple:

1) No girls.
2) No grown-ups.
3) No bad *Mzungus*.
4) No *Mzungus* except me, who is not really a *Mzungu*.
5) No bad anyones.
6) We are independent.
7) Our country first, everything after, enemies last.
8) We will *pigana*, fight, to the last boy to preserve our freedom.
9) We will attack other countries that threaten our freedom.
10) Spies must be killed. Violently.
11) Girl spies must definitely be killed.

Secretly, I resolve that one girl, even if she spies, won't be killed. How can we kill Gretchen? I think I love her. It's her blonde hair and trusting blue eyes. I've told Mum, but she says I'm silly. Far too young. There's a drippy song by someone they call Nat King Kong, they play at the club on dance nights. It goes 'They try to tell us we're too young, too young to really be in love...' It's a conspiracy, got to be.

On our third trip to our home country, we discover Becky and Gretchen have established their own country only twenty yards along the hillside. They call it Chola. Also a meaningless word. Love would have flown out the window, if there were one. Is there nothing we can do without copycats?

As soon as they leave, we raid. There's little to plunder. Like Kichoncho, Chola's a bankrupt state. The best we can do is use a helmet to gather up hyena and jackal droppings on the hillside, and leave them as calling cards. That'll teach them! It doesn't strike me as strange to leave feral faeces as a present for the girl I love.

We're coming down the hill from Kichoncho when we walk into a near-riot on Top Road. There's a crowd of more than twenty at the turnoff to Compound Hill. I've never seen so many *watu* together in Geita. They're in an ugly mood.

Mlozi has finally realised he is, in fact, God. The one and only. He's unwisely elected to announce his decision at the top of his voice, yelling over and over that he is *Mungu*, who created everything in the world, all the way from Geita to Biharlomoulo, forty miles distant. There, as everyone knows, the *dunia*, or world, ends. Where does he think the *Wazungu* come from, I wonder? Or the *Wahindi* or Indians, the *Wachina* or Chinese?

It's gone down badly. A small group of *wasikini* beggars is one thing, but this crowd is different. He's still performing when we get there, jumping from foot to foot on his flat rock, technicolour ribbon-hair flopping, *Kimbo* tin rattling, anklebones jingling, and froth bubbling from the corners of his mouth. He's blissfully unaware of the effect of his words. The crowd is not having this blasphemy. There is no humour here.

'*Tu chinje!*' a furious man says. Let us slaughter him! Several bend to pick up rocks. There's going to be a stoning. Right here in front of us! A *masikini* was stoned to death nearby a year ago. He was a *mwizi*, thief. He stole a *Kimbo*-tin of *karanga*, or groundnuts, from another *masikini*, who hysterically denounced him. There were no convictions, because the only witnesses were living participants, and. . . Mlozi's life is in the balance.

'*Ngoja!*' shouts an *mzee*, or old man, in a *kanzu*. Wait! I know this old man. He brings chickens for Umali to kill. He's a Muslim, but squeamish. Umali says he's got a big *shamba* and at least three wives. The stone-gathering stops. Some pebbles drop. The *mzee*'s got authority. His printed *kanzu*, or loincloth, is clearly expensive.

Umali says this *mzee* has *phedha mingi*, a lot of money. Based on a herd of *ng'ombe*, the strange hump-backed, long-horned local cattle. They say they're immune to sleeping sickness, transmitted by tsetse flies, which kills horses and most breeds of cattle. We never see those in Geita. The *mzee* in the expensive *kanzu* is an important supplier of animals to the Ishmaeli butchers. The crowd falls silent.

'Who said you are God?' the *mzee* shouts at Mlozi. He's cunningly shifting this from execution to interrogation. Clever. There are disappointed murmurs, respectfully muted.

'The sayings said,' Mlozi yells.

'What sayings?' the *mzee* spits.

'The sayings of God.' Some *watu* chuckle.

Others are indignant. *'Blurryfucken-dammit!'* one shouts. Another joins the refrain. *'Gotohellyoubastar!'*

*'Blurryfuckenbitch!'* a young man in a red shirt yells. Becky's told me what bitch means. How can they call him a female dog? It would be funny in other circumstances.

'You hear God?' the *Mzee* yells above the rising clamour.

'I hear,' Mlozi says. The Mzee turns to the others.

*'Pumbafu!'* he announces with authority. A fool.

There's a murmur of agreement.

*'Lazima'*, naturally.

*'Ndio'*, yes.

*'Kabisa'*, absolutely.

Some are amused.

'He's not evil,' the *mzee* adds. Whispers of reluctant condescension. It's not as if it's a normal person saying such things. They've always thought Mlozi's mad. Or is he possessed by a *Jinni* or *djinn*? Some stalwart *watu* still look angry, but the fury of the moment is broken. They begin to wander off. Lutoli and I too.

# Ten

Growing up fatherless is not only sad. It's arduous. It's worse if the status is unique to you. Unfair, unkind, poignantly lonely. The *wakoloni*, or colonial, community in Geita is patriarchal, macho, both. Only men are given contracts to work on the mine. When wives are employed, it's strictly 'off contract', meaning they have no rights, and can't even expect notice if their services are terminated. That said, a contract doesn't stop management from summary firing of anyone, nor does it mean anyone can expect a pension. All it does is give men status, and 'proper' permission to work, at the same time sending a message that women are less.

When Dad dies, the 'contract' matter should, in normal circumstances, ensure we'd leave the country on the next mail-ship. Two hundred pounds won't last long in Cornwall, Mum says. Then it'll be the poorhouse. Becky and I live in terror. I won't even have a gun, I think. How will I protect them? Poorhouse sounds awful.

For once, and never again, Mr Snel, the manager, decides to alter the rules. He does so, he says, out of respect for Dad, whom he admired. A pity he never showed that while he was alive. He gives Mum a contract, meaning she keeps her job, remains in the house with free water and electricity, and has the benefits of a contract-holder.

Crucially, the mine pays children's fees at boarding school anywhere in East Africa. Mum becomes an honorary man. Many years later in South Africa, I see 'honorary white' status applied to black people by the government when it suits them. Hypocrisy in race. Echoes of gender hypocrisy in Geita. Meantime, the poorhouse threat recedes.

Despite her status, Mum's a woman. The expat community know it too well, and some people treat us with disdain, patronisation and even overt cruelty. Mum is vulnerable. Having gained a unique favour, it can be taken away with ease. She can't afford to make enemies of 'higher ups' on the mine, or their wives, and *we* can't upset their children. Mum has no choice but to keep her counsel, sometimes in vexing circumstance.

Mum lectures Becky and me ceaselessly about the goodwill

of the company, and its necessity for our survival. How we, as children, should behave in exemplary fashion, and never be impolite or naughty in front of Europeans. If we behave badly, or swear, the consequences will be our doom. She'll lose her contract and job. We'll be 'packed off' out the country, and end up on the street somewhere. We'll starve. I'm only five, and begin to develop genuine aversion to people of my own colour.

Contrasting with my feelings about *Wazungu*, and particularly the English, who occupy nearly all senior positions in Geita, is my unbridled love for the *watu*, with whom I can fluently, and often vulgarly, discuss any topic without fear of anger or retribution. Further driving this is the cruelty of children. Particularly from Top Road.

Dad has only been dead a few weeks when 'posh' white kids from Top Road use his death against Becky and me. 'Your Dad's dead, and my Dad can beat your mother up,' is typical. 'He's just a skeleton now', or 'worms are eating him'. I never get that from my *rafikis*, or their elders. They never even mention Dad's death, or that I have no father. Their own life expectancy is short, and most of the *totos* have lost one or both parents. Shared suffering does bedfellows make. They know what it's like, especially Lutoli.

Despite trying to obey Mum's orders about deportment and behaviour, I fail. I suddenly find myself the man of the family. My duty is to protect the others, for Dad's sake. Protection means vigorous response to threat or unpleasantness, not beating a retreat. Mum's messages are ambiguous. On one hand she ceaselessly praises Dad's courage, his heroism and strength, and tells me to be like him. Then, she says, I shouldn't challenge people, should walk away from confrontation, be sworn at and not swear back. The two don't gel.

I'm taught to deal differently with adversity by my real friends, Lutoli and the *watoto rafikis*, into whose company I am more and more driven. I learn from them not to start a fight or argument. If I'm on the receiving end of unkind attention, however, there's only one-way to deal with it: vitriolic, abusive, profane and, if necessary, violent riposte.

My playmates are arbiter on the contradictory instructions from Mum. It suits me. I'm angry. Cross with God, furious at the taunts of white kids, afraid for the family, morbidly curious about death, confused. I'll fight for survival and dignity, against anyone threatening either.

I'm less that six when it becomes known to all that 'Jimmy is a tearaway', he swears in Swahili at anyone he disagrees with, he stands his ground, and he argues with adults. Mum can't control me. I don't know then, but those early days after Dad's death are a crucible for future anarchist tendencies. I will always hold a jaundiced view of authority.

'Speak Swahili, Dammit!' I yell at Mrs Snel, the manager's wife, when she orders me to stop slashing the club's flowers with a stick.

Not only does she only speak English, which is bad enough, but she's also got a strong, nasal, Canadian twang. I can't understand a thing she drawls. It's Sunday, and I'm callously rearranging the club garden-bed with roundhouse swipes. I'm very good at this. Swish goes the stick, decapitating ten blooms. She shouts something in gobbledygook. I stand my ground. I'm not frightened of God, so who the hell is *she?*

'I will not speak Swahili,' she answers, 'but you will stop cutting down the flowers!'

'Eat your willy!' I swear in Gallua, taking another ten blooms down. The only Gallua I know are swearwords. Just like the *watu* here. They say they hate Galluas, but they admire, and therefore adopt, their invective. I don't care if Mrs Snel doesn't have a willy. I add she has a vagina like a snake, in Swahili, and round it off with *'youblurrybitch!'*

My fluency and diction leave her flummoxed. But my tone and expression, and the last word, don't. She recognises open rebellion. Later, I'll damage my reputation further through the game of *uchi maji mti kimbia*, or naked-water-tree-running.

I have oaths and swearwords for every occasion. My *rafikis* witness my outbursts, giggle, and laugh, clutch their sides in glee to see me abusing powerful *Wazungu*.

In *watu* circles, and among villagers, my name is known. I am 'Jimu', the *'Piri-Piri'*, or Chilli-Pepper. I cause much laughter. Unlike other *Wazungu wakoloni*, or colonials, I'm fluent in Swahili, having learnt the language so early, and used it ever since.

I can converse about every manner of thing with elders, have good knowledge of local things and customs, have an obvious preference for African company, am not fazed by matters of biology or sex, and am more dismissive and opposed to *Mzungu* authority than even them.

I am a hilarious anachronism. I have also moved to the centre of Umali and Amina's lives. They never have their own children. Now they have me. White, yet un-white. I am aware of ever-closer bonds between them and me. And, of course, Lutoli.

My connivance with servants, plus my abusive and dismissive attitude, makes me widely unpopular with *Mzungu* adults. They are undermined before their hirelings, angry, but powerless. They take the only open courses: they discuss me among themselves, 'report' me to Mr Snel, the manager, or make forays to talk to Mum.

It becomes a regular part of life: 'Mrs such-and-such says you swore at her,' or 'Mr such-and-such says you threatened to burn his house down.' I develop *kiboko*, or rhino, skin, and unhearing ears. I don't expect kindness from those quarters. I'll give as good, or better, than I get. It's a dangerous path, and will lead to unpleasant consequences.

It becomes habitual and inevitable that 'Jimmy' is blamed for anything untoward, conceivably caused by a child. If a window's broken in an empty house, Jimmy threw the stone. If a plant's destroyed, Jimmy did it. Sometimes the allegations are justified. Often they aren't.

My notoriety grows. I'm ever more alienated from the expatriate society to which I allegedly belong. My only solace and comfort is with Mum and Becky, Umali, Amina, Lutoli and the *watu*, who the *Wazungu* call 'natives'. And Sandy.

Sandy becomes my close friend and constant companion. She follows me everywhere. Bedroom, where she sleeps, head on pillow, much to Mum's annoyance, toilet, kitchen, chicken run, even swimming pool, where she dives in and swims abreast of me.

For Christmas Mum buys me a high quality, four foot long rubber dinghy, in which I'm frequently seen furiously paddling or languidly floating on the green lake water of the huge pool, Sandy perched half inside, front legs raised on bow, head held like a commander viewing the vessel's progress. She loves being with me, and never chooses to disembark when I give her the chance by paddling to the pool edge.

One day when I'm six I need a theme to live by, a rationale and philosophy to sustain me in this world grown cold and harsh. It comes to me in bed, while I'm thinking about Dad and how I'm going to survive without his warm, friendly face, his manly-tobacco smell, the confidence his strong hands gave, the surety that with him I was protected and safe.

A homespun proverb comes to me. It's simple. 'I am my own father', it says. It has three meanings. One, Dad's within, because I'm his son. Amina said that. Two, anything I do is with his authority, which I inherited. Three, even if he isn't with God, who I may have killed, if I am *he* I can watch over myself in his place. Sad though it is, it gives me direction and hope. I have the right to fight adversity. I have a licence to stand up for myself. Who else will? I resolve never to run away from anyone. They will have to run from me.

Umali's a bush psychologist. He knows how disturbed I am by Dad's death, and shows great compassion. He's always trying to make me laugh, sometimes using filthy Swahili, of which I am so patently fond. His expletives are unparalleled. Why should he say he 'went to the bathroom', when he can graphically pronounce he's defecated, urinated, and passed such wind it blew a hole in his trousers?

Poor Umali. He has an irritable bowel. He suffers a lot from diarrhoea, and likes to talk about it.

'*Nili kunya Kimbo sita,*' he proclaims. I shat six *Kimbo*-tins-full. Mum resorts to giving him raw flour stirred in water.

'To bind you up, *kufunga*,' she says, her Swahili always improving. It does. Three days of constipation, a day or two in-between, then many *Kimbos* again. He's never completely well.

Despite trying never to show emotion, it's evident Umali dotes on me. He's constantly amazed at my Swahili, flattered by my returned affection for him, Amina, the *totos* and *watu*. When he sees me looking sad, he cracks jokes to make me laugh, or tells stories of lions and *fisis*, the fearsome hyenas, striking delicious terror in my heart. Humour and terror. Better than emptiness. He avoids Dad's death. I think he knows about Tembo's puppy, and Mr Valari (senior), but never broaches the topic.

I ask him a grave and serious question. 'Where do people go when they die?'

'This is a big thing,' he says.

'Tell me old one, *tafadhali.*' Please.

'They go to meet with their elders.' What kind of Muslim is he? Ancestor worship?

'*Sababu?*' I say. Why?

'*Biashara ya Mungu,*' he says, looking into my eyes. A business of God. Umali knows me well. What if he knows about Tembo's puppy and Mr Valari (senior)? He witnessed my attempt to shoot God. '*Biashara ya Mungu tu,*' he says. Only God's business.

'*Sababu?*' Why?

'*Nimesema,*' he says. I have spoken. He will be drawn no further into my morbid thoughts.

'*Sikiliza,*' he says, changing the subject. Listen. '*Mimi ata fundishe wewe kutega samaki.*' I will teach you how to bait fish.

'*Wapi?*' I ask. Where?

'*Ko* dam.' At the dam, which brings lake water to the mine, halfway from Nungwe Bay.

'*Ndio,*' I say delightedly, 'yes'. My thoughts about death evaporate. I really want to learn to fish. From that day our relationship takes on another dimension. Mum says what an old rogue Umali really is, how he goes fishing when he should be working, on the flimsy pretext of teaching and looking after Jimu.

Our equipment is basic. Sisal, a kind of cactus, grows wild in Geita. Making a fishing line begins with chopping off one of the great thorn-tipped leaves, then beating it with gusto against a tree trunk, until the pulpy green skin is removed. By then fibres are visible, and we pluck them out, then roll them together on our thighs. It's incredible how a little rolling inseparably connects lengths. I continue until I make thirty foot of twine, then hang it next to Umali's to dry overnight.

We fashion hooks from thin rusty nails. We cut off the heads with pliers, then beat the lower shaft to a U. At the top a closed bend makes an eye. At the short end of the U, using a rusty file, we sharpen the point and cut a barb. It's hard and tedious. Floats are bits of balsa-type wood found everywhere. Weights, ingeniously, are 'forked' spark plugs discarded by the mechanic Spiros at the mine garage. It's confusing, 'cos they're straight, not forked. For fishing poles we cut lengths of bamboo. Our kit is environmentally friendly.

There's a catch. The dam's five miles away, a long walk in the hot sun. Umali persuades Mum to take us in the morning before work, and to fetch us after five. She agrees because she knows Umali will never let anything happen to me, and because she welcomes my interest, at last, in anything other than death and dying. Mum's learnt to drive since Dad died, and has bought an old car. She drives us to the dam in that elderly *Morris Minor*, Maisie. The little black car has had umpteen owners, and is held together more by serendipity than science.

There isn't much choice of cars in Geita. Only two are sold in fifteen years. Mostly they're thrown away, completely worn out, like Puncture-Car. Maisie, for all her shabbiness, is the only entertaining thing we have. There's no television, and the shortwave radio can't pick up signals beyond Congo, due to the magnetic iron ore in the ground. Bends radio waves. Mum takes us on little drives, sometimes just two or three miles. Barrat stores. The club. Sometimes, daringly, to the grass airstrip down the bottom of the wooded valley two miles from the camp. We love Maisie. Particularly when she starts.

Mum leaves us at the dam, with strict instructions not to drown. Sandy, who refuses to stay behind, takes the warning seriously, watches me like a *mwewe*-hawk, and whimpers when I approach the water's edge.

The dam's huge. A half-mile long reservoir, where the builders cast a concrete wall across the valley, and installed a pump to bring water ten miles from Nungwe Bay. All round is dense green bush. To approach the water I have to take off my sandals and squelch through thick, glutinous mud. Umali never wears shoes. He digs with bare hands in the mud for fat bloodworms. We put them on our hooks, toss our lines out, and make dry seats from banana leaves.

Tilapia here, in the main, only grow ten to twelve inches long, and rarely weigh more than a pound and a half. But they're pretty fish, and, for their size, give quite a fight. Umali tutors me. He shows me how to sweep my fishing pole overhead, and get the line far out on the water.

When I try to rush things he gives me a singular and valuable piece of wisdom. *'Haraka-haraka, haina baraka!'* he says. Speed-speed, it lacks blessing. He watches my float, and tells me to strike when it bobs under. When I catch my first fish he whoops with delight, and takes it off the hook for me. It's small, and he calls it *mkundu wa mbilikimo*. A pygmy's anus. The next one is better. I catch five fish that time.

Sandy shows a true spirit of cooperation. Each time I pull a fish onto the bank, she grabs it in her mouth and brings it to me. While I'm removing the hook, she makes spitting noises. It's the funniest thing. Sandy doesn't fancy raw tilapia. Umali says she's a person who died and came back as a dog. He's a Muslim who believes in reincarnation.

After just a few trips to the dam, I'm a *fundi* at tilapia fishing. Umali prefers catfish, which live on the bottom, so he doesn't use a float. These fish are sometimes as big as his calf, and appear most hideous to me, whiskers and strange mouth, a deformed cat.

# Eleven

We bring home fish, small and large. We don't throw them back like people in England. Why catch them? That idea wouldn't work here. Amina cooks. Umali's friends, and passing strangers, come to share. Amina boils the tilapia whole in a heavy-duty iron pot, or *sufuria*, with wild spinach gathered in the bush, chillies grown next to the hut, onions and sweet-potato chunks. When it's ready, she takes it off the fire, and places it beside a steaming mound of *ugali*, or stiff maize-meal.

We sit in a circle on the ground, dip fingers into a bowl of water, take handfuls of *ugali*, and roll them one-handedly into balls. We dent them with our thumbs, and fill the recesses with fish and gravy by scooping into the fish-pot. Popped in the mouth and chewed slowly, it satisfies through a wonderful combination of taste and texture. No other food comes close. It doesn't matter how many *watu* are there. Somehow, there's always enough.

The fish meals exacerbate our habit of eating with the servants, and Mum begs us to eat with her for a change. One day we decide to acquiesce. There's been a torrential rainstorm that afternoon, and the flying ants have erupted from the ground to flutter briefly before losing their wispy wings and falling in a heaving, squirming carpet of life. They're eagerly collected by the *watu*.

Becky fills a china pie-dish. She's just come in the front door with her writhing pot when Gretchen calls from the garden. Becky puts the dish on the dining table, covers it with a lid to stop the ants escaping, and goes out. She completely forgets her dish. I go out with her. I haven't seen my blonde Gretchen for a long time.

The dining table's laid. Mum's friends, Mrs Moore and Margaret Miller, a prim and upright expat wife from Darlington in Yorkshire, are coming. Mary O'Rourke, of *Sportsman* cigarette-bribe fame, has left Geita. In the kitchen, Umali's been labouring for hours. A fine roast chicken, *chinja*'d earlier by himself with an Islamic incantation, potatoes and cabbage are in the offing. Becky's covered pie dish is from a set, and the matching salad bowl is also on the table. There's nothing out of place.

After washing our hands, Becky and I take our places at the table. It's strange to eat so high up. The big people greet us. They've been talking about us, Mum says. 'Going native' and 'running wild' have been mentioned. She's been at pains to deny it.

Umali enters, carrying his delicious-smelling roast chicken on a platter. Mum takes the lid off the salad bowl. Margaret Miller lifts the lid off the pie-dish. Pandemonium ensues.

'Maggots!' Margaret screams in her Yorkshire accent, recoiling so violently she tips her chair backwards and falls, striking her head on the floor.

'Oh God!' yells Mrs Moore.

'Jim!' yells Mum.

'Not me!' I shout.

'Sorry,' Becky whispers.

'Oh, my head. . !' groans Margaret, sitting up, probing a gash in her scalp, where a thin arterial jet of blood pulses three inches high.

The dinner party's a resounding failure. Our notoriety grows. We aren't going to see much of Margaret Miller for a while. Umali can't hide his delight. He finds the repugnance of white people to good flying ants amazing. He and Amina dine in style on roast chicken *with* flying ants.

It's shortly after Becky distinguishes us with the flying ants that I make my own contribution to Mum's sense of unease. Mum is asked, in addition to her job at the mine store, to 'run' the guesthouse, a small building with a big verandah on Top Road. This means supervising Thelemani, the *pishi* or cook, cleaner and do-it-all, and ensuring all's as it should be for important visitors.

Sir Gordon Wearing is a 'bigwig' in the mine head office in London. I wonder if he has a big head to fit the wig. He comes to Geita once a year. Apart from *ugali*, Thelemani can't cook at all. Umali can. When the bigheaded man comes, meals will be prepared in our kitchen, and Thelemani will take them to Top Road on a covered tray. Thelemani's a very tall and agreeable man, much younger than Umali.

Sir Gordon arrives by Land Rover-taxi from Mwanza a little

before four in the afternoon. He's been told Mum's name, and his driver asks a toto playing beside the road where to find her. All the *watu* know where each *Mzungu* lives. Mum's still at the mine store.

I'm whittling a stick in the garden. Sandy's sleeping on the ground beside me, twitching when flies bother her. The big *Mzungu*, dressed in a fancy white safari-suit, introduces himself and asks for Mum.

Sandy growls and shows her tiny teeth, which seems to amuse him. Standing, she's less than a foot high. I tell her to *nyamaza*, be quiet, and say Mum will be home soon. He's welcome to wait for her, or I can give him a tour of our house. I'm determined to do the right thing.

Mum's told me a man is coming from London, and Mr Snel asked her to show him around. She isn't home, so I'll do it. Though look closely, I can't see that his head is especially big, and there's no sign of a wig.

When Mum comes home she's met by a very amused, if embarrassed Sir Gordon. 'Jimmy gave me a wonderful welcome,' he says with a strained smile, a half-glass of orange juice freshly squeezed by me in his hand. He tells her what I've shown him. The lounge, the dining room, the bathroom, the bedrooms. I've told him the history of each piece of furniture. I've shown him the washing basket where we put dirty clothes. All my toys. The chest of drawers in Mum's bedroom. I've explained what she keeps in each drawer, opened them to show him. I've displayed her 'posh' knickers and bras, as well as her 'normal ones'.

Mum says: 'I didn't know where to put my face.'

I just can't get things right. Abuse the *Wazungu*, trouble. Be nice to them, still trouble. Sir Gordon has a lovely tale to tell at the club. Jimmy, his funny little dog, orange juice squeezed with grubbly hands, and, as *coup de grâce*, my mother's knickers.

Thelemani, meanwhile, is a natural philosopher. He speaks of many strange things. One day he introduces me to the concept of bisexuality. *'Iko wageni,'* he proclaims. There are others. 'They go and do *jigi-jigi* to someone, then return and are *jigi-jiggied* by someone else.' I muse on this a long time.

When I ask Umali, he says Thelemani is a *majinga*, fool, and speaks out of where he should only *kunya* to relieve his obviously overfull bowels. Thelemani's going too far for a six year old. Even Umali, as profane as he is, has limits. He tells Thelemani his mother is a *fisi*. Thelemani is most affronted. He says his mother doesn't even look like a hyena, whereas Umali's wife has a distinct resemblance to a catfish. Everybody laughs. Umali has met his match.

From five, the expatriate children attend the mine 'junior school' in the mornings. The building has one big room, with a cloakroom in one corner. The number of children varies from six to ten, aged five to six. It's on Bottom Road, between the African hospital and *kifo nyumba*.

There's only one teacher at a time. Before I go, there have been five young ladies from England in four years. Each time, the 'peaches and cream' faced arrival has been spontaneously pounced upon by sex-starved bachelors. Geita never lacks for those. They're pregnant, married, or both, 'before the *jogoo*, or rooster, crows', I hear it said, and not necessarily to their impregnator. Another replacement is found. Another bachelor, and at least once a married man, steps forward.

My teacher is Alice. She's from Hampshire. I'm five and a half when she comes. My memory of her relies not only on then, but years after, when she's married to Bob Hawk, surveyor, thirty five years her senior, and until then a sworn single man.

Alice is plain. She lasts in post a year, unlike her predecessors, because young bachelors think her too plain. Mice frolicking in the absence of cat means sixty year old Bob tries her charms, in spite of boozily declaring he 'wouldn't let a woman' in his life. Geita is amused. Soon Bob's gathering wild flowers in his garden. Someone says they aren't lilacs, and it isn't spring. People note what time Alice's light goes out.

'She's marking your work', Mum says, embarrassed when I suggest they're doing *jigi-jigi*. Umali sagely says I'm right. Of course it's *jigi-jigi. Lazima!* Naturally! It takes six months before the swelling of her belly heralds a not-so discreet trip to Mwanza, from where the Derby and Lolita of Geita return as Mr and Mrs Hawk.

Before and during her pregnancy, Alice tries to teach me for a year. She isn't used to children 'run wild', and, though impressed by my Swahili, she finds it has disadvantages. I express profane opinions of her and old Bob to the cleaning maid, knowing it's safe. When Alice complains 'Jimmy's saying things in African,' Mum's alarmed.

'What have you been saying?' she asks.

'Bob likes her *kuma*,' I say. Her vagina. Mum laughs in spite of herself, and calls Umali. He's the only person I listen to.

*'Usisema,'* don't say it, Umali says, turning to me when Mum has finished regaling him with her fears. The teacher will tell the manager, Mum will be fired, we'll have to go away, and he'll lose his job and quarters in the garden. He's trying not to laugh.

*'Kwa nini?'* I ask. Why?

*'Wao baada ya wewe mbali,'* he says. They'll send you far away.

*'Nini niseme?'* I ask. What should I say?

*'Mambo mema,'* he replies. Nice things.

'But isn't a *kuma* a nice thing, Umali? Don't you like Amina's?' Umali loses control, hoots with laughter. Mum digs him in the ribs.

'You're as bad as him!' she exclaims, unable to keep her face straight. Her Swahili is coming on, I have to admit. I'll have to be more careful.

It isn't Mum, or Umali, who take action to curb me. The next time I speak Swahili at school, though I'm only telling the maid I don't like the teacher, Alice grabs me by an ear, drags me to the bathroom, bends me over the low basin, turns on the water, and forces a piece of Lifebuoy soap between my lips.

'That'll wash the filth from your mouth,' she says when she lets me up. It doesn't. I tell her what to do with her fat vagina, and her tits while she's at it. She doesn't understand, but gets the gist. From now on we're sworn enemies.

I'm thrilled to hear of Alice's bust-up with Mrs Snel, the manager's wife. It's just days after the soap incident when, sunning herself topless in what she presumes is the seclusion of her garden, she causes an accident.

Driving down from Top to Bottom Road for an early sundowner, Vito Parelli, an Italian bachelor who's shunned her virtues before, applies his Land Rover's brakes to prolong his view of her naked bosom from his high vehicle. Unaware of the go-slow ahead, Mrs Snel slams her Volkswagen Beetle into the back of him. Instead of lying about why he's stopped, the terrified Vito points out Alice.

'What do you think you're doing?' Mrs Snel yells at Alice from the road. 'You're that new teacher, aren't you?' Alice leaps to her feet, holding a T-shirt in front of her chest.

'This is Africa, you know,' Mrs Snel yells, you can't go naked round here!'

Soon the story of the *uchi*, or naked, English teacher is old news in Geita. Not really fair, she was only topless. I don't care. Alice and Mrs Snel are never to be friends. It may have been hard for Mr Snel and Bob Hawk, but, being old drinking pals, they decide to ignore the petulance of women.

For me the bust-up is heaven-sent. Talk about *schadenfreude!* I don't like either. They can kill each other for all I care. I'm unknowingly anticipating the thoughts of Mao tse Tung. Somewhere in his little red book are the words 'my enemy's enemy is my friend'. If it ever comes to it, I'll help either kill the other.

I'm six, Becky eight. Umali and Amina are run ragged during the day, too exhausted to look after us at night if Mum goes to the club. In desperation they introduce Jackson, Amina's long lost nephew, tell Mum he's a super chap, and persuade her to employ him ad-hoc to babysit.

Jackson's in his early twenties when we meet him. He's always dressed in clean shorts and shirt, which in a district where most *watu* wear *Kanzus*, long wrap-around cloths, or tattered, filthy remnants of western garb, is unique. Unlike his aunt, he has a mouth full of brilliant white teeth. He plays the guitar. An old, battered, much repaired one. He strums it with enthusiasm, if not skill, and sings, in what he thinks is *Kiingereza*, or English.

Once, sometimes twice, a week for two years, before I go to boarding school, and later during holidays, Jackson is our evening companion. He's always gleaming and freshly bathed, smelling of carbolic soap, wearing a wide grin, and carrying his beloved guitar. We welcome him, Mum gives him instructions not to let me run riot with a knife, or stick nails into electric wall plugs, and to keep the doors bolted in case of lions or *watu mbaya*, bad people. Then she drives the half-mile to the club in

Maisie.

We love it when Jackson plays his guitar. At least two strings are usually missing or replaced with fishing line, and the other four aren't in tune. He strums it, beats a drum-sound with his thumb, and sings. That's the best. His English, which he insists on using, is atrocious, mispronounced, non understandable and wonderful. We sit in a circle on the floor, and listen.

Jackson sings lots of songs. Popular ones throughout the British Empire, ubiquitous and defining Englishness. He's heard them on his crackly wireless. For me the real words, meanings and pronunciations will take years to permeate, let alone replace these first renditions. Everything I hear later is, to me, fake, a re-make, and a less likeable version of the 'original'. *Gorde Sieve Our Greasious Quinn* is my favourite. Sieving the greasy queen would get the bad bits out. I also like *We'll mate again*, and *Tack a massage to Miree*.

About this time the *BBC* begins random-time broadcasts to Geita in diverse style, manner and smell. I don't know who starts it, but the craze sweeps through the camp like a locust-storm, and soon we're all doing it. The rule is, when you feel you're going to break wind, you clench your buttocks, hold it in, stand to attention, salute, shout 'London News!', then let go. We are updated by the news at random times of the day for several years. There are foreign, as well as British announcers.

'Der London Newses!' Dieter shouts. 'Pffffpfff.'

'Newsa da London!' It's Antonio. 'Bwaaapff.'

'London News,' Gretchen says sweetly, 'pfff.' Girls are always so gentle, even when they *jamba*. Specially Gretchen.

Even Lutoli gets into it. *'Newsi ya Congo!'* he pronounces before he lets rip. Perhaps this news coverage explains my early take on world affairs.

Jackson's so relaxed and tolerant, we begin to take advantage. We tell our friends we can do anything we want when he's minding us. They come to see for themselves.

There are evenings when the Blüger pair, Sophia Fortuna, Becky's Italian friend, and the two of us congregate at our house and listen to Jackson's songs. Then we play games, usually starting with good old hide and seek. When we tire of that, we make up others. We play doctors and nurses, which means we ask each other what's wrong, health-wise, then flash our private parts. It's quite cursory, and I wonder why we bother. It hasn't got any meaning. Unless I can look at Gretchen.

Our most exciting game is Becky's invention. It's called *kuruka chini*, or 'to jump down'. She pulls the mattress off her bed, and puts it on the floor under the built-in wardrobe. Then she empties the shelves on one side, and leaves the door open. This forms a ladder, which we climb in a queue, to sit on top of the wardrobe, and then launch ourselves into space. We have to shout the name of a wild animal in mid-air, then emulate the sound it makes before crashing onto the mattress.

'*Nyani*-wah-thump!' monkey.
'*Fisi*-hee-hee-crash!' hyena.
'*Simba*-roarrrr-bump!' lion.
'*Tembo*-woo-hoo-bang!' elephant.
'*Chui*-arrrghh-wack!' cheetah.
'*Twiga*-chew-chew-biff!' giraffe.
'*Nyoka*-ssssss-wallop!' snake.

We live charmed lives. Not one broken limb in hundreds of jumps.

One evening we again persuade trusting Jackson to let us play *kuruka chini*. We file into Mum's bedroom, unpack half the wardrobe, drag the mattress off Mum's bed, and start jumping, to jungle sounds and hoots of laughter.

Unnoticed by us, the door opens and in steps Umali. He's heard the racket and come to investigate. Sometimes time stops. This is one. For a frozen moment he stands staring up at the top of the wardrobe, where Dieti, too late to stop, is launching into space, the trumpeting of an elephant breaking from his pursed lips. Umali's eyes go wide as baked-bean-tin-tops, and his mouth opens and closes like a freshly landed tilapia. Time catches up. Dieti thumps into his chest, knocking him sprawling.

'*Scheise!*' Dieti exclaims, rolling off Umali's body. Shit!

'*Shetani!*' Umali wheezes, struggling to sit up. Devil! When he recovers he tells us his thoughts in graphic terms. He's unamused. He tells Mum he went to investigate loud noises, and '*Geremani ndogo ari ruka ju mimi!*' A small German jumped on me. It takes a long time for Umali-relations to thaw.

123

'Tell that Dieter not to jump on Umali!' Mum says.

# Twelve

I prefer Lutoli's company to anyone else's, except Umali. We get along so well, and play inventive, amusing games together. The *Wazungu* don't understand or sympathise. They say I've 'gone native'. It makes me mad. I won't be forced to abandon my oldest friend just because the *Wazungu* say so.

One of our best games involves 'volunteered' animal participants. In Geita there are huge flowering trees called *Spathodea Campanulata*, which produce eight-inch long seedpods. When they fall, and dry in the sun, they split into two brown, boat-shaped, halves. They have sharp prows, and perfectly shaped hulls. There's even a squared-off transom. They float, and are completely waterproof.

Lutoli says these are *Mungu's*, or God's, little *mashuas*, open sailing dhows, like the fishermen use on Lake Victoria. We make holes and insert sticks for masts, then attach bits of rag for sails. Faithful to the *mashua* design, we attach a flat stick to one side aft, as steering-oar. Traditional *mashuas* don't have central rudders.

With boats ready, we head for the dam above top road. We check which way the breeze is blowing, then look for passengers. There are always ants in Geita. Termites, safari ants, little brown ants, red ants. They're never difficult to find. Using a stick or leaf, we deposit several outraged little passengers in our *mashuas*. Then we launch them downwind. The craft are surprisingly fast.

Within minutes they're fifty yards away. Sometimes they go all the way to the far bank. We run round, and watch our seafaring ants disembark. As they step on land again, they look confused, and fan out into defensive positions. I can imagine their thoughts. What the hell's happened? Sometimes the breeze dies when the boat's in mid-water, and our passengers are becalmed. We don't know if any swim for it.

One day my *mashua* is sailing along with its unwilling passengers, when there's a sudden disturbance on the surface of the water. To our astonishment a big frog leaps into the boat. We don't know if he's after the ants, or likes sailing. He crouches there, on the deck, his thick throat billowing, watching with slit eyes as his commandeered craft continues into the middle of the dam. He's a frog pirate, I say. Lutoli doesn't understand.

Just then there's a loud splashing sound, and something like a long undulating black rope flashes out of and back into the water. It's gone. So is the frog. The *mashua*'s swamped. It's sinking.

'*Nyoka ya maji!*' Lutoli screams, retreating from the bank. Water snake. '*Blurryfucken!*' he adds for completeness. Even Lutoli's learnt from the English. With *blurryfucken* snakes like that, we go in search of other adventure.

Later, at Mum's office, I tell Mr Hessler about the snake. I leave out our adjective. Hessler is the man who knows everything, Mum says. At his request, I describe what Lutoli and I saw, and what happened to the frog, which was stealing my boat, and. . . Mr Hessler holds up his hand.

'*Ach zo,*' he says, peering at me over his half-glasses, with the sunlight from the window illuminating his bald head, 'zat iss der Barotse vorter snake. Der proper name iss *Crotaphopeltis barotseensis* – I know ziss von!' He's triumphant. I've stumbled onto his passion, water snakes. 'Zey eat small sinks, like leetle fish und frogs, but, to us, zey are harmless.' That might be, I muse, but I'm not ever going in that water.

Lutoli's waiting outside. He agrees with me. What does the bald *Mzungu* know, anyway? Does he know the *watu* call him *Kiwanja*, for *Kiwanja ya ndege*, or landing-place of the bird? An airport. Some call him *Embakasi*, the name of Nairobi's airport. So are bald *Mzungus* called. We head for my house.

On our way along Top Road, we come to the junction of Compound Hill. Mlozi's there, on his *mwamba*, or flat rock. It's been a while, maybe a year, since he narrowly escaped stoning for blasphemy. We're so busy, we don't go this way often, and we mostly keep to bush paths. Mlozi's changed. He's slimmer, looks older. He's got even more coloured ribbons braided into his locks, and there's more *mifupa*, or bones, around his ankles.

More importantly, he's built himself a home. It's only six foot by four, and four foot high, made of sticks and mud, roofed with bundles of tied banana-leaf. There isn't a window or door. It's just behind his *mwamba*-stone, which now serves as patio. When he sees us he does a little dance, shaking the bones, but he doesn't rattle the dreaded *Kimbo*-tin and stones. Lutoli says some *watu* are beginning to be afraid of Mlozi. Say he's not mad, nor *jinni* or *djinn*-possessed, but an *mchawi*, or witch. He shudders saying it.

The *machula* is a collector and carrier of *mavi*, or faeces. That's his occupation, like many people did before waterborne sewage.

The camp has separate water-borne systems for each house. They built them all the same, and the length of transit is twenty yards. The destinations of the outlets are concrete-covered septic tanks, with vents lidded by concrete stoppers.

They say expanding and explosive gasses force the lids up, thus venting and reducing pressure. This delights us, and we want to hear our septic tank fart. We'll take a whiff, get a thrill, run away, breathe fresh air, and laugh. Problem is, despite equatorial heat, supposed to exaggerate and expand foul gas, venting never happens while we wait. Must occur gradually, unexplosively. Maybe at night. Or it holds it in till our backs are turned, and does a 'sneaker'. We have to prise the lids off, stick our noses in, and inhale deeply. There isn't a smell at all. What a letdown.

The *machula* couldn't be more different. The *mavi* he carries is raw, rotten, stinking, nauseating downwind. In the grassy waste between the houses are eight corrugated wood and iron privies, with steel buckets under the seats. These are removed, emptied, and replaced through a rear trapdoor every week. This is *machula* work.

The post is undesirable, the waiting list short. Incumbents are placed by fate on the lowest rung of humanity. All have, at least, squint, cast eye, partial blindness, old age, bent posture, abnormal gait, small stature and low self-esteem. They are the true *wasikini*.

I'm six when *machula*-baiting begins. It's to become an obsessional pursuit for me, my *Mzungu* friends and African *rafikis*. A game of *machula*-baiting can't be pre-arranged like other sports. The *machula* is wily, knows his terrain, and that his best defence is to reduce exposure by randomising his timetable according to chaos theory. A serious mathematician when not carrying *mavi*.

We never know when he's coming, before, unexpectedly, the cry of *'machula, machula'*, sung to the tune of 'King of the castle', rings out.

We can rely on one thing. The *machula* comes by day. The task of emptying buckets of *mavi* into bigger buckets is precarious enough, without doing it in the dark. To top that *fisis* or hyenas, the cause of such fear among *watu*, are keen diners on *cordon bleu* human excrement, and can smell a thimbleful a mile off. They can't open the privies to gain their culinary delights themselves. A *machula* doing it for them, in the dark where they alone can see, would be a *fisi* dream come true. They'd dine on the delicacy, and wash it down with fresh *machula*. The crafty *machula* comes by day, and generations of wistful *fisis* live out their lives in eternal hope, and ultimate disappointment.

He comes in the shimmering heat, with a dark three-foot-wide halo, faithfully following above his bent head. These are the bluebottles, or 'shit-flies', moving like the *'Interahamwe'* of Rwanda in later years, 'as one'. There's a low buzz, which by ears unabused by modern life can be heard for hundreds of yards.

Closely following, like the second horseman of the apocalypse, is the honk. Not a stink, not a stench. Worse. Faeces stinks. Faeces rotted more out of the bowels than in, stinks worse. Rotted in temperatures above 40 degrees, mixed with urine, carried in open buckets, garlanded with shitflies, it produces an olfactory sensation for which there is no word. Honk has to do.

Under the moving, humming cloud, and out of the nose-banging honk, the struggling *machula* staggers into range on thin legs, yoke over shoulders, buckets swinging, breathless from exertion, heat and toxic fume. With enough warning, we can be in position, out of sight in the grass, waiting with breath baited by anticipation and revulsion. The range closes.

In an ambush you shouldn't open fire too soon. You should hold your fire 'till you see the whites of their eyes'. John Wayne said so, and he can't be wrong. When you open fire, the enemy must be in range, unable to retreat without suffering significant casualties. Hence subterfuge, camouflage, and careful placing of artillery and machine-gun out of sight. Military strategy. John

Wayne's a trusted expert. He always wins against Red Indians. We take him seriously.

We have to let the *machula* into range before we attack. That's rule one. Here, Sandy proves, for the first time in her life, to be an unreliable ally. Though she creeps with us silently to our ambush positions, she finds it impossible to contain her excitement as the *machula* comes closer, and, before he's in range for the attack to begin, she leaps on her short legs from the cover of grass and thornbush to deliver a wild, yelping bark, and high-pitched snarl, giving away our position and sacrificing the element of surprise. She sabotages two ambushes, and I am prevailed upon to lock her in the house when a *machula* attack is planned. When I do, Sandy ignores me for an hour afterwards. But she can't keep it up.

Sandy-less, we're able to concentrate again. After maintaining the surprise element, the second matter of importance is to have lots of ammunition ready, so to deliver a sustained fusillade. Verbal abuse, like anything else, which may give the game away, has to be withheld until the last moment. The *machula* must 'walk into it'.

This is vintage John Wayne. Gretchen tells me a joke she heard about him. Someone told her dad. John Wayne wants to have an Indian squaw, which is *IS*. He goes to the Indian Reservation, which is *IR*. He enters the Indian Tepee, which is *IT*, and asks the Indian Chief, which is *IC*, for an Indian Squaw, *IS*. He gets badly beaten up by the *FBI*, which is a Forkin Big Indian. I laugh, because otherwise she'll think I don't understand. I've heard the word fork used like this before. When a car engine doesn't go, it's forked. That's what Spiros the Seychellois mechanic says when he throws his spanner down.

There are five, sometimes six or even seven of us. We need sufficient combatants to outflank and surround our quarry. Our numbers depend on how quickly we can recruit after a warning. All are sworn to join if called, and close enough. Sometimes we are only *Mzungu* children, other times several *totos* join in. There are never more than five minutes to organise and get into position. The *machula* shuffles determinedly. He stops at each privy. If uninterrupted, he can move between all of them, and be gone in ten minutes. Timing's critical.

In the early evolution of the sport, our artillery comprises only pebbles picked up and pocketed *en-route* to the battlefield. This is unsatisfactory, and serves only to harass and annoy our target. Soon, however, technology being what it is, we make catapults. This changes not only the results, but also the rules of engagement. Now we can award points for hitting particular targets, on or off the *machula*.

Top points go to knocking his bucket off the end of his yoke, or causing it to overturn. Lesser points are for striking the *machula* himself. There's kudos too, in missing, but putting him to flight, particularly if he knocks over or spills the buckets himself. A negative or 'minus' point is deducted if the *machula*, responding to the attack, hits you with his own ammunition, a handful of *mavi*.

Pitched battles occur up to ten times a year. There are so many that the exact disposition of troops, position of the enemy, accuracy and success of the fire, and final outcome, can't be recalled for each occasion. What is memorable is the predictable diction of an ambushed *machula*.

'*Blurryfuckenbastars,* fokin you. . !' he yells, scooping the contents of a bucket and hurling it in our direction. I think he'd use the same words even if he *did* know the meaning.

One fine day in 1958, a year and a half after Dad died, it's school holidays, and everyone's at home in Geita. I'm a little over seven, which makes Becky and Gretchen nine, Dieti seven, and Antonio Barelli eight. We're playing cops and robbers in the garden of the Barelli house. The girls have little choice. If they want to play with us, they play our game. Dieti's being a robber who just happens to be hiding, after a bank-heist, in the branches of a very large tree. This affords him a great view over the camp, and particularly the open ground and latrines.

Dieti, unlike his sister, still has a strong German accent, and suddenly, instead of being quiet and maintaining his hiding place, he yells, '*Ze machula ist Komink!*' This is the end of cops and robbers. We drop our toy guns, grab handfuls of stones, and dash headlong into the elephant grass to set up our ambush. The girls are as keen as us, and collect stones in held-up skirts.

'Jeem, eef I heet the *machula*'s bucket weeth thees stone,' Antonio whispers as we lie peeping through the grass, 'you must geeve me one chicken-gum.' He means chewing gum.

On this occasion, we're too slow. By the time we get our ammunition ready, and deploy, the *machula*'s gone. We decide we have to plan ahead, not leave the initiative to the enemy. We'll get him, before long, and it'll be us who choose both time and terms of engagement.

It's Christmas holidays of the same year, when we decide the time has come to spring a major ambush. Thus far we've only held sporadic skirmishes against the *machula*, and the outcome's been undecided. It's time for a strategically planned, devastating attack, to 'teach him a lesson'.

Dieti's father was in the *Afrika Korps*, so there's military talent in the family. Dad was in the Royal Navy, and I'm bigger than Dieti, so I also qualify. Antonio's dad surrendered with thousands of other Italians in Ethiopia, so Antonio comes along as a simple trooper, not to partake in strategic planning.

'Anyvay, yor fadder iss ein alcoholic!' Dieti adds for good measure.

'Why you says thees?' Antonio asks. 'I hearded him singink in der club,' Dieti says, 'und he vos singink "arrived drunk in ze boma!" '

'Thata waasa *Arrivaderci Roma,* Goodbye Rome,' Antonio mutters.

'Vell, he shood say zo.'

Antonio's brother Stefano is only five, too small for action. Gretchen and Becky are nine, and keen, though they've no weapons skills. Girls! They don't even know how to shoot a catapult. Frankly, I think, they're a liability to any self-respecting army.

The offensive has to be bold to be effective. We anticipate the 'shock and awe' American bombing campaign of Baghdad more than forty years in the future. We have new weapons, in addition to tried and tested stones and catapults.

It's Dieti who comes up with our gunpowder plot. In those days in Tanganyika there are problems with baboons raiding the *shambas* or kitchen gardens of the *watu*. Someone imports large red fire crackers, or *bangers*, from China, which the *watu* buy to throw at the baboons, which, it is hoped, will flee and never return. They're called *'bobejaan bangers'*, from the Afrikaans

131

for baboon. In fact, these giant three- inch long bangers are bought more for fun and frightening people than by baboon-harassed *watu*. The buyers in chief in Geita are us, the armed wing of the *AMF*, or Anti Machula Front.

Dieti, adopting his best military planning pose, draws on the ground with a stick. We've seen films where generals do that. 'If ve take big bamboo,' he says, 've can empty powder uff four oder five bangers in it, und make vun cannon.'

'How will we set it off?' I ask.

'Vid der fuses,' he says. 'Ve make a hole in der back, und pull der fuse out. Zen ve light it!' 'Whata willa we shoota from ita?' Antonio wants to know.

'Anysing. Stones, hoont-sheet. . .' Dieti says.

'How many cannons?' I ask.

'Two. I make zem. Ve haff big bamboos at mein *haus*.' Dieti goes off   to make his cannons. Antonio and I collect smooth round pebbles from the stream near the club. For the cattys. The girls say they'll come to shout abuse, and maybe toss a few stones. That's a worry. Stones chucked by them may go in any direction. Including ours. We tell them to stick to abuse.

Meanwhile I consider the enemy. The *machula* always comes from the west. We know this, because he collects *mavi* in the evenings, when the sun is going down behind him, throwing long machula-shadows on the thorny ground to the east. With the enemy in bold outline against the orange East African sun, there's a disadvantage. The sun'll be in our eyes, not his. How to overcome that? I decide to consult an old military advisor. Umali.

'*Sababu, mdogo wangu?*' he asks when I explain our mission to disrupt the local sewage system. Why, little brother?

'*Ninapenda,*' I say. I like it.

'*Atatosha,*' he says, smiling wickedly and showing his teeth. It will suffice. 'If that's what you want to do, I'll advise you how.'

Umali draws on the ground with a stick. Also a bit of a general. 'The *machula* comes from here,' he says, pointing to one side, 'and the sun's behind him?'

'Yes.'

'You have to attack from behind. Wait until he's halfway up

the slope, then attack from downhill, where he came from. That way the sun will be behind you, and will blind *him* when he turns.'

'*Asante,*' I say. Thanks. I relay the revised plan to Dieti, who's delighted, because shooting cannons into fierce evening sunlight is difficult.

Unfortunately, our latest, and boldest, attack has to be postponed because of the intervention of a scorpion. Dieti and I are intricately planning the attack. It's a hot, sweltering day, and we're sitting on the floor in our lounge. We don't like the wooden armchairs because our feet don't reach the floor. I yawn and stick my right hand under the edge of a big rug. It's so strange how, in the heat of day, it feels so cool on the fingers in the space between wooden floor and rug.

The *Buthidae* family of scorpions are the most dangerous to man. The genus *Parabuthus*, of which there are several species, is commonest. *Parabuthus granulatus* is the culprit in most fatal scorpion stings in East Africa. They grow up to three inches long. They're light brown, with paler striations across the body. They hold their tails high, and on them are hook-like extensions to deliver the sting. The poison they inject is a neurotoxin, which, in sufficient dose, causes difficulty speaking or swallowing, inability to pass urine, a rapid heart rate, incoordination, panic and respiratory arrest.

Scorpions don't, as a rule, choose humans or large animals to sting. Their prey is other insects. But they seek out cool, dark places in the heat of day. Places like the space between our wooden floor and the rug.

It's difficult to describe the sensation. Everyone knows what it's like to hit a finger with a hammer. This is indescribably worse. Like someone's injecting petrol into my fingertip. I scream in agony, and pass out.

I come to with a bumping, rocking movement. I look up to see the underneath of Amina's face. She's running, breathing like a locomotive, carrying me. It's the road to the hospital. Her mouth is open as she gasps for breath, her two big teeth protruding. We're almost there, and only seconds later I'm staring up into the worried face of Dr Weiss.

'You vill be fine,' he says, as I feel a sharp prick in my left shoulder, 'zis is ze treatment for ze scorpion sting. Ze maid vos very clever.' He holds up an empty, lidded jam jar, with a crushed scorpion at the bottom. 'Zis is vot stinged you, and I know zis von. Today iss your lucky day.' He pricks me with another syringe. 'Zis is adrenalin.' He puts his stethoscope on my chest and tells me to breathe. 'If I didn't know vot stinged you, zat vood be bad, but ze maid she kilt it, und bringt it. She iss very goot!'

The sharp pain in my finger subsides, but now a throbbing begins. I lift my hand and am shocked. My finger's dark purple like a *bringali* or aubergine, swollen to twice its normal thickness. I wince more with alarm than pain. Beside me Amina tut-tuts.

'*Pole,* Jimu, *pole.*' Easy, Jimu, easy. I feel her hand on my shoulder. Good old Amina. Not a wicked witch at all.

'*Das ist fur der pain,*' Dr Weiss says, injecting me again. It's my first experience of morphine. The pain recedes like magic, and I enter a pleasant, dreamy world. It's almost worth being stung by a scorpion. Pity I couldn't just have the morphine. As I drift into euphoria-land, I giggle to think of the *machula* recruiting a scorpion. It's stopped our attack before it began. With what would a *machula* pay the scorpion? Obvious.....

Convalescence is so boring. Josef Weiss orders I stay in bed, without visitors, for five days. Mum insists I obey, and persuades Umali to police me. I'm not feeling well the first two days. I have a banging headache, and my finger still throbs. I lie with Sandy, listening to the sounds of the bush at night, of *watu* talking and Land Rovers going up and down the road in the day. I'm woken each morning, as always, by the raucous crow of our rooster or *jogoo*.

By the third day I'm fatally bored, and Umali finally agrees to let me sit outside, while he and Amina hover, just in case. They keep an anxious eye on the road, lest Mum come home early and catch me out of bed. Equally concerned for my welfare is Sandy, who at a year old looks like a shortened Dachshund, a brown teddy bear with a big black button-nose. She's lain on my bed since I was bitten, and now sits solicitously close, studying my face with unblinking, doleful eyes. Together we watch the *kukus*, or chickens. I've never paid them too much attention before.

The *kuku* run is huge. Twenty yards by ten, fenced with wooden poles and chicken-mesh. We have thirty fowls, all hens except one. The exception is the *jogoo*, pronounced jog-awe, or rooster. The females are small and drab, but the *jogoo* is magnificent, proud, and twice as big as his ladies. He's black and white, with a collar of reddish brown, and a scarlet comb like a ripe pomegranate on his head. There's a cruel curve to his beak, and his beady black eyes glare with menace and disdain. As I watch, he stalks the run like a slave master, stopping either to drink from an upturned WWII helmet, or to briefly mount a hen.

'*Na tengeneza mayai,*' Umali says. He's making eggs. Doesn't make sense. We only get two eggs a day, if we're lucky. As I watch, the *jogoo* mounts his sixth hen in an hour. He knows I'm watching him. Between thrusts, he glares at me. He wants to be my enemy. He came after me last time I fetched eggs, but thought better at the last second. A coward, despite his crowing and posturing. I'll teach him one day.

I don't need to bother. Only a few weeks after the scorpion, Mum buys a young male turkey from a chicken and orange merchant. Moses is from the *waGallua* at a *shamba* near Biharlomoulo, a large village forty miles away, where many Gallluas live. He's a serious *mpengu* or gap-tooth. His top front teeth are missing because, in the age-old Gallua custom, he's knocked them out with a rock, because gaps in the teeth are deemed *maridadi*, attractive to maidens, and allow 'better' kissing. His remaining teeth are badly decayed, and two are only black stumps protruding from his gums. His short curly hair is as white as the distant snows of Kilimanjaro, and his face as wrinkled as dried fruit. He's very slim and stooped. He broke his back as a child, he says, when he fell from an *umstafehli* tree.

Not everything about Moses is decrepit. His dark eyes, always darting about, as if looking for danger, are bright and mischievous, and he has an enchanting, if lopsided and dentally challenged, grin.

There are twenty orange trees, six lemon trees, five *umstafehli* trees, and a grapefruit tree on his *shamba*. When the fruit is ripe, Moses trundles it to Geita. His transport is an aged bicycle without handlebars, pedals, chain or seat. Just the metal frame and wheels, which were once part of a bicycle. The front wheel forks are wired to the frame to prevent turning. Attached to the top bar there is a *baruti*, or dynamite, box. Moses fills it with fruit, and pushes his strange two-wheeled cart all the way. It makes sense, because the footpath to Geita is narrow and overgrown, and won't allow a four-wheeled cart to pass.

Becky and I like Moses, and he finds Mum a compassionate, and therefore gullible, customer. By the time he emerges from the dense bush, and pushes his contraption up the hill, he's exhausted, parched, and breathless. He comes to expect that he will be given cold water from the fridge to drink, and Mum will surely buy all his fruit to save him further labour.

The average load in his box is fifty large oranges and half a dozen lemons. The oranges are huge, almost the size of a grapefruit. They're green on the outside, and never change colour, no matter how ripe. Inside they're a rich orange, almost red. When cut in half and squeezed, one produces half a tumbler full of sweet, tangy juice. In Geita we don't buy Coca Cola or other bottled drinks, except at the club. Umali squeezes the oranges, and fills several pint glass bottles, which are kept in the spare fridge in the pantry. We drink glasses full whenever we're thirsty.

Once a year the *umstafehli* trees each bear a single fruit. A massive dark green thing, twice the size, and roughly the same shape, as a rugby ball. The green skin is soft, and the fruit easily bruised or burst by contact. There are inch-long green spikes on the surface, but they're illusory. Like the rest of the skin, they're soft and fleshy, and easily bent or crushed. Nature using trickery for protection. They look like thorns, but don't have the same effect. Must keep some gullible fruit eaters at bay. The *umstafehli* is linen-white inside. The soft flesh is separable into spindle- shaped segments, each with a large black pip in the centre. If a segment is squeezed, milky white juice runs out.

An *umstafehli* has to be chilled in the fridge for maximum enjoyment. When it's sufficiently cool, we gorge. The taste cannot be likened to any other. Sweet and sour at the same time, fragrant and tantalising to the taste buds. Once eaten, never forgotten, and the next *umstafehli* is passionately longed for. That's the problem. One tree, one fruit, one year. Not exactly available. Only favoured customers get one, and we get two, sometimes three, each year. We're lucky indeed

In addition to tending fruit trees, Moses rears chickens on the *shamba*. When they are half grown he forces them into little baskets made of twigs and twine, six to eight at a time, leaving them so little room that their heads protrude and they can't move their wings or bodies.

A basket is suspended from each end of a long pole, which he hefts on his shoulders for the trip to Geita. Moses knows Mum won't let him continue to carry a burden in the hot sun, and can't see animals in distress without rescuing them. Fortunately for us, he's usually sold half his chickens before he gets to our house. Mum buys the rest, and they're set free in the chicken run. After, that is, the little black lice which stick to the outer edges of their eyes are removed, using a fine cloth and a dab of turpentine.

Our chicken run's a flat piece of wire-fenced ground twenty metres square. There are two chicken houses, made of wood planking, raised from the ground on stilts a foot high. They're roofed with corrugated iron. Each has an entrance just big enough for a chicken to squeeze through. Inside there are wooden perches running across, where the fowls cuddle close to each other at night. On the ground there are six upturned army helmets, filled with water. It's hot in Geita.

The number of *kukus* varies. At times there are as many as forty, at others as few as fifteen. In Geita you can't buy an oven-ready chicken. Squeamishness and sentimentality are out. Our *kukus* are for eggs, and eating.

One day Moses brings a different kind of bird, a *batamzinga*, which strangely translates as cannon-duck, but is known to *Wazungu* as a turkey. It's a feisty, very angry young male. He's a handsome thing, all reds and browns, with huge hanging bits on his chin and under his fierce, curved beak. He has tail feathers all the colours of a can-can dancer's skirts. He's contorted in a tiny woven-grass cage. Of course, we buy him.

When he's released in the *kuku* run, he does a high-speed dash around the perimeter, scattering sand and pebbles. He's relishing his freedom. The *kukus*, and even the *jogoo*, look taken aback. Life's going to change round here.

From the outset, the *batamzinga* dwarfs the *jogoo*, and he continues to grow. The *jogoo* tries to ignore him, but the hens overlook his gigantism, and adopt him as one of their offspring. It's hilarious watching Snow-White, our favourite hen, leading her six newly hatched chicks round the run, with a huge gawky turkey youth in tow. Sometimes, when she digs up a worm, she even gives it to him. People don't believe us till they see it. We've had the turkey three months when he first makes the call by which we'll name him.

He stands in the centre of the chicken run, spreads his magnificent tail feathers like a huge technicolour fan, thrusts his magnificent head back, opens his huge beak wide, and shrieks. 'Gooloogooloogooloogooloo,' in an unbroken challenge to all. A *coup d'etat*.

The *jogoo* is supplanted. From now on, though he still announces the sun's rising, and services the hens, he'll never strut again. His eyes lose their threat. The dictator of the *kuku* run is Gooloogooloo now. The *jogoo*'s a broken bird.

Moses has a brother, Iwe, pronounced ee-weh, which means 'you' in Gallua. This causes much hilarity. If he says, 'I like you', he'll be saying 'you like you.' There are many delightful possibilities. You could marry you. You could even do *jigi-jigi* with you. I wonder why his parents named one son You and the other after a Hebrew Patriarch. The brothers live with their wives and children on a *shamba* six miles away in the bush. Iwe is absent much of the time, as a guest of the Tanganyika Territory Correction Service. He pursues a more nefarious occupation than his brother. We're hugely amused by him.

Iwe is even older than Moses, and is a notorious criminal. His crime is illegally producing a poisonously alcoholic drink from maize and sugar, distilled to a potent spirit called *'moshi'*, or 'smoke'. This he sells to tribesmen and women far and wide, including those at Geita. The *selekali* or police try to stamp out illegal brewers and distillers because, being so potent and so cheap, illiberal consumption is at the root of many murders and maimings, and, more importantly, Her Majesty's Colonial Government in Dar es Salaam receives no excise.

Caught red handed many times, Iwe has just as often moved the location of his distillery, each time rebuilding it deeper and deeper in the bush. He disguises his enterprise by sinking the bins in the ground, planting vegetation, and only lighting fires in deep holes. His efforts only protect him briefly, because he only ever gets one production to market before the *selekali* pounce, smash his equipment, and remove him to jail. Iwe doesn't remember how many times he's been locked up, but knows it's a lot.

Mum takes pity on Iwe, and finds him a likeable rogue. She asks him why he's always in trouble. Iwe can speak no English, but he has heard the words of the magistrate many times, and he takes them as total explanation for his woes. 'I didn't got the line-sense,' he says, and the meaning is unclear. What sense is there in a line? I ask Mum. He means a licence, she says. He doesn't have a brewing licence, so he isn't allowed to distil alcohol. Many times over the years he disappears because, yet again, he's in jail. Each time we see him again he gives the same explanation. Mum tries to get him to look at the matter more broadly.

'If you haven't got a line-sense,' she says, 'why do you do it, and get into trouble?' He cocks his head and looks confused. Maybe he wonders if the *Mzungu* woman hasn't imbibed too much *moshi* herself, talking in riddles like this.

'Because,' he says at last, 'it's my work.'

'Yes, but the *selekali*, the police. . .'

'They won't give me the line-sense, *blurryfucken!*' Mum blushes, but controls herself.

'But you have to stop. . .'

'*Memsahib*, are you, too, working for the *selekali?*' He eyes her quizzically. 'Do you want Iwe to become *masikini*, a poor man, and blind him in one eye so he can beg?' There's no winning. Each time he's freed from jail, Mum makes him a big mug of sweet tea, and he regales us with the latest chapter in his continuing infamy.

We've got to give Iwe his due. He's an entrepreneur. Doing his own market research, he branches out into growing *bhangi*, or cannabis, beside his jungle stills. It's noticed the known drunkards among the *watu* seem ever more detached and carefree. As a consequence, Iwe's stays at Her Majesty's pleasure are longer, and we see ever less of him. Still, he steadfastly pleads, it's all simply due to the lack of a line-sense.

# Thirteen

In January 1959, at seven and a half, I go to boarding school. There's no school in our district, and Arusha is a long way from home. Becky, two years older, has been boarding there for two years. Now I'm going with her. I neither know how far it is, nor how long three-month terms will seem. I have no inkling how different it will be to live in close company with other boys, nor what discipline is like. Such is the naivety of youth.

I'm excited. I'm going on a journey. It will be an adventure. Becky and Mum don't try to persuade me otherwise. I wonder why Becky cries when she has to go back after holidays, but that's girls for you.

Buying clothes for school is a new experience. The uniform for boys is short khaki trousers, dark green short-sleeved shirts, grey stockings and brown lace-up shoes. Most of these are available at *Boma Duka*, that collection of Indian shops at the *boma* near Geita.

The shirts are only available in white. Mum's a *fundi* at dying clothes, and dyes the white shirts green in a cauldron heated on the *Belling* range. I'm measured for my khaki shorts, which are stitched in the hour on a *Singer* treadle sewing machine by an ancient Indian lady dressed in a flowing pink sari. There's a red dye-mark on her forehead. She's Hindu. The dot means she's married.

She speaks continually as she deftly pushes the cloth under the whizzing needle, and pedals the machine. Beautiful Swahili. So I'm going away to school. She wishes she'd been to school. Could have succeeded in life. Too late now. She's just a poor old widow. Has to work her fingers to the bone. Do her children care? Not at all. All they want is money, which she earns with her life-blood.

I'm called back into the *duka* by Mum. Plimsoles or *tackies*, stockings, underpants, vests. I've never worn a vest before. Too hot in Geita. Arusha's colder, Mum says. She isn't buying shoes. Margaret Miller says I can have Andrew's old ones. They're a size too big, but what the heck.

My clothes are packed in a tin trunk. Last night at home. I'm excited, and don't heed Becky's dark warning. 'It's really going to be horrible,' she says. As the end of the holidays comes nearer, she becomes more and more morose, and sometimes she has puffy eyes, like she's been crying. It's just girls, and she's trying to spoil things.

On the last night we go to bed early, though I take ages to fall asleep because I can't wait for morning. Even Sandy sleeps fitfully, her little legs pummelling my side as she chases an imaginary *leguaan*.

Mum wakes us at four. It's black outside, cool and strangely quiet. There isn't much sound in the bush. The crickets, cacophonic at night, are sleeping. The maniacal giggle of the hyena, the screech of the crickets, the mating calls of bullfrogs, all are absent. Chill, dark, impenetrable silence. The jungle waits for the day. Everything sleeps. Except us.

I'm up, washed, and dressed in my new uniform. Becky's slower getting ready. Umali, bleary eyed and cursing, is clanging about in the kitchen, making a cold breakfast. There's no fire in the range, just ash in the grate. You can't cook this early in Geita, unless you get up even earlier to chop wood and light a fire. Umali looks really funny. It's his shirt.

Umali's shirt has died and decomposed, and would have gone to meet its maker if it were not that its fragmentary, string-thin remains still adorn his scrawny neck, and briefly extend to cover one nipple. It was a shirt once. Over time it grew holes. They merged. Now the whole thing's a hole. Mum buys him three new shirts. He's so happy. He wears one. And wears, and wears it, until it, like it's predecessor, is all string-and-hole.

'Why don't you put on another shirt?' Mum asks.

'Because,' he says, 'I haven't finished this one yet.' His short trousers aren't much better, and Mum's many attempts to improve them meet the same fate. Umali is a dedicated rag-wearer.

At five to five a loud horn honks in the darkness. It's Fritz, the non-talkative driver with the pencil-line moustache and German accent, and his long-wheel-base Land Rover. Someone says he's sixty-four years old, though he doesn't look it. His history is known to Eugen Blüger, who tells Dieti, who tells me.

In World War One Fritz is an *Askari* in von Lettow Vorbeck's *Schutztruppe*. His father is a staunch ally of the

Germans, and gives him a German name. During the war, when the Kenya-based *KAR* or Kings African Rifles invade *Deutsch Ost Africa*, now Tanganyika, Fritz fights against them with detachments of African troops and German Officers. They harass and harry the far superior British forces throughout Tanganyika, and as far south as Rhodesia. In an outrageous display of cheek, they actually seize, and, for some days, occupy a British fort there.

Fritz is involved in many ambushes and skirmishes, sometimes followed, when the enraged British bring overwhelming force to bear, by strategic withdrawal across the Rovuma into Portuguese East Africa, or Mozambique. Frustrated and outwitted, the British forces are ordered to respect Portuguese sovereignty, and only cross the frontier in pursuit on negotiated terms with the Portuguese. This buys the resourceful *schutztruppe* precious time.

In this way von Lettow Vorbeck's guerrilla troops, one of whom was Fritz, tie down a force several times their size for four long years, and only surrender to the British when World War One ends, and the *verdamte* order comes from Berlin itself. Fritz, after giving his all for so long, is perplexed and bitter. He's worked hard at becoming German, then, after not losing one single engagement, his beloved *Obersti*, or *Oberstleutnant*, has to ignominiously surrender to the enemy!

Fritz speaks fluent German, and everything about him, apart from his African ethnicity, is Aryan. He's tall and slim, and has a proud and arrogant bearing. He shaves his moustache in a straight line on his upper lip, and he's always immaculately turned out in military style khaki safari suits. He speaks little, and very guttural, English.

Fritz even tells Eugen an amusing war story. One day close to Kilwa, a hundred miles north of the Mozambique border, the *Obersti*, as the *Schutztruppe askaris* fondly referred to *Oberstleutnant*, or Colonel, von Lettow Vorbeck, is asked to exercise his jurisprudence in a tribal dispute. A villager brings a complaint against his neighbour, that this man ate his grandfather. Understanding that cannibalism isn't quite as eschewed here as in Europe, Vorbeck reaches a judgement, and orders the offender to pay the complainant a dozen hens.

Plaintiff and defendant 'walk off as good friends, one with the other's grandfather in his stomach.'

'Parp-parp' the hooter goes impatiently, cutting the dark silence like a bursting balloon.

'That Fritz is so impatient!' Mum exclaims, sitting on Becky's bulging suitcase, trying to close the zip. Then he's loudly knocking on the door. He isn't from the Geita area, and his tribal language is Gallua, though he resembles his tribesmen not at all, not having the usual tribal scars, pierced and stretched earlobes, nor even front top teeth knocked out. He's a stranger to his tribe, every bit as much as he's a convert to German-ness. He can speak Gallua, but prefers not to. He understands Swahili, but thinks it common. German is his choice, and he seizes the chance to speak it when Eugen Blüger comes to Geita. When not out driving the Land Rover, Fritz has become Eugen's shadow, they say.

'Ve vill be late!' he barks when Mum opens the door. He grabs a suitcase impatiently, and carries it lightly in one huge hand. On the way to the car we hear him mutter crossly, 'Vy zey say ve go early, zen be late?' He's not as chatty, or friendly, with us as he is with Eugen. Only likes Germans.

Five minutes later, luggage aboard, headlights carving glowing yellow shapes on the surrounding bush, the Land Rover growls from our uneven driveway, and gathers speed as Fritz changes gears and stabs the accelerator to show his impatience. Framed in the verandah window, Sandy cocks her head on one side and looks bereft. Umali says she whimpers for hours after we leave.

I sit back, thrilled at everything. The darkness, the stillness, the expectancy of the road to Mwanza, the prospect of a train ride for a whole night and day, a night in the railway hotel in Dodoma, and a twelve hour bus ride to Arusha, which is the 'big school', where I'll feel important and fulfilled, and have exciting adventures.

Fritz drives the Land Rover up Compound Hill in four-wheel drive. No two-wheel drive vehicle ever makes it to the top. The engine whines and groans. Then we're at the summit, and Fritz freewheels the heavy vehicle down the other side.

Soon we're in deep bush, the Land Rover rattling and

banging as we hit potholes, with rustles and thuds from leafy branches on roof and windows. Tsetse territory, the peeling black and white warning signs giving us just enough time to close the windows before the aerial assault. It seems shorter between Her Majesty's 'close windows' and 'open windows' signs. Happy anticipation does that. I fall asleep.

I wake up to find we're going even slower than usual. In front of us is a lorry, piled twice its height in bundled raw cotton. It's from the ginnery twenty miles away, where the freshly picked cotton is threshed, washed and deseeded. This one treats cotton from plantations in a radius of a hundred miles. Then it sends it on a 'gin-lorry' to Mwanza, from where it's shipped on the lake to Kenya for further processing.

There are several ragged *watu* perched on top of the high cotton cargo. It's a tradition here – lorries pick up *watu* on the road. As always when we're behind a struggling gin-lorry, our trip is badly slowed.

The ferry's waiting, and there's room. I get out and walk about, watching the water boil on one side, where the big engine thrashes its propeller round, the blades just exiting the surface of the green water.

I amaze the crewmen with my Swahili, and amuse them with bawdiness. Mum laughs. Her understanding of the language, though better than most, is limited to 'kitchen Swahili'. She enjoys seeing me 'talk like a native'. I think she'll enjoy anything I do. That's mothers for you.

Mwanza is only twenty miles after the ferry. My excitement grows. We reach town at ten-thirty, five and a half hours after leaving Geita. That's good time. Fritz drops us at the Mwanza hotel, and goes on to the bank for Mr Snel, the manager. The train leaves Mwanza station at six pm, so we have time to kill.

Down the road, two hundred yards from the hotel, is an iconic shop, 'Lake Printers'. We always take Becky there before she catches the train. She buys comics, and Mum's always generous at these times. She won't be seeing Becky for three months. Now she won't see me either. This is my first opportunity to share in 'off to boarding school' largesse.

In 1959, and for years after, there's a comic series, which, in ceasing publication, will leave the world a colder, poorer place.

*Illustrated Classics* tell the greatest stories in the English Language, in script and beautiful coloured drawings. *Treasure Island, Twenty Thousand Leagues Under the Sea, A Christmas Carol, The Man in the Iron Mask, The Three Musketeers, From the Earth to the Moon,* and *The Amazing Tales of Baron von Munchausen.*

Becky calls the last the 'Astonishing story of Policeman Higginson', after the boss of the Geita police force. I don't know what astonishing means. Something to do with polish or fishing. She must have heard it from big *Wazungu.*

Lake Printers always have good titles, and we buy every one. They also have *Beano, Topper,* and other comics. On the train, and at Arusha School, these'll be our treasures, until we swap them for other treasures.

At the hotel we sit on the verandah, drink ice-cold Pepsi's through straws, and begin reading, while Mum fusses that our cases are properly packed, she hasn't forgotten toothpaste, soap and shoe polish, and that her letters to the headmaster are properly sealed, and protected from crumpling. From the verandah the turquoise-blue of Lake Victoria is visible down a palm-lined avenue.

At six o'clock that evening the train pulls out of Mwanza station. The locomotive wheezes and chuffs, and blows a stinking column of greasy black smoke into the air as it gradually, and very slowly, builds up speed. Becky is crying inconsolably, sticking her head out the window and trying to keep Mum, standing waving on the platform, in view. I'm not sad at all. This is my great new adventure.

Including Becky and me, there are six children, and a teacher has come from Arusha as escort. We're in two compartments, each with four bunks. Becky and I share our compartment with Gretchen Blüger and the teacher, a very old-looking, wrinkled lady called Mrs Shuter. Dieti Blüger is in the compartment next door, with two boys who live in Mwanza. Gretchen looks lovely in her dark green uniform. Her golden hair is in a ponytail, and she looks older and more grown up than her ten years.

From the outset Mrs Shuter stamps her authority. Firstly, she says pointedly to Becky, there's to be no sticking heads out the window. If you do, you'll get soot from the engine in your eye.

Secondly, we're not to go anywhere, not even to the toilet at the end of the carriage, without asking permission. Lights out is an hour from now, so there's just time, if we hurry, to go to the dining car and have supper. Listening to her, I begin to realise that, adventure though it may be, there's a downside to this.

East African Railways & Harbours, with the *EAR & H* badge and logo on its trains, has rolling stock from the early twentieth century. The carriages are fitted out in beautiful teak and oak. They're real masterpieces of craftsmanship. The furnishings, like the wall panels and windows, are hand-made for the trains.

Must have taken a long time for the builders in faraway Birmingham and Northampton to complete a single carriage. These trains are symptomatic of a different time, when things weren't rushed, mass produced in plastic or chipboard, or hurried to market without pride.

The dining car's a spectacle. The oiled teak panelling glows like filigree gold. Velvet drapes on the windows, tied back and hooked, are ocean blue, and bear the *EAR & H* logo in gold italics. The tables have snow-white tablecloths and starched napkins in shiny silver holders. The cutlery, also silver, is confusing in number and complexity. Small and large knives, a fish knife, a spoon, small and large forks, and a very small fork with one prong shaped like a knife. This, Mrs Shuter says, is a cake-fork. Salt and pepper pots are silver, and *EAR & H* embossed.

The waiters are solicitous and friendly. They carry several hot plates at a time, and remain upright as the train bumps and sways into the gathering gloom. Despite my misgivings about Mrs Shuter, I feel a deep thrill of excitement and anticipation. This is still my first great adventure.

The four hundred miles from Mwanza on Lake Victoria to Dodoma in the southeastern hinterland is a sixteen-hour journey. The train stops at lots of lesser stations, as well as Shinyanga, a hundred and twenty miles, and Singida, three hundred miles from Mwanza, before the last hundred miles to Dodoma.

After dinner we get into in our bunks. We'll arrive in Dodoma next morning at eleven. Meantime it's thrilling to hear the locomotive chuff, the wheels click on the rails, and to feel the surge and sway of the train.

Dodoma's a dusty town of no importance, apart from the railway, which links Lake Victoria to Dar-es-Salaam on the Indian Ocean, and the lunatic asylum, which is the only facility for mental illness in all Tanganyika Territory. Here we disembark. The bus which will take us the hundred and thirty miles by dirt road to Arusha is only expected next morning at six, so we walk the quarter mile dirt road to the Railway Hotel.

The hotel, the only one in town, is a beautiful old German building, built of red brick at the turn of the century. It still sports long arched verandahs on each of its three floors, with a crenellated outer wall resembling the battlement of an ancient Hapsburg castle. It originally serves as a regional social centre under the German colonial administration of *Deutsch Ost Afrika*. After the British accept von Lettow Vorbeck's, but not his *Schutztruppe*'s, surrender at Mbala on the shore of Lake Tanganyika on the twenty fifth of November 1918, the territory changes hands. Now the hotel is the local social retreat of the British.

The lounge has faded grandeur. A great portrait of von Lettow Vorbeck, in *Schutztruppe* officer uniform, ostrich feather in hat, and *Mauser* pistol in fastened side-holster, still hangs imperiously on the long wall. It's dated in the corner, in German. *Neunzehn funfzehn.* Nineteen fifteen, Gretchen says authoritatively.

Funny, I think, German military pictures on the wall after all these years. This here, from the first war, that other one in Geita, of Eugen Blüger, Gretchen's dad, and Ernst Rommel, chief of the *Afrika Korps*, from the second. I'm in the company of German war-heros wherever I go. 'A nice painting,' Gretchen says beside me. Not as nice as you, I think. Someone says they never take Vorbeck's picture down because he's still so fondly remembered.

There's a large dormitory with two metal beds and six bunks, in three tiers of two, which open through a heavy wooden door onto the verandah overlooking the main street, which, though tarred at some distant time, has all but decayed to a dirt road again. On either side are rusting corrugated iron 'shops', where *Wahindi* and *Warabu*, Indian and Arab, traders sell a limited range of wares.

147

The teacher, Mrs Shuter, takes one of the beds, and assigns us to bunks. After a shower and a change of clothes, we have a dinner of hard fried eggs and baked-beans on toast, in a shabby dining room, which was once grand. Then it's time for bed. We have to be up by five in the morning. The bus to Arusha is at six.

The bus is ancient, and gaudily hand-painted in all the hues of the rainbow, and some not in the rainbow. On the door-side there's a logo in hand-painted purple. *'Duma Upesi'*. Fast Cheetah. We board with blustering people of diverse origins. Indians on business, tribesmen and women travelling to villages en-route, with sacks of maize flour, live chickens in grass cages, and a couple of unhappy-looking goats. There are two very weathered and haggard white big game hunters, complete with bolt-action rifles, who take great care that their elephant tusks and other trophies are securely attached to the rusty iron rack on the roof. I wonder why they don't have a Land Rover.

As the *kunguru* bird flies, it's a hundred and thirty miles from Dodoma to Arusha. But the Fast Cheetah lacks the freedom, and speed, of a crow.

The Pienaar Heights lie on the edge of the Masai Steppe in the Kondoa district, halfway from Dodoma to Arusha. A great barren, windswept escarpment looms after a grinding, gut-wrenching ascent from the wooded plateau. Here, a winding road snakes along the lip of a vertical fall of thousands of feet. Clouds drift past, a long way down.

The heights are named for Major General Dan Pienaar of the *SAOEV*, or South African Overseas Expeditionary Volunteers force, which joins the fight against von Lettow Vorbeck's *Schutztruppe* in the fourteen-eighteen war. Not even Pienaar and his huge South African army can corner the wily Vorbeck.

The bus hurtles down the stony road to terrifying oblivion. After an hour of pure panic we level out onto the valley below. I relax, then fall asleep again.

When I wake we're cruising along a straight, level dirt road on the approach to the town named for its original inhabitants, the *wa-Arusha*. Finally we roll onto the tar road. It's a small place, with some western-looking shops in the centre, less salubrious buildings of corrugated iron, wood and adobe everywhere else. From there it's a short way to Arusha School.

The school's a privately run institution, a pleasant, and, for Tanganyika, cool little town in the foothills of the great twins, mounts Meru and Kilimanjaro, or *Kilima Njaro*, as the locals call it. *Kilima* means hill. *Njaa* means hungry, so I think Kilimanjaro means hungry hill, or hill of hunger. Unlike Geita, here it is lush and green, and cold rivers and streams from melting snow on the mountains criss-cross the land.

The school takes boarders, the only reason we're sent there. In the nineteen fifties less than one percent of African children go to school. The European and Asian population in Tanganyika never tops ten to twelve thousand. Thus there are very few schools of any description. Arusha School is the biggest and best in the country, and caters for the children of the expatriate community from all over the territory.

It's modelled on an English public school, though nobody says which one. The headmaster in 1959, and for the five years I'm there, is a very upper class English don by the name of Mr Houghton. His deputy, the assistant head, is a mild tempered and pleasant, baritone-voiced, sports loving, Welshman, known to all as BL Thomas. Someone says BL is short for 'bloody'. A worrying thought.

The buildings are English styled, late Victorian in design and construction. The main buildings are built around two large quadrangles of lawn, a hundred yards square. On one side is a row of classrooms. At the two far ends are boys' dormitories, juniors one side, seniors the other. Facing the classrooms is a linen store and tuck room. Between the grassy quadrangles is the dining room, with big windows, and kitchen. This part of the school is joined to the female dormitories by a curved and covered walkway thirty yards long.

I sleep in the junior dormitory. Sadly, my memories have more to do with enemies than friends.

I meet Marais. For a long time I don't know his first name. He's a rarity in Tanganyika – a *Boer*, or Afrikaner, from South Africa. The *watu* call them *Kaburu*, because they can't pronounce *Boer*. Plural is *waKaburu*. I don't like Marais. He's a thug and a bully. There is a family of Afrikaners, or Dutch as we call them, in Geita. The van der Westhuizens. All I know about them is our *ayah*'s always give them a wide berth or they get abused. *Boers* don't like the *watu*.

I'm less than seven years old when I'm shown to my bed. I'm choked with homesickness, ill from crying. Realisation has dawned: this is not a holiday, it's banishment. Becky and I are here, Mum's alone in the house in Geita. How did I get conned into this? I'll have to do something about it.

If I survive the twelve long weeks of this term, and I've never thought about such a long stretch before, I won't come back. My throat aches and I have a pounding headache. Dr Weiss said I'd have headaches after the cerebral malaria. I find I only get them when I'm upset. I'm screwing up my eyes to avoid the sun's glare through the big glass window, because it makes my head worse.

I instinctively dislike the matron, a middle-aged spinster called Miss Baxter. She's very businesslike, and not at all friendly. She's also stout, ugly and lacking personality. But she's in charge, and determined to thoughtlessly exercise her duty. To begin with, she lets me know who's boss by calling me Francis. My name is Francis James Penhaligon. I rather like it. But I'm used to being called by the abbreviated form of my second name, James. I'm Jim in Geita, and Jimu to the *watu*.

'Francis,' she announces, 'this is your bed.' She grimaces, like I learn to expect. I have encountered the 'put-down'. Marais is in the next bed.

From the outset, Marais bullies me. He's older, in third year. He's eight, a foot taller than me. He's lanky and tough. He has a strong Afrikaans accent. His parents farm a hundred miles away and speak no English. His only weakness is asthma. For that he has a bell-shaped glass bottle with a rubber tube sticking out the top. On the end is a hollow rubber ball. When he gets wheezy, he puts the bottle near his open mouth and squeezes the ball. This produces a spray, which he gulps into his lungs.

I have no compassion. Marais is irritating in all ways. I hate the way he looks and talks. I can't stand his wheezing, and the sound of his spray-bottle is like hard chalk screeching a blackboard. I'm to have this for company every night, eighteen inches from my bed.

Marais knows I'm not in his fan club. He sees me wince when he speaks, feels my agitation when he wheezes and splutters. He can't miss me sticking my head under my pillow as I attempt to escape his Marais-ness. Despite his poor health, Marais has advantages. Age and size. He uses them against me.

It begins with a shove in the back. I'm standing in line to enter the dining room. Breakfast time. I'm not happy. I've had a horrible night. My worst nightmare for a long time.

Mum's buried the other side of Mrs Williams. She's trying to get to Dad, but can't, no matter how hard she tries. Mrs Williams's coffin's in the way. It's made of something stronger than iron. Digging under it's no use, because it moves. It's determined to keep Mum and Dad apart. There's a horrible sound. Cruel, evil laughter. Stroessner, the murderer. Half his head is missing, and there's brains and gore on his leering face. 'You can't, you just can't. . !' he laughs satanically. *'Kaa peke yako Memsahib!'* he continues, switching to Swahili. Stay on your own, Madam! Mum's getting desperate. Her fingers are torn and bleeding. It's normal for the dead to bleed.

I'm awake for several minutes before I'm completely sure it's just a dream. When I get up I feel so sad. It's physical, like there's a heavy bag of potatoes on my back. My legs feel leaden. I'm nauseous. I'm depressed, but I don't know that word.

Marais shoves. I'm forced to take a half step forward to stop myself falling. I almost collide with Miss Baxter. Marais's face is impassive. Miss Baxter says I'm playing the fool, and sends me back to the dormitory.

I miss breakfast. I don't care because I'm not hungry. But Marais has just started. There'll be more, much more. Other boys have told me what he's like. From the outset it's clear to all new boys that 'snitching' is not allowed. Whatever happens, you never snitch on anyone to teachers or matron. Particularly not older boys. This serves Marais well. When he returns from breakfast he's not only wheezing, but gloating as well.

*'Ja, Rooinek,'* he says, *'dit sal jou leer!'* Yes, Redneck, that'll teach you! Afrikaans. Difficult enough having to talk English nowadays. Now I learn Afrikaans too.

I resent the *English* bit. I'm Cornish. Dad said we're British, not English. Loyal, not Royal. Cornwall's only 'cledged' onto England by a tiny spit of land at the river Tamar. A couple of sticks of gelignite, and we'll be an island. Stick together, us

Cornish. 'One And All!' That's the motto. Mum told me.

I can see myself manning a machine-gun on the west bank of the Tamar. I'll be like Dad. Fierce and brave. The enemy will be the English. Odd that. Dad fought for them against the Germans. Why did he do it? He liked Eugen, and fetched the Lotanga for Otto. I like Germans too. I'll never fight against them. Now the Afrikaners, the Marais of the world, that's different...

There's tons of gelignite in the cold store at Nungwe Bay near Geita. A man-made tunnel at the water's edge leads to a cave right under the lagoon. Ingenious. Cool like a fridge. A perfect store where explosives won't explode. Brainchild of a man called Harold Norris, who has a jutting chin, and tells stories which never go anywhere. The under-lake explosives magazine comes to him in a dream after two Gallua miners are blown to smithereens by *baruti* left too long in the sun. Dynamite. I wonder if I could pinch some and send it to Cornwall. How much is needed to blow Cornwall from England?

Starting now, life gets worse. Marais likes destroying my Saturdays. After applying *blanko* to my tackies, I turn to find they're streaked with brown polish. It's inspection time, too late to re-*blanco* them. After inspection we're allowed access to our 'tuck boxes', can take five sweets. That's a week's allowance. If shoes or tackies are found wanting I miss out on tuck. Marais celebrates. *'Verdamte Soutpiel,'* he wheezes. This is worse. Damned Salt-Prick. One foot in England, the other in Africa. Prick hanging in the salty sea. Afrikaans is endearing itself to me. Prick means willy.

Sand in my bed, mud on my shirt, and worse, comes my way. I'm a bed wetter. It only stops at nine. It's infrequent and irregular, and usually happens when I have nightmares, invariably containing jumbled stuff about people, animals and death. In the dreams I'm visited by intense anguish, like on the day Dad died.

I see Mr Valari (senior)'s waxy face and accusing eyes, the half-skeletonised *mzoga* of Tembo's puppy, and visions of Mum, Becky, or Dad, dead and rotting in the ground. I'm told I moan, grind my teeth and thrash about. I wake to find I've wet my bed. In Geita I've been bed-wetting about once in six weeks. It continues.

Bed-wetters are treated in a special way. I have to tell Miss Baxter. I'm given a harsh talking-to in front of everyone, and then have to strip my bed. I carry the wet mattress, on my head, into the centre of the quadrangle and place it on the grass. The timing is for when the boys on one side, girls on the other, are queuing for breakfast. They enjoy a grandstand view. It's morning cabaret.

It's hard carrying and scrubbing a wet mattress to the giggling attention of boys, and more so girls. Marais leads the mocking. 'Jimbo has peed his bed again,' he says in his heavy accent, just loud enough for the children, not Miss Baxter, to hear. He imitates a hyena's giggle, which infects the others. When the matron turns and asks why everyone's sniggering, Marais says, in a husky voice, 'Nothing Miss. . . nothing'. My hatred grows. Somehow, sometime, I'll teach him a lesson.

My unhappiness and disappointment at Arusha School extinguishes my school excitement and optimism like *mvua ko moto*, or rain on fire. Becky told me, and I didn't listen. Now I know she was right. From this time forth, I will never want to go again. I'll stay in Geita, no matter the consequences. This decision will have consequences for me, and for what I'm beginning to think of as 'them', or authority.

# Fourteen

In 1959 Arusha is a small market town in the heartland of the *wa-Arusha* tribe, not yet a national Capital. The snow-capped peak of Mount Meru, the smaller sister of Kilimanjaro, is visible from most parts of town. From elevated positions the blue-grey slopes and white hat of *Kili*, though almost forty miles away, interrupts the sweep of the horizon.

The *waArusha* have an ancient belief. Meru and Kilima Njaro, or Kilimanjaro, were born as twins, but Meru got arrogant, and tried to out-do her big sister. In response, Kilimanjaro bashed Meru so hard on the head that she's been shorter ever since.

The surrounding countryside, four thousand six hundred feet above sea level, is alpine green. Pines and conifers cluster in groves between vast expanses of green, luscious grassland. To me, from the arid, hot flatlands near Lake Victoria, the countryside can't be more different. Arusha town is a motley collection of buildings, some European-style, others built of a variety of materials, including stone, mud, corrugated iron and wood.

On Saturday mornings after shoe inspection, providing we haven't 'blotted our copybooks' during the week, or failed to properly clean our shoes, we're allowed to go into town. We line up in rows, boys one side, girls opposite, smallest and youngest one end, biggest at the other.

We find ourselves facing our age or size equivalent of the opposite sex. Then, at an order from the escorting teacher, we hold hands, and form a column, teacher in front, smallest children behind him or her, biggest at the back. Thus regimented, we walk the mile into town.

I'm a junior misogynist. The touch and feel of a girl's hand is more repugnant than a snake. It takes willpower not to toss my little lady-partner's sweaty hand aside. With the cloying touch and feel of a keener grasp than my own, I proceed into Arusha town. I make it clear small talk is not allowed. It would be different with Gretchen, but she's ten, and I'm seven, so she is in another group. The thought of her holding some big boy's hand brings a hard lump of jealousy to my throat.

There's a pattern to our Saturday morning trips to town. First we're taken to a little take-away where we buy burgers. The sign on the window says *MISTREES YUM-YUM-TUM SPECIAL BURGER BAR. TASTIE AND DILICUSS.* Yum-yum I understand, but not dilicuss. Someone says it means nice tasting. 'Oh,' I say, *'tamu!'* Being here is a welcome break from loathsome hand holding, and maybe it's because these are my first burgers, or just because they're not school food, that they're the most delicious burgers in the world. *Tamu sana.* I love them. They're scrumptious, and I never miss the opportunity to gorge at Mistree's Dilicuss Burger Bar.

Next is Arusha Printers, a bookshop with all the regular comics from England. We buy *Beano* and *Topper*, and us boys get war comics about heroic British troops fighting Germans and particularly evil Japanese. The Germans shout *'Blitzen'*, *'Englander'*, *'Achtung'* and *'Schweinehund'*, and the Japanese yell *'Banzaai'*. Becky says that's a small tree. She's mad. Having stocked up on reading material, we proceed to the most important shop of all, *FATTI ALIDALI'S NICE-SWEETS EMPORIUM.*

Here is a magical cave, packed with *Rowntree*'s fruit gums and pastilles, *Sherbet fountains*, *Crunchies*, *Cadbury*'s chocolates, and all things dreams are made of. We're only allowed a shilling each on sweets, so we form syndicates, buy as many kinds as our money allows. There's bickering and argument later, when it comes to dividing spoils. Generally the silly girls come out worse. What they deserve, holding our hands so keenly.

We're told to pray for forgiveness of sins. The bearded preacher keeps saying we must, from the pulpit of the little church by the river. Suddenly, aged nearly seven, far from home, feeling lost and lonely in this foreign, colder, greener place, almost as bad as I remember England, I undergo a spiritual awakening. So it seems.

It's apparent to me the preacher knows all about me. He knows what I've done. My spying on the corpse of Mr Valari (senior), killing Tembo's puppy, and above all, shooting God! How can he, who has never met, or talked, to me know all that? Only one explanation. God knows everything. Obviously I have not killed him. Just made him very, very angry. And he's told the preacher. Instructed him to tell me from the pulpit to repent and mend my ways.

At bedtime in the junior dormitory we have to kneel beside our beds and pray before lights-out. Until now I've closed my eyes and thought of Geita, Mum, Dad, Umali, Lutoli, Amina, Sandy. Now I can't afford such indulgency. God's on my case. *Ata Kamata mimi*, I think. He'll catch me. I still think in Swahili. It'll be years before I can think a whole thought through in English, and not mentally translate. *Mungu* has found me out now, and I have to make peace. Dodging my bullet hasn't gone down well.

I kneel by my bed in awakened knowledge of my evil and badness, and try to find a proper prayer to do the job. Difficult. I'm not even sure I'm sorry I missed God. He took Dad, didn't he? Then he presided over me leaving Mum so far away, to come to a hellhole. But I have to apologise. The bearded preacher has talked about hell and punishment. What if God decides to take Mum, or Becky, or Umali, seeing taking Dad hasn't taught me my lesson? I had better put my ideas in order. Apology beats apocalypse.

'Dear God,' I begin hypocritically, 'please forgive me for my sins. Help me never to sin the same sin again. . .' I don't apprehend that what I'm praying for is variety in sinning. After asking for forgiveness and avoidance of past sins, I decide it's okay to ask a favour. After all, I've humbled myself, apologised. If God is merciful and kind, and other things the bearded preacher keeps saying, when not threatening us with the abyss, then surely he can grant a small wish to a contrite sinner.

'Please look after my mother and father,' I pray. Can't leave Dad out because he's dead. He's up there with God, isn't he? So close enough to be looked after by him. 'And my brothers and sisters, and Gretchen and Dieter, especially Gretchen, and Umali and Amina, and Lutoli, and Tembo, and his dead puppy, and Sandy, and all my relations and friends, and everybody who I know and who I don't know, even the *wasikini*, who are poor, and the *machula*, who stinks. . .' I'm casting the net very wide, asking a lot. But what if I *don't* pray for someone, then something happens to him or her? I can't bear the guilt. I can't bring myself to pray for the *Wazungu*, or Europeans, as a group. I don't like them. I don't even like being one. I pray all the harder for those I choose.

'Let them live a long, long time,' I pray, knowing it's strange to ask for Dad, who's dead, to live a long time, but not prepared to relegate him to second class-ness. I can't pray 'let him be dead a long time', can I?

'And let them be happy,' I conclude. A happy *machula* seems a contra-something. Mission. No, dission. I don't know. I give up. 'Amina,' I say, not knowing 'Amen', and then I hop into bed. It doesn't strike me as odd that I end my prayers with my old *ayah*'s name. Just to be sure God has heard me, I pray it all over again, three more times. Hello, Obsessive-Compulsive Disorder. Isn't there something obsessive about monks chanting the same words over and over? It's from now I'll have to resist an urge to re-do things many times, then check and re-check they're done.

Before ending my praying session, I allow myself one extra appeal I'm not too sure about. God might think it's opportunistic and greedy. On the other hand, if I don't ask, I certainly won't get. Recklessly, I ask for it: an ever-lasting lollipop.

That done, I allow myself the luxury of imagining I'm at home in Geita. Walking in the bush with Gretchen. I wallow in this muse for a long time, before moving on to something else, which is my own, unencumbered by other people, and gives me a great sense of peace. It's amazing how powerful the imagination of a child can be. I create something all mine, with vivid colours and real sounds, replete with everything I need, and without the things, which trouble me.

My imaginings in bed at night, with my head under the blanket to dampen the racket of Marais snoring, are simple. I'm with Lutoli in our hillside republic of Kichoncho. The only sound is the peaceful cooing of the *njiwa*-bird. We're lying on the ground, looking up at the aching blue sky. High up there on a rising thermal current drifts a magnificent *mwewe*, its great wings immobile, its all-seeing yellow eyes searching hundreds of square miles for prey. It's great to be here watching this. It lasts a while, then I conjure something else.

My restless mind searches for ideas. That's it. . ! I have a canoe. Very strongly built, closed in on top, with a small hatch for access. I have stores of things to eat and drink, and the inside is cushioned with foam rubber. I get in when the rainstorms begin, and seal the hatch. Everything that can possibly go wrong has been thought about, and prevented.

After a while in the darkness, I imagine the canoe begin to move as storm-water nudges it towards the river. Then the rocking of flotation, and a sense of drifting downstream. I'm safe in my canoe. Nobody can touch me. There's no teachers or matrons, no Marais, nor anyone to worry me. I'm alone. I feel better. My rushing thoughts slow, and calm descends.

Eventually my drifting canoe reaches the sea and is swept far out into the blue vastness. I eat sweets and biscuits and dried fruit, drink from a bottle of lemonade or *Coke*, and take a peek at my whereabouts through the hatch. When storms brew on the horizon, and the sky darkens, and the winds begin to howl, I batten down the hatch, make myself comfortable, and enjoy the feeling that, though the elements and world conspire and try to kill me, I'm safe and indestructible in my canoe.

I fall asleep with a sense of enclosure and inviolability, then my dreams take over and continue in the same vein. When, that is, *mzogas* dripping blood and gore don't suddenly come at me.

Only much later do I realise what I'm doing in these perambulations of my mind. Vicarious escape from intolerable circumstances, in which I have no control. I don't want a life without Dad. I don't want Mum to be a widow. I don't want to be away from her, or Geita. I don't want to be terrorised by Miss Baxter, the teachers, and Mr Houghton, the headmaster. I don't want to sleep next to wheezing, nasty Marais. I want nothingness. Only my canoe, out there on my imagined sea, offers me the refuge I seek.

As the end of the first term approaches, there's a mood of excitement at school. The first sign is a reduction in bullying of smaller children by big ones. A miracle. Suddenly they stop calling names, shoving in line at pre-dinner inspection, and streaking mud on whitened tackies or plimsoles. Why are they so unkind in the first place? Why do they change, just because it's close to end of term?

Suddenly there's a relaxation of rules. Lights-out is no longer so strictly enforced, and Miss Baxter leaves them on as long as twenty minutes after eight. She doesn't pounce out of the dark to catch us talking after lights-out or 'playing the fool', with her usual frequency or ferocity.

The last Saturday shoe inspection isn't as rigorously carried out. The biggest boon is that, on the last Saturday, we're allowed, after shoe inspection, to empty our tuck boxes. This leads to gorging, which is what went on in Sodom and Gomorrah. Excess. The bearded padré is obsessed with that. The evil ones practised excess, and the Lord struck them down. It's obvious the Sodomites ate far too many sweets. I pray to God to make me like sweets less, to avoid Sodom, 'cos it's awful what the priest says.

There's a rhyme I learn at the end of the first term. It has to be used only two days before term ends. 'Today's the brush, tomorrow's the comb, next day I go home.' There's never sweeter poetry. The older kids have a rude version. 'Miss Baxter's bush, Mr Houghton's bum, take me home – I want to come.'

Finally the last night comes, and we're given our cases and trunks to pack. By this time law and order has completely broken down. People call each other by first names. Miss Baxter laughs and jokes, instead of shouting and threatening. There's a festive spirit. We pack our neatly pressed clothes, our shoes, comics, and whatever toys we still have. That night supper is informal, and there's no queuing for hand inspection. Even the food's different. Almost, but not quite, edible.

Last night. It's impossible to sleep. I don't need the canoe. Just thinking about going home, after twelve never-ending weeks, is enough. In the small hours I drift to sleep. Then Miss Baxter's shaking me awake.

'Your bus leaves in forty-five minutes,' she whispers, not to wake snoring Marais. His father's fetching him later. 'Bath before you dress,' Miss Baxter says. Three quarters of an hour go by in a flash. Bath, dress, quick bowl of porridge in dining room, collect case, check trunk has been put out front.

The headlights of the bus illuminate the main building, where I meet Becky, Gretchen, and Dieti, and the boys from Mwanza. It's six in the morning, and dawn. An icy wind from Meru and

Kilimanjaro penetrates our clothing. We board and the bus glides out the school gates, *en-route* to Dodoma. I make sure I'm sitting next to Gretchen. Does she know how I feel? She doesn't say.

Dodoma at six pm. We don't stay at the Railway Hotel, but meet the Mwanza train at seven. On board the *gari moshi* we sleep as if drugged. At six next morning I look out the window. Only four hours to go. The train has descended to flat country, and there are signs Lake Victoria's near. In the early light I see the great, smooth, cheese-coloured boulders strewn on hillsides and perched on plains. Igneous rock, or granite, submerged for millenia by a much higher, deeper Lake Victoria, before, also aeons ago, it finally broke through at Jinja in Uganda, to form one of the sources of the Nile. Then the lake level fell by over a hundred feet, exposing the rocks eroded smooth by long submersion. They have huge emotional content for me. They say I'm nearing the water, and, more importantly, getting close to home. The sun rises above the horizon, beaming down intense white heat, and it is day. Soon, in a few hours, I'll see Mum and Fritz, and we'll set out for Geita.

By nine o'clock we see glimpses of blue lake as the train snakes on towards Mwanza. My beloved boulders are everywhere. Our excitement's too much to contain. The escort rasps her voice telling us to stop leaning out the windows. We don't want to miss any of this.

The train splutters into the station and squeals to a halt. Becky and I spot Mum on the platform. Fritz is beside her, Teutonic and black. While the locomotive hisses and exudes steam and stinking smoke, we're locked in an embrace of three.

Fritz stands alone, aloof, impatient. His moustache is shaved straighter than ever. How does he avoid cutting his lip? I can almost hear his thoughts as we hug. 'Vy you do zis?' Doesn't he ever hug anyone? He's impatient to drop us in town and go off on mine business. He'll collect us from Mwanza Hotel at two o'clock. That gives us time to buy anything we want not available at Barrat Stores or *Boma Dukas*.

We're in a state of high excitement and bliss for the next four hours. After stocking up on comics at Lake Printers, and sweets from two different shops, we lunch on the verandah of Mwanza Hotel. Cool and shady here, red cement floor, wicker tables and chairs. Homely atmosphere. Apt, I think. Home.

Fritz drives up at precisely two o'clock. He wordlessly helps us load our luggage in the back, and then we're off, Geita-bound. Exit Mwanza, car ferry across lagoon, into bush and tsetse belt. The Land Rover groans and creaks, sometimes almost losing the struggle along the rudimentary road. In spite of our excitement, Becky and I lose our epic fight to stay awake.

Mum wakes us as we fight towards the summit of Compound Hill. The Land Rover's positively groaning. It must be the steepest hill in the world. It's seven thirty, and the sun has gone. A moonless night, only the yellow lights from the Land Rover pierces the black cloak of night. It's cool at last. Even cold. The back of my shirt is wet with sweat, and now it's like an icepack. The engine whines in a final agony as we crest the top of the hill. It's visceral. As the engine relaxes, so do we. Like an apparition in a magical fantasy, the fairy lights of Geita camp appear before and below us. We freewheel down the steep road, Fritz applying brakes to thwart a headlong plunge. The houses separate as we approach. Then there is just one before us now. Our house, *home!*

The Land Rover crunches on the driveway gravel, and has not rolled yet to a halt before the front door opens. Silhouetted against the light, the unmistakable form of Umali appears. He runs down the steps towards us, the prancing profile of Sandy at his heels. Now we're really home.

As I step from the car I'm embraced by Umali, then Amina. Sandy jumps up and whimpers in happiness, the little bell Mum put on her collar tinkling merrily. Fritz bids us a guttural farewell, and drives off in a cloud of dust and a shower of small stones. He has a family at home. I hope he's more avuncular with them.

The house looks so daintily decorated and furnished, so clean and polished. I've forgotten how house-proud Mum is, how hard Umali works. From the kitchen comes a delicious aroma of roasting chicken and potatoes. Umali has made a special effort. I'm almost overwhelmed with happiness. I'm home for four whole weeks. I won't even let myself think about going back. That will spoil the holiday.

Gooloogooloo, our *batamzinga*, has entrenched his hegemony

over the chickens. The lady *kukus* haven't suffered. Before the coming of the turkey, they're subjugated by Mr *Jogoo*. Then it's he who has first choice of tasty morsels cast over the fence, to him they give way at water basins, and his the right to ravage them at will. The ravaging continues, but *Jogoo*'s rule over the *kukus* is now only as vassal to flamboyant Lord Gooloogooloo.

The days whizz by too quickly. In a frenzy we re-establish our lives. It's never going to be the same, no matter what we do. There's a calendar now, a countdown to disaster. That's what we think about going back to school.

I try valiantly to put the horrible thought out of mind. I visit old haunts. The club and swimming pool. The golf course, the African compound, the many *watu* who know me. I enjoy Sundays when we go to the club. We swim, eat crisps and drink bottles of icy *Pepsi*. We wait excitedly for Sunday night cartoons, newsreels and black and white movies. We play Germans and English at war, or cowboys and Indians. When we tire of that we spring a poorly planned and abortive *machula* campaign, barely hitting his full buckets with a few stones, and singularly failing to overturn them, or even delay him in his determined limp from privy to privy.

Dad has been gone two years. 'Uncle' Adrian, a dashing Afrikaner with huge handlebar moustaches who manages the mine 'reduction' works, begins to visit Mum, and accompany her to the club. Becky doesn't mind. At first I'm incensed. He's taking Dad's place. Yet Mum looks less unhappy than before. I'm torn. He's an Afrikaner. Like Marais and the van der Westhuizens, that strange and reclusive 'Dutch' family on the other road. But I have to admit he's not really like them. Firstly, he's nice-looking. Becky says he's handsome.

There's something gallant about Uncle Adrian's moustache. It's huge, just like his car. That's a two-tone blue and white *Chev* with great big wings, like a spaceship. He drives that, while all the other men drive beaten-up Landys. He's also very generous. Always sending *Pepsis* and crisps out to us kids on the verandah at the club. What can I do? What *should* I do? In fact, Uncle Adrian is so generous, he spends all his money every month. Mum says he hands over half his pay to Ishmael, the club barman, and the other half to Barrat's stores. Asks them to tell him when it's finished. It's just like that song that's so popular these days: It starts with *'I was born one mornin' when the sun didn't shine, picked up my shovel and walked to the mine'*, and ends with *'I owe my soul to the company store.'* Many owe their souls, and more, to the company store.

Uncle Adrian buys things for people all the time. He's always 'standing rounds' at the club, or buying presents at Barrat's. He wears crisp new white shirts on Sundays, and never wears the same one twice. Sunday nights, he gives them to his 'house-boy' who makes a fortune selling them to other *watu*.

I decide to do nothing about Uncle Adrian, for now. Anyway, due to his generosity we're able to buy more sweets at Barrat's store, as well as more *Pepsis* and crisps at the club. Also, in a strange way, it feels good to have a man around. Less empty, less lonely for all three of us. With a sense of guilt about Dad, I decide I won't do anything to drive Uncle Adrian away. At least, not now.

I'm woken by blood curdling shrieks. They're coming from the *kuku* run. Pandemonium and panic from thirty straining *kuku* throats, and as many pairs of wildly pounding *kuku* feet. They're zooming about, squawking as loud as they can. Something's very wrong.

'What's happening?' Becky shouts above the din. It's woken her and brought her running to my room, which overlooks the run.

'Dunno,' I shout.

'Stay there you two!' Mum yells, dashing past my door to the kitchen. That's the way out. Torch there. On shelf, for going out in the dark. We're a yard behind. Won't let her go out alone. Sandy's at my feet, barking. The *kuku* shrieks and foot-pounding is louder. Mum flicks on the torch. She opens the door. We're running down the steps, following the pencil of light. No way will we let Mum go on her own.

*'Memsahib!'* It's Umali. Invisible in the dark. Mum swings the beam. He's naked apart from a *kanzu* round his waist. There's a glint of panga-blade in his hand. We're at the *kuku* run. They're dashing about like creatures possessed, colliding with the wire mesh, bouncing off, dashing the other way, shrieking at the tops of their hysterical voices.

Mum shines the torch. Under the wire near our feet is a mound of earth, which wasn't there last night. A tunnel. Even as we watch, something mottled brown and black, a foot high and three long, torpedoes from the hole and disappears into the elephant-grass. Umali hurls his panga after it. It clatters uselessly against a rock.

'*Nguchiro!*' he shouts. Mongoose! No point going after it. It's gone. The *kukus* are spooked. Takes them ten minutes to stop dashing about. Three lie dead in pools of coagulating blood. Their throats are torn open. Later we realise one's gone. A black and white speckled hen. The killer must've carried her off when he dashed past.

One young hen has her wing half-torn from her body. She's a pretty one, white all over. She's feeling very sorry for herself. Her wing-bone's broken, and there's a scarlet streak of blood on her snowy feathers. Standing together silently on one side are the *jogoo* and Gooloogooloo. There's no posturing or crowing now. In the torchlight both look bewildered and frightened.

'*Wapumbafu!*' Umali shouts at them. You fools! He stamps his bare foot. 'Why do you just stand, *blurryfucken?*' He stamps again. He does this when he's angry. 'What kind of guardians are you?' He's disgusted. They should have done something. Not just stood around as if this is entertainment. He's right. These two are much bigger than the other *kukus*. Particularly so 'Emperor' Gooloogooloo, regent and show-off extraordinaire.

We take the injured hen into the house. She's in shock. She's the one who adopted Gooloogooloo when he came. Mum wraps strips of torn sheet around her body, holding her broken wing in place. There's little chance she'll survive. Umali cuts some grass with his panga. In the dark, he cuts his leg too. Mum wraps another piece of sheet round his shin. We put the grass in a cardboard box, and make a bed for Snow White. That's the hurt *kuku*'s name now.

She lies in the box and stares at us unblinkingly. Mum opens her beak and puts a tiny piece of aspirin on her tongue. She tries to eject it, but swallows instead. May as well try something. She's going to die anyway. Mum gives her a handful of chicken-food mix. Dried maize, groundnuts, sunflower seeds. It's in a little dish. Another's got water. Snow White looks pathetic all bound up.

'Mongoose?' Uncle Adrian says next day. 'No, don't think so. They take what they kill. Don't kill so many and only take one. This is the work of something else. I'd say a Civet Cat. That, or a honey badger. Much more likely.'

*'Nyegere?'* Umali says. Honey badger? He shakes his head emphatically, *'Hakuna hapa.'* There aren't any here. *'Ngawa?'* Civet Cat? *'Labda. . .'* Maybe. . . He shakes his head again. *'Alakini ni nguchiro!'* But it's a mongoose! Umali's not one to admit he may be wrong. *'Blurryfucken nguchiro!'* he spits.

'Enough of that!' Mum says threateningly. Umali grins. 'Solly *Memsahib*,' he says.

We nurse Snow White in turns. She's a model patient.

There are naughty pawpaw trees in our garden. Two produce rude-shaped fruit. Like a bum, or a lady's privates. Another grows a man's willy and testicles. Mum wants the offending trees cut down, but Umali says the fruit's the sweetest of all.

One Sunday afternoon the Mwanza priest who conducted Dad's funeral pops in. Mum sits with him and Becky at the garden table made from a wooden cable-drum. Just five yards away is a huge hanging pawpaw in the shape of a lady's thing. It's very detailed. The priest and Mum look assiduously the other way. I arrive home from the bush, and announce the unannounceable.

'It looks like. . .' I begin.

'Yes, Jimboy please get the sugar,' Mum says, her face reddening.

'But you've got sugar!' I exclaim, 'and that pawpaw. . .'

'Yes, now please check if Sandy's okay.'

'Sure, but the pawpaw is just like your *thing!*' I spurt. The priest chokes on his tea, then coughs into his handkerchief. Mum takes time forgiving me.

'You showed me up,' she says.

'It's the naughty tree,' I say.

There's that peculiar family living in a house down the road off to the left. They're quite reclusive, though not as bad as the Valaris, the 'secret' Italian family further up the hill, who nobody ever sees, apart from Mr Valari, who's seen at work, but

165

nowhere else. The van der Westhuizens are from the Orange Free State in South Africa, home of the 'Dutch'. Like Marais. They're different, everyone says. 'Only speak Afrikaans,' someone explains, 'they're common as muck.' Muck is common, I admit, it's everywhere.

They're a strange family. Unlike the Valaris, they don't hide in their house all day, but always seem to be in the garden. Our *ayahs* give their place a wide birth, because these *Kaburu Wazungu* don't like *watu*. When they walk anywhere near, they're shouted at. By adults and children, of which there are several, all dirty and snotty-nosed.

*'Kaffir'* is a word the van der Westhuizens like. It means nigger. *'Ek sal jou bliksem'* means 'I'll lightning you'. How will they do that? The *watu* don't like the abuse, or the van der Westhuizens. Neither do I.

'They shout me *blurryfuckenkaffir* every time I walk past,' Amina laments to Mum, 'Why they *blurryfucken* do that?'

One of the sons is nicknamed 'Skokie'. Afrikaans for 'Shock'. He put his thumb into a big electric plug-thing on an outside wall near the head office. I don't know what it was for. He got a 'helluva shock', they said, and the end of his thumb was burnt off. The plug-thing was removed from the wall.

There's worse. The van der Westhuizens cut off puppies' tails. I don't believe Dieti and Gretchen when they tell me. The van der Westhuizens' dogs have puppies. They're Boxer-lookalikes, because there are no pure Boxers here, and the mother's tail's off. All she's got is a funny little stump she wags furiously. They're going to cut the puppies' tails off today, Skokie tells Dieti when he walks past the house. Why does he do that? Why tell him? To frighten us, says Becky. That's why. They're horrible.

Becky and Gretchen refuse to come. They don't want to see puppies' tails chopped off. It's cruel. We agree it's cruel, but is it worse if we see it?

Dieti and I watch the house. At four o'clock Mr van der Westhuizen comes down the back steps. He's a big, bald man. His kids are bald too, at least the boys are. They really are strange. He's carrying a big basket. Three of his bald sons are with him. He walks to a tree stump, puts the basket down. He takes a long knife from a sheath and extracts a little brown bundle from the basket. It's a puppy. He puts it on the stump, positions it. There's a glint of steel in the sunlight, then a spurt of bright blood, and a pitiful whimper from the puppy. He's cut its tail off. There's shouts of delight from his kids. Dieti and I are sick in the grass. Told you so, says Becky.

During my absence at school, they've built a concrete circular, above-ground children's paddling pool next to the club pool. It's just two foot deep. In the middle is a concrete plinth with a big steel pipe in the centre. Topping that is an upside-down steel bowl four foot wide. Water shoots out the top, jets down the inside curve of the inverted bowl, and cascades in a solid curtain to the pool, where it hits the surface with the force of hail. It's so loud we can't hear someone shouting from inside. Indeed, the water-sheet's so thick we can barely see anyone inside. This is 'watercave', and becomes the venue for secret meetings when we don't want anyone to know our plans. We can go anywhere for secret meetings, but *anywhere* doesn't have the appeal of water-cave.

I choose watercave to tell Gretchen I'm planning to run away.

'Run a what?' she yells, trying to make herself heard above the thunder of the water.

'Run away,' I shout in her ear.

'What away?' she yells.

'Run,' I bellow.

'Okay,' she shouts, 'let's!' What an offer she's making. I don't seize the chance. I'll regret it one day. Not now. All I can think is watercave's not an ideal place for conversation.

In the last days of the holiday we invent a new game. *Uchi maji mti kimbia*, or naked-water-tree-running. It starts in our garden, when someone turns on the hose. In panic, we dive for cover. Big trees. The trunks are two foot wide, and the icy jet can't get round. At first Sophia, Antonio, Andrew, Gretchen, Dieti, Becky and I take turns to be *Shetani-maji*, or water-devil. Soon, like all games, it needs spicing up.

Dieti shows great imagination by suggesting running for cover should only be done 'visout clozes'. In addition, taking turns is too predictable. Gretchen suggests anything should be allowed. You shouldn't know who'll be the next ambusher. This introduces new, exciting, danger-elements. From now, the rules go, hose-ambush can happen anywhere, anytime. When it does, it's forbidden to find cover unless stark naked.

A further development in the game of naked-water-tree-running occurs and teaches me an important lesson. It's Dieti, again, who decides we need greater challenge. It isn't enough to strip off before running for cover from water attack. Boring. What we should do under attack is *not run* away naked, but nakedly hop away on one foot. It's a hop too far.

The gang has slavishly obeyed the rules thus far, but sheer complexity now makes it impossible. Failure to comply, along with interest, is lost. The game withers and dies under the weight of bureaucracy. I find out that complicating things can kill them.

Snow White is making remarkable progress in the kitchen. She hasn't got an infection in her wound, which is amazing, because her wing is not only broken, but also badly lacerated. Mum's given her a bit of aspirin every day. She's convinced that's why she's doing so well. Poor thing doesn't seem to mind having her broken wing strapped to her body, and she's really quite taken with living in a cardboard box. She lies there quietly, but clucks gently when someone approaches her. She only gets out her box to relieve herself. After a few days we experiment. We leave the back door open.

Snow White gets up, exits her box, walks to the door, and goes gingerly down the steps. Stares disdainfully at her erstwhile companions in the run, until Gooloogooloo spots her and comes to the wire. It's amazing. They stand like prisoner and visitor on either side of a barrier, making gentle clucking sounds at each other. It's conversation. Tiny adoptive mother advising overgrown adopted son. Eventually she walks away, relieves herself, wearily climbs the steps, pads across the kitchen floor, and climbs back in her box.

She's eating and drinking, and starting to look positively happy. The wing's stiff, and she'll never be able to fly. It won't matter. We trim the feathers on one wing of the *kukus* anyway, to stop them nesting in the trees. Learnt that early in Geita. When Mum and Dad first had *kukus*, they perched in high branches, and had to be shot for dinner.

Snow White is endearing herself. She's got a disbility now,

which makes her *kuku masikini,* or poor chicken, Umali says. But she hasn't got a cast eye, I say. Not *yet,* Umali replies. Many chickens in the bush have cast eyes. She'll have that, and worse, if she doesn't vacate his kitchen soon. When Mum's out he whispers that, though Mum doesn't like his language, Snow White survived an attack by an *nguchiro,* or mongoose, and a *blurryfuckenbitch* one at that.

# Fifteen

The holiday draws too soon towards an end. The last week is spent getting our things sorted out and packing. I try not to think there's only days left. Something will happen to prolong our stay. Maybe we won't have to go back at all. If I pray hard enough, maybe God will intervene. If he's got round to forgiving me shooting him. Also, if I ignore the matter, maybe it won't be true. But going comes closer. Soon it's the second last day. Umali has noticed my mounting depression. He suggests we go fishing.

'Why you cross, Jimu?' Umali asks on the bank of the dam. Lying beside us are our bamboo fishing poles, lines stretching out parabolically to the floats. We're lazy fishers. 'Why you angry?' Sandy whimpers. She wants to know too. I turn to Umali.

'I don't *want* to go back to Arusha,' I say fiercely. I spit several yards into the water. There's a long silence. Umali considers my words. Suddenly my float disappears beneath the still surface, and I grab my pole and strike. Flash of silver near surface. Fish on hook. I run up the bank, tugging. Sandy barks. A fat tilapia glints in the shallows, and I haul him onto the bank. Sandy grabs him in a deft movement, runs a few steps, and drops him at my feet. He's at least a pound and a half. Sandy makes that spitting sound. It's amazing how she fetches them, when she hates the feel in her mouth. She's almost as good a spitter as the *watu.* Can't let myself laugh when I'm in serious conversation with Umali.

'*Samaki muzuri,* ' Umali says, breaking his silence. Nice fish. He grins. I take the fish off the hook and throw it further up the bank. It didn't even eat the worm off the hook. I cast again, landing my float near the original spot. I'm getting very good.

'You fish well,' Umali says. Big compliment. When he first brought me here I hadn't a clue. He's a good teacher. I concentrate on my float, or try to. The thought of going back to Arusha brings tightness to my throat, and pounding to my chest.

'You don't want to go back?' Umali says.

'*Sitaki!*' I say vehemently. I don't. I spit again. This is serious business.

170

'Jimu, that is your school, if you don't go, how will you know to read, to get work of a *Mzungu?*'

'*Sitaki,*' I say. I don't want.

'*Usi pigana,* Jimu,' he murmurs gently. Don't fight, Jimu.

'*Nami kukimbia,*' I threaten. I'll run away.

'*Apana,*' Umali tuts. No. You won't run, and you won't fight.'

'*Kwa nini?*' I ask. Why not?

'Because your mother cries a lot. She works long and hard for you.'

'I want to stay with her and with you,' I say.

'Think Jimu. The *totos* stay at home. They won't read, they won't get good work. . .' I'm silent. Umali is agreeing with Mum. I have argued and pleaded with her so many tearful times, to no avail. Here's my best friend in the whole world taking sides against me.

I decide it's time to stop fishing and go home. Umali comes too. He's caught two fat catfish. There's little conversation on the road. I go ahead, fish in a bag tied to my pole, Sandy at my heel. It's a long walk home.

That night I lie in bed and think about this place, Geita, my home. Anyone from outside would imagine a little mining camp deep in the African bush would be a backwater, cut off and isolated from the world. But nothing is further from the truth. You only have to scratch, and the world outside is with you, in the present, and in history.

There's *watu* here, of different tribes, plus Indians, Chinese, Germans, German Jews, British, Italians, South Africans, Seychellois, and Mr Snel's wife is Canadian. They all have different backgrounds, languages and ways, and it colours the culture here.

There are *askaris* who fought in WWI with von Lettow Vorbeck's *schutztruppe* against the British. There are the German-Jewish survivors of German extermination camps in WWII, Dr Weiss and his wife, and Mr Hessler, who works with Mum at the mine store. There's Eugen Blüger, Dieti and Gretchen's dad, who served with Rommel in the *Afrika Korps* in WWII, and his cousin Otto Müller at Lotanga, who sailed in German *Kriegsmarine* submarines.

There's Higgs and Kaizer, the mine *askari*, who fought with the *KAR* in Burma, as part of General Slim's army taking the war to the Japanese between 1942 and 45. Several of the British people on the mine also served in theatres of the war, though none with such distinction as Dad.

Geita is no backwater. The important events of the first half of the twentieth century are all represented here, in the memories of living, breathing people. I love this about Geita. It looks isolated from the world, but nothing is more untrue. Where else, I wonder, can I actually talk with the very people who were involved in so many momentous, world shaping, events?

Next day I go in search of my old friend Kaizer. There's no television, nor clear radio reception apart from Radio Congo, but Kaizer's wartime tales more than compensate. He's a mine *askari*, or policeman, who served with the *KAR* in the war. The force has its roots in Nyasaland, or modern Malawi.

In 1899 a British Captain Lugard of the Norfolk regiment founds a small army called the *Central African Rifles*, in order to defeat a notorious slave trader called Mlozi. Same as our Geita ribbon and *Kimbo*-tin man. Was *that* Mlozi as crazy as ours? Was his insurrection madness-driven?

When 'Mlozi-the-first' is dealt with, 'natives' from colonies in West, Central and East Africa, are recruited into the *KAR* to serve under British officers. In post World War I Tanganyika, sixteen battalions of *KAR* are raised, many from among ex-*askaris* of von Lettow Vorbeck's indomitable *Schutztruppe*. I wonder why Fritz, the German-accented driver, didn't join the *KAR* like so many others. Did he dislike the British too much?

I ask Kaizer to tell me about the war in Burma. He scratches his greying hair, smiles, and begins. He loves to tell stories as much as I love to hear them.

In World War II the *KAR* is deployed in Abyssinia, Somaliland, Madagascar and Burma. It's so compelling. My beloved *watu*, from right here in little Geita, fighting big wars far away. In Burma, battalions of the *KAR* form part of the Eleventh East African division in General Sir William Slim's Fourteenth Army, the largest mobilisation of Commonwealth troops in the war. In all, over a million men are deployed through different phases of the war.

In 1944 General Slim's army launches a major offensive against the Japanese in Burma. The East African Division fights its way down the great river system of Burma, one brigade crossing the Chindwin, another striking the Japanese in the Kabaw valley. It's in the Kabaw valley where Kaizer wins his commendation for bravery.

Do I know, he asks, that Mr Higginson, the chief of the mine *askari*-force, fought in Burma too? That's interesting, even if Kaizer's own story is delayed.

Kaizer smiles. Then he begins again. Captain Reginald Higginson, known even then as 'Higgs', is an officer in a Tanganyika-based battalion of the *KAR*, in which, by 1944, there are only a few former *Schutztruppe askaris* left from 1918. But the tradition of their gallant predecessors is evident in their discipline and fighting prowess. When Higgs is disbanded from the army in 1946, he gets a job forming and running the small private police force for the gold mine in Geita. Half a dozen of his *askaris*, from the area originally, come with him, to form the backbone of the squad.

They say about Higgs that his years serving with African soldiers turned him into an African himself. Soon after arriving at Geita he is stricken with malaria, and will surely die, if not nursed back to health, in a tent, by an African woman. She's Kaiser's sister, and an ageing spinster at twenty-two. She thinks she's that age, because her mother said she was born six years after Vorbeck's tragic surrender in 1918. They say Higgs is so indebted he marries her. I doubt that's the only reason, because I know Higgs and his *bibi* very well, and they're a close and loving couple.

Higgs commits the worst transgression in British Africa. He dares marry a black woman. While they decide to keep him as police chief on the mine, it's a unanimous decision to socially black-ball him, and, of course, his wife. They can't ban him from the bar at the Lone Cone Club, because that would be 'going too far'. Fellow drinkers know how thirsty it gets in that heat. To deny a man a cold beer is inhuman, old bean. Nevertheless, he's told his wife is not welcome, and he must avoid too much conversation with 'decent white women'. They may catch something.

Kaizer, so named by his *Schutztruppe* father, is a man in his mid forties in 1959, when I'm eight. He served with Higgs in the King's African Rifles, in Somaliland and Abyssinia, and finally Burma.

There is always an *askari* stationed outside the Lone Cone Club. Why, I don't know. In Geita they're only armed with a wooden baton, which won't do much against a rampaging lion or a man with a gun. Kaizer insists on the club posting. There are two reasons. One, he loves Higgs more as a brother than a brother-in-law, and thinks his former officer, and current, boss may get so drunk he'll need help to get home to his *bibi*. The other is that Higgs, who loves Kaizer too, is wont to bring him out an icy bottle of *Whitecap* several times an evening.

Kaizer sits on the low stone wall outside the bar. He loves to talk. His English is very limited. Army commands, mostly. Even in Burma he was posted with other Swahili-speaking *askaris*, and the British officers spoke good Swahili. He's fond of me, and enchanted by my fluency in his native tongue. I sit outside with him on many occasions, from as young as five. By the time I'm eight we're old *rafikis*, or friends.

One day I ask how they march in the King's African Rifles. He jumps to his feet, smoothes his khaki shirt and shorts, and, stamping his right foot mightily on the ground, raising dust knee-high, stands to attention. Shouting *'kushoto, kulia, kushoto, kulia,'* lifting his knees almost to his chin, he marches towards the flowerbed. *Kushoto* is left, *Kulia* is right. He reaches the edge of the bed, and executes a high-stepping, stomping about-turn. He's so proud, so erect, so correct, so enthusiastic, even though he wears car-tyre rubber sandals, not boots and puttees. A born *askari*.

'Tell me about fighting the Japanese,' I say to him. This time he'll talk about himself, I hope, not Higgs.

*'Hawa,'* he says, 'them'. I relax. This is what I want. Fighting the Japs is what I'd like to do, and I pretend the war isn't really over. Soon as I'm big enough, I'll be off. Hearing Kaizer's story will prepare me for future battle. He finds the Japanese are formidable fighters in the jungles of Burma.

'In the Kabaw valley I am once with a small patrol, sent to find how close are the Japanese. We walk carefully, hiding behind one tree, then another. It has been raining days, and mud sucks at our boots. Sometimes my boot comes right off, stays behind in the mud, and I take my next step in my sock.' I nod my head in empathy.

'There are flies and small insects everywhere, and we have to be quiet, not smack them on our faces or legs. A slap can be heard a long way. We pick the insects off one at a time. Can't keep it up. Just leave them, even though we feel their crawling. We are even afraid to breathe.' He smiles in reminiscence.

'It's hotter and wetter than here. The sweat runs, the insects crawl and bite.' I shudder. I have a sudden itch on my cheek, and have to scratch. Kaizer laughs.

'We've been walking, and hiding, for four hours, when we find the Japanese.'

'You find them?' I ask.

'They find us,' he laughs. 'Those Japanese, they cover themselves with leaves, and crawl through the jungle. You can't see them at all.' He shakes his head in remembered surprise. 'We say they have narrow eyes to stop the bush getting in.' He laughs. Then he's serious again. 'Suddenly a machine-gun opens up. . . *kak-ak-ak-ak-a*, bullets are spitting on the ground about us. *Plop-plop-plop* they go, leaving round holes in the mud. One *askari* screams. He's got one through the knee. They have to cut his leg off.'

'Do you shoot back?' I ask, captivated.

'At what, little *Mzungu*, at what? We can't see anything!'

'What do you do?'

'We fall flat on the wet ground and nearly *kunya* in our trousers.'

'And?'

'There's a huge explosion, right near us.'

'What is it?'

'Mortar bomb. Blows one *askari*'s head right off, just like a chicken. His name is Arozi, and he's a friend. Comes from Geita, like me.'

'Then. . ?'

'I, and another *askari*, crawl to the right, to get behind those Japanese *nyokas*. That's what they are to us, snakes with narrow eyes. It's slow work, and the insects won't leave us alone.'

'And?'

'We come up behind them, but there's only one. He's lying in the grass, between two bushes, and has a mortar-launcher and three bombs. He doesn't know we're there. I take aim with my Lee Enfield, and, *ka- boom*, I miss him!'

'What happens?' I ask, the tension overwhelming. Kaizer smiles indulgently.

'It's alright *Mzungu ndogo*, little European, can't you see I'm still here?'

'Yes. . .'

'The Nippon, he rolls over and tries to stand when my bullet hits the ground by his head. The other *askari* shoots him with his Sten gun, *Brrr-aa-a-ppp*, six bullets in the chest, knocks him backwards like a toy. Nine millimetre.'

'Dead?'

'Completely dead. *Anakufa kabisa.*' He dies completely. 'Can you believe, he has strings in his hands to the triggers on two machine-guns, which are tied to trees, sighted where he knows we would approach. Just one Japanese...' Kaizer shakes his head. 'They are very clever.'

Now Kaizer smiles and gets to his feet. The story is over. Those Japanese are tougher than they look in war comics. In them they're all thin, short, knock-kneed, buck-toothed and bespectacled, and the only word they yell is *banzaai*, which means 'charge'. Handicap that, having nothing else to shout than 'charge' if you happen to mean 'retreat'. And *banzaai* is not a midget tree like Becky says. I can't imagine a Japanese soldier yelling 'Midget Tree!' on the charge. Anyway, perhaps I shouldn't really fight the Japanese. They're dangerous. I tell Kaizer it's a great story, and one day I'll write a book about him.

'*Asante, ndugu ndogo,*' thank you little brother. 'You have *hakiri*, and you will do it one day.' Brains.

On the way home my throat feels really tight. Distraction from going back to Arusha only works momentarily. It's still there, closer with each click of the old wind-up clock on the sideboard.

At home a visitor's waiting in the compound. Lutoli. I haven't seen him since I've been home. We're delighted to meet up again, and for a couple of hours I almost forget my misery.

He tells me he's been away with his mother, visiting his late father's relatives in Biharlomoulo. He knows I'm going back to Arusha soon, but hasn't realised it's tomorrow. We talk, practise shooting with our homemade catapults, and eat a meal of *ugali* and *mboga* with Amina and Umali. When we part, Lutoli cries shamelessly.

'You're my best friend in the world,' he sobs, 'a friend to beat all.' He makes me cry. There's something very sad about Lutoli. Like a premonition, if there is such a thing.

Umali doesn't show anger about my temper tantrum at the dam. Instead, he tries lifting my spirits by telling me one of his funniest jokes. A Swahili one.

'There's a man with two willys, or *mboros*. His wife is fed up, because when one lies down, the other stands up. Finally, exhausted by double *jigi-jigi*, she sends *Two-Mboros* to the doctor to have one amputated. When he reaches the clinic, after many days on the road, the nurse tells him to wait, as *Three-Mboros* and *Four-Mboros* have come first.'

When he's got me laughing, he makes up rude rhymes:

> *Kwa kibiriti ya kupata matiti,*
> *katika Dodoma kupata kuma,*
> *lakini kwa rungu kupata mkundu!*

> For matches you get tits,
> in Dodoma you get a vagina,
> but for a *rungu* (wooden club), you get an anus!

Reality returns brutally. It's been a break to think about something other than going back to Arusha. Kaizer's stories distract me from the harsh here and now. So do Umali's jokes. For a while. Maybe I can get help from another source.

I've tried praying, begging, hoping for a *novus actus interveniens*, or 'new intervening event'. It hasn't worked. I'm still going back to school. My scheming and plotting have come to nought. Perhaps I should take a completely different tack. What about Mlozi? It's not just Lutoli who says he's a *mchawi*, or witch. There are others.

Just behind his flat rock or *mwamba*, is Mlozi's tiny hut. It's so small, not even tall enough for me to walk in without bending, if I wanted to. It's made of bent sticks, twigs and mud, and roofed with banana-thatch. He sits on his rock all day, then crawls into his hut at night.

There are mutterings about Mlozi among the *watu*. It's been a long time since the *ng'ombe*, or cattle-rich, *mzee* intervened to stop the crowd stoning him to death. Since then, some *watu* have begun to believe he's neither mad, nor possessed by *jinni* or *djinn*. That leaves only one explanation for his lifestyle and appearance: he's *mchawi*, witch-sorcerer. Some think no further, others avoid him, lest he curse them. Then there are the *wasikini*. Begging for a living is an insecure occupation. They need all the luck they can get.

One day Mlozi tells a *masikini* that if he begs at the green house beyond the baobab tree, he will receive blue trousers. The *masikini* does, and it happens. The *masikini* oracle is born. How, or with what they pay him, I don't know. But I've got money. Of my fifty shillings pocket money for next term, Mum's already given me five. Suddenly I know how to spend it.

*'Jambo,'* I say next morning. It's my last day in Geita. Time is running out. I'm standing before Mlozi's *mwamba*. It's one o'clock in the morning. Swahili-time for seven am. Once I got the idea last night, I couldn't wait to get here. The sun's already scorching, and Mlozi's sitting in his usual place. He's bent over, and his ribbon-tied locks obscure his face. He's murmuring softly in there. The murmuring stops. A hand on the end of a thin wrist heavy with copper-wire bracelets reaches up and parts his plaited locks. Coal-black eyes are staring.

*'Nini Mzungu?'* What, white person? asks that strange, reedy voice. This is not simple. It could be 'what do you want?', 'what white person are you?', or even 'what now?' implying I've been before. Suddenly I'm struck with dread. I can see why the *wasikini* fear and respect him as *mchawi*. Anyone who with just two words can bring such confusion has very strong *dawa*, or medicine. How do I answer?

'I have come. . .'

'You have come?' His voice is spooky. High-pitched, yet gravelly. He can see I have, yet he asks. There's more to this. He knows why I'm here. Just wants to hear it from me. I feel a tingle in my spine. What am I doing here, seeking out this strange, strange man?

'*Ku ulisa,*' I say. To enquire.

'*Aw omba?*' Or beg, even pray? He's playing a game with me.

'To ask *hekima,*' I blurt. Wisdom. I'm not here to pray.

'My *hekima?*' A thin laugh. The anorexic figure suddenly straightens, and he sweeps his ropey locks aside. His face is even thinner than before. Bony. Amused, he looks like a laughing skeleton. I want to leave this place. It's eerie, even so early in the day. But I've got a mission.

'I don't want to go back to Arusha,' I plead.

'*Uta rudi,*' he says. You *will* return. He adopts his faraway look and begins a mumbling speech with no one. It's like I'm not here, as if he's consulting the sky.

'You'll go back,' he suddenly says. He spits expertly at the ground. 'You'll return both there and here.' He loses interest. That's it. He's not even looking at me. I'm dismissed by the *mchawi*. My hand's in my pocket. I feel the five shilling coins. I'm devastated. He's robbed me of hope.

There's a crippled *masikini* standing nearby. He's been waiting, watching with one bright eye. Clearly he's next in line. I extract a shilling and place it on the rock. Mlozi doesn't shift. The *masikini* does. For a cripple, he moves with dazzling speed. The shilling disappears into the folds of his ragged clothes. Mlozi doesn't notice, or care. He is not a material man. I go away to nurse my bitter disappointment.

After two hours of wasted tearful pleading with Mum, though she's as distressed as me, I go to bed. But I can't sleep. I lie in the dark, trying desperately to hatch an escape plan. I can't run away in Geita, because all directions lead into the bush. Foolish anyway, because Geita's where I want to be. This is the opposite of breaking out from prison. I want to break *in* to where I already am. How can I do that?

I wrestle my thoughts. The only prospect I have of altering things is to change Mum's mind. If she decides I can stay, that'll be that. How can I persuade her? All my pleading, all my tears, have failed completely. Out of my confusion comes an idea.

If I escape on the way to Arusha, and disappear for a while, that'll make Mum realise how serious I am. I have to make my move between Geita and Arusha. Geita to Mwanza is no good – jungle. Mwanza to Dodoma, on the train? That's difficult, because when the train stops there are lots of people on the platform, and everyone looks out the windows. The hotel in Dodoma? The dormitory – difficult to sneak out. Someone's sure to wake up.

I'm getting desperate. I'm thinking myself closer and closer to Arusha, without escaping. It will have to be the bus. It's the only option. I'll jump out the bus.

I force my mind off the subject. It can wait till Dodoma. There are so many other things to think about. What about Higgs and Heathfield? Thinking of them will take my mind off my dilemma.

Higgs and Heathfield are reprobates in the eyes of the *Wazungu*. Higgs because of his black *bibi*, Heathfield because they say he's 'homosensual'. Thelemani told me about it. Men and *jigi-jigi*. The *mutu* who does *jigi-jigi*, then gets *jigi-jigied*. Not that I really grasp it. It's a no man's land of knowledge. Higgs, on the other hand, doesn't only live with his *bibi*, but has a troika of half-caste children. People say this in lowered voices. The shame of it!

Being socially unacceptable to other club members, the semi-outcasts come, nevertheless, reliably and regularly, every time the sun tips the western hills, to drink at the great maninga-wood bar at Lone Cone Club. The far right hand end, because everyone else occupies the middle and left, and proximate tables and chairs.

They drink heavily and share only each other's company, except for the occasional interlude when a more sympathetic and less bigoted member of the middle-to-left assembly forays over to show slightly embarrassed solidarity with the outcasts. A joke, a pat on the back of one, usually Higgs's rather than Heathfield's, his folly being less reprehensible, for homosensuality is worse than miscegenation, a beer ordered against the tab, then a retreat to more hallowed surroundings. Quizzical looks and 'tut-tut's from those who remain unpolluted from mixing with the unmixable.

Higgs and Heathfield are always last to leave, ordering more

*Whitecap* lager when Ishmael, the barman in white *kanzu* and red *fez*, rings the bell for last orders. They drink till the beer's finished, the lights off, and everyone's gone. They stagger outside, and Higgs takes Heathfield home on his *Harley Davidson*, before finding his way down the dirt road to his own house .

In 1958 there is a most curious thing. It will live forever in Geita folklore. It's so strange I have difficulty persuading people in Arusha that it's true. The drunken outcasts, Higgs and Heathfield, lurch out the club into the parking area. They're even drunker than usual.

Higgs finds his motorbike and pulls it off its stand. He straddles it and kick-starts the engine. Heathfield has disappeared, and Higgs calls for him impatiently, gear engaged clutch held in. He feels a weight alight, Heathfield's warm body against his back, moist breath on the nape of his neck. Heathfield can get rather clutchy and a little pathetic after ten quarts of *Whitecap*. Higgs is used to it. He lets out the clutch with his left hand, and rolls up the revs with his right. The big *Harley Davidson* roars, and the unsteady bike trundles away up the gravelled road.

Then Heathfield really starts to exceed himself. At first Higgs feels his arms move up from holding him round the hips, to grasp his shoulders. 'What the hell you playing at?' he shouts above the roar of the engine. No answer. Now Heathfield begins to dig his nails into Higgs's shoulders. The pain is excruciating.

'Stop it, you fool,' Higgs yells, but the nails dig deeper, and begin to scratch painfully down his back. The agony is so extreme that Higgs, rounding a corner, loses control, and he, Heathfield and bike, plummet off the road into the undergrowth.

Higgs hears his bike hit something. He finds himself on a bed of soft branches, and suddenly feels very inebriated. To hell, he thinks, and falls asleep. His last thought is 'where the hell is Heathfield?' and 'I'm not taking *him* home again.'

At seven in the morning Higgs awakes to searing tropical sunshine, buzzing of myriad insects, and a skimpy memory of last night. When he tries to rise, he finds his back and shoulders are in agony. Gingerly he feels the scratches, and discovers deep lacerations running from shoulder-tip to waistline.

He limps to where his bike lies on its side by the trunk of an *Mbuia* tree, and is astonished to see the near side of the petrol tank has four deep dents. He pulls the bike up, and finds the same on the other side. One dent has a hole in it. Protruding from the hole is a very large, bloodstained claw-nail. Higgs's clingy friend last night was not Heathfield. He, on staggering into the fresh air, feels awfully tired. He sees an inviting flowerbed, and subsides into it.

Higgs's passenger is a full-grown leopard. The news spreads like bush fire. Some *Wazungus* say he's making it up. Whites who marry blacks are probably liars, and worse. But how can they explain his lacerations and the holes in the tank? The claw? Why does Heathfield admit sleeping in a flowerbed? Higgs brought him to the club, and his bike wasn't damaged then.

Did Higgs sneak out between drinks, disable and puncture his own petrol tank, insert what is undeniably a leopard claw into the hole, severely lacerate himself, then sidle back in and act normally? Wouldn't someone notice the blood? Even if not, how did he get rid of Heathfield on the road? Unless he and Heathfield are making this up together. But why? Why would these two men, no matter their faults, play a prank like this? It doesn't make sense.

Three days after the incident, while Higgs is still receiving daily injections and dressings for his wounds, a leopard is shot just two miles from the club by Marcello Barelli, Antonio's father and our great white hunter. His rear right foot is missing a claw, and the toe pad is torn and septic. When his back feet are placed against the fuel tank, the claw positions match the punctures. The incident is closed.

The leopard weighs two hundred pounds, and is fully nine foot from nose to tip of tail. He will be remembered for years as the 'Geita-Night-Rider', who hitched a lift with the constabulary. When Higgs recovers his limited dignity, he's often heard to brag, after several *Whitecaps*, that 'I gave that sod a lift half a bloody mile!' The legend of The Astonishing Tales of Higgs the Policeman grows. I think 'astonishing' means funny.

Higgs isn't bad, I muse. In fact, he's a good man, a kind one. Yet the cruel *Wazungu* make him an outcast. During this holiday I go to his house. I meet his *bibi*, Maria, Kaizer's sister, again.

She makes me lemonade from a fresh lemon she picks off her tree, squeezes, mixes with sugar and cold water. Higgs comes home and is hugely pleased to see me. Doesn't get white visitors. I ask where his children are. Visiting at Kaizer's *shamba*, he says. 'You're a big friend of Kaiser, aren't you?' I confirm I am. 'He's Maria's brother, you know?' I do know.

I notice a whole wall in the lounge is filled by a built-in bookshelf. It's crowded with books. All sizes and colours. I've never seen so many together. Higgs is a big reader. How many of the *Wazungu* know that? He's cleverer than them by far.

I can't sleep. I don't want to let my mind wander back to my Arusha-school-escape plan. Too much thinking, and I'll be exhausted before I start. I'll have time aplenty for planning on the horrible train, and in the Railway Hotel in Dodoma. There are other things about Geita I can think about now. Anything to stop thoughts of Arusha. I fall asleep trying to think what to think.

I wake while it's still dark. I know what I should have thought about. There is this other story, the coffee-planter's one, which is funny and sad at once. Such things don't happen anywhere else than in the Tanganyika bush. The Land Rover may be coming for me, but not yet, and I've got my mind to play with as I want. It's a defence against the coming dawn, which will see me on the road away from home again. A road I don't want to travel. I haven't heard Roger Whittaker singing *'Morning Please Don't Come'*, yet I share the sentiment. And they can't stop my thoughts.

Higgs and Heathfield are not at all unusual in Tanganyika. By comparison with some people, they're pillars of propriety and conservatism. I turn over in bed. Geita is such a wonderful place. I don't want to go tomorrow. Why can't I just stay, like Lutoli? I feel sad when I think about him. I miss the times we spent together. Why do I have to be a *Mzungu*, and go away to school? It's happening again, I'm thinking about Arusha.

I force my mind back. There's no end to interesting things, which happen. The coffee planter's story for example. It's a good one. It's stories like this which give Geita, all Tanganyika, that special something which makes it home. Not like the soft green wetness and tiny houses, which is all I remember of

Cornwall and Germany. This is a man's country, I think, and suits me because I'm a man.

In 1959, a visitor comes. Don't know why, but he does. Probably because he likes his beer cold, and the word is out there's a good fridge at Lone Cone Club. Terence Worthing is his name, and he farms coffee a hundred miles away. Ex-servicemen were encouraged to start the industry in yet another attempt to make the colony pay. Terence stays a week as personal guest to Mr Snel, General Manager. They met long ago in the war. Snel was in Gibraltar, where Terence was a Navy diver.

Terence is a big, bearded man, who smokes a pipe, drinks prodigious amounts of *Whitecap*, and loves regaling people with his escapades. He tells several stories at the bar. One stands out, and joins Geita folklore.

The coffee plantations are three years old, spread out in a crescent over ninety square miles of sun-scorched scrub. A dozen new farming ventures halfway between Mwanza and Musoma, and ten miles inland from Lake Victoria. Young coffee plants stand in long rows on cleared fields; living conditions are basic. Most planters still sleep in tents, or huts of corrugated iron and roughly hewn planks. Their energies are focused on bringing irrigation from rivers feeding the lake, grading roads and planting coffee.

Blistering hot days in the open, and bush-loneliness, lead to a meeting of minds at one's *shamba*. A decision is reached. At a point equidistant from their properties, designated *Timbuktu*, a clearing is cut. A huge round mud and wattle hut, open above the waist, is built, and roofed with *makuti*-style elephant-grass. A bar is constructed from crudely sawn *maninga* planks, and tall stools of hides and sticks are commissioned from local *watu*. The *pièce de la résistance* is a large paraffin refrigerator, which arrives by lorry from Dar-es-Salaam, five days distant. *Club Timbuktu* is in business.

Hard-working men shouldn't drink every day, four planters' wives declare, so they only open on Sundays. The Sabbath 'holy communion' becomes a riotous, drunken and very *spirit*-ual occasion.

Early in the history of *Club Timbuktu*, the revellers see a most remarkable sight. 'We are thoroughly under the affluence of incohol, really sizzled,' Terence says, 'and don't know if it's real or imagined. Sun and booze, deadly together.'

A dozen tribesmen and women emerge from the bush. They aren't from tribes the planters know round there. These are the much feared 'bush people', of whom the *watu* speak with dread. They are cannibals, they say, who worship a monkey-king, or, some think, a great crocodile. No one is quite certain. They wear animal skin moochies over their genitals, and nothing else. How can a cannonball eat people, I wonder. Before or after being fired?

Carried at shoulder height by the leading four apparitions is a stretcher of wooden poles and plaited grass. Regally perched on top, perfectly balanced and smiling a greeting, is a white man. He's unmistakably European, despite his deep-copper tan and black fur moochi. Apart from that diminutive garment, he's stark naked.

'Hello,' he says in a lah-de-dah Oxbridge accent, 'I'm Joe'. The planters burst out laughing. This is high comedy, a joke by one of their number. They're always playing tricks.

'Good show!' one shouts, clapping. They 'play the game', greet Joe and offer him a drink. Joe gives a command, and his bearers set him on the ground. While his entourage watch, Joe joins the *Wazungu* drinkers in a 'bender to end benders'.

It turns out Joe is, in a previous life, an Oxford law graduate who goes into colonial service after university. He's helped by contacts of his wealthy family, who live in a grand estate in Hertfordshire. 'It'll make a man of you, show you the world, and teach you responsibility,' his crusty barrister-father tells him. 'Oh, and don't come back until you've got yourself a real woman, not another floozie. And ask her to show you how to do up that damnable tie.'

Joe joins the colonial office, undergoes two weeks' training, which comprises cocktail parties in Chelsea, and drunken debauched forays into Soho with six colleagues and two heavy-drinking 'trainers'. He's sent east as a junior in the legal section of Hong Kong's colonial administration. There he meets his first wife, daughter of the third most powerful man after the Governor General. Married, and with a baby due in an indelicately short time, the couple move into their own home.

By this time Joe is twenty-six, and deeply bitten by the 'booze-bug'. He begins to have symptoms of alcohol dependence. He tells the planters, who listen in rapt concentration, 'I begin to have a drop in the morning, to ease the shakes.' He takes a swig of neat gin, grimaces, and swallows.

'Then I start to hide a bottle in the drawer at work.' Soon he's topping up his alcohol level throughout the day. His young wife, now with daughter, whose only occupation is 'screaming and shitting', finally begins to resent his drinking. Arguments flare. He starts lying about his drinking, hiding bottles where she won't find them. He avoids going home when he can't face the rancour. 'Office floor's comfortable when you're pissed.'

After yet another 'bender' with a friend in the Chinese bars of Kowloon, Joe returns home to find two things. 'She's up and left, with baby, and written me a note saying sorry Joe, can't take this anymore. Melanie.' There's another envelope, a brown manilla one with a seal. 'Know that anywhere. Bloody colonial office. I'm informed that, due to unprofessional and thoroughly reprehensible behaviour. . . my services are no longer required by the Hong Kong administration.'

Joe grins. 'At the bottom it says I'm being given two months severance pay and a second class ticket home on the steamship *SS Orion*. Departing Hong Kong for Cape Town, Mombasa, Dar-es-Salaam, Suez, Port Said, Genoa, Barcelona, Gibraltar and Southampton, on 27th instant. That's three days.' The planters are impressed. They can't reel off a list like that. Not 'affluenced' as they indubitably are.

Joe drinks his money before *Orion* reaches Dar-es-Salaam. Desperate for a drink, he tries his luck ashore. For a few pennies he buys enough homemade Nubian gin to 'slay an elephant'.

'And so,' he says, grinning with black teeth, 'I decide to hell with the ship. I don't want to see Mombasa, Suez, Port Said, Genoa, Barcelona, Gibraltar or bloody Southampton. I have a paradise, here in Tanganyika!' There's applause from the planters, who all think Tanganyika's a good place. They pour him another glass of neat gin.

Joe hangs around Dar a few months, finds he doesn't need a fixed abode when the *Warabu* and *Swahilis* offer food and a floor mat to sleep on. But he 'begins to be noticed' by the 'damnable Brits'. It's unheard of for a white man, an Englishman-to-boot, to mix with the natives like this. . . 'First I'm arrested, thrown in a cell for a night, and lectured on race mixing by the superintendent. Bugger them.' It fails to reform him, and a policeman breaks his arm with a baton. 'Stronger advice, the bastards!'

Joe decides to head inland, away from authority. It's 1936, and there's a lot of construction work in different parts. Every day lorries leave Dar, loaded with cement and material for places with exotic names, like Shinyanga, Dodoma, Iringa, Mwanza and Musoma. A *Chagga* driver offers him a ride.

'I don't give a bugger,' he said, 'all I want is peace and quiet, and something to drink.'

Somewhere near Musoma, ten miles from where he's telling his tale, the lorry noisily blows a head gasket. Joe is no mechanic. He thanks the driver, and takes his chances on a footpath into the hills, a bottle of Nubian gin clutched in one hand.

'That's 1936,' one of the planters says, 'It's 1959 now, twenty-three years. . .'

'Exactly,' says Joe, 'time flies when you're having fun. I even manage to avoid the war. Only hear about it in '51.' He holds his glass out for a refill. The planters appraise him. If he was twenty-six or seven when he left Hong Kong, he's fifty or thereabouts now. Okay, he wears nothing more than a moochie, and his teeth are black, but there isn't a grey hair, or a single wrinkle on his face.

'I think you should meet the *bibi* and kids,' Joe pronounces. 'Marina, *kuja hapa, leta watoto.'* Marina, come here, bring the children. A dark, wrinkled, bare breasted, elderly looking woman detaches herself from the watching clan, and several light skinned men and women, plus a couple of teenagers, join her. 'This,' Joe says proudly, 'is my family.' His family smiles, but look bewildered. According to Joe, he is the only *Mzungu* they've ever seen until today.

'To what do we owe this visit, Joe?' a planter finally asks.

'Gin,' he said. 'Ivory for gin.' He snaps his fingers and yells, *'Leta meno ya tembo.'* From the edge of the clearing two young men come running, bearing between them a huge elephant tusk.

'You shoot elephants?' the planter asks.

'Naw, find dead ones. Elephant cemetery, you know. Have to die sometime.'

'Well,' says another planter, eyeing the tusk. 'Ivory's selling for. . . what is it. . . several pounds a pound. This one's heavy. . . I think we can do business.'

Thus begins a most unusual commercial and social relationship. Native Joe, as they name him, has to wait a week for his first two cases of gin, but he and his *watu* don't mind. They camp patiently at *Timbuktu*. Next Sunday the planters return with the gin. Someone has a delivery of irrigation equipment from Dar, and contacts his supplier. After another drinking binge with his *'Mzungu* tribe', Joe embarks imperiously atop his stretcher, gin bottle in hand, and waves goodbye. Everyone shakes their head as the strange procession filters back into the fastness of the bush.

'We're onto a good thing,' Terence Worthing tells his audience. I'm listening raptly. I'd love to meet this wild man of the bush. I have much in common with him. 'Native Joe brings us tons of ivory. Tusks like we've never seen. By George, it pays! All our booze, and more. He comes every six weeks, ten times in all, his poor sweating devils divided between those carrying him on that ridiculous litter, and those lugging ivory. All the time he sits swigging gin from a bottle. Never seen anything like it.'

'What then?'

'All good things end, I suppose,' Terence muses, staring into his empty beer glass. Someone takes the hint and buys him a *Whitecap*. He pours, takes an appreciative swig, and continues. 'One day Joe kicks the bucket, out in the bush. His adopted *watu* don't have a clue what to do. See, they're ancestor worshippers, have rites and rituals when one of them croaks. With Joe, they don't know what to do.'

'What they do?'

'Truss him up under a pole, like a deer, carry him three days through the bush. We'll know best, they think, how to send him to his ancestors. Joe liked us, and we are his *kabila*, or tribe. Of course it's the gin he really liked, but what the heck. Course it's a bloomin' Sunday, like they arrange it specially. They come out the bush, carrying his stinking corpse on a pole, flies all over.'

'They brought him to the club?'

'Too right. Luckily we've had a few by then, makes it easier. Once we understand the poor heathens have carried him through the bush, in that heat, we think we'd better do something. We dig a big hole, or they do, three foot deep, 'cos that ground's as hard as bloody steel. We put Joe in, stick a bottle of *Johnny Walker* with him, cover him up, and make a show of praying to impress them. My oppo, Bruce the Aussie, holds the friggin' exercise book, which we keep the tabs in, upside-down, and makes a speech. 'G'bye Joe,' he says, 'hope there's shitloads of gin where you've gone.' Joe's poor *bibi* never stops wailing, and nor do his youngsters. We give them the cash in the kitty, and that's that.'

'That's it?'

'No. Same evening, all boozed up, we run out of grog.'

'And?'

'Need more booze. . .'

'You don't. . ?'

'We do. Dig the old bugger up again.'

The digging up bit doesn't worry me. I dug up Tembo's puppy, didn't I? But I'm worried about Higgs. He married a *bibi*. Joe married a *bibi*. Joe's dead. I hope that's not going to happen to Higgs. Please God, I pray, don't let Higgs die too. I wonder how much he'll listen to my prayer. Can someone who killed Dad have mercy? Or someone who makes me go to boarding school?

# Sixteen

Finally I fall asleep, Sandy's head beside mine on the pillow. It seems only minutes before it's five am. Fritz is hooting outside. Quick wash, get dressed in school uniform. Lug my trunk to the front door with sleepy Umali. Get in the Land Rover. By the time we get to Mwanza I'll have firmed up my plan. I'll escape. It'll be before the Dodoma-Arusha bus. I'll pretend I've given up the struggle for now, act normally, buy comics for school at Lake Printers, and get on the train with only limited emotional display. Don't want anyone pre-warned.

The same children as before, parents seeing them off. Mrs Shuter is escort again. Horrible old bag. Becky sobs a lot. I sob a little, though my feelings are mixed. Gretchen sits next to me and tries her best to engage me in conversation. Mum asked her to. Mum knows how I feel about her.

'It's not so bad, Jim,' she says.

'It is,' I say. Much as I adore her, I'm too busy thinking to have a chat. Competing with the dismay and foreboding I've felt the whole holiday is another feeling. Excitement. Anticipation, exhilaration almost. I'm going to turn this thing on its head, and only I know. I'll put an end to the nightmare.

When I've been missing a few days, they'll know I'm not prepared to go to Arusha under *any* terms. They'll give up and let me stay at home. They'll all know soon enough, I think, watching Mwanza Station and the distant figures of Mum and Fritz growing smaller. Mum's looking so sad. Fritz is erect and, as always, aloof. I noticed, this morning, that on shaving his pencil-line moustache, he's nicked the edge of his lip. There's a scab. Did he say *Himmel* when he did it?

The train journey's the same, only this time I've changed attitude and intention. As the miles roll by, the sun's glare hurts my eyes. After several blinding hours comes the welcome sunset. The landscape grows gentler in early twilight. I think how different this journey is to last time on the same line. Then I was keen, excited about adventure. Now I know better.

There's nothing to be happy about. They're taking me where I don't want to go. A place where I'm alien, where I don't fit, where I'm unhappy. All for my 'own good'. Why don't they

190

listen to me? Mum. . . surely she, of all the people in the world, should listen? But she hasn't, no matter how I pleaded, cried, begged. It's seven thirty, Becky says, showing off her new watch.

The sky grows dark as the blood-red sun plunges off the end of the world. A three-quarter moon softly lights the arid land. Trees cast eerie shadows. Somewhere ahead the locomotive belches. The brakes clunk on, iron wheels screech on iron rails. The train judders and slows. A naked light bulb attached to a wooden pole, surrounded by giant fluttering moths, beams jaundiced light on a disintegrating cement platform. A station.

We squeal to a halt, and judder again. Why is that? I don't know. Nobody gets off or on, and the locomotive doesn't need water or coal so soon. Not that those are here anyway. Gretchen is fast asleep. Her head has slipped to one side, and is resting lightly on my shoulder. Her breath is sweet and warm. The only people on the platform are two tired-looking women vendors in *kanzus*, trying to sell roasted *mahogo*, or cassava. I don't see takers. The train shakes and groans, and starts again. The vendor-women look disappointed.

At eight thirty Mrs Shuter says go to bed. I lie on my narrow bunk, listening to the clicking of wheels on track. It comforts me. That, and the gentle roll of the carriage. Tomorrow's another day. I'll show them I mean business. But I can't sleep. My mind's somewhere between ensconcement in my imaginary canoe, and the train trying to rock me to sleep. Even the *gari moshi* is in on the plot. The thought keeps me from slumber.

I'm awake when we roll to a halt in all the little stations, as well as Shinyanga and Singida. I remember the sounds well from the last trip. Noisy bartering. Women's shrill voices, deeper tones of African rail crew beating prices down. Swish of water feeding locomotive boiler. Clanging boots on steel plate. Hissing from restless engine.

I doze, and then it's morning. The dazzling white sun-orb is up already, beginning its relentless obsession with cremating creation. Breakfast in dining car. A tatty one this time. Faded, flyblown, hand-written *EAR&H* sign. I hardly eat. My brain's grinding out a plan without me. It's visceral, involves the gut. I always think important things there. We sit in our compartment more searing hours.

I doze again, and wake, my head aching from heat and discomfort. Trouble with sleeping sitting up. Head lolls all over the place. Lips dry too, cracking. Taste blood when I suck them. Nobody has lip-ice or Vaseline. I just lick them. Becky says it'll make them worse. Gretchen agrees.

Four in the afternoon we pull into Dodoma station. The Railway Hotel's the same. Miserable. Can I escape here? Von Lettow Vorbeck's painted eyes look stern. Does he know my plans? I consult my stomach-brain partnership. No answers. Not many routes out. Just the rail-line we've come on, and the road to Arusha. Last place I'll be running to. Cross-country. Where that will take me, I've no clue. Seen glimpses from the train. Dry, arid places, no water anywhere. Dust bowls. Could get lost out there. Like Lawrence of Arabia, only worse. He had a camel and a gun. There's places where it's green, but no road, just windy footpaths back to the railway line. No point. I'll go round in circles, come back to the rails every time.

There are other places, where lions lie sunning themselves, flicking their tails at flies. Look like big pussycats, but they aren't. Don't fancy a one to one with them. Not without a gun. Rhinos, they're about too, massive grey tanks with pointy fronts and big bums. Bad tempers. Wish I could have Dad's *Wesley Richards* 375 Magnum. Not that I could carry it far. The *watu* don't even speak Swahili round here, they say. Can't tell them 'Speak Swahili, dammit!' Not in English either. What will they do with me, a small Swahili-speaking *Mzungu*, or whatever they'll call me? All in all, escape prospects are lean.

Morning. Surprisingly, I've slept in the old hotel. Not even a dream. Must be mental exhaustion. We've had breakfast, though I only managed half a dry bread roll and a glass of juice. The gaudily painted bus is parked out front on the dusty circular driveway. Same one, the *Duma Upesi*. Only I know it's not so upesi! More like *pole-pole*, slow.

The driver's a young chap in blue overalls. He's flirting outrageously with a nubile cleaning maid. He speaks Swahili. I don't know if she does. She's giggling as he reaches out and squeezes her breast. *'Nina penda ku tomba,'* he says. I'd like to do *jigi-jigi* with you. She skakes her head. Doesn't understand. I would laugh, but this is Last-Chance-Saloon. After this it's Arusha. I don't fancy an escape from there.

'Everyone on the bus,' the old bag shouts. Why she has to be so loud, I don't know. Likes bullying smaller people. Becky and Gretchen get on with the others. I don't. I'm glued to the spot. Don't want to get on. My plan's not ready. I haven't got it sorted out. How am I going to escape? Can't let this bus carry me even closer to school. My plan's going downhill, approaching irretrievable. If I don't act, *do* something, it'll be too late. 'You, Francis,' the ugly one says, noticing my lack of movement, 'on the bus, sharply now.'

'Yes Miss,' I hear myself say. It's automatic, not considered. Unknown to me, my brain-stomach partnership has reached its limit. I climb the two iron steps, enter the bus. Becky and Gretchen have kept a seat for me.

The diesel engine roars into life. The driver's parted from his sweetheart cleaning lady. He doesn't believe in formalities. The gearbox grates, the old bus roars out the drive, scattering pebbles and raising a cloud of dust. I'm still standing. I hold onto the seat beside me. Then something happens. The secret conspiracy within takes over. I'm amazed to feel myself running, bumping against metal seat-sides.

The bus plunges forward. I accelerate the other way. At the last moment, just before I collide with the back, I jump. Breaking glass, flying, still running, hit the road, dragged backwards by momentum. I'm still trying to run when I tumble and fall. I hit the unyielding ground with my face, and roll.

I'm lying there, bleeding. The bus is braking, skidding on the road. I get dizzily to my feet. Blood drips from my cheek. People are running towards me. I've got to get away. I take a step. Sharp pain sears through me. I've twisted my ankle. Mrs Shuter's there. She's gasping, breathless. 'What happened?' she says. Becky's just behind her. The blue-overalled driver is behind Becky.

'Ouch,' I cry, and fall on the stony ground in a faint.

I awake with a burning face and throbbing ankle, and it feels like sword-fighters are fencing in my head. I'm lying on the back seat of the bus, which is moving again. The window I broke is above me, taped up with cardboard. Becky and Gretchen are staring anxiously at me from the seat in front.

'Are you okay?' Becky asks. Her face is paper-white. Like when Dad died.

'My face and head,' I sob, 'they're sore!' I notice long cuts on my arms. Not so deep, but they burn like petrol.

'He'll be fine,' says Mrs Shuter, 'so sit down, you two. We don't want more injuries.' Becky and Gretchen sit reluctantly.

'Is he okay?' Gretchen asks Becky. Just then the bus swerves violently, and a rumbling vibration shakes us like dolls. We roll unevenly to a stop. A tyre's burst. It takes the driver an hour to change it, because he can't find the jack-handle.

We arrive in Arusha, and I expect the worst. Or is it the best? I'm in trouble, all right. What will Mr Houghton do? *Fukuza*, chase, me? I hope so. Expansion is the word they use. He'll expand me from school and I'll just have to go home. That'll be a result. Success, after all.

Sadly, they don't punish me in the way I hope. I don't know why, because I've broken the bus window. They put me in the sick bay and everyone is strangely kind. There's a huge scab covering my whole right cheek, which looks scary in the mirror. I can't believe it. No lessons, no sermons, nothing. Just the sweet nurse-lady, and the visiting doctor. They give me headache tablets. My ankle's sprained, not broken. For four days I lie in a comfortable bed, read comics, and sleep when I like. School's never been so good.

But all things end. On the fifth day I reluctantly go back to my dormitory. What was it all for? My plan has failed completely. It's like I never tried.

There is one good effect. Everyone knows I jumped through the bus window while it was moving. That takes courage, and I'm not someone to mess with. The exception is Marais.

Arusha. Saturday afternoon. Swapping comics with Andrew Miller. He gives me a Classic. *Mutiny on the Bounty*. Bought at Lake Printers in Mwanza. Their stamp is on the back. Tanganyika advertising. I've never heard the word 'mutiny' before, but the *mu* bit in 'mutton', 'mud' and 'muck' is pronounced *muh*. How or why a crew seizing a ship from the captain can be like mutton, I don't know, but there it is. Surprising, though, 'cos what I know of sheep is they're timid, not rebellious.

These white people are very strange. I know I'm one, but that's different. The Bounty author must mean mutton is connected. Maybe too much mutton makes sailors revolt against their captains. Turns them rebellious. Life at seven and a half is confusing, especially with my English.

I give Andrew *Around the Word in 80 days*. 'Here's *Mutiny on the Bounty*,' he says. He pronounces it 'mewtiny'.

'It's *muttony*,' I correct him, 'as in mutton.'

'No it isn't,' he says. A bad-tempered argument ensues. It's settled by Miss Baxter.

'*Muttony*, indeed!' she laughs, shaking with mirth. I hate them both. Why do they always have to be right?


Marais has other enemies. Andrew Miller, for one.

'We must get him,' Andrew says. Marais has put mud on his tackies once too often.

'How?' I say. He's bigger than us.

'I've got friends,' Andrew says. He stares at me. 'Are you in?'

'Yes,' I say, unsure what it means.

Next day is Sunday. Everyone goes to play down by the river. We wade in the shallow, cold mountain water, throw pebbles, skip them off the surface, and dig tunnels in the soft riverbank. People say a boy was suffocated once when a tunnel collapsed. It doesn't stop us.

After breakfast Andrew sidles up. Behind him come two others. English twins. Jed and Jack. I can't tell them apart. They sleep on the other side of the dormitory, and keep to themselves. I wonder how Andrew has befriended them.

'We're gonna do it now,' Andrew whispers.

'Do what?' I say.

'Marais.'

'What we gonna do to him?'

'Tie him up, shove him under his bed.'

'What?'

'Teach him to mess with us.'

'How?'

'Come and see.'

We're walking towards the dorm. Jed or Jack saw Marais go in. The other one's pulling a long piece of string out of his pocket. I ponder as we go. I don't like Andrew, but I like Marais less. Using one enemy against another could be a good idea. Like Mao-tse-Tung said, 'my enemy's enemy is my friend'.

'What you buggers want?' Marais says as we stride up to his bed. He's sitting and looking into his locker.

'You,' says Andrew.

'Me. . ?' Marais sees the other three of us. His voice is different now. Quavery. This is it. . . this is something I've longed for. We jump on him. We push him down on his bed. He doesn't resist. The twin with the string winds it round his wrists, forcing them together. Andrew pulls Marais' dressing-gown cord out and gives it to me.

'Tie his ankles,' he says. Obediently, I wrap the cord round and round. Marais is trying to speak. He's wheezy. Who cares? Jed or Jack's got one of his socks. He shoves it into his mouth. His twin has a roll of sellotape. Must have pinched it from art class. These boys are organised. He pulls tape from the roll, puts long pieces across Marais' mouth to keep the sock in. A gag, he says. Andrew's tying Marais' belt round his knees, pulling it tight. Marais doesn't resist.

'Right,' says Andrew, 'under the bed.' We lift him between us, and push him under his bed. 'Counterpanes,' Andrew says. Jed or Jack pulls one side of the counterpane down so Marais can't be seen by anyone coming in. The other fetches his own counterpane. Shouldn't be noticed where his bed is, in the far corner. He puts it on the bed, pulls it down the other side.

'Let's go,' Andrew says. He should be an army officer, a kernel maybe. Or is that maize? Maybe an *oberst*.

The sun's shining down at the river. We join the other boys. They're doing what they always do. Chucking pebbles, wading, digging, and arguing about nothing. We've got a secret. We've got a prisoner. While we're strutting about here, we're punishing someone we hate. It feels great. Only, what if his asthma gets bad? He sounded wheezy when we were tying him up, and then there are the socks in his mouth. I don't like Marais, but I start to get really worried.

'Maybe we should go and check on him,' I say to Andrew.

'What for?'

'He might choke or something.'

'Good if he does,' Andrew says. Jed and Jack grin widely. They don't talk much. Someone said they're *auto*-something.

'But we can't just leave him. What if he dies?' Andrew frowns. The twins look anxious, though not as much as Andrew.

'Okay,' Andrew says at last, 'go check on him, we'll wait here.'

Marais has been trussed up under his bed for half an hour. He's completely immobilised, and the gag has made it difficult to breathe. His asthma, fortunately, has not got worse. He had an attack just before we jumped him, and took his spray.

I pull up the counterpane and bend down to him. He's breathing. My heart's beating like a drum. I've had terrifying thoughts. What if he's dead? His pupils are wide in the darkness. He blinks in the light. I breathe more easily.

'Hello,' I say, trying to hide my panic. I must free him, but make sure he knows there's a new order now. 'If I untie you, will you stop bullying me and the others?' His head nods, his eyes still blinking. 'If you don't,' I continue, 'we'll tie you up again and, and. . .' I search for something we'll do. I should have asked Andrew. 'We'll throw you in the river,' I whisper threateningly. He nods his head.

I get down on my knees, and drag him out from under his bed. It's difficult getting the sellotape off his mouth, and it leaves a nasty red mark. He spits out the sock. He doesn't speak. He's too frightened, and his mouth's too dry. It takes forever to undo all the knots. Finally he's undone. I leave. Andrew is angry I let our prisoner go. I was only supposed to check on him, not 'spring him'.

There's no more Marais-trouble. After a while I even feel sorry for him. It's worse when he starts following me around and giving me sweets. I've never befriended enemies before.

'You helped me,' he says one day, staring at the ground.

'Well...' I say, embarrassed. I did, but then I also helped tie him up.

'I won't forget,' he says. I'm his friend now, because I set him free. I don't know what's worse from him, persecution or adoration. I tell Becky what we did, and she tells Gretchen.

Gretchen says she doesn't want to get on the wrong side of me. I take that as a compliment, or is it complement?

At the end of term we're flown back to Mwanza instead of going by bus and train. I think it's because they've decided it's safer with me. I won't jump out a plane window. The plane is an East African Airways DC3, otherwise known as a *Dakota*. It's a twin-engined aircraft of World War II vintage, and is fitted out to take thirty passengers. It never has that many, and most seats are occupied by mailbags. It comes from Nairobi, lands at Arusha, goes on to Mwanza, then returns to Nairobi. I'm about to discover airsickness.

The door to a Dakota is at the back, where the steps go up. After climbing them, I'm faced with a narrow aisle between the seats. It's very steep. The *Dakota* stands very high at the front, very low at the back. There's a strange and unpleasant smell. I come to know it. Aviation fuel, pressurisation, and previous passengers being sick. I struggle to my seat. Becky, Gretchen and the others are in theirs. The rear door's closed. Pilot and co-pilot squeeze past. Smile at us.

The engines explode into life one at a time. The plane taxis, speeds up, then we're in the sky. There's buffeting, rising and falling, sideways jolts and every kind of movement. I'm terrified. This is worse than the *Argonaut*. But, before my panic can reach crescendo, nausea intervenes. As the plane drops into a sudden trough, it leaves my stomach up there, and I vomit all over the back of the seat in front. I want to die. Two more hours of unmitigated hell, heaving stomach and burning throat. Becky's ashamed. Gretchen is kind and wipes my face with tissues.

'It's horrible to be airsick,' she says. Her German accent is long-gone, unlike brother Dieti. The others in the plane are amused at my illness. None of them feel even a bit sick.

At Mwanza aerodrome Mum's shocked how pale I am. It takes a long time to feel better. I get the first real smile I've had from Fritz. 'Ze plane iss make you sick-yes?' he says. I smile weakly back. He likes to see suffering.

# Seventeen

First day home in Geita, Becky, Gretchen, Dieti and I capture a *shenzi* dog, and give it a bath. We corner a little black and white one against the mine-store wall, and rush him home. He's only a few months old, but already jumping with fleas and festooned with fat black ticks.

Like Sandy, his Dachshund genes are declared by the shortness of his legs and his small size. First we pull the ticks off and pop them underfoot. Black, inky blood squirts out. We dust him with Sandy's flea powder. After allowing a few minutes for that to work, we run a warm bath, and pour in half a bottle of Mum's treasured bubble bath.

The bewildered and quaking captive makes no effort to resist. We scrub him from end to end, inside his filthy ears and under his tail. All the while Sandy stands up at the bath, watching with interest. We use one of Mum's best towels to dry the trembling waif. Finally, Becky and Gretchen use Mum's hairdryer and a brush to finish the job. Sandy watches it all.

We take our gleaming prisoner to the kitchen, and give him a tin of braised steak and a bowl of diluted *Nestlé* milk. He stops quivering and laps with gusto. He doesn't look *shenzi* now.

'Let's keep him,' Becky says.

'Yes,' I say.

'Our *Vati* vill go mad if ve take him in our haus,' Dieti says.

'We can call him Dickie,' Becky announces.

'Why Dickie?' Gretchen asks.

'Nice name,' Becky says. Just then Mum comes home. She sees the little dog, the wet towel, the hairdryer, and makes up her mind.

'He can't stay,' she says, despite our pleading, Dickie goes back to the tough *shenzi* life. But his story isn't over.

It's Christmas Eve 1959, and the astonishing saga of Higgs the policeman marches on. Gretchen and Dieti's parents get a special Christmas parcel from Germany each year. It's filled with goodies, and makes their festive occasion. Today a couple of *totos* who caddy for the *Wazungu* on the golf course climb in through an open *dirisha*, or window, and make off with the

199

special parcel. When its loss is discovered, a distraught Mrs Blüger sends her *haus-boy* running down the footpath to fetch the police. In Geita this means Higgs.

The redoubtable Geita constabulary roars into the Blüger driveway on the battered and rust-streaked Harley Davidson of leopard-taxi-fame, petrol-tank still deeply dented, with the Blüger's *haus-boy* riding pillion, wide-eyed and struck dumb after a wild, erratic and deafening projection up the dirt road. There's no headlight. It came off when Higgs ploughed into the bush.

He dismounts and strides purposefully to the front door. The sway in his gait declares his inebriation, standard by six-thirty of an evening, but he's determined to act professionally. The *haus-boy* found him where he predictably would be, at the club. Ishmael the barman said someone outside had a 'seryus massage' for him. And serious he deemed it was, to be so summoned. He knocks loudly, as officially as he can, on the door. Eugen opens it.

'A robbery, is it?' says Higgs, trying but failing to suppress a beery belch.

'*Ja,*' says Eugen, astonished at the wild-eyed, red faced and moustachioed spectre of the *askari*-chief.

'Tell me,' says Higgs, extracting a tatty notebook from his shirt pocket, 'do you have a pencil?'

'Come in, I haff vun som-vere,' says Eugen. Dieter, Gretchen and Mrs Blüger sit glumly in the lounge.

'Vood you like ein nice cold *Vitecap?*' Eugen asks, passing Higgs a pencil and motioning him to a big German armchair with ashtrays built into the wide wooden arms.

'What a capital idea,' says Higgs, collapsing delightedly into the deep chair.

An hour, plus six bottles of *Whitecap,* later Higgs has forgotten why he came. He has thoroughly enjoyed himself, taken no notes, but has bonded with this affable, if difficult-to-understand, man, who, though German, and therefore the enemy, was once a soldier, like Higgs himself, and therefore a 'good sort', not to leave out his generosity with beer. Higgs returns the pencil to Eugen, unsure why he's got it anyway, gets up, makes for the door, trips over the rug, and falls over another chair.

When he sits up he's clutching his arm. It's broken.

Credit where it's due. Somehow, despite the Plaster of Paris lumpily applied by an annoyed Dr Weiss, who himself has to leave the bar to go to the hospital, Higgs somehow apprehends the guilty *totos* next day, which is Christmas, and the parcel, or most of it, is returned to its grateful owners.

'Zese *totos*,' says Mrs Blüger, 'you chust can't trust zem!'

'But Higgs is goot, even iff he iss alvays trunk,' says Dieti.

'*Ja*, he iss,' says his father, shaking his head, 'but how, I chust don't know...'

Our Cornish heritage is important to us. Though patriotically 'British', in his whole life Dad never said he was 'English'. As I already know, Cornwall is just 'cledged' onto England by a tiny bit of land next to the river Tamar. It has only been ruled by the English for six hundred years, and is a separate 'Duchy', not 'county'.

The Cornish have a long history of fighting against rule from London, examples being the rebellion lead by Michael Joseph, known as *Angoff* the blacksmith, and Thomas Flamanck in 1497, which ended tragically at the Battle of Deptford Bridge, the prayerbook rebellion of 1549, when Cornish speakers revolted against English prayerbooks being foisted upon them, and the Jacobite uprising of 1715. Our history cannot be forgotten.

Mum learned to make Cornish pasties from her mother. She mixes a short pastry, using flour, butter, salt and water. It's kneaded in a big bowl, then rolled out on the scrubbed kitchen table. She cuts the pastry for each pasty round a dinner plate.

Chopped potato goes on first. On this she puts a handful of diced onion. Then a generous handful of finely cubed filet steak. A knob of butter follows, then chopped fresh parsley, a pinch of salt and a sprinkling of fresh ground pepper. The outer rim of pastry is painted with egg white using a brush. Now closing and crimping.

Mum seals the pasties with an even zigzag along the top, neat as a zip. She paints the pasties with milk, pierces the sides with a fork, and puts them on a baking tray. When the tray's full, it's into the hot Belling woodstove. Thirty minutes, and out they come, golden, fragrant and delicious.

Every Lone Cone Club attender has tasted Mum's pasties, and loves them. They're a miracle of creation. A square meal of meat, vegetables and pastry in one handy package. Smell like heaven, taste even better. They make a welcome change, mean not having to cook. A year after Dad dies, Mr Snel, the Manager, tries one. He's so taken, he insists she choose a Sunday, let everyone know, and make enough for all. The club will pay for ingredients. Mum calculates that if each adult eats two, each child one, they'll need more than a hundred.

Umali recruits Amina, and the irascible couple spend hours chopping onions and potatoes. As Mum zips up the pasties and fills the trays, Umali puts them in the oven. The first batch of twenty-five is ready. Umali walks down to the club carrying the cloth-covered tray on his head. He's mobbed by hungry *Wazungu*, most of who have to wait for the next batch. It's the same next time, and next. The experiment is a great success and a failure. Success because they love the pasties. Failure because they love them so much they want more, much more.

Mr Snel calls Mum to the bar for a conference. This can be a nice sideline for her, he says. Becky and Jim need things, and her salary isn't enough. How much does it cost to make a hundred? Thirty shillings. Sold at a shilling each, that's a hundred shillings. The people will be happy to pay that. Now, a hundred pasties went nowhere, did it? Better make two hundred, no two hundred and fifty. Shall we say once a month, every last Sunday?

So begins the Geita pasty factory. Soon, extra labour being required, it won't raise eyebrows to see, in addition to Umali, diverse and hitherto jungle-bound, ragged tribesmen sprinting downhill towards the waiting *Wazungu* at Lone Cone Club, trays full of Cornish pasties held aloft, or balanced on their heads.

In 1960 we have an unexpected visitor. Communication here is as rudimentary as it was in Von Lettow Vorbeck's days. There's only one unreliable radiophone at head office. At least Vorbeck had runners for when the telegraph failed.

I don't know who it is when the stranger knocks on the door. I open it and stand staring for several seconds at a tall man in a white uniform, a funny round hat on his head with writing on: *HMS GAMBIA.* Whatever that means. He obviously knows who

I am, because he says 'Hello Jim.' I don't like the familiarity.

'Mum,' I yell, 'there's a strange man here.'

'I'm your brother,' says the stranger.

'No you're not!' I say. Mum comes to the door. There's a brief pause, then she throws herself into his arms.

'Fraser,' she gasps, 'oh Fraser!' She's crying.

'Mum,' he says, kissing her cheek, and hugging her. This is crazy. Who is this interloper? I can't bear to hear him call her 'Mum'. She's *my* Mum, not his. I try to slink away in indignation.

'Jimboy,' Mum says, 'say hello to Fraser.'

'Fraser?' I ask, turning back. The name Mum uses so many times. I have a big brother in the navy. Another one, not Bertrand. Fraser. He went away when I was two. I'm eight now. Can it really be him?

'Your brother,' Mum says. She takes Fraser by the arm and leads him into the house. He has a long canvas bag-thing hanging from one hand. A navy kit bag.

'Say hello properly to your brother,' Mum insists. I stick out my hand. I'm not going to hug him. Okay, he must be my brother if she says so. But this is all too quick. Anyway, he'll be just like Bertrand, the other brother who pitched out of nowhere, partied at the club, and buggered off again. Haven't heard from him since. What is it now? Two years, maybe longer.

# Eighteen

Fraser is intrigued by his little brother-in-the-bush. I'm wary of him. I ask what *HMS GAMBIA* means. Her Majesty's Ship, Gambia, he says. A royal navy light cruiser. Named after a West African Country. All navy ships belong to the Queen. The Gambia's currently in Gibraltar. Somewhere near Spain. Spain's a country, isn't it?

Fraser arranges transport to see Dad's grave at Samina. The midges drive us off in short time. He visits the club only briefly, has a mandatory beer with Mr Snel and Dr Weiss, and comes home early. He's quieter, this big brother, than the other one. He seems more thoughtful, much sadder about Dad. Mum says he 'worshipped' him. One morning I watch him sit alone on the bench in the front garden. He notices me.

'Come here Jimboy,' he says. I go. 'You're sad about Dad, aren't you?' I am, of course I am. Doesn't everyone know that?

'I am too,' he says gently. 'Sit down, I'll tell you about Dad.' Tell me about Dad? What is there to know? He was handsome, brave, and strong. I loved him. God killed him. I tried to shoot God. I sit. It's a crude bench of unsanded maninga on two dead tree-stumps. The table is an old cable-drum, painted green.

'Mum told me what you did with Dad's gun,' Fraser says quietly, 'you must have been very cross.'

'I was and I still am,' I say, bursting into tears, 'he took my Dad, and I still want to shoot him. . !'

'I'm your brother, Jimboy. I loved him too. He was also my Dad.' I look at him again, through a film of tears. He really does look sad. Maybe he's genuine. He hasn't gone to the club all the time. He doesn't laugh and joke like Bertrand. I step closer. He puts his arms around me and gives me the first masculine hug I've had since Dad died. I feel his chest heave. My big brother's crying! We stay like that a long time. Then he talks.

'I'll tell you about Dad, so you know where you come from, Jimboy,' he says. I rather like that name. Nearly as good as Jimu. 'Living in the bush, there's lots you don't know. You come from a good family and you should be proud. Especially about Dad.' I nod. I later discover Fraser is the family historian. He knows everything.

'Dad was a Cornishman, born in a house in Fairmantle Street, Truro. His family was wealthy in those days. His father, Edgar, was a Warrant Officer in the Royal Navy, and retired to become harbour master in Truro's old river port on Lemon quay. Sailing ships came from round the world. Dad had an older sister, Natalie. Our surname, by the way, existed in Cornwall long before William the Conquerer won the battle of Hastings in 1066, and our family history in Helston goes back nine hundred years.'

'Really?' I ask.

'True,' says Fraser, 'really. It's quite a history.' He continues, and this is what he says:

Edgar's father, our great grandfather, is Joshua. He is born in Helston in 1850. Just over five foot tall, with an enormous moustache, he's one of richest men in Cornwall. He buys and sells antiques. They say he's "been up and down the Mississippi on paddle steamers, trading antiques, when most cousin-jacks haven't crossed the Tamar to England." He's famous in Cornwall for his ostentatious wealth, knockout punch, love of animals, devotion to wife and children, and paradoxical, almost casual, infidelity, which continues into his eighties.

There's an enduring friendship between Joshua and the mayor of Truro. They are of a type, and, though "pillars of Cornish Victorian society", like nothing better than to depart from time to time on a stagecoach to London, without telling their wives. Anonymous in the capital, they indulge in wild drinking, gambling and brawling, and many is the public house which suffers serious disruption and damage from their visitations. After a month, or sometimes two, they sheepishly return to their wives, who forgive them and nurse them back to health. Until next time. They last abscond in their seventies.

One day Joshua sees a big man whipping a tethered horse. He tells him to stop, and the fellow attacks him with a club. Joshua punches him once. Sadly, the man hits his head on a lamp post and dies. Fortunately, the presiding judge at the inquest is the mayor.

'He deserved to die,' I say, 'anyone who whips a poor horse, or any animal, should be killed.'

'Quite,' Fraser laughs. He's really quite nice.

Joshua's long suffering wife, Helen, is dedicated. She thinks he's "involved with the widow Smith", and threatens to "go round and smash in her windows", to which he replies "Old Josh will just have to put them in again!" '

'What do you mean by "involved" with the widow Smith?' I ask.

'Well,' Fraser says, blushing. I've never men blush. 'Let's say he likes her. . .'

'Were they doing *jigi-jigi?*' I ask.

'Jimboy,' Fraser says, 'You're terrible. Where do you hear these things?'

'Everywhere, everyone,' I say.

Despite everything, Joshua is popular, wealthy, and the hero of many a widow or single woman, several of whom live rent-free in his houses in Truro, St Ives and St Austell. Helen and Joshua only have one child, our grandfather Edgar.

Edgar grows as big as his fierce father is small, and has a temperate, retreating nature. At thirteen, in the year 1890, he goes to sea as cabin boy on a French barque. This annoys Joshua, because he wants him to continue the antique business.

Edgar returns after three years at sea, sixteen years old, six foot tall, broad, suntanned, and worldly-wise. After two months he joins the *Andrew*, or Royal Navy, as boy seaman, Joshua using influence with a captain.

From 1893 to 1918 Edgar serves on several ships in the fleet. He's a pioneering underwater diver, using an experimental helmet fed with compressed air from the surface in Falmouth Harbour. His old helmet is a family heirloom. He serves on a battle cruiser in the battle of Jutland, when Admiral Jellicoe's *Grand Fleet* chases Admiral Scheer's *High Seas Fleet* all the way to its German home ports, never to emerge as a serious threat for the rest of the War.

'Wow,' I say. 'Were they really big boats?' Grand Fleet sounds, well, grand.

'Huge, Jimboy, *ships*, not boats.'

In 1918, a week after Armistice Day, Joshua suddenly 'gives up the ghost and dies'. Sounds voluntary. Edgar attends the funeral, to see his distraught mother crying out 'not he, he not be dead, no, *not* my Josh,' before trying to jump into his grave.

Even in death, the ninety-year-old rogue commands love. Three hundred pack the church, many weeping inconsolably. It's rumoured there are several broken-hearted widows among them.

Edgar is forty in 1919, when he retires from the navy and returns to Cornwall. At first he lives at home with his mother in number nine Rosewin Row, off Mitchell Hill, which enjoys a splendid view of the newly built Truro Cathedral. The house has five bedrooms, an indoor bathroom and toilet, and a panelled study where Joshua kept business journals and files. Within a year Edgar meets, courts and marries Loveday Rowe, a thirty year old spinster with crossed eyes, beaked nose and a sweet nature. She's granny, the *Mzungu masikini* I met on that holiday in Cornwall. Edgar and Loveday move into their own home, a two bedroomed terraced cottage at thirty-seven Fairmantle Street. Here, our aunt Natalie, and two years later our father, Richard, are born.

'D'you know what's happened to that house?' Fraser says. 'Number nine Rosewin Row is still a lovely old terraced house, and you can still see the cathedral. Thirty-seven, eight and nine Fairmantle Street are joined, and turned into an undertaker's premises. On the other side there's a frozen food shop. They say one side there's chickens, the other side people, both frozen.'

*Mzogas.* Can I never get away from the dead? Before Dad died, I never even thought about them. Then Tembo's puppy, Mr Valari (senior), and all the dead people in my nightmares, like Stroessner, who murdered Mrs Williams, Mum, dead and trying to dig her way to Dad. Fraser continues.

Richard is sickly, suffers with asthma from an early age, and fails to thrive. Asthma means a bad cough. Edgar despairs of his son making adulthood. Loveday dotes on him.

Adding to his Royal Navy Pension, Edgar is also paid as harbour master. Great ships come up via the Carrick Roads near Falmouth, bringing cargoes up the Fal and Penryn to Lemon Quay in the centre of Truro. Now the harbour's gone, the river silted up, and where ships used to dock stands a Tesco supermarket. The coming of the railway killed river freight. Truro harbour dies of neglect, the river chokes on silt.

When Dad (Richard) is three, his grandmother Helen follows her beloved Joshua to the grave. She's buried beside him at

Kenwyn Cemetery. Edgar and Loveday move to Nine Rosewin Row. It's not clear if they sell thirty-seven Fairmantle Street now, or if that's the later work of aunt Natalie. Richard's earliest memories are from Rosewin Row.

Richard's frail build, his asthma and proneness to pneumonia, worries his parents. 'He'll never make old bones,' Edgar warns Loveday, but she never gives up, staying up all night nursing him through many illnesses, some he isn't expected to survive. Richard's health remains precarious throughout his childhood and adolescence. He uses that cunningly, allowing his mother and Natalie to cater to every whim. Once when he and Natalie walked past the cathedral *en-route* to school, he threatens to bang his head on the cathedral wall unless she carries his satchel. She does, for several years. He grows up protected by women, and distant from Edgar, who laments he'll never endure the rigours of a sailor's life. Steeped in maritime history, preferring to walk a deck rather than a road, Edgar suffers in silence.

Despite his weakly appearance, Richard determines by six years of age that he *will* go to sea. When he says so, Edgar laughs. He can't see Richard as a sailor. He tries to be gentle, exaggerate the hazards of the sea, the rewards of work ashore.

By twelve Richard has caught up with other boys his age. He knows Edgar won't use his influence to get him a seagoing berth. It hurts, because Joshua helped Edgar.

It's half way through his thirteenth year he decides to take action. For months he's watched freighters come upriver from Falmouth to dock at Lemon Quay. One day there's a three masted Norwegian schooner, loading cargo for New York. Her name is *Bergen*.

Richard persuades the master to employ him as cabin boy. Without telling his parents or Natalie, he steals away one evening at dusk, taking only a few clothes tied in a blanket. Within the hour, taking advantage of a high tide and favourable wind, *Bergen* slips away from Lemon Quay and heads downriver to Malpas, the Fal, the Carrick Roads, then west into the English Channel. By nightfall she's rounded Lizard Point, and is reaching with a northeasterly wind into the wide Atlantic.

'Dad ran away. . ?' I say. Fraser sees what I'm thinking. Looking for a precedent to justify jumping out the bus at

Dodoma. Mum's told him.

'It was different,' Fraser says. 'He went away to make a living, not to escape school.'

'But he wasn't sent to boarding school,' I say.

'Enough,' says Fraser, grinning in spite of himself. He continues with Dad's story.

Richard soon regrets his action, but he's committed now. Seasick and missing home, he tries to learn the duties of cabin boy. He doesn't know he has already come under the malign surveillance of the first mate, a bearded giant called Jensen.

Jensen has his reasons for his Anglophobia, but these are never clear. He hates the English so much, it's like an illness. Someone must have done something bad to him or his family, to so drive him to vengeance and retribution at any opportunity. He's a man in his thirties when Richard comes aboard. Seeing the twelve year old 'English' boy answer a Nordic prayer. His day has come. He doesn't know the Cornish aren't English. He bides his time. Vengeance is a dish best eaten cold.

'We're Cornish, not English,' I say. Dad always said that.

'Too right,' Fraser says. At last he agrees with something I say. I warm to him.

A week into the North Atlantic, Jensen shows his hand. Richard is carrying a tray of crockery to the master's cabin, when he passes the big man. 'I'm going to get you, English swine!' he hisses. Richard is startled by the naked hatred in those pale eyes. His dream cruise has just turned sour.

The captain is a gentleman, fatherly and kind. He gives Richard small luxuries from his table. Perhaps it's because the captain likes Richard that Jensen waits. But he never misses an opportunity to scowl and whisper threats when alone with him. He makes suggestions about Richard's mother, claiming to have known her intimately. This is an error, for certain things are sacrosanct. One is Richard's mother. Jensen will pay, regardless of cost or time.

The violence begins with a slap across the head in a corridor. Then a punch in the face, causing a black eye. There are shoves in the back, bringing falls and broken crockery. A bruising poke in the ribs. The captain notices the marks and asks questions. For Richard this vendetta in't for sharing. He will resolve it on his own. Jensen is *his*. He won't share him. He lies. He fell against a door handle. He slipped on the wet deck and struck his ear on a lifeboat. When Jensen sees the boy isn't telling, he takes if for fear, and redoubles his efforts.

One evening, in a wild and pitching sea, he shoves Richard in the back, causing him to fall down the stairs and break his leg. It's a fractured tibia, and the ship's carpenter makes a wooden splint. It's fortunate, because Richard is unable to work the rest of the passage, which keeps him away from Jensen. The captain commiserates, but Richard never tells how it happened.

'He should have shot him,' I say.

'You like guns, don't you Jimboy?' Fraser says, grinning again. 'I know all about you.' He continues the story.

*Bergen* docks in New York, and the captain sends Richard to convalesce with friends near Manhattan docks. They are a retired sea captain and his wife, whose children have moved away. Richard has a comfortable time. In three months his leg is better, and he begins looking for a new ship. Despite his experience, he already loves the sea and ships. Maybe it's inherited from Edgar, the father who despaired his son would ever make a sailor.

He serves on five ships in four years, and learns the trade of seaman. He grows in strength and stature. In 1923, three years after he last saw her, while standing in the prow of a schooner edging into Hong Kong harbour, he spies a familiar shape. *Bergen*.

Within an hour of docking, Richard boards the Norwegian ship and asks for Jensen. He comes on deck. He's been told someone called Penhaligon wants him. Jensen is surprised at the change in the cabin boy. Richard challenges him to a fight. The crew form a circle. It's one sided. Jensen wins. Richard is carried back to his ship.

Six months later he spies *Bergen* in Auckland, New Zealand. Literally – he's looking through a spyglass at the time. He goes on board. A man called Penhaligon wants you. Jensen comes up. The crew form a circle again. Some take bets. It's more even. They fight until neither can stand, and both are carried away.

It's a year before Richard sees *Bergen* again. Jensen is slower coming up this time. Richard knocks him out with a single punch. He's been practising on the ship's coiled-rope fenders.

There's one more time, and Jensen refuses to come out on deck. Cowers in his cabin. Richard is prepared. He takes out a white feather from his pocket, and sends it down to the coward. At seventeen Richard has solved the problem. He never sees Jensen, or the *Bergen*, again.

'That'll teach him,' I say 'but I would have shot him!'

'That's not the kind of man Dad was,' Fraser says. 'You see, Jimboy, he was kind and gentle, but never ran from danger, never let fear get to him. He was a determined, brave man. He didn't need a gun with Jensen. He used big guns in the war, but only to do his duty. That's why he died. Because he did his duty, no matter what.'

'But Jensen was *blurryfucken*,' I say.

'Geita has done wonders with your vocabulary,' Fraser laughs, before continuing.

Richard is seventeen when his parents see him again. Although only five foot seven tall, he's filled out and gained muscle. When he ran away he was a frail twelve year old. He returns as man and sailor, and Edgar and Helen are overjoyed. After two weeks at home in Rosewin Row, Richard is ready to go back to sea. In his last two days he spends time with his father.

They go sailing in a Falmouth Bassboat on the Carrick Roads and Falmouth harbour, and drink *St Austell's IPA*, Indian Pale Ale, at the Heron pub in Malpas. Richard regales Edgar with things he's seen and done. He's been to many countries, even served eighteen months on *Cutty Sark*, the most famous of all the tea clippers. Richard recalls those few days with his father as the best they ever have together.

When he returns to sea in 1924, Richard is soon noticed. He has the qualities to be a bosun. These include quiet disposition, seamanship, respect for authority, and a knockout punch. Those days the bosun has to 'deal with' seamen who disobey officers or fought. In 1927 Richard is persuaded to join the Royal Navy. Soon he comes to the attention of an officer with an unusual task - selecting gifted tallship sailors to loan to the United States navy for an expedition.

Admiral Jonathan Evelyn Byrd of the United States Navy purchases an elderly Norwegian square-rigged wooden ship called *Samson* in 1927. She was built in 1882, as a whaler with a hull of oak ribs and spruce planking, toughened to resist the crushing ice of the arctic. She's refitted, renamed *City of New York*, and sails from Hoboken on the twenty-fifth of August 1928, bound for the Antarctic at the other end of the world.

It's the beginning of the famous Admiral Byrd's first Antarctic expedition, which will last until 1930. Byrd has asked for, and got, experienced sailors from the Royal Navy. One is Richard. It's something he's very proud of.

Seven years after leaving the Royal Navy, while working as a rigger on a South African gold mine, he rejoins as able seaman in 1939, at the outbreak of hostilities. 'If my country's at war, I'm at war,' he tells Mum, who he leaves standing with three small children on the dock in Cape Town.'

'Which country?' I ask Fraser.

'England,' he says. Right. That's clear. I thought we were Cornish. I can't fathom big people. They change what they say all the time.

Dad serves on *HMS Hood*, before being transferred weeks ahead of her fateful battle against *Bismarck*. He's posted to a converted trawler, adapted for convoy escort duty to Murmansk in Russia. When *HMS Turtle* is attacked and sunk by *Dornier* bombers sixty miles off Grimsby in August 1940, he's the last man to leave the ship, and single-handedly shoots down three enemy aircraft from the listing deck of half a ship. The other half has broken off and sunk. He saves the lives of the captain and a boy seaman.

He's one of only eight survivors from a crew of sixty-eight, and spends four hours clinging to a wooden hatch cover in near-freezing water. This causes him to get rheumatic fever, and leaking mitral and tricuspid heart valves. He's awarded the Distinguished Service Medal, or *DSM*, by Lord Mountbatten, in the company of King George VI, at a decoration ceremony in Portsmouth.

'Not many of those given out,' Fraser says.

'Decorate?' I ask. Images of Christmas. Fraser knows what I'm thinking. Funny thing to *decorate* a man. A tree, perhaps, not a man.

'They just use the same word, nothing to do with Christmas,' he assures me. He grins. He thinks I'm funny.

Because he worked on a gold mine at Brakpan on the East Rand near Johannesburg before the war, the Brakpan Times puts Dad on the front page. 'Brakpan Man Decorated by King' it says, above a half-page photograph of Dad.

'Dad was famous?' I say.

'He was, I suppose.' Fraser lights a *Navy Cut* cigarette. Made by *John Players*. I've got sharp eyes. How can I get one from him?

Serving in the Far East Dad sustains a serious head injury. While he's being treated in hospital in Rangoon, he hears from another patient that his cousin and best friend, Major James Penhaligon, who he knew and loved from small, has been killed by the Japanese. It happened in April 1945, not long before the end of the war. Dad is heartbroken. He's also very sick.

Dad re-joins the navy in 1939 as an '*A1*' fit man. He is discharged in '46 with leaking heart valves and epilepsy, and a naval health grading of '*E*'. He's thirty-seven years old. After a year in hospital for epilepsy, he reluctantly takes a shared job with Mum, running a store in Zululand. That's why I'm born in Nongoma.

'Dad had no choice but to come to Geita. He couldn't get a job anywhere else,' Fraser says.

'Why?' I ask.

'Because he was sick. Here, in Geita, they didn't examine him before they gave him the job on the ropeway. Anywhere else, he'd have been examined, would have failed the medical.' A lot falls into place. I've wondered why we live here, in the bush. I love it dearly, of course. Wouldn't want to be anywhere else. . . not that I know anywhere else. Apart from Arusha or Cornwall, and I wouldn't want to live in either.

'Dad was too weak, too damaged by the war, to get better when he got malaria,' Fraser explains. 'So now you know, Jimboy,' he says, 'you can be proud of your name. Of Dad. There weren't many like him. When you grow up, try to be like him.'

'I will,' I say, my chest swelling with pride, 'I will. But I would have shot Jensen!' Fraser laughs. He's been talking for two hours. I've listened. Not been bored. His words are precious.

Bring me closer to Dad. Poor Dad. He paid with his life, just so he could be our breadwinner. Like Mum said.

I feel a welling of love for my thoughtful big brother. He knows so much, takes so much trouble. He also looks, and acts, so much like Dad. I haven't noticed before. It's as if five years haven't happened. Like Dad is talking. Fraser's leaving in a week. A new sadness descends. Can't anything be other than sad?'One thing more you should know,' Fraser says.

'What?'

'Aunty Natalie, Dad's sister.'

'What about her?'

'She's the reason Dad was poor, why we're all poor.'

'Why?'

'Aunt Natalie fiddled the old folks out of all their money. She was a bad businesswoman. She kept opening shops, then losing all her money, and every time Granddad Edgar bailed her out. In 1947 he died. By then Grandma had lost it up here. . .' He taps his temple. Ah, Dodoma, the lunatic asylum on the Dar railway.

'Then Natalie really went to town.' I thought she lived in town. Never mind. 'She persuaded the old girl to sell Nine Rosewin Row and give her the money. Plus three other houses and a row of shops in Lemon Street. That's in Truro.'

'Why did she?'

'Because she could. An evil woman. She blew all that too. That's why Dad and Mum didn't inherit anything. I told you Joshua made the money. Edgar spent some of it. Natalie blew the rest. That's why Dad took the job here in Geita, why he's dead now.'

'It's not fair,' I say.

'No,' Fraser says. 'They say it's clogs to clogs in three generations. That's what happened.' I feel a surge of resentment against Aunt Natalie. *She* killed Dad. Not just God. Mum says I met Natalie when we went to Cornwall that time on the *Argonaut*. It's so long ago now, I can't remember, try as I do.

Mum says Fraser shouldn't say such things about Aunt Natalie. Dad wouldn't like it. He was never nasty, not even about her.

Fraser walks in the garden. Under the acacia tree, he finds Lutoli and I smoking cigarette butts collected at the club. We're nine, and seasoned smokers. I try to hide my fag end in a cupped hand. My smoking is widely known about and condemned. Mum's given up the fight. I'm a man, I say, and men smoke. Lutoli has no reservations or fear. As Fraser stares, he takes another drag, inhales deeply, lets smoke curl from his nose. I can do it too.

'Don't hide that,' Fraser says, 'I saw you from the verandah.' There's a shocked look on his face. 'How long you been smoking Jimboy?'

'Since Dad died,' I say, 'or I think so.' I drop my burning butt and stamp it into the ground.

'Mum know?'

'Yup.' This is an inquisition. Lutoli's butt has burnt to the end. He extinguishes the end and ambles away. He doesn't follow *Kiingereza* or English, but knows when things are getting unpleasant.

'Right,' Fraser exclaims, 'I've got an idea.' An idea? What idea?

'What are those cheap cigarettes the poor *watu* smoke, you know, the beggar-ones. . ?' he asks. I'm surprised he remembers those little cigarettes. I've forgotten he lived in Geita two years before he joined the Navy.

'The *wasikini?*' I ask.

'That's them. The beggars. What are the cigarettes called?'

'Ten Cents,' I say. He says he remembers them. The awful Ten Centies. Known to the watu as *Centie Kumis*. Tiny packets of ten thin, filterless cigarettes, filled with dark, vicious tobacco. People say it isn't tobacco at all, but lion *mavi*, or shit.

The name's in the price. Ten cents. The original price. When dinosaurs roamed the earth. In 1961 it's eight times that. *Infatuation*, Dieti said, causes prices to go up. Happens all the time. There's a hundred cents in a shilling. Twenty shillings in a pound. At eighty cents, you can still get twenty-two packets of *Centi Kumis* for a pound.

'They're the ones,' he says. He fumbles in his pocket for change. He extracts two ten-cent coins. They can't be called *small* change. They're huge, with a big hole in the middle. It's so the rural *watu* can keep them threaded on a string. Wear their money like jewellery. Not the *wasikini*, they hide their money.

It'd spoil the image. 'Go to the store and buy me a packet,' Fraser says.

'One or two?' I ask.

'Just one, I'm sure it will do,' Fraser says ominously.

Barrat stores, to which so many owe their souls, sells everything. Food in tins, fresh vegetables from Mwanza, sweets from England, alcohol, cloth, shirts, trousers, ammunition. And tobacco. There are no restrictions on who can buy what. Mr Barrat nonchalantly gives me the *Centi Kumis*, and soon I'm back with Fraser, who's been joined by Becky under the tree. He's asked her if she smokes too. Yes, she says, unwilling to be a wimp. At twelve, she can't be seen as inferior to her ten-year-old brother.

'Okay,' Fraser says, grinning wickedly, and tearing open the cheap paper packaging. 'Who's first?' What does he mean, first? He sees our bewilderment. 'You're going to smoke this whole packet,' he says 'five each.'

'Okay,' I say, unphased. Why not? I like smoking. I've never smoked a whole *Centi Kumi*, though. Too strong. Burns the throat and makes you cough. Are they really simba *mavi?* Umali swears on it. Anyway, can't let Fraser think I'm scared. Especially not now, Dad's heroism so recently recounted. He lights one and passes it to me. I take it as casually as I can, and puff deeply.

Mistake! The taste and smell is horrible. *Must* be *simba mavi!* The burning in the back of my throat is intense, like petrol. I once swigged some from a ginger-ale bottle at the garage, unaware Spiro the mechanic kept petrol in it to pour into carburettors. Priming, he said, whatever that is. I thought I was going to die. Spiro never stopped apologising. 'You must be careful,' he said, ''cause if you drink petrol you'll be forked.' This is similar, but worse. Fraser's waiting.

'Come on,' he says, 'smoke it.'

'Yes,' Becky says, joining the winning side. Always does that. Crafty. Not crafty enough for Fraser.

'Here's yours,' he says, passing a lit one to her. She's lied about smoking. Apart from a tentative puff or two when she choked and went red, neither she nor Gretchen are smokers. She takes her *Centi Kumi* gingerly, pretends to draw on it.

'Deeper,' Fraser Commands. She tries, splutters, jumps to her feet and runs, coughing, indoors. 'One down,' Fraser says, 'one to go.' His turns his attention back on me. I take another hateful puff.

'Inhale, Jimboy, inhale. . .' he commands. I inhale. The acrid smoke sears the lining of my lungs. I cough and cough.

'Again,' he says. The thin cigarette's almost burnt out now. No problem, he's already lighting another. By the time I've smoked five *Centi Kumis* I'm as green as a *leguaan*. I'm trying to puff the last of the fifth, when my stomach contracts and I spurt my lunch out on the ground. Only then does Fraser relent.

'Now you know what smoking can do,' he says, 'I'll leave it to you.' He goes inside, his good deed done. I'm as sick as an *umbwa*, or dog, the rest of the day. All I learn is never to smoke *simba mavi*. It's *blurryfucken*, like Lutoli says. Now I know what he means.

To this day I can't help wondering what they do with animal droppings in zoos. Do cigarette-manufacturers have a secret deal?

# Nineteen

It creeps up on me that there's competition for Fraser's attention and affection, not just from Sandy, who follows him everywhere. I should have noticed earlier that, ever since he arrived, there's been an unusual, doting presence.

I'm nine, and Gretchen Blüger has just turned twelve. She's changed. I haven't thought about it before, but suddenly my jealous eyes see things they never saw before. Gretchen's a tomboy no longer. Gone are the wild hair and scabbed knees of yesterday. Gone the multi coloured, much-patched dungarees and T-shirts.

Suddenly, clean-scrubbed, wearing fashionable dresses in light colours and whites, and smart shoes instead of battered sandals, and smelling of strange, alluring perfume, is a swan in place of a chicken.

It's been a long time since she played naked-water-tree-running with us. Won't now, far too sophisticated. What a pity. I've never thought her pretty before, but now she's beautiful. Her natural blonde hair framing her aquiline face and perfect nose, her piercing blue eyes.

Why haven't I seen it before? Something else. She's changed shape. Her legs are no longer sticks. Her waist is narrow. She has curves. She isn't flat chested. Becky says she wears a bra. Amina finds this particular *Mzungu* women's device hysterical, and describes them as *mifuko ya matiti*, or tit-bags. The though of Gretchen wearing a bra is simultaneously alluring and repulsive. Lacy cup-shaped things with straps. Gretchen in tit-bags!

What impresses and worries me even more are not the physical changes, but something else. Attitude. Behaviour. It's changed completely. I'm used to her running amok with us, climbing trees, throwing stones, abusing the *machula*. Here's something completely new. Here's a smart, curvaceous, beautiful young creature, who overnight is an adult, has time no more for childish things. She isn't spending her days at our house to be with Becky and me. No. It's *Fraser*. I feel two separate, equally powerful, quite debilitating, streams of resentment and jealousy. It makes my chest so full it's going to burst.

I've only just decided to love Fraser. He's my long-lost big brother, and, like me, he's sad about Dad. That's a thought. He's a gunner in the navy. Won first prize in the shooting competition at *HMS St Vincent* in 1954. Wherever that is. Like Dad, he's a crack shot. Where was he when I tried to shoot God? We could've made a proper job of it. Anyway, now I've found him I don't want him to go, ever. He should stay here, with me, in Geita. I want to be like him, walk like him, talk like him. I'm King Louis in *The Jungle Book*, and he's Mowgli. Mum says I want to climb right into him.

Now here's this girl. I know her, but I don't. She's different. First, she's spotlessly, almost unhealthily, clean. That's not our way in Geita. We're grubby, no matter how often we bathe. We play with so many things. *Kukus*, dogs, wild animals. We dig holes, climb trees, and run through elephant grass. Nobody's like this. She's shiny-clean, and has no scratches or scabs on her face. Her hair hasn't got brambles and grass in it. There's something else. Poise. I don't know the word, but I know the impression.

Gretchen's *maridadi*. Beautiful. She's smart, fragrant, un-rough, un-tough, and no longer flat chested. She's quiet, discreet, polite, and obviously infatuated. She sits on the verandah, pretending to talk with Becky, but I see where her big, adoring, blue eyes are looking. Fraser's is drinking a bottle of beer, oblivious. Gretchen's in love. With my big brother. How dare she come here, just when I've found him, and then fall in love with him? How dare she stare at him that way?

The other surge is worse. I haven't thought about Gretchen, or any girl, with deep affection. Not *that* deep. Girls are girls. Weaker, less able, less reliable version of boys. They're a pain, and handicap. Not fun, I've thought, trying to outrun a rampant lion if a girl's with you. Girls are dyspraxic. Don't know where I read the word. They can't throw a stone for toffee. Useless aim. Waste of time. But this is different. She isn't trying to outrun a lion or throw a stone. Nor climb a tree. Naked-water-tree-running is out of the question. This is new. Completely new. This, I later come to know, is my first experience of bewitchment of woman by man. Not a fully-grown woman, but a beguiling one nevertheless.

This is reverse jealousy. It's no longer only anger at her attraction to Fraser, who belongs to me. I'm painfully jealous that it's *him*, not me, on whom she's focusing. How dare he come here and steal my darling? That's new. I've never thought of anyone as 'darling'. From now I think of Gretchen no other way.

The last week of Fraser's visit is fraught with emotion. Mum is tearful several times. She's coped better than she could have expected after Dad died. But now she has Fraser home, and he's so like his father it's almost like having him back from the grave. Becky is strangely quiet. I think it's too much for her. She always withdraws into her shell at emotive times, never shows her true feelings.

I ride a roller coaster. Alone with Fraser, I feel a welling of devotion. When I see Gretchen I feel it too. When she's talking with him, hanging on his every word, laughing with the voice of an angel, doting on him with her eyes, I feel rage. At both of them. It's a conspiracy. I'm the victim. I have to get away. I escape to the garden, sometimes beyond. Once, after running until out of breath, deeply scratched by thornbushes, I throw myself on the ground, lie in the elephant grass, and sob myself to sleep.

When I awake it's dark and safari ants are exploring my face. That's even more startling than the close-by footfalls and sniffing of a foraging hyena. What shocks me is no one notices I'm gone. Gretchen is still worshipping at Fraser's altar when I come back.

We're sad when he leaves. Gretchen's the worst. She comes to see him off at the house. She's asked her parents if she can go shopping in Mwanza, so she can be in the Land Rover with us. They said no, and when she comes her eyes are red from crying. Fraser, who's been amused by the hero-worship until now, is embarrassed to see how heartbroken Gretchen is. My feelings are also intense. Heartbreak and relief, each vying for supremacy.

We fly back to school. It's been decided that's best, although nobody's saying it's because Jimmy jumps through bus windows. I'm airsick before the plane takes off. The smells of pressurization and stale old vomit are enough. Becky makes sure she doesn't sit by me.

I've gone to Arusha since 1958, the year after Dad died. Then it's all-European, the colonial government not permitting the admission of black, coloured or Indian students to any school where white pupils attend. By 1960, when I'm nine, *uhuru* is close on the horizon. The European-only policy is suddenly reversed. This year several black pupils are admitted to my school. Among them is a young man of eleven, called Robert Matwiga.

Matwiga comes from a rural village, and is elated at the prospect of attending a European school. The poor chap suffered polio as an infant, and his left leg is withered and as thin as a broomstick. He more than compensates through a very strong right leg and immensely powerful shoulders and arms. In fact, he turns out to be the best sportsman in the school, often beating not only other pupils, but even teachers, at tennis, cricket and any other sport. He has a strange, almost vaulting walk, his thin leg acting as prop or pole-vault for him to pivot forward onto his good one.

For several weeks after he comes to the school, the boys follow him, imitating his walk. Whenever he goes for a stroll there's a single file of suddenly crippled boys, as many as ten, vaulting behind in gay abandon. The novelty soon dies, fortunately. I don't think the question of cruelty or harassment arises.

Matwiga is a courageous chap, replete with wicked humour and intelligence. In his village there is no water-closet toilet, or anything resembling a flushing western facility. The first time he goes to the toilet, he comes out glowing with enthusiasm, energy and delight, and exclaims in Swahili, face shining and eyes bright, that his deposit in the bowl resulted in a strange and unique sound, which went *'Tum-Bui.'* To an English ear it would sound like 'Toom-Buwee'. It was accompanied, he says, by an upward splash of fingers of water, like a fountain, which was ice-cold on his *mkundu*! 'Plop', the old word, is redundant henceforth. Soon everyone says they're off to do a tumbui.

Like me, Matwiga speaks Swahili better than English. This disadvantages us in school, but forges a special bond. It also allows us to say funny things about others, without danger. We are called the 'black and white gigglers'.

Matwiga inescapably becomes one of our gang, joining me, Schmedjie the Finn, and an English boy, David Allen, in an unholy clique. We will embark on many a nefarious enterprise together. The thought occurs: Matwiga is a *mutu*. Lutoli is a *mutu*. Matwiga is at school with me. Lutoli goes to a mud and wattle 'school' building near the *boma*. He has to walk barefoot, three miles on a jungle footpath each way.

I wonder if Mr Snel, the mine manager, who agreed to pay my fees from mine funds, can be persuaded to pay for Lutoli too. It's only fair. I'll ask him when I get home. Meantime, I'm stuck in Arusha. Colourful Swahili curses come automatically to mind. *Mapumbu* and *matiti* are in them. Testicles and tits.

Mrs Androupolos is, unsurprisingly, Greek. A teacher whose subject, of all things, is English. She's short and fat, and very Grecian. Her husband is never mentioned, but must have existed, because she has a son, Georgios, same age as me, but, like his mother, short and fat. It's obvious why. He's always sucking a sweet, and never without a pocketful.

Neither Georgios, nor his mother, speak good, or even much, English, and they do so with strong Greek accents. I can't work out how Mrs Androupolos convinced the school, and particularly the erudite and posh head, Mr Houghton, to employ her as a teacher of English. For the sake of my memories, however, I am very glad she did. If she had failed, my life would have been anecdotally the poorer. Because of her accent, we decide it isn't English she teaches. It's *Greklish*.

Mrs Androupolos is a stickler for discipline. She spends three quarters of a lesson disciplining us and very little time teaching. I think she doesn't know enough English to teach, and practises diversionary tactics to fill the void.

'Gude morning cluss,' she says, standing in front of her desk.

'Good morning Mrs Androupolos,' we chorus. 'Gude. Nauw, ohpen desks and tak grammahs from eet. Poot on desk and ohpen pudge twenty-foive.' There is rustling and shuffling from the class. Then she sees something.

'Allen, why ees yoor shit bouttons ohpen?'

'*Me,* miss?' Allen says, fingering his shirt to check his buttons. She points at him with her pencil.

'Don' spik mi buck! Kum heere een fraunt.' Allen shuffles to the front. 'Hwy yoo spik?'

'Sorry Miss.'

'Hokay, go buck yoor desk.'

One morning Mrs Androupolos takes the first class of the day, just after breakfast. It's English grammar, and she stands, as usual, hands on hips, facing the class.

'Toddaye we tuk ther grummars,' she announces. 'Nauw feerst ees ther nouns. A noun ees a theeng, sigh ufter me, a noun ees a theeng. . .'

'Ay noun ees a theeng,' we chorus dutifully.

'Ay noun ees a wud for a theeng.'

'Ay noun ees a wud for a theeng,' we echo. There's sniggering from Schmedjie and Allan, but I manage to contain myself.

'Hwat ees ther wud for a theeng?' Mrs Androupolos asks, holding her palms upwards.

'Eet ees a noun!' we chorus, fighting to control our laughter. 'Hwat ees a noun?'

'Ay theeng,' we shout as one. Then it happens. Matwiga, until now unusually quiet, stands up and fumbles with the flies on his shorts. Then he pulls his willy out. Holding it between thumb and finger, he raises his other hand in question. A deadly hush descends. Mouths are open. Mrs Androupolos turns blotchy purple, stops walking, talking and gesticulating in mid pace, sentence and gesture.

'Please mees, ees thees theeng a noun?' Matwiga asks with angelic face and genuine curiosity. The silence hangs. Not a rustle. The cooling window breeze takes a break. The purple of Mrs Androupolos's face blotches white, pink and angry red. She explodes. Spittle flies.

'Poot eet ahwaai, yoo feelthy buoy!' she bellows with a quavering voice. The tension breaks, and we burst out laughing. Matwiga prods his offending organ back into his pants. He sits down, grinning hugely. He's rewritten English.

'Hwy yoo luff?' Mrs Androupolos roars at the tittering class. 'Hwat ees so funay?' We lose our remaining control. 'Thees ees no luffeeng theeng!' she yells. We convulse. Mrs Androupolos stalks from the room. The laughter continues. It's beginning to abate when she stalks back.

'Took yoor puds,' she shrieks, 'end wraite wun hunderd taimes "Ai weel nort shauw my theeng een cluss!" ' Fresh oxygen. We re-lose control. After a few minutes, Schmedjie begins to write the first of his hundred lines, 'Ai weel not shauw my theeng in cluss!' He shows us, and, sniggering, we begin to copy his example. We're still giggling when Mrs Androupolos announces, 'Ai am goh nauw. You geeve yoor lines for me tomorrow. Robert Matwiga, Ai report you for Meester Houghton.' She picks up her books and scuttles away.

School slang is quick to change. 'Willy' is immediately replaced by 'noun'. 'Joe's got a longer noun than Mark.' Schmedjie writes a catchy poem. *Only a clown plays with his noun.*

Apart from teaching Greklish, Mrs Androupolos runs the school tuck shop. This is a small affair, and takes place in a classroom next to the quadrangle on Saturday mornings. There is limited choice, and the merchandise is confined to bottles of *Coca Cola* and *Fanta, Sherbet fountains, Rowntree*'s fruit gums and pastilles, *Dominion* salted crisps, *Kit-Kats, Crunchies*, and bars of *Nestlé*'s and *Cadbury*'s chocolate. Sometimes there are also oranges and bananas, but that's rare.

It's soon apparent why Georgios helps his mother in the tuck shop, and why he is so fat. He gobbles sweets and chocolates all the time. He eats all the profits, or pay, his mother earns from her extra-curricular activity. A change is due, and Schmedjie and Matwiga come up with a plan so brilliant I'm filled with admiration.

'You get caught,' Schmedjie says, 'when you look guilty.' We're sitting on the bank of the river, bored and thinking how we can do something illegal, and get away with it.

'So don' look guilty,' says Matwiga, tossing a pebble into the river. Schmedjie looks thoughtful. Everyone knows he'll come up with an idea when he looks like this.

'Tuck shop,' Schmedjie announces, 'that's what we should do!'

'Do what?' I ask. Matwiga and Schmedjie talk in riddles.

'Rob it,' Schmedjie says, 'we should rob it. . .'

'But don' look guilty,' Matwiga completes.

'Rob the tuck shop. . ?' Allen asks, joining the debate.

'Exactly,' Matwiga confirms.

'But Mrs Androupolos and Georgios are there,' I say.

'That's why this plan is so good, you see?' Matwiga says, turning to me with a grin.

'What plan?' Allen asks.

'This one,' says Schmedjie, getting to his feet. 'Imagine you are Mrs Androupolos and Georgios, and I'm coming into the tuck shop.' He smoothes his blond hair, puts on a stern expression, and paces towards us.

When he's six feet away he pretends to scoop up goods from an imaginary shelf, and puts them in a non-existent bag, all the while keeping his eyes fixed on what he's doing, his mouth set in a bored grimace, as if for all the world he'd rather be somewhere else. Having put the 'goods' in the 'bag', he makes eye contact with us, nods condescendingly, turns on his heel and strides, 'bag' in hand, out the 'tuck shop'. It's stirling stuff, leaves us speechless.

'But you didn't *look* like you were stealing,' Allen says.

'Exactly,' says Matwiga. He likes that word.

'Can it really work?' I ask, fear blunting my enthusiasm.

'Did I look like a thief?' Schmedjie asks, shaking his head in answer to his own question.

'Who dares wins,' says Allen, catching up, 'they say that in the British army, or something.'

'Of course we win!' laughs Matwiga, clapping his hands. 'Of course we win!'

'They say you should have a, what is it. . ?' I say, struggling for the right word, 'a division!'

'What you mean, exactly?' Matwiga asks, looking serious.

'Something to make them look somewhere else,' I say. 'Then Schmedjie can walk in, take some things, and go. . .'

'Who said I'm the one to do it?' Schmedjie says angrily. 'I didn't say I would!'

'Straws,' says Allen, breaking off elephant grass for the purpose, 'whoever gets the shortest is 'it'.' He turns to show his fist clutching four stalks of grass. He proffers them. Reluctantly, we select one in turn. Schmedjie's is the shortest.

'There,' exclaims Allen, 'it's you anyway.'

'Shit in buggeration,' swears Schmedjie, who's learnt the term from me, after I heard it from an older boy. Lovely expression.

'You do it?' Matwiga asks, staring into Schmedjie's eyes.

'I don't know if. . .' Schmedjie stammers, for once losing his silver tongue.

'This Saturday,' Allen exclaims, enthusiastic now someone else is 'it'.

'Wait a minute,' Schmedjie shouts, 'what about the. . . *division?*'

'That's it,' I say.

'Diversification,' says Allen. Clever clogs!

'Yeah, what about that?'

'Easy,' says Matwiga. He stands tall on his good leg, pulls his shoulders back, and limps forward. 'I go in the shop, we all go in, 'cept him, who do it.'

'Why?' asks Allen.

'We keep them busy while Schmedjie does it.'

'What we say?' I ask.

'Hello, Mrs Androupolos, can I have *Mars* bar, packet crisps, and *Coca Cola*, please,' rattles off Matwiga.

'So while she gets them, Schmedjie walks in, takes the stuff and walks out?' Allen says in wonderment.

'Exactly,' says Matwiga.

'I'm not sure. . .' Schmedjie begins.

'Can't refuse now,' I say, 'you got the straw.'

'No, you can't,' echo Allen and Matwiga together.

'Okay, if I do it, who's next time?' Schmedjie asks.

'We draw more straws,' Allen says. There's a long silence. Finally we all nod. Boredom is banished. There's a purpose in life. And exciting danger.

'We better practise,' Allen announces, ''cos the one doing it must not only not look guilty, but look official too.'

'Official?' I ask.

'Yup, like he's just collecting stuff, routine-like. For a teacher, boring.'

'Exactly,' says Matwiga.

'Innocent and official,' says Schmedjie, 'I think I might laugh.'

'If you do, we are caught,' growls Matwiga, 'so you better don't.' The plan is practised over several days. The venue is perfect, because it's our classroom, which, on Saturday mornings, becomes tuck shop. It's never locked.

We take turns being Mrs Androupolos, Georgios, and the thief. Allen loans a small cardboard suitcase for the venture. It looks official and non-guilty. We can pack the spoils in it. What thief, after all, would brazenly display a container for his loot? The fourth one of us, not playing thief, Mrs Androupolos, or Georgios, takes the role of 'divisonary' customer, giving Mrs Androupolos a long list of requests. It's so exciting, we can hardly wait for the real thing.

# Twenty

Our first raid is planned. It has to be on a Saturday, the only day the tuck shop opens. We've practised our techniques of diversification and official-looking 'taking', which we prefer to 'stealing'. We're only 'liberating' what is rightly ours, Allen says, and Matwiga gleefully agrees. It isn't fair, we concur, that fat Georgios has so many sweets, and we so few. Six days before the raid, on the preceding Sunday, we find, to our horror, that our nefarious plan is known in a very high place.

Schmedjie, Allen, Matwiga and I sit down on our seats in the front pew of the little church. We have just been singing *Onward Christian Soldiers*. The grey-bearded padre is looking our way as he stands in the pulpit and opens his big leather Bible. He pauses a long time. Then he clears his throat and begins:

*'And the Lord spake unto Moses, saying, If a soul sin, and commit a trespass against the Lord, and lie unto his neighbour in that which was delivered to him to keep, or in fellowship, or in a thing taken away by violence, or hath deceived his neighbour; Or hath found that which was lost, and lieth concerning it, and sweareth falsely; in any of all these that a man doth, sinning therein: Then it shall be, because he hath sinned, and is guilty, that he shall restore that which he took violently away, or the thing which he hath deceitfully gotten, or that which was delivered him to keep, or the lost thing which he found. Or all that about which he hath sworn falsely; he shall even restore it in the principal, and shall add the fifth part more thereto, and give it unto him to whom it appertaineth, in the day of his trespass offering. And he shall bring his trespass offering unto the Lord. . .'*

He closes the Bible, raises his eyes, and stares directly at us.
'God knows all things,' he bellows unexpectedly, making us jump. 'Even that which you may think he does not!' Schmedjie shifts uncomfortably. 'There is no secret you can keep from his all-knowing eye, no matter how small. . .'

Matwiga's eyes bulge. Deep down, he's very superstitious. His whole village is. He swallows hard. 'All knowing, wise and compassionate, he knows our deepest secrets, our hopes and our dreams.' The padre's eyes bore into mine. He knows I tried to shoot God. He knows I went to Mlozi to get witchcraft to avoid school. Not that it worked. He knows about our planned tuck shop raid!

'Yet he allows us, allows us to sin, not because he is weak, but because he is strong. He grants to us free will. He allows us to sin, but trusts we will not. He knows our every weakness and vice. He knows our temptations, which are of Satan. Yet he does not act to prevent our sins. He watches and waits. He is all-knowing.' Even Allen has a spooked expression now. Matwiga can no longer meet the accusing gaze. It gets worse.

'We pray to God for those things we want for ourselves. For the welfare of those we love, for happiness, for the delivery of those in peril. . .' I feel a sudden tightness in my throat. I do all those things, ask God to protect and look after Mum, Becky, my brothers, Umali, Gretchen, Lutoli, Dieti, Sandy. . . Now the padre's definitely staring at me. I avert my eyes guiltily.

After staring at the parquet floor for several seconds, I glance with bowed head at Matwiga, and meet a gaze of naked terror. His eyes protrude frog-like. I feel the same. God knows about our tuck shop plans. We are being warned. The sermon continues, but I can't concentrate. We're in big trouble with God. The padre's eyes lock on mine. I'm the worst sinner of all. Worse than a Sodomite.

'Let us pray,' the padre intones, his eyes finally looking down.

'Our Father,' the congregation chorus dutifully, 'Who Art In Heaven. . .'

'Hello, what's Your Name?' Matwiga prays loudly.

'Jesus is his name,' whispers Schmedjie crossly. People are looking at us. Particularly BL Thomas, Vice Principal. This is worse and worse.

'*Ana jua!*' Matwiga blurts as soon as we're in the fresh air. He knows. His eyes hold superstitious dread.

'*Ndio, najua,*' I agree. Yes, he knows. I share his horror. The preacher knows our plans, he's made that obvious. And if he knows, God, his boss, manager, whatever, knows too. Doom is imminent.

What's that stuff. . . brine, that's it, no, it's got a rock in it, no, a stone. Brimstone, that's the one. That and. . . fire. Fire and brimstone. I don't like the sound of it. Wonder what kind of stone is a *brim*. Maybe they use them to edge things.

*'Tuwatche!'* Matwiga hisses as we form up to walk back to school. Let's leave it. 'If God knows, and we do it, there will be great *hatari*, danger.'

*'Kabisa!'* I agree. Absolutely. A shudder of dread runs through me. I'm in enough trouble with God.

The tuck shop is safe. Our arrangements are like the nuclear standoff between Russia and America – all preparation and no action. Oh yes, then there's the matter of BL Thomas. He looked most annoyed when Schmedjie whispered to Matwiga. As if reading my thoughts, Schmedjie turns to Matwiga.

'It's not Our Father, Which Are In Heaven, hello, what's your name? It's Hello *is* your name!'

'You mean they call Jesus "Hello?" '

'Yup,' says Schmedjie, 'because God is the alpha and he's oh-mega.'

'What?' I ask.

'Mega's big, but he's also the beginning and the end. At the beginning you always say hello. So it's "hello-is-your-name".'

'Funny,' says Matwiga. I agree. We have to *tell* God his name?

Fortune is with us on one thing. BL Thomas seems to have forgotten our disturbance of the Lord's prayer. We do, however, come to his early attention on another matter altogether.

Our minds are ever seeking. It isn't long after our big fright with the almighty when Schmedjie discovers a hitherto unknown athletic secret. It starts, like most great discoveries, by accident. He's very light skinned, and rubs on sun cream before going in the sun. It's too late when he realises he's used toothpaste on his legs. We're outside, and BL tells us to lap round the field. Schmedjie makes his discovery.

Toothpaste on legs makes you fast. He tells us. Soon we, and half the school, are at it. Mint cools the skin. The chilled air feels quick. Even Matwiga tries it on his good leg, and says he walks faster.

The only problem with our speed-enhancer is so many use it,

everyone's faster, so the cheating doesn't help. It comes to a head when Schmedjie openly rubs it on his legs on the field, and BL asks what's up. There's a strange, minty smell around track events lately, and he's determined to get to the bottom of it.

'Toothpaste!' he declares in his singsong Welsh accent, 'and *why* are you putting it on your legs?'

'To go faster,' Schmedjie mumbles.

'Speak up, boy!'

'To go faster...'

'What... *faster.* . ?' BL looks incredulous. 'Faster, eh, I suppose you *believe* that?' Putting it this way, it *does* seems silly. Some of us giggle. Even BL struggles to keep his expression stern. 'Showers,' he roars. 'Get it off, and double back. Last one does twenty press-ups, and three laps without toothpaste. In future, read the label, it's *tooth*-paste, not *leg*-paste.' In the showers we mock Schmedjie. Stupid Finn!

'Shark-fin,' Allen taunts. What a ridiculous notion, toothpaste indeed! Schmedjie doesn't apply for a patent, or a potent.

It's Allen who suggests pyjama-leg-cripple-running. It has to wait till after lights-out. We remove our pyjama trousers, and put our bent knees back down the legs. This binds calves tightly to thighs and forces feet against buttocks.

Thus shortened, and compelled to 'walk' on bent knees, we lower ourselves from our high beds, and race each other down the aisles between the beds. Excitement comes from the risk element, knowing Miss Baxter can appear, torch in hand, anytime. Handicapped, it will be hard, if not impossible, to get away, harder still to get back into bed.

We tell Matwiga he doesn't have to play, but he refuses to be left out. For him the rules are modified. He can climb down from his bed before rearranging his pyjamas, and keep his thin leg out of his pyjama pants. Despite his lopsidedness he's as quick as anyone. The game is compelling. We play nightly. For several days we get away with it. It's Matwiga who cops it.

We've been racing ten minutes. We don't hear a footfall, or the door open. She sneaks up. Like a trained *German Shepherd*, she's a silent assassin. Suspects something. Some of us, mainly Schmedjie, can't help sniggering while we hobble about. Miss Baxter is expert at not showing suspicion. She comes, waits a bit, seems to go, then sneaks back.

The beam shoots out from nowhere. It lances the darkness in a white, terrifying cone. There's subdued scuffling as we scuttle desperately to avoid the torchlight, which marches determinedly up and down the aisles. I reach my bed, and manage, by herculean effort, to pull myself up. I've just got my legs under the covers, when the searchlight catches Matwiga.

He's been desperately trying to squiggle to his bed, but now, like a rabbit in headlights, he's stationary and blinking. His startled face is lit up like a clown, and his expression brings giggles from several quarters of alleged sleepers.

'What have we here?' Miss Baxter says. She's invisible behind the beam. Matwiga neither moves nor speaks. Terror is on his face. He blinks rapidly.

'Speak, boy!'

'A game,' Matwiga mumbles.

'*Game,* tying yourself up like a turkey, crawling about the floor?'

'Yes Miss.'

'Yes Miss *Baxter!*'

'Yes Miss Baxter.'

'Undo yourself and get back in bed,' she says. She turns to the wall, snaps on the light. We're blinking. 'He's not the only one, is he?' she intones menacingly. 'All of you, bedclothes off..!' she yells.

There's no escape. We lower the covers. All our legs are doubled up in our pyjama pants.

'Right,' she intones, angrier than before, 'undo this nonsense, then line up here.' She points at the floor. We know what's coming. 'All except you, Master Matwiga. You will write one hundred lines – "I will not demean my body". '

'What that mean?' Matwiga says softly.

'It means you find out and write a hundred lines. Before lunch tomorrow.' She reaches in Allen's locker, takes out his plimsole. He's got the biggest feet here.

Three of the best from Miss Baxter is very sore. I jump, turbocharged, back in bed after my turn, my backside on fire.

'I'm fed up with this dormitory,' she announces after the last boy has made an agony-powered leap into bed. 'I know about the toothpaste, and I'm shocked what you were doing tonight. Let's have no more of it.' She clicks the light off and is gone. My pain begins to ebb. Somebody sniggers, then we all giggle. There's always a funny side.

For a while there's a moratorium on new games.

I get airletters from Mum three times a month. They're those blue, folded things which double as writing paper, and envelope in one. Mum says she'll write every week, but sometimes doesn't quite manage, or else one letter a month goes missing. I look forward to her letters all week.

When it's post time, in the evening after supper, I wait anxiously to see if there's one for me. Miss Baxter takes the letters out of the bag one at a time, and announces whom it's for. The lucky ones jump up and grab their letter. Each one which isn't for me is a disappointment. Then it's me, and my heart surges. Other times she finishes, and I'm not a lucky one.

Mum's letters are always much the same. Her writing, which she learnt long ago at another boarding school, is a beautiful copperplate script. 'Darling Jimboy, her letters begin, I hope you are well, and that you are happy.' She then says something about home. 'Gooloogooloo is well, but he tried to peck Amina yesterday. Sandy misses you, and I have to let her sleep on my bed while you're away.' Then there's usually something about someone on the mine. 'Rosanna has been very sick, but she's better now,' or 'Higgs broke his ankle when his motor-bike fell over.'

There's always a part about Umali and Amina, and sometimes Lutoli. 'Umali says he misses fishing at the dam with you.' Or 'Amina drank too much again, and got into a fight with the *ayah* who works for Mr Snel.' Her letters round off here, about two thirds of the way down the inside of the air letter. 'I miss you and love you. You'll be home soon, and I look forward to that. Your ever-loving, Mum. XXXXXXX (hugs and kisses).'

There may never be anything new in her letters, but that's not what I love them for. They are from Mum, from Geita, my home, and they've been there more recently than me. I take my letters reverently to a quiet place where I can read and re-read them over and over. I also smell them, and rub them on my face, because it's the closest thing to home. In my banishment in this alien, far-off place, they evoke a feeling that my real world, that which I love so dearly, still exists, even though it's so far away.

For five weeks in a row I get a letter from Mum every Friday. That's unusual, for two reasons. One is she never manages a letter every week. The other is they usually arrive on different days of the week. There's something very unusual going on. I check with Becky, and she's also had a letter every Friday for five weeks.

We compare letters. Apart from our names, the contents are almost identical. There's more. The letters are very brief, and the handwriting looks shaky. Not like Mum's usual confident copperplate hand. They're all written in the same pen. We check previous letters and confirm our suspicions. Those were longer, and written with a variety of pens. I go to Miss Baxter and tell her I'm worried about Mum. I think she's written the letters all at the same time. Why would she do that, and then date them differently?

'Your mother's fine,' Miss Baxter says. She's telephoned the mine. I don't know how that works. There's only a radiotelephone there, the one in Mr Snel's office at the head office on Top Road. 'They told me she's fine, so run along and don't worry any more.' I tell Becky, and she says everything must be okay, so we mustn't worry.

# Twenty-one

At night I lie in bed and think about things which happened here in Tanganyika. Eugen Blüger told Dad about the first time the *Schutztruppe* were bombed from the air. Dad loved to tell me the story. I must have been five at the time.

A British biplane first appears in the colonial war, near the mountains of Oldorobo, in 1915. It comes from nowhere, and bombs the *Scutztruppe* position. The English have sent tribal spies ahead, to tell the people that the aeroplane is a 'new *Mungu*' (God), and that this *Mungu* will surely seal their doom.

The *Mungu* is hit in the fuel tank by a well-aimed round from an *askari* with a smokey old *Mauser* '71 pattern rifle, and crashes in flames. The pilot runs screaming from the wreck with his trousers alight. His trouser-fire is put out by a German officer with a blanket, but not before his buttocks are thoroughly singed. The *askaris* celebrate, shouting, '*Mungu nyupa si Mungu!*' The new *Mungu* is not a God!

The plane has done damage. A 50lb bomb has exploded close to the troops. *Oberstleutenant* von Lettow Vorbeck, reconnoitering the battlefield, encounters an injured *askari* lying in the grass, his left arm blown off from the elbow.

'Don't worry, *Obersti*,' he says, smiling through his shock and pain, 'I have another one, I can still fight!'

An awkward thing has developed with Marais. Ever since imprisonment under his bed, and being set free, he's undergone a metamorphosis where I'm concerned. Whereas he used to glower, he smiles warmly at me. In place of whispered threats, are offers to help clean my shoes, fetch things for me.

Schmedjie says I've gained a 'side-kick'. Matwiga says a *silav*, meaning slave. They want me to order him to do silly things, like put his head in the toilet bowl and pull the chain, or abuse Miss Baxter or drop his pants in front of the girls. I won't do it. He may not be a friend, but he's trying to make up for the past. How do I know if the change is genuine, or if it'll last? Dad had a saying: 'Trust everyone. If they let you down, don't trust them again.'

I suppose I never gave Marais a chance. I disliked him from

the outset. In the next bed, he was a constant reminder I was far from home. His wheezing didn't endear him, especially when it kept me awake. I didn't like his accent, nor his gaunt *mzoga* build.

It's four o'clock Friday afternoon. The kids who live nearby are going home for the weekend. Those from further afield sit glumly on the grass beside the circular driveway, where parents collect their darlings. It's not jealousy, we convince ourselves, though we don't talk to Schmedjie at these times, 'cos he's one of 'them', not us.

An ancient-looking green long-wheelbase Land Rover with a canvas back pulls up. A huge, muscle-bound, bearded, *Mzungu* in khaki shorts and shirt gets out, and I see him embrace Marais. His farmer-father. They talk animatedly. Marais points at me, and his father walks my way. For a moment I'm seized with terror. Is this retribution for my part in his kidnap?

'*Jan het gesê* you kom wid us fore die veek-ent,' he says in pidgeon-English. 'You like eet?' My mouth is dry, my heart pounding. It takes seconds to register. 'Eef you vant eet, ve talk die matron, yes?' His is a very strange accent, almost, but not quite German. My relief is huge. Rather than coming to kill me, he's offering me an escape from school, even if just for two days. Marais, who I should call Jan now, is grinning.

'Yes please,' I say. Who'd have thought? I turn to Matwiga. He's not smiling. I'm breaking the unsaid rule. Like Schmedjie, I'm abandoning my friends.

Twenty minutes later, we drive out onto the bumpy dirt road out of town. Mr Marais is a man of few words, like his son. The Rover bounces its dusty way to the east, then turns left at a fork, and heads towards a range of distant red hills. The snow-capped peak of Meru is visible to the right behind us. Though there are no clouds, and the sun is bright, there's a cool, refreshing breeze, unlike on the lake-plain of Geita, where even at this time of afternoon it swelters.

The dirt road deteriorates to a track, formed, I'm sure, simply by the passing of vehicles. It winds around obstacles, like giant anthills and rocky outcrops. Without talking, Mr Marais points out herds of *wildebeest*, *kudu*, and even a pair of grazing rhinos.

The sun drops down to meet the horizon to the west, a great

blood-red disc bathing the whole world in pink. It's seven o'clock, and three hours since we left Arusha. One moment the sun's there, clinging to the edge of the world, then it plunges completely away. It's only momentarily dark, for then a golden moon, and myriad stars, suffuse the land in gentler light. We erupt onto a great plain ringed by distant hills, black and mysterious. Then we're stopping. The big man gets out and pushes open a wooden gate. He drives us through, then closes it behind. We have reached the boundary of the farm.

The wood-built house is fully half a mile from the gate. We pull up and get out. I'm stiff as a stick. The light from the windows is strangely pale. Jan reads my thoughts.

*'Ons het nie elektriek nie,'* he says. We have no electric. 'Use de hurricane-lamps.' At the door his mother and two sisters greet us. His mum is a thin, smiling lady, who speaks no English. She says 'velkom' several times. One sister is called 'Meisie', which means girl. I don't know if it's a nickname, but find it strange. Meisie's thirteen, and goes to a 'farm-school'. She's pretty, in a red-haired, freckly way, and has a ready smile. I can't see the colour of her eyes in this light. The other sister is Doreen, which I also find strange among these tough people. She's eleven, dark haired, and serious.

*'Julle moet eet,'* Mrs Marais says. You must eat. She leads us into the warm dimly lit kitchen. I haven't realised how cold it is. It's like that on the high plateau in the evening. Three hurricane lamps make wheezy blowing sounds, and cast yellow light and shadow around the room. There are rows and rows of copper pots and pans hanging from a wooden beam above an open fire, where orange flames dance, casting flickering light and shadow. We sit on long benches, like those in church.

Mrs Marais and Meisie bring a big pot of boiled potatoes, and another with delicious-smelling stew. *'Kudu,'* she says, smiling, *'geskiet gister by Pa.'* Shot yesterday by father. After boarding school, it's delicious. Meisie can't keep her eyes off me. I look up several times to find her staring. She grins, but doesn't look away. Jan talks to her in Dutch, then tells me she thinks I'm handsome. No one's ever said that, except Mum. I say she's pretty too, and we grin at each other like two monkeys. I feel a stab of guilt about Gretchen. But, then, she doesn't know.

The Marais family goes to bed early. I share a room with Jan, which I don't mind now. As soon as we're in bed, he snuffs out the whooshing hurricane lamp. I fall into a dreamless sleep.

They rise early. At six the sun bursts through our un-curtained window, and the farmyard comes to life. It's ice-cold outside. We wash in a small outbuilding. It's simple. There's a handle-powered pump, which you push to and fro until it draws a stream of water from the well, which runs out a tap into a bucket. When the bucket's full, you ladle freezing water over yourself with a small metal jug. Soap all over with the pierced bar of *Lifebuoy* on a string. Rinse off, and you're done. The toilet's in the shed next door. Pit latrine.

After breakfast of fried *boerewors*, a long spicy Afrikaans sausage, and eggs, Jan and I go exploring. The plowed earth runs away forever in furrows of deep red-brown. Forty thousand hectares, the farm, Jan says. Too big to contemplate.

There are fields with rows and rows of baby maize just beginning to erupt from the soil. Other fields are half-grown, tiny cobs just starting to show. Some places are covered in fresh, peppermint-green grass, grazed by fat black and brown cattle. They don't have humps, like our scrawny Geita beasts, and they're not troubled by flies. This is a different world. Everywhere are sprinklers shooting revolving jets of water. It's amazing what the hand of man can do.

There's a barn with a massive haystack. Jan, Meisie and I climb it and have a midday snooze. Doreen doesn't come. She's playing alone in the house.

'Did you got a girlfriend?' Meisie asks, a piece of straw in her mouth. I notice her eyes are bright green.

'No,' I say. Why does she want to know?

The weekend ends too soon. We go back to Arusha, bearing huge packets of *biltong*, dried spiced game-meat, and homemade *beskuit*, an Afrikaner sweet rusk, to dip in tea. From now on, I don't hate Marais, I mean Jan, any more. My friends won't be convinced so easily.

We're only back a week, and I haven't done that convincing, when Jan gets very sick. It starts with an asthma attack in bed, and gets worse and worse, in spite of his inhaler-bottle, until he can hardly breathe at all and his face is mottled blue. In a panic I run and call Miss Baxter. She looks at him for a second and gets the school doctor out of bed. Jan needs support to walk out of the dormitory. A Land Rover-ambulance takes him to hospital. Next day Miss Baxter says it's pneumonia, and he's 'very ill indeed'.

At lunchtime the grey-bearded school padre who sussed our tuck shop plans holds a special prayer for Jan. Andrew, the English twins Jed and Jack, and I, avoid his gaze. I'm sure he knows what we did to Jan. I betrayed him. I didn't like him then, because he'd been horrible. Now I hate my co-kidnappers. It was their idea, and I went along with it. I wanted revenge. How hollow it feels now! Thank heavens I let him go that day, but still I feel bitter remorse for my part in the affair.

That night the padre comes and breaks the news to us in the dining room. Jan Marais died an hour ago.

What is sorrow? What is grief? What is God's plan? What is his message? I go to bed that night, next to Jan's achingly empty bed, which is stripped of blankets, sheets and pillows. I feel an overwhelming mixture of emotions. Guilt. Sadness. I cry bitter tears, but feel dishonest. He wasn't a real friend, was he? I hated him so long. Yes, he was much nicer to me, and I've just had a weekend with his family. What about pretty, green-eyed, smiling Meisie? How is she feeling now?

Maybe Jan Marais would have become a good friend. If I convince myself he would, will it be because he's dead? Did I kill him with my hatred?

I dream about Dad and Mr Valari (senior), and Tembo's disintegrating, stinking puppy. In my dream I talk with Jan, who says death's quite nice, actually, and I should try it. Meisie's standing just behind him, smiling and nodding.


The whole school's in shock. Everyone knew Jan had asthma, but they didn't expect this. His funeral service is held on Sunday at the church. The family are Dutch-Reformed, or *Much-Deformed*, Andrew says unkindly, and there isn't that kind of church in the district. I sit with Schmedjie, Matwiga and Allen, as far away from Andrew and the auto-twins Jed and Jack as I can get. I'm never going to mix with them again.

Jan's coffin is of light wood and has shiny brass handles. It's resting on two trestles in front of the altar. The Marais family are seated next to it. I only see the backs of their heads, except when Meisie twists round during the singing of *Abide With Me*. She stares at me. I don't know if it's an accusing look in her green eyes or not. She's still pretty, even with red eyes and tears streaming down her cheeks.

At the end of the service the coffin is carried by six men, including Mr Houghton and BL Thomas, to the old Land Rover, and pushed in the back. He's going to be buried in the farm graveyard. The family walk stiffly out of the church, looking neither left nor right, and drive away.

The shock lasts weeks, and I feel strangely detached from day-to-day things. I can't believe what's happened, and I keep imagining I see Jan. Once I think I see him in the bathroom, coming out of a shower cubicle. He disappears as I look, and I realise it's only the shower curtain. Another time, just as I'm drifting to sleep, I feel someone touch my shoulder, and Jan's voice says 'hello *Rooinek*, do you miss me?'

I jump upright in bed, but there's nobody there. Only darkness, with a narrow glimmer of dull moonlight from the high window. I wonder if his ghost is trying to contact me. For days I walk alone in the places where Jan used to go. It's silly, but I can't help it. I avoid Schmedjie, Matwiga and Allen.


One Saturday afternoon, while the old gang is playing down by the river, I sit alone on my bed, staring at the still-unoccupied bed beside mine. I hear a footstep, and Miss Baxter is there. She contemplates me a long time in silence. Finally she speaks.

'You didn't do it,' she says softly. She's reading my thoughts. I feel I did. Killed everyone who ever died. Dad, Mr Valari (senior), Tembo's puppy, and now poor Jan. My chest is full to bursting, and tears roll down my cheeks. She sits beside me on my bed and puts her arms around me. I never thought a hug from her would be welcome, but it is. I feel deeply comforted, and understood by another person for the first time since Jan died. Finally she wipes my face and eyes with a tissue. 'Come to my office,' she says, 'I think a piece of cake and a cup of tea will do you good.'

From this episode I learn two things. You can't hate someone always, and even people who are hard can be gentle and kind. Miss Baxter talks to me about Jan whenever I feel the need. After a month I feel better, if still sad, and, thank heavens, the nightmares stop.

Many concepts are posited on lazy Saturday afternoons by the river. We muck about with water and pebbles, and dig tunnels deep into the sandbanks. Later we lie in a group on our backs, enjoying the late afternoon sun. That's when we ruminate.

Petrol explodes in engines. It takes a lot of deliberation and argument to persuade the gang. Matwiga says it's impossible, for two reasons. First, he says, we would hear the explosion. Since the sound of a car, which he can very accurately reproduce, including the grating of gears or the engine struggling up a hill, sounds nothing like a bomb going off, there can *not* be explosions in the engine. Second, if there is an explosion, people will be blown up and killed. Since that is clearly not what is happening to the occupants of that car driving down the school road over there, explosions are out of the question. It's simply the 'strength' of the petrol, which drives the car. Conclusion: 'strong' liquid powers a car.

The former spawns a further hypothesis. In Allen's opinion it should be possible to drive a car on elephant wee. Elephants are big and very powerful. It's logic that their wee must also be strong It follows then, being stronger than any other wee, it is comparable to petrol. We agree to look into it. Big money can be made, if nobody beats us to it.

Allen says there's a thing called a patent, where they write down your invention so no one can steal it. It's a *potent*, I say. Sounds better for elephant wee. We'll get a *potent*, we agree. Will we keep elephants at fueling depots, I wonder, or just take their wee there? Won't it be a bugger persuading an elephant to pee into a car tank?

Our midnight 'feasts' are a lot less grandiose than the title. We scrounge around for things to eat for days. The obvious, and always first-raided stock, is that of grudging Schmedjie himself, who always has a large square tin full of home-baked shortbread biscuits. His mother makes them, and he brings them after weekends at home. His parents live just forty miles away, at Moshi, in the foothills of Mount Kilimanjaro. We're envious, and take vengeance by raiding his tin.

There is otherwise a sad lack of victuals to take to our midnight feasts. One fairly reliable, and, given the shortages, essential, contribution comes from the grove of lemon trees between the football field and library. I have never seen lemons like these. They're a paradox. On the outside, they're the biggest, yellowest lemons. But therein lies the lie. The peel's an inch thick. When removed, the fruit inside is the size of a plum. The strangest thing is the peel is incredibly sweet, and, we find, very edible.

All that's required to plunder the lemon-source is to amble over that way in the half hour between showers and suppertime. It's essential to wear a baggy jumper, with the bottom tucked into the waistband, to put pilfered lemons in. Looking strangely and bumpily pregnant, all we have to do is make it back to the dorm and deposit the loot in our bedside lockers. So, pregnant-boy-detection by a prefect, Matron or wandering teacher not being too frequent, our stock of said item is usually replete. Lemons are available year-round here.

Schmedjie's biscuits and lemons. Not much to feast on. But there's also our 'kitchen hook'. Woodwork is never my interest, apart from making crude things in Geita. But Schmedjie says we should join woodwork classes, and use the tools and materials to build a 'stealing-hook' he's designed.

Schmedjie has, among his collection of artefacts, a key he found on the playground, which, to his amazement and delight, fits the lock on the kitchen door. He's snuck in there several nights, locking the door behind him. The food's locked away. But, and this is what excites him, there is a large pantry-cabinet in one corner. It's filled with cakes and bread. The cabinet is a wood-framed thing, but the sides are only wire mesh fly-screen. Not only that, but in the far right corner there's a hole three inches wide. Schmedjie takes me on a night-scout of the kitchen. Sure enough, there's the hole. We can get a hand through, but the cakes are three feet out of reach.

Schmedjie shows me his drawing. It's a three-foot-long carved stick, with a moving wooden hook at the end. At the top-end, and near the bottom, are holes – for string to pull the hook-swivel up and down. With this masterpiece, he's sure, we can reach and retrieve the cakes in the fly-screen cabinet.

We attend three woodwork lessons, in which we are pleased there's little supervision. Schmedjie has carved the hook-bit when the teacher asks what it is. 'Art,' Schmedjie says. The teacher smiles and walks away. He likes art. By the third lesson's end we've completed our work. We smuggle our device to the dormitory and hide it under Schmedjie's bed. We never go to woodwork again.

Our machine works. It fits through the hole in the mesh, and the point of the hinged hook easily penetrates both cake and bread. We pull the string, lift them up, then withdraw them to the hole. With eager fingers we break them up to fit through, and we have more for our midnight feast.

The feasts occur after lights-out. The venue is under my bed. The beds are high steel ones, with a three-foot space between floor and springs.

We burgled the kitchen last night, and our lockers are full of sweet-skinned lemons. Schmedjie's mother has just replenished his biscuit tin, and there are two homemade shortbreads each. I've contributed a packet of *Kool-Aid*, which, mixed with water, makes a very artificial-tasting drink. Robert and Allen have nothing to bring, so they made the lemon-run.

Tonight, as always, lights-out in the dormitory is at eight o'clock. We wait half an hour after Miss Baxter clicks off the light. It's difficult to contain our excitement. Not that we're going anywhere, or doing something new. It's just that what we're doing is strictly forbidden, and getting caught will result in very sore bums. Excitement has strange roots.

Schmedjie, who has a luminous *Oris* watch which glows green in the dark, is our timekeeper. At the agreed time of eight thirty, he rises from his bed, casting werewolf shadows on the wall in the moonlight from a high window. 'It's time,' he whispers.

'What you guys doing?' comes the voice of a boy none of us like, and who we've refused entry to our gang of four, which we say can't have a fifth member on account of its name.

'Mind your business,' growls Matwiga, invisible in the

darkness. The questioner shuts up. Matwiga's already punched him once.

The counterpanes and blankets are draped over the sides of my bed. The sprung wire links underneath make a perfect suspension point for a hunter's lantern. They are popular in Tanganyika. Short, square torches, with lens and bulb on one side, perfect to hang under a bed.

We feast. Schmedjie biscuits, lots of sweet lemon skin, some sour lemon, cake and stale bread rolls from the kitchen raid, and toothbrush-mugfuls of Kool Aid. Not much, but stolen fruit and cake is sweet.

Christmas approaches, and the dining room and dormitories are decorated with Christmas trees, tinsel and raffia-paper. We rehearse carols for a performance in the assembly room. Boys from the big-boy's dormitory teach us new versions:

*While shepherds watched their flocks by night,*
*all seated on the ground,*
*a choir of angels it came down,*
*and glory shone around.*

Becomes:

*While shitting on the rocks at night,*
*a great big furry hound ,*
*a roll of tissue it came down,*
*and bum-hole it was bound.*

And:

*Once in royal David's city,*
*stood a lonely cattle shed,*
*where a mother laid her baby,*
*in a manger for his bed.*

Becomes:

*Tell why you are so witty,*
*why such muck is in your head,*
*how you got to be Miss Baxter,*
*with a face like the long-dead.*

And:

*Good King Wenceslas looked out,*
*on the feast of Stephen,*
*when the snow lay round about,*
*deep and crisp and even.*

Becomes:

*Wenceslas is just a Kraut ,*
*creep and tit and heathen,*
*everyone knows he's a lout,*
*full of farts and piss-en!*

It's a great introduction to carol singing.
'What's a lout?' Matwiga asks.
'A thing what crawls in your hair,' Schmedjie says, 'if you've got lots they call them *louses.* '
'Lice,' Allen corrects him.
'Is that 'cos they's the same size as rice?' Matwiga asks.
'Course,' I say. It's logic.

245

# Twenty-two

At home Mum makes a confession. Did we suspect anything wrong last term? Well, she's been very sick. Pneumonia and pleurisy, and Dr Weiss was so worried he had her flown to Nairobi, and from there to Johannesburg in South Africa. She spent three weeks in the Hospital, having oxygen and antibiotics. They said she had a 'tropical infection', whatever that is.

Before she goes, Mary Miller suggests she write post-dated letters to Becky and me, so we won't know. She lies half-dead, writing six air letters each. She's so ill, so short of breath, she has to make them brief. Knowing me, she says, she doesn't think I'll be fooled. But Mary insists, and Mum doesn't have the strength to resist.

What would have happened if she died? Who would have told us? How would they have explained the letters? They were forgeries, weren't they? If putting a wrong date on, and pretending it's an up-to-date letter is a forgery. For the best possible reasons, Mum deceived us. This goes to prove the correctness of my most fundamental beliefs. One, you can't trust *Wazungu*. Two, you can't trust grown-ups. Three, I can't even trust my own mother.

I have nightmares, and Mum dies in all of them. In one I have to bury her next to Dad, on the other side from Mrs Williams, who, disintegrating and smelling like Tembo's exhumed puppy, is sitting on her gravestone, directing my digging. Becky says I'm silly. She doesn't get nightmares at all.

During the long, hot days of the hols, we get so bored we have to do something new. Over the years we exhaust many options. Sometimes we go out looking for distraction. Baby birds fall out of nests, and we take them to the girls to nurse. Then they die. We find pythons sleeping in the shade of the big steel pipes carrying the roadside ditches under crossroads. They're only dangerous if they're very big, you're very small, and they can get at you. We're too big and too quick. We throw stones at them, and they undulate off into the undergrowth.

The monsoons in northwestern Tanganyika occur in winter and summer, though that close to the equator it's almost impossible to tell which season it is. Most of the time it's hot, cloudless and dry. Suddenly, in a matter of minutes, the sun is cut off and the sky darkens with great pregnant black storm clouds. Rolling thunder echoes between the hills, ear-piercing lightning bazookas between ground and sky, and the rain comes. In a deluge so dense that it's hard to breathe if you're caught in it. It's as if you're underwater. If you're in a car, you have to stop. Windscreen wipers are useless. You can't see through the wall of gushing water.

This is when we surf the ditches from Top to Bottom Road. Who cares about pythons? We use small planks like boogie-boards, held in front as we hurtle down in torrents of brown, muddy water, oblivious to scratches and bruises gained én route from colliding with the sides, or from boulders which, like us, are swept down in the fierce cascade.

Scaring *leguaans*, metre long insect and berry-eating lizards, which look like dragons, and have long, darting tongues, amuses. They live underground in tunnels, to escape heat and predators. They're seldom seen by day, coming out to hunt and forage by night. We know how to find the entrances to their tunnels. We bless them with unexpected shocks while they try to sleep away the day.

Those *Bobejaan* bangers, or 'baboon' crackers, are large red explosives, two and a half inches long, and an inch in diameter. They have long white fuses. They're meant for farmers for frightening away crop-stealing baboons. Barrat Stores aren't fussy who they sell to, and at ten for a shilling they're a bargain. At first we light the fuse and drop one down a hole. Muffled explosion, terrified *leguaan* dashing out different hole. Bombardier Dieti refines our technique.

The fuses are three inches long, take half a minute to burn. We bind three or four bangers together, fuses cut different lengths, twirled together. This achieves a series of explosions. Taking our advanced ordinance, we return to the *leguaan* tunnels. Dull thud underground, frantic scurrying, second thud, more scrabbling, third bang, half a dozen *leguaans* bolting from holes, blinking in daylight, nostrils twitching, legs pumping in naked terror. Next explosion, they run faster. Anywhere. *Leguaan* Armageddon! Weapon breakthrough, atomic bomb class. No lizard can rest in peace.

We cluster-bomb the *leguaans* many times, before this, like everything else, grows mundane and boring. Discussing the problem, we decide to turn our focus on humans. Who else than the Valaris?

The Valaris are that very private, even secretive, Italian family. Worse than the van der Heevers. Mr and Mrs Valari have two children, a fat daughter, Anna, and a son, Gino. When they came to Geita in 1956, they brought Mr Valari's father, Mr Valari (senior). The old man who died in 1957, shortly after Dad, whose *mzoga* I saw in *kifo nyumba*.

Neither Anna, four years older than me, nor Gino, my age, socialise with other children. They don't go to school, and only speak Italian. I've only seen Gino a few times. It isn't possible to talk with him. Swahili and English draw a blank response. He has the same thin, rangy, look as his father, and the *mzoga* of his late grandfather. There are no laws about withholding children from school in Geita, or else they aren't enforced.

Mr Valari is the only one who leaves the house. Every day he drives his rusty Peugeot to work at the electrician's building on Top Road, and every evening he returns to park in the dusty spot beside the wooden house. Nobody, not even those he works with, know much about him.

There's an echo of Boo Radley in Harper Lee's *To Kill A Mockingbird*, about the Valaris. The children in that seminal novel try their best to 'make Boo Radley come out'. We'll make the Valari's come out, whatever it takes. But first we need a quisling. An Italian traitor, who will advise and teach us to abuse our victims in language they understand.

Antonio Barelli is the older of two sons of Marcello and Marula Barelli. Marcello is a gung-ho Italian, in his forties when I'm ten. Unlike the Valaris, who have never socialised in Geita, Marcello does it enthusiastically and energetically. He's known for two things: drinking to excess and singing *O Caro Mia*. His drinking often leaves him semi-paralysed and incoherent. We imitate his song as *'Oh Kamasutra'*, the meaning of which we have no clue, but which delights adult club drinkers, particularly when Marcello, too inebriated to notice our words, sings with us. There's another one of his songs called *'O sole mio,'* which we sing as *'arsehole-meeow'*.

Marcello's also famous for shooting Higgs's night-rider leopard, and many an innocent elephant, whose feet he turns into gruesome wastepaper bins to give to every woman on the mine. The ivory, it's said, he sends to Italy by 'devious means'. Marula, his wife, could easily be a Valari. She's reclusive by nature, and lives in the shadow of her raucous husband. It's said she doesn't even eat, because she's as 'thin as a rake'. We unkindly say a rattlesnake. It sounds right, although I don't hear her rattle. I've never seen a rattlesnake. They're American, not African. Marcello more than compensates for Marula's non-exuberance.

Antonio is a few months younger than me. His brother Stefano is four years behind him. At six, Stefano is catastrophic. Skinned, festering knees, face bruised by countless collisions, snotty nose, often bleeding, and no other language than Italian. A pocket-sized manic Italian accident.

Antonio becomes our quisling.

'Why Ai shooda do thees?' he asks when we make the suggestion.

'Becos, if you don't, ve kill you,' Dieti growls, confident in our numbers, if not his size.

'Hokay,' Antonio says, suddenly seeing the light. He's an affable chap. He's over a recent bout of chagrin at our mis-sung Italian songs. Catapults, stones and abuse will be our assault weapons. Dieti suggests adding baboon-bangers to toss at the house, and we agree. Can't have too much assault. Abuse, however, is something else. How can we abuse someone who doesn't understand the abuse?

Here Antonio makes his invaluable contribution. Becky, Gretchen, Sophia, who, though Italian herself, says she doesn't know bad words, Dieti, Charlie Praze, the Cornish assistant manager's son, and Andrew and George Hunt, the sons of the family from Yorkshire, and I, make up the group. Antonio will train us in Italian swearing. Gretchen has reverted back to tomboy since Fraser left, but I feel different when I'm close to her. At thirteen her loose jeans and oversize shirt cannot hide the shape of her hips, or that her chest is no longer flat.

'What you thinking?' she asks me one day as I stare and try to visualise her shirt open. Her blue eyes are mocking, and tell me she knows. Teasing. It makes me angry. I'm diverted by our quisling.

'Sheet,' Antonio says, 'ees murder.'

'Vot?' says Dieti.

'Sheet, sheet, sheet!' Antonio explodes, 'eet ees murder, *murder!*'

'Vy?' asks Dieti.

'He means the sheet een the toilet, and eet ees murder, spell *m-e-r-d-e*,' Sophia explains, blushing as soon as it's said. Unguarded moment.

'Oh, *m-e-r-d-e!*' I say.

'Yes,' Antonio says.

'Vel, zat iss vun verd,' Dieti sighs.

'Pees ees *Pee-s-ci-a-re.* . . say eet,' Antonio continues patiently, *'p-i-s-c-i-a-r-e,* or say *pisa, p-e-e-s-a-h.*'

*'Pisciare,'* we chorus, *'peesah.'*

'Bum ees *culo,* say *ku-lo.*'

*'Kulo, ku-lo.*'

'Vagina ees *va-geen-ah,* spell *v-a-g-i-n-a,* say *vah-geen-ah.*'

*'Va-geen-ah.'* I catch Gretchen grinning. She finds this funny. If only she knew. I'm falling in love. Find it difficult to breathe when she's near.

'Testicle ees *testicolo, test-i-colo.*' Gretchen and Becky fall about laughing.

*'Testicolo, testicolo.*'

*'Jigi-jigi* ees *rapporti, ra-port-ee,*' he says, making the universal finger-in-hole sign. I avoid looking at Gretchen.

*'Rapporti, ra-port-ee.'*

'Preek ees *pene,* say *peh-neh.*' Becky and Gretchen snigger.

*'Pene,'* we echo, *'peh-neh.'*

'Stop luffing!' Dieti hisses.

The training goes on for an hour. Then we're ready for the Valaris. It's midday, and Mr Valari and his Peugeot will be at work. That leaves his wife and children alone. At our non-existent mercy.

I wonder what poor Mrs Valari, Anna and Gino think when we launch our assault. First we hurl and catapult stones onto the tin roof to attract their attention. When they come to the window, they see their little wooden home is completely surrounded. Just like in those Western movies, when the Red Indians surround a homestead. The first to shout abuse is, paradoxically, our quisling Antonio. He assumes he has not only to teach us the invective, but also demonstrate its use.

'*Merde,*' he yells, and another hail of stones clang on the roof, to a chorus of '*pisa, culo, vagina, pene, testicolo*' and '*rapporti!*' It's jumbled and punctuated with Sandy's frantic barking, but has the clarity of opera, where, though people sing, talk or stab themselves all at once, every word is heard.

Dieti lights a *bobejaan*-banger, holds it in one hand as the fuse burns down, then hurls it just in time. It arcs towards the window, and explodes. It's like a thunderclap, and echoes from the hills. There's an awed silence. Dieti's a great bombardier. No wonder the Germans gave us such trouble.

The faces at the window are horrified. The curtains close and they disappear. We shout more Italian abuse, shoot more stones, and then withdraw. The first battle of the Valari war is over. It has been a resounding victory. A rout, or is it a *root?*

In a way our raid has a result. Soon, Gino Valari, like Boo Radley, will come out to play, but nobody will want to play with him. So he'll just go back in again.

I go home, thinking not of the Valaris, but of Gretchen. That night I dream she says she loves me. That she meant it when she said she'd run away with me that ancient day in water-cave.


'No,' Mr Snel says when I ask if he'll pay for Lutoli to go to Arusha with Becky and me. I've waited for Sunday, when I knew he'll drink a lot at the club. Drink makes people more amenable, they say.

'Why not?' I ask stubbornly.

'Because it's ridiculous,' he says, putting his glass of *Whitecap* down on the bar. The two men sitting next to him have fallen silent. No spine, I think. Worms!

'Why's it ridiculous?' I'm standing with my arms crossed. I always do that when I'm about to abuse a *Mzungu*.

'Take him away,' Mr Snel says, looking over my head. He's high on his barstool. Mum has come up behind me. He's talking to her. I'm dismissed. I draw a big breath. Before I can let rip with what I think of him, and all the *Wazungu* in Geita, I'm forcibly bundled out of the bar, onto the verandah.

'Don't you ever talk like that to Mr Snel!' Mum says when the door is safely closed. 'I'll lose my job, we'll have nowhere to live.'

Lutoli says he told me so. The *Wazungu* will never do something good. Why did I ever think they would? It's not in their nature. What about my nature? I ask. That's different, he says, I should know that.

The little black and white shenzie dog we captured a year ago, de-ticked, de-flead, bathed in bubble bath, fed on steak, and named 'Dickie', has never forgotten his experience. Life on the outside is tough. He's not able to leave where the miracle happened.

We try persuading Mum to let us have him, but she won't budge. One dog's enough. For a while he just hangs around the garden, hoping for a change of fortune. Before long, he draws Tembo's lonely attention. Ever since his puppy died, for which he unshakably holds me responsible, Tembo has pined for another friend.

Now the *shenzie*-convert, like him outcast, lonely and living on the fringe, draws ever closer to Tembo's cooking fire, gratefully gulping down thrown titbits, coming ever closer to the patient little man, until finally they embrace, and he moves into Tembo's little room. From that day the two are inseparable. We've done something good.

I come home from fishing with Umali to find I missed Moses, but he's sold Mum a *batamzinga* wife for Gooloogooloo. She's less than half his size, about as big as Mr *Jogoo*, and white all over. A drab affair compared to the groom.

Now Gooloogooloo shows his true colours. Barely an hour after Mum puts her there, just as Umali and I reach home, there's a horrible hullabaloo from the *kuku* run. Hysterical cackling of *kukus*, pounding of Gooloogooloo feet on dry earth, thrashing of wings, sharp, triumphant cries, blood-curdling screams from the new bride.

Umali, Mum and I arrive together. We're far too late. Gooloogooloo has *jumped* her alright, but not like *Mr Jogoo*. Tembo, watering the vegetable garden, has seen it all. Gooloogooloo stared at his new wife silently awhile. If he needed conjugal inspiration, Mr *Jogoo* provided it by jumping three *kukus* in fifteen minutes. Gooloogooloo watched and decided what to do.

'*Akaruka,*' Tembo says, coming towards us. He jumped.

'*Wapi?*' Umali asks. Where?

'*Juu ya mke wake,*' Tembo says. On top of his wife.

'*Alafu?*' And then? Tembo is infuriatingly slow.

'*Yeye kuuawa yake,*' he says, pulling his finger across his throat. He killed her by the throat.

The young turkey-lady lies crushed in the sunshine. Her neck has a gaping wound, and crimson blood spurts, to a diminishing range, from a torn artery. The only other movement is that of her smaller feathers wafting in the hot, dry breeze. Her body quivers briefly. She's dead. We've just registered this when Gooloogooloo leaps, in a single bound, mighty wings flapping, on top of the henhouse. He steadies himself, fans his spectacular tail, throws back his head, opens his bloodied scimitar-beak, and screams defiance at the world. '*Gooloogooloogooloogooloo. . !*' He does a follow-up '*gooloogooloo*' for good measure. Look what I've done, lesser creatures, I've killed the bitch!'

Mr *Jogoo*, as far from the murder-scene as he can get, tries to make himself small, finds sudden fascination on the ground, scratches at it with rare interest. How the mighty are humbled!

'*Haipende wanawake,*' Umali says. He doesn't like women. Just then Amina emerges from the servant's quarters.

'*Yeye mbaya,*' she says, clucking. He's bad. 'He likes to bite me too.'

Murderous though he obviously is, I find something alluring about this huge and arrogant bird. There's a meeting of souls. I don't give a bugger for rules, and nor, evidently, does he.

'Show me,' I say. Amina grins one-toothedly.

'*Leta kikapu,*' she tells Umali. Bring a basket. A *kikapu* is a large woven grass basket. The *watu* use them for shopping. We keep two in the kitchen. Umali goes, brings one. She places it round her bum and ties the handle-bits together in front with string. Then she opens the gate and steps into the *kuku* run. She's gone just four paces towards the dead turkey-lady, when Gooloogooloo, seeing space behind her, leaps from the henhouse roof and dashes at her. He pecks the *kikapu* viciously, and, though unhurt, Amina screams.

*'Shetani!'* she yells, trying to hit him with her hand. Devil! He ducks his head like a boxer, pecks at the *kikapu* like a left jab.

*'Wanaume?'* I ask Umali. I'm intrigued. Men?

*'Ana penda,'* Umali says, grinning. He likes them.

*'Kweli?'* True?

*'Kweli!'*

'Should I try?'

*'Try, Jimu, try.'*

Amina runs from the *kuku* run, Gooloogooloo pecking at her *kikapu* till she slams the iron gate on him. I wait a second, then open the gate and enter. Gooloogooloo stops in his stride and stares. There's something very bullfight here. Will he start pawing the ground? There's a vicious glint in his eyes. Naked terror seizes me. What am I doing in here with this sadistic murderer? I don't even have a *kikapu*. Then, before I can turn and run, Gooloogooloo puts his be-bobbled head on one side, makes a gentle clucking sound with his tongue, and comes towards me. I'm frozen with fright. I can't believe what's happening.

When he's very close, he puts his forehead against my knee and closes his eyes. A vibration runs through him. Soothing. Almost like a cat's purring. This murderous bird loves me. What can I do? I put my hand out carefully. He stays as he is. To applause from Umali and Tembo, I stroke his neck. It's the beginning of my love affair with a psychopathic misogynist.

It's the talk of Geita that we have a woman-hating turkey. Before long, Gooloogooloo's entertaining the populace with his own special cabaret. When they come, expat wives and daughters, to verify the rumour themselves, though they don't really believe it, they're cautious nevertheless. They ask Becky and I to demonstrate. Into the *kuku* run I go, without fear or *kikapu*. Up strolls Gooloogoolooo, long neck stretched out for me to stroke, eyes misty with love. He makes that clucking, purring sound deep in his throat. Out I go.

Becky's debut. In she goes, *kikapu* firmly tied round her bum. Gooloogooloo's electrified. A female! Out fan the feathers in his massive tail, out bulge his eyes. He gallops, dust and small stones flying, and furiously assaults her *kikapu*. Nobody can doubt his hatred, or the damage he will inflict on unprotected female buttocks.

By now the females in the audience have to choose: go in with or without the *kikapu*. None chose without, and all are grateful. He never attacks men, though he doesn't let them stroke his neck like me.

It takes a long time to think of experimenting with Sandy. She's female. Will he attack her, or will she, like the hens, be exempt from his wrath? Sandy isn't keen to find out, and I have to shove her into the run and slam the gate. Gooloogooloo doesn't hesitate. His feathers fan, he paws the ground like a bull, and begins his death-run. I only just let poor, quaking, whimpering Sandy out millimetres from his rapier-sharp, reaching beak. Tembo doesn't like the idea of testing with Dickie. I'm trying to kill his dog all over again.

I explain Gooloogooloo never attacks males, and Tembo relents. Dickie goes in, walks around nonchalantly, nothing happens. Gooloogooloo doesn't even unfurl his tail feathers. He hates all females, except for *kukus*. Snow White's particularly close. She's the oldest *kuku* when he came, and he's bonded with her. A fifth of his size, she's his adopted mother, and her sisters are his aunts. As we watch, she ambles stiffly up to him, and there's affection in both *kuku* and turkey eyes. How can this be? Of all females, only *kuku* ones are exempt from murderous hate.

Umali laughs. When Gooloogooloo came to us he was very young, he says. The *kukus* were kind to him. Good sisters and mothers. Snow-White especially. He's never forgotten. It's the only explanation. But why the hatred for all other females? He was abused by his mother, Umali says, what else? In his egg, or after?

At three years, Sandy has grown into a remarkable little dog. She's almost as low to the ground, and as long, as her Dachshund ancestors, but her other, chaotically assorted, genes have given her a most unusual appearance. The 'seams' running up her legs and down the middle of her belly are, to Becky and I, proof that, like a teddy bear, she was stitched together in a factory. She has the nondescript, yet loveable, brown face and stubby black snout of a little hyena, which is why Umali teases us by referring to her as *fisi ndogo*. Like that namesake, she is, for her small size, extraordinarily strong. Mum says she lifts weights when we aren't looking, because her seamed legs bulge with well toned muscle.

Sandy adores Becky and me. She's never happy unless she's with us. Easy when we're together. When we aren't she has problems. Which one should she be with? She can't make up her mind. At night when we go to bed, she splits her time in each room. It becomes part of our soundscape to hear her nails click the wooden floor as she trudges the corridor. Arriving in my room, she jumps on my bed, nuzzles me briefly, then lies down beside me. She closes her eyes, and falls asleep instantly. Ten, fifteen minutes later, she opens her eyes, stares at me awhile, then jumps off the bed and clicks her way back to Becky. It goes on all night. It takes a girl's ingenuity to harness this resource.

We have, between us, a sizeable collection of *Illustrated Classics* and other comics, including *Topper, Beano* and *War* series. There's no television to divert us. In Geita, too, owing to its remoteness, and, it's said, those radio-wave-bending effects of magnetic iron in the ground, there's no radio reception, apart from Radio Congo. This broadcasts a continuum of Swahili love songs or patriotic ditties, interspersed with official announcements.

'*Leyo katika Stanleyville, Congo, selekali walisema. . .*'. Today in Stanleyville, Congo, the police said. . . Who cares what they said? We know the words of all the songs. *Katerina, Katerina, Katerina, mpenzi wangu. . .* Catherine, Catherine, Catherine, my girlfriend. . . *Mwalimu Julius Nyerere alisema jano katika Dar es Salaam, eti. . .*' Teacher Julis Nyerere, soon to be president of an independent Tanganyika, said yesterday in Dar es Salaam that. . . Music. Same tunes over and over. *Malaika, ninakupenda Malaika*. Joyous guitar and *marimba*, played with soul. Makes you want to dance. In Kenya, the Kenya African Democratic Union, or *KADU*, is demanding the unconditional release of its president, Jomo Kenyatta, from permanent internal exile and restriction, after his years of imprisonment by the Imperial British. More music. *Kondukitor, kondukitor, nyipe tiketi. . .* (bus) Conductor, conductor, give me a ticket. . .

Apart from running wild, there isn't much to do. That's why

we get up to so many disreputable things. At night there's Radio Congo, or comics. We read and re-read them constantly. When we get fed up with ours, we swap. Tiresome, dragging ourselves from room to room. That's where Becky gets her brainwave.

'You got *The Count of Monte Cristo*?' I yell from my room one evening. 'Yeah,' she shouts back.

'Can I have it?'

'Okay,' she yells. There's a pause. 'Where's Sandy?' At the sound of her name, Sandy's ears twitch. She's lying on the foot of my bed, watching me.

'With me,' I shout.

'Sandy, Sandy, Sandy,' she calls. Sandy leaps from my bed and scurries to Becky's room. Click click click on the floor. Half a minute passes.

'Call her,' Becky yells.

'Sandy,' I call. Click click click click. She's beside me. Grinning. She always looks like she's grinning. Rolled up and tucked into her collar is The *Count of Monte Cristo*. Eureka! This is much more exciting than the comic. Carrier pigeon, nothing, here's a carrier-dog.

The radio crackles. There's trouble in the copper-rich Congo province of Katanga. Moise Tshombe is stirring up nationalism. He's only after the copper, which makes Kinshasa rich. It's rumoured he's going to secede Katanga from the newly independent, bloodstained, Congo. Somebody calling himself President Mobutu in Kinshasa has arrested the old President, Patrice Lumumba. He won't stand for Tshombe breaking up the country. Forces are mobilising. Mercenaries are being recruited in Europe and South Africa. Music break. *Malaika....  Nasindwana nakupenda, we, nineku owa Malaika.* I was beaten in love for you Malaika, or I'd have married you. *Malaika* means angel. Also a name for a girl. I switch off the radio.

'You want something?' I shout.

'*From the Earth to the Moon*,' Becky yells. I leaf through the pile on my table. Find it, roll it up, and shove it through Sandy's collar.

'Call her.'

'Sandy, Sandy. . .' Sandy dashes off. Clickety-click click.

'Got it,' Becky laughs. 'You want something?'

'Anything.'

'Call her.'

'Sandy . . .' Click click click. She's brought me a *Beano*. I roll up *From the Earth to the Moon*, and as I reach to put it through her collar, she takes it with her mouth. I'm dumbstruck as she click-clicks back down the corridor to Becky. We've invented *Umbwa*, or dog mail. The possibilities are endless. A *Wells-Fargo* hound! From now on we'll never lack a delivery service.

There's a knock on the front door. I get up wearily and go to see whom it is. Oh hell, it's Boo Radley, I mean Gino Valari. He's come out! Thin legs like yellow sticks protruding from oversized shorts, pinched face, pale like milk, narrowed eyes blinking in the fierce sunlight.

'Hello,' I say. Nothing. More blinking. He looks exactly like his late grandfather, Mr Valari (senior), or, at least, his *mzoga*.

'Jambo,' I say. Swahili's best. Still nothing. I smile. He doesn't. Is he out to avenge his family? Doesn't look like it. He hasn't got a stick.

'I wanna. . . *play*,' he stammers in a low voice.

'Well,' I say, dumbfounded, 'we're not playing right now.'

'Hokay,' he says, obviously relieved. I realise coming here isn't his idea. It's his mother and sister. They've sent him on a peace mission to their attackers. I'm overwhelmed with shame.

'Would you like some sweets?' I ask, remembering I've just come back from Barrat Stores, and have a whole roll of Rowntree's fruit gums.

'Yessa pleeza.' There's actually a little smile on his wan face. Everyone loves sweets, even Gino Valari. I reach in my pocket for the gums. I've half a mind to break the roll in half, but resist and give him the whole roll. His eyes go wide, and his smile takes over his face. I don't think his parents buy him sweets.

'*Grazie,*' he says, pocketing the fruit gums and walking away. Thanks. It's a strange feeling, pity for your victim, guilt, all that. And I never thought I'd give all my sweets away to an enemy. Maybe he's trying to be a friend. What would I call that? A frenemy. An *Italo-frenemy.*

# Twenty-three

The *fisi* or hyena's Latin name is *Crocuta crocuta*. They superficially resemble dogs, but are more closely related to cats and mongooses. Adults weigh from 80 to 190 pounds. They are powerfully built, with rough, mottled coats and steeply sloping backs caused by an apparent imbalance between their massive forelegs and short rear quarters. This endows them with a strange, menacing, almost comical, loping gait. Their large ears are erect and constantly scanning, and their muzzles broad and dark.

The combination of razor-sharp teeth, and the most crushingly powerful jaws in Africa, enable hyenas to sever a deer's limb with a single bite, or break open bones and access the marrow with ease. They are not only scavengers, but also fierce hunters who kill and devour wildebeest, zebra, buffalo and other large and small animals. They live and hunt in large groups called 'clans'. The relationship of the hyena with man is very old. In ancient Egypt hyenas were even domesticated and bred for food.

There was always reverse predation of man by wild hyenas, which accounts, at least in part, for the rich African folklore which links this creature with the supernatural and witchcraft. The insane 'giggling' or laughter hyenas make when excited, which they also use to alert other members of their clan of a food source, is enough to send shivers down the spine of any superstitious *mutu*. It's a horrible, secret language of the night, in which they celebrate murder most diabolical. In Sukuma folklore, *fisis* are up to their thickset necks in the occult.

'If the *mchawi*, sorcerer or witch, wants to kill you,' Amina says on many frightening occasions round the fire, 'he can change into a *fisi*, and tear you to pieces. . . in the morning they find your pitiful remains, that which he has not devoured, on the ground, and there are *fisi* footprints, even droppings, but the *fisi* himself will be long gone, having changed back into the witch-doctor.'

Sometimes people have followed the fisi's tracks all the way to the *mchawi*'s hut, where they suddenly end. The evil one has taken pieces of his victim into his hut, and they are still there, but no sign of the *fisi* is seen. This is why you must behave.' I tremble. Will I one-day find human parts outside Mlozi's tiny hut? One thing's for sure, I'm not going anywhere near his rock at night.

The stories aren't entirely made up. They're based on the real beliefs of a deeply superstitious and fearful people. I see Amina and Umali shudder, their eyes wide, at the sound of the insane cackle of nocturnal hunting *fisis*. That terrifying sound, and the stories about witchcraft and being eaten, is enough to make Becky and me tremble with fright at the mere mention of this dreaded spectre. Our fear is a tool of discipline to Amina, because she only has to mention *fisi*, and we obey.

The big bad wolf, or monster, of European fairy-tales may strike fear into children, but the *watu* of Geita fear a reality, not a fairy-tale. Umali and Amina, like most *watu*, have their own *shamba*, or farm, 'in the bush', as the *Wazungu* say. There live elderly relatives, tending a patch of maize, a couple of goats, a flock of scrawny chickens. It's ten miles distant as the *kunguru-bird* flies, but accessed only by a tortuous footpath, not a straight crow-path. When, once a month, Umali and Amina go home, they never lack for company.

So pervasive is *fisi*-fear, that nobody ever walks to their *shamba* after nightfall, unless accompanied by several others, and everyone in the party is armed with a *rungu*, a knob-ended fighting stick, or a homemade spear. The *shamba* goers, up to a dozen, assemble at day's end, usually in the garden of our house, because Umali, being who he is, is a natural organiser. The group talks loudly, like excited children, to show they aren't really afraid of the *fisi* at all. If there's a full moon, their path is lit, and we watch them until they disappear into the bush.

On darker nights, at least one person in the party illuminates the way with a torch, or, if there's an underground mine-worker, he walks in front, carbide-helmet-torch on, yellow finger of light weakly probing the path. They are swallowed by the darkness.

Somewhere a *fisi* giggles. Somewhere else another replies. There's silence. Then the crickets start their din, and the invisible frogs go *'reddit, reddit, reddit. . .'* They've red-a-lot. It's spooky here in Geita at night, but I love it dearly. The fear outside makes being safe in the house, with electric lights, the cosiest, best feeling in the world.

When they return from their *shamba* odysseys, Amina and Umali have tales to tell, always starring the *fisi*. It's difficult to separate what's genuine, made-up, or imagined in the darkness of the meandering bush footpath, with spine chilling *fisi*-cackles hastening the travellers on their way. All three are probably true.

'Last night,' Amina says, 'we saw a *fisi* who wore the crocodile-tooth necklace of a *mchawi*.' Wide-eyed look of horror. 'This *fisi* says unless you behave he will come for you.'

*Mchawi*. Lots of *watu* think Mlozi's one. So do I. Does *he* go out at night as a *fisi?* One of Lutoli's friends says he saw a big *fisi* going into Mlozi's hut late one night. Terrifying. It sends tingling feelings up and down my spine. But if he really is a sorcerer, perhaps he can cast a spell for me. He didn't last time, but maybe persistence is needed.

Who knows how a *mchawi* thinks? I won't see him in *fisi*-state, I hope, shuddering at the thought. Sunlight destroys *fisi*-mchawis*, they say, which is why they only hunt by night. I'll go in the day. Put on a brave face. There must be something he wants. I'll get it. Then, maybe, I won't have to go back to school. I decide I'll talk to Mlozi when the courage is with me.

It's May Day 1960. A Sunday. There's a big celebration at the club. All the children are dressed for the occasion. They've put up a Maypole for us to run round, holding bits of coloured ribbon. Before we do that, there's another ritual. The May-Queen. Becky's been chosen. I don't know why. I think she's ugly, but Mum says I shouldn't say so.

Somebody's conspicuously not joining the children. Gretchen. She's over twelve, and thinks she's an adult. She's standing with the ladies, drinking her Pepsi from a glass. It's even got ice in it. She's wearing a dazzling white dress. Her mum made it specially. Her blonde hair has been permed. That's why, Becky says, it's not hanging all over. She's got lipstick on. Red. She really looks like a lady. I hear her talking to Mrs Snel.

'Yes,' she says, sounding oh-so-mature. Then she laughs. It's like crystal glass breaking. I've never thought of a girl's voice being like crystal glass breaking.

I'm standing three yards behind her, wishing I was in the group. But I'm just a kid of nine, whereas she's now a lady. As I watch, her slender hand reaches round, and her fingers furiously scratch her bum. *That's* my Gretchen, I think. Can't leave an itchy bum, no matter what. You're still one of us. One day, you're going to be mine. All mine. One day I'll marry you, and we'll be so happy. It's nauseating to realise I'm in love. But worse not to think about her.

Gretchen can only act the lady sometimes. At heart she hasn't changed. It's a conflict in her. How to play with her friends but be a lady. Sometimes she gives up, reverts to form.

Doctors and nurses. A game with sinister motives. About seeing each other's privates, but pretending there's another *raison d'être*. A child's version of big people's 'coffee' invitation after a party. Medical intervention is no more on the agenda in one than coffee in the other.

We play the game a lot, from when I'm five or younger, because I can't recall the first time. Indeed, supporting this notion is the undoubted fact that the suggestion to play the game never shocks or surprises us. It's as normal to suggest it as hide and seek. We're used to it. It's almost humdrum.

There's no point trying to detail more than one particular game of doctors and nurses, because there's so many. One of the last stands out particularly.


I'm nearly ten and the gang is in Mum's bedroom, on the bed and floor, feeling bored. There's Becky, twelve, Gretchen, thirteen, Dieti, ten, Antonio Barelli, ten and his chaotic baby brother, Stefano, six. Including me, that's seven. Gretchen's more-or-less back to her old self today.

I don't know who suggests we play doctors and nurses, but suspect it's Gretchen. She looks like she's reverted to her former rough and ready appearance and ways since Fraser went back to the navy, and she played the lady at the May-Day party, even if she did scratch her bum. Even so, there's something more adult about her than the rest of us. It isn't just her chest. Today she's got on a loose denim shirt over her swimming costume, so her shape's not obvious anyhow. Everyone agrees doctors and nurses is a good idea. With Gretchen playing, I think it's a *very* good idea. I don't dare imagine what I might see.

There's only one 'doctor' in a game, and everyone else is patient or nurse. There can only be one nurse, so, barring doctor and nurse, five of us will play patient today.

It's blistering hot and we've been down to the pool at the club, where we swam for hours in the tepid water. Nobody's changed back into his or her clothes, so everyone's in a costume. Only Gretchen's wearing a shirt. It's an old one of her dad's. We've walked like that to Barratt stores to buy sweets. Sweets are important for doctors and nurses.

Gretchen announces she's been a patient too many times, so she's doctor today. I vaguely recall being the doctor who examined her last year, or was it the year before? She cheated. Said, 'One-Two-Three, Quick-Look,' and whatever she flashed was gone before I could focus. I'd like a longer look, but can't say so. I give in. Maybe we'll play a second round, with me as doctor.

Stefano's excited. He's only six, and it's his first game. He wants to be first patient. Becky announces she's today's nurse. She doesn't like being examined, or is it that being examined by another girl is meaningless?

Doctor Gretchen and nurse Becky go into the consulting room, which is the bathroom off Mum's bedroom. Stefano's jumping up and down by the closed door, impatient to go in and be a patient.

'Next!' comes the nurse's stern command from within. The door opens, and I briefly see doctor Gretchen sitting on the toilet, Becky's standing beside her. Stefano enters and the door closes. There's a hush in the bedroom. Everyone's straining to hear what's happening.

'Now, what's wrong with you?' we hear Gretchen ask Stefano sweetly.

'Nuffink. . .' we hear Stefano whisper, overawed. He hasn't expected this.

'There must be something,' Becky says.

'Eet eesa my feenger,' Stefano proposes.

'Well, take off your costume,' we hear Gretchen order.

'My. . ?' Stefano says in a strangled voice.

'Pants,' Gretchen finishes for him.

'Off,' orders Becky.

'Now!' barks Gretchen. There's a long silence. 'Take two of these,' we hear her say. The door opens, and out walks Stefano, naked, carrying his bathing shorts in one hand and two Smarties in the other. He looks bewildered.

'Next,' Becky bellows through the door. Nobody moves. The consultations are frightening today.

'Jim, you come in,' Becky shouts, 'it's your turn.' What the hell, I think, why not? Do as must do. Maybe it'll set them an example for later.

'And what's the problem with you today?' Gretchen smiles sweetly from the toilet seat. Her denim shirt's unbuttoned from the midriff up, and I can see her costume. It's a white one, contrasting strongly with her suntan. This is no accident. She was buttoned up when she went in.

'It's me dick,' I sigh, knowing it'll come to that anyway.

'Take off your costume,' Gretchen says. I knew she was going to. I take them down. She has Becky's ruler in her hand. What kind of medical instrument is *that*? She prods my willy with it, and says, 'that doesn't look good at all.' I stand there, waiting for the prescription. 'Take two of these,' she says, handing me two Smarties. The others go in and show their wares. All get the same medicine. Pharmaceutical options are few. Then the girls announce the game's over. There won't be a second round. I'm crushed. They're laughing. We've been fooled again.

Donald Coutts, the bachelor Scotsman, competes with Eugen Blüger's timber business, but unlike Eugen, who has ten lorries, he has only three, and they're older and smaller. He doesn't need much. A single man with frugal tastes, he has no one to support. How much does it cost to stay sozzled on *Johnny Walker Black Label?* He earns enough.

At the club, Donald becomes expansive, and ever more Scottish, when he's had a few 'wee drams'. He's heard from one of his *tunnyboys* that I want a holiday job. The *watu* always know everything I'm thinking.

'Jimmeh,' he says, 'whad ye like ta wurk fur mae?'

'Yes please,' I say. I'm ten, and it's time I earned some money.

'D'ya know what you have to do, as tunnyboy, loon?' I thought that meant lunatic, but I'm reassured it's 'heeland' for *lad*. Of course I know what I have to do. There are six tunnyboys on the back of a lorry. They get the name because they lift 'tuns and tuns' of wood.

'Load wood,' I say.

'Reeght then, I'll pay ye the saime as t'uthers. That's two shilling a day. Start tomorrow. Thae lorry leaves at seven.' He turns back to his drinking friends. I'm dismissed. But I've got a job.

Mum is worried. I'm far too small. The tunnyboys are young men, not little boys. Don't wreck my career, I tell her. Dad would have wanted me to earn for the family, and I'm going to do it. Becky says I won't last the day. Dieti says I should have asked his dad, and I can't trust Donald Coutts. He doesn't like *Scotch* people. Especially *Scotch* people who drink *Scotch*. It's cannibal!

The morning breaks. The sun's shining through where I left the curtains parted last night. Couldn't risk not waking in time. I'm up, dressed in old clothes, and ready to go when the old Bedford lorry creaks into our drive. The driver and young men on the back all know me. *'Kuja,* Jimu,' one shouts. Come, Jimu. I'm helped up onto the back. It's a tipper, has a sloping floor.

The gears grate, and we trundle down the hill, turn left by the club, and rumble along Bottom Road past *kifo nyumba*, the little church and African hospital. Half a mile, and we turn off onto an overgrown bush path, created not by bulldozer or road-machine, but by trucks like this forcing their way. The lorry bucks and undulates over scrubby ground, and we tunnyboys bend and duck as branches sweep inches above our heads. Sometimes we're too late, get hit and scratched. The boys are teenagers, and, despite ragged clothes, are a happy lot. We talk and joke in Swahili.

'You want money?' one asks me, smiling.

*'Ndio,'* I nod.

'To help your mother?' asks another.

'Of course.' They laugh.

'Jimu is small, but he's a real man!' says the first. I'm happy with that. I like my new workmates.

The lorry bundles through low-hanging bush. Then we emerge onto a man-made wilderness. This is where they have been harvesting trees for years, and have created a clearing several miles wide. Only short dead stumps interrupt the barren landscape, and even small bushes don't thrive here.

'Everything's in the trees,' says Obani, the friendliest tunnyboy. 'Everything here is *of* the trees, and when they take them, they kill everything.' It certainly looks that way. The cleared ground is bone dry, and dust rises up to choke us. Man making desert from paradise. We drive over the uneven surface and park at the edge, where tall trees cower and await their fate. It's eerily quiet. Not even a *njiwa*-bird makes its call. It's like they know.

We decamp the lorry. There are three two-handed saws. Six men get to sawing down three tall *maninga* trees. They have incredible strength and energy. I sit on a stump, watching. The driver has orders I'm not to touch the saws. There are some leftover logs lying around, and he tells me to load them. The first one's three foot long, a foot wide. I'm shocked by its weight. Several tunny boys stop sawing to watch me. They laugh at how I struggle. It's almost impossible to lift. I strain, make a huge effort, and heft it, cradled in both arms, up to my belly. It's so heavy I feel the rough bark scratch me through my cotton shirt. I struggle towards the lorry.

The driver engages the tipping mechanism and brings the back down to my height. I'm being watched by seven pairs of eyes. I can't drop it. I'm a man, and I must prove it. I get to the lorry, brace the log against it, and then heave up with all my might. It moves only slowly, and tears through my shirt at the skin on my stomach. It reaches the lip, and I make a final effort. It rolls down and clangs against the steel floor of the tipper. The tunnyboys and driver applaud. I'm breathless, sweating, and my stomach burns like fire. I look down. My shirt is badly torn, and soaked in blood.

'*Hi ni ngumu,*' says Obani. This is hard. 'Sit a little, then take logs small-small.' I sit on a stump, which once was a giant tree. The tree felling goes on. The sun is like a furnace-blast. I know furnaces, because I once stood near the smelter when they opened it. I was almost roasted. The suns burning my neck, and the scratches on my stomach sting. I don't think I like this job.

I get up and look for small logs. Even two-foot ones are

heavy. While living trees groan as they begin their long fall, then crash to the ground with heavy impact, I load small logs. One of the tunnyboys pulls a whipcord and starts a powered saw. It's one they leave out here, covered with canvas. It's on big wheelbarrow wheels, and has a circular toothed blade two foot wide. They push it up against the fallen tree-trunks. It cuts through them with a grating, shrieking noise, hurling wet sawdust and wood fragments in all directions.

Thus the noble trees are reduced to logs. The loud saw stops, and everyone joins in loading the lorry. We've been here for five hours. It's afternoon already. I can tell by the scorching sun. It's time to go. We clamber onto the timber pile and sit where we can. It will be more precarious than before. Raised on top of the logs, we can't duck for cover from passing branches. The driver goes very slowly. After an eternity we reach Bottom Road and turn left towards the weighbridge. I feel sick and I've got a pounding headache. There are sword-fighters in my head again.

By the time we reach the weighbridge, I'm no longer able to concentrate. Obani's worried. '*Pole* Jimu,' he says. Pohl-eh. Take it easy Jimu. 'You'll be home soon.' I faint against his shoulder.

Mum thinks it's cerebral malaria again and she and Umali put me to bed. They dab my forehead with cool, damp cloths. Amina goes for Dr Weiss. 'Sunstroke,' he says, looking at my tomato-red face. 'He vill niffer learn, und *vot* a muzza you are,' he says to Mum.

It takes days to recover. I never work as tunnyboy again. Worse, I'm not paid for my day's work. I should have heeded Dieti. Whisky-swilling Donald Coutts can't be trusted, and I'm not built for hard labour in the tropical sun.

# Twenty-four

In 1960 the talk is of *uhuru*, freedom, for Tanganyika Territory. The British government is grooming Africans to take over from the colonial administration. *Mwalimu*, 'Teacher', Julius Nyerere is leader of the Tanganyika African National Union, or *TANU*, and is tipped to be president.

In Geita, because of its remoteness, plus the absence of television or radio reception, news comes late, and in incomplete or garbled form. The most reliable information comes from English newspapers posted by sea and rail, two months old, and not much concerned with affairs in this insignificant corner of empire. Tanganyika never makes front page, and articles about its future are limited to short, telegrammatic, columns on pages three or four.

The bush telegraph is more effective. Just as the call of *'nyoka'*, snake, lights a bush-fire, magically assembling *watu* to chop the reptile to pieces, the call of *'uhuru'* from Dar-es-Salaam reaches across salient, plain, mountain, forest and lake, to every corner, every village, every hut and every person. Groups of *totos*, or children, from toddlers who can barely walk, to young adults, brandishing paper flags with green, yellow and black stripes, begin to assemble at the workplaces and homes of foreigners, there to dance and sing over and over a new song.

*'Oh-oh-TANU, wa jenga nchi,'* goes the opening line. Oh-oh-*TANU,* of nation building.'

*'TANU,'* a solo voice sings. *'Wa jenga nchi.'* chorus the rest. Of nation building.

*'TANU.'*

*'Wa jenga nchi.'*

When the singing and dancing ends, the leaders abuse and threaten the foreign *Wazungu*, or, at different places, *Wahindi*, Indians, or *Wachina*, Chinese.

'This our country, go home! We will seize your house!' Not our house, I muse, the mine's.

One day Lutoli is with a group of twenty dancing, singing *totos* outside our house. I don't blame him. I know he wants *uhuru*. They sing the *TANU* song of nation building. Mum is at work. Umali, Becky and I sit on the front steps watching the performance. When the song ends, after many repetitions of the chorus, a *toto* of twelve steps forward to demand we leave the country.

'*Apana!*' Lutoli exclaims. No! 'This is Jimu, our friend of long- time. Not like the other *Wazungu.*' Poor Lutoli. He's a patriot, and wants Tanganyika to be free, like he wanted for Kichoncho. He can't let these demonstrations go on without him. Then he encounters this – me, the nearest he's got to a brother, bearing the brunt.

'*Ni kweli.*' It's true, the lad who began to harass us says. Lutoli relaxes. Everyone knows Jimu. When they're gone, Umali turns to me with a worried expression.

'What will your mother do after *uhuru?*' he asks.

'*Sijui,*' I say. I don't know. 'I think we'll stay.'

'*Mungu ata saidia!*' God will help! Will he, I wonder. I've had an on-off relationship with him. More off than on.

'*Allah hafiz,*' I say out of respect for Umali's Islam. God willing. Do they have a different God?

In December 1960 Tanganyika is plunging headlong towards *uhuru* within a year. The British government in Whitehall can't wait to sever their links with the unprofitable colony. *Mwalimu,* or 'teacher', Julius Nyerere is touring every region to make speeches to local branches of *TANU.* His taught before he went into politics. He flies with a small delegation to the mine airfield in Geita in a *de Havilland Dragon Rapide* biplane. A beautiful old thing.

Mr Snel has arranged a welcoming committee. The mine-works close early, and all the Europeans are lined up next to the dry grass runway as the old-fashioned, high-nosed, double-winged, twin-engined aeroplane taxis to a very noisy halt in a cloud of dust and bits of flying grass stubble. It looks like an antique from the First World War. On the side in bold red letters is emblazoned:

*CASPAIR CHARTERS – DAR ES SALAAM*

Mr Snel and a smartly dressed Adrian Venter escort the entourage of five from the plane. The *Wazungu* are dressed in shorts and shirts. The visitors wear bright tribal gowns and skins.

269

We had a lecture about being polite to important guests, even though they're black. I find that very rich, coming from people who talk about animals better than black people. *Mwalimu* Nyerere is a dapper man, only six inches taller than me at the age of nine. He has grey hair, a broad smile, and a friendly manner. He walks along the line of assembled *Wazungu*, fly whisk in hand, and shakes hands with every man, woman and child. When he smiles he shows even white teeth.

After the inspection, he climbs into a police Land Rover which came from the *boma*, and they roar off in a new cloud of dust. Our moment of excitement is over. We remove to the club.

There's a nine-hole golf course beside Lone-Cone club. The first tee is next to the bar, and the ninth hole just across the way. Golfers start and end their game next to the venue of real interest – drinking. Almost all the *Wazungu* men, and several of the women, take up golf. This is in no small part because everyone knows promotions, favours, perks and permissions to go on leave are agreed with John Snel, the mine manager, on the golf course, or in the bar, known as the 'tenth', or 'nineteenth', hole, depending if you go round once or twice.

Geita mine is up on the hillside along Top Road. From there the three parallel connecting roads run down. The club's on Bottom road, where the flat land begins. The golf course is there. Because the area is semi-arid and very hot, it's not possible to cultivate grass to be mown and rolled for a 'green'. They resort to 'browns'. The earth is tossed through a big sieve to remove stones, and then raked smooth. After each game a *bibi*, or 'wife', drags a log around on two ropes to remove shoe-prints and ball-tracks.

The fairways are created by removing trees and cutting the wild grass with a tractor-drawn mower. On the edges the bush remains as before, and continues for many miles every direction. Bordering the golf course it's dense with trees and thornbushes, and inhabited by myriad beasts, birds and insects.

As the sun goes down in the evenings, golf-stragglers are subjected to a cacophony of wild African sounds. Through the background screech of crickets, comes a distant high-pitched giggle of a hyena, the grunt of wild pig, frog croaks from hidden places, and even the bone-jarring roar of a lion. There is tangible relief when the players reach the sanctuary of the bar.

The caddies are African boys aged eight to eighteen. I know all their names, and some are good friends. They're paid a pittance to caddy, but take revenge by 'losing' balls in the rough, then 'discovering' them later. They sell them back to the club. Some balls have changed hands many times.

The caddies also play. They have no manufactured clubs, so they make their own. One design is a length of steel concrete-reinforcing with a right-angle bend three inches from the end. On this short piece a stone is bound on for weight, then sealed with the sticky sap of the blue gum tree. At the top, a rag is wound to form a handle. It's quite amazing how these urchins, with such homemade clubs, hit a ball. It's 1961, and I am ten, when Mr Snel invites the caddies to play against him and four other *Wazungu*.

The caddies wipe the floor with them. Embarrassment. Grown white men, posh equipment and clothing, humiliated by ragged, illiterate child-caddies with homemade clubs. The caddy who beat Mr Snel is Lutoli's cousin. He's only twelve. The invitation is never repeated.

'Tell your little black friends that's the last time they play,' says a scowling Mr Snel to me. I'm with four white kids, but he singles me out. He wasn't this way about black people when *Mwalimu* Nyerere came. The caddies say his attitude just proves he's *blurryfucken*.

With my *rafikis*, friends, I'm a *mutu*, like them. With the *Wazungu*, I'm a *Mzungu* kid. Different things are expected of me. I can't be half-and-half. I'm complete in each role. My mind, loyalties, ways and speech are identical to my *rafikis*, and then I have to snap into *Mzungu*-role for the whites. The roles have to remain separate. There can be no *enosis*, or union, no blending, because there is no middle ground. Except when very young, and even then in a limited way, African and white children don't play together here. African children don't speak English. White children don't speak more than *kitchen-Swahili*.

I am unable to use one set of thought and language in the other setting. I'm constantly at risk of 'too much blackness' or 'too much whiteness', depending who I'm with. It won't do to 'moderate', because then I'll be less adroit in both settings. The problem is I also share both groups' ideas and prejudices. As a Swahili, I despise *Wazungu*. If I don't, I'm a sellout. As a *Mzungu* I despise *watu*. If I don't, I'm a 'savage'. How's that, love and hate for the same people?

I'm becoming not just a hypocrite, but the very embodiment of one. Both my peer groups are constantly amazed at what a chameleon or *kinyonga* I am.

'I don't know how you do it,' Lutoli says. 'One second, ours, next second theirs.' Another day he says 'Jimu, you are a black person in the skin of a white!' Multiple personality, here I come....

The *Wazungu* kids play on the golf course too. There, we discover, during the day when the big people are at work, is a great feeling of tranquillity and freedom. We don't have to limit ourselves to golf. We play tab, and hide and seek, which means skulking behind bushes next to the fairway. Or else we just walk and talk, feeling in that wide place we are the only people on earth.

One day I walk with Lutoli, George Hunt and Sandy on the fairway of the third hole. George is nine, like me. His parents came to Geita with him and older brother Percy a year ago. They're from York. He's a rogue, and always up to something. Unlike me, he has a fierce father to protect him. It's always safe to blame Jimmy. Since Percy and George came I've been blamed for more things than ever. The Hunt family speak in a thick Yorkshire accent which I find difficult to comprehend.

We come to a dense copse of trees, where the real bush begins. Sandy stops dead like a midget Pointer, her nose pointing one way and her tail the other. Who knows what she's inherited in her *Shenzi* lineage? From deep in her throat comes a low, grumbling growl. As we stare, we see something remarkable.

It's a little man, just four foot tall, with snow-white hair and beard and wrinkled mahogany skin. He's dressed in animal skins. Above his waist, up to his chin, he wears a zebra pelt, the black and white stripes matching the patterns of sunlit ground and shadow all around. Below his waist he wears just a furred leather moochi, attached by a leather thong between his legs and round his waist. As George delicately whispers, 'ya can see 'is whole loonch-box from t' side.' In one hand he holds a *gabori*, a homemade flintlock rifle, taller than himself. Over his shoulder is slung an animal horn with gunpowder.

*Gabori* is the Swahili name for muzzle-loading guns. The tribes round Lake Victoria made copies of Arab *jazails*, brought to the region by slave traders in the eighteenth century. They even carved some of the Arabic designs on the stocks, though they had no clue what they meant. By now such guns have almost disappeared. But there are people who still make and hunt with them. The mysterious 'pygmy' tribes who live in the jungle. They hold a great mystique to their larger, village-living brethren, who believe the small people have powerful witchcraft, and can cast devastating *dua*, or spells, on their enemies.

'It's alright, Sandy,' I say to my growling little canine. She stops and wags her tail. Sandy has a lovely nature. If it's okay with me, it's okay with her.

The little man speaks no Swahili, and we have no idea what his language is. But he doesn't seem afraid, and doesn't run away when we approach him. We communicate with smiles and hand signs. He seems pleased to encounter us. With strange and convoluted gestures, he tells us he was hunting all day, but has not been fortunate. It's a long way to his home, deep in the bush, and he's setting out now. He points to the south with his *gabori*. Somewhere Bushirondo way, to us the great unknown. European explorers had a habit of disappearing out there years ago. I ask if I can examine his gun, by pointing and grinning. He hands it to me.

This *gabori* is an amazing blend of art and cunning. The barrel is a length of one-inch water pipe. Where he found that, I have no clue. One end is sealed, welded closed by being bent and beaten over a fire. The stock is of carved *maninga* wood, smoothed by rubbing with powdered stone. There are three steel hosepipe-clips holding the barrel in place. On the side of the barrel next to the stock is a depression, with a small hole. The flintlock mechanism is formed from beaten iron nails, and a tight bend holds a fragment of white flint.

I return the *gabori* to the pygmy, and make gestures of shooting. I have to see if it works. He grins hugely, and unslings the buckhorn from his shoulder. He shows us its contents by removing a wooden stopper. It's a dark grey, with the gunpowder smell of exploded fireworks. Umali tells me the pygmies make their gunpowder from ingredients they find in the bush.

The little man pours powder into the end of the *gabori*'s barrel. Then he inserts a wad of dry leaves, and rams it in with a long, thin stick. He produces a leather pouch, much like his immodest moochi, and unties a thong at the top. He withdraws a steel ball- bearing an inch in size. Where he got them I can't fathom. He drops it into the barrel, and follows it with another leaf-wad. He carefully prods the barrel. He holds the *gabori* in one hand and pulls back the 'hammer', which holds the flint. He trickles powder into the depression, then replaces the horn over his shoulder. He points at a baby tree thirty yards away, and motions for George and I to stand aside. He sights his *gabori*.

There's a loud click, a brief pause, and an ear-piercing blast. The little man disappears in a cloud of black smoke. Before it clears we race to the target-tree, though Sandy, scared witless, bolts for the bush. The tree, five foot high and three inches wide, is cut in half. We turn to congratulate the shooter, but he's gone. Sandy emerges, ears down, from behind a thornbush.

'What the *fook* was that?' says George.

# Twenty-five

A month later George steals a box of a hundred 0.22 bullets from his father.

'Won't he find out?' I ask. The box is labelled *'BSA 0.22 calibre'*. The bullets inside have shiny brass cartridges.

'Ee don't nauw owt,' George says, 'ees allus too droonk.' George is never complimentary about his dad. He isn't wrong, though. I've seen Mr Hunt staggering out the club. Mrs Hunt too.

'What we going to do with them?' I say.

'Mak a goon,' George says, 'an' shoot summat WI' it, *ka-boom!'* He makes a pistol of thumb and index finger, and grins. A gun. A good idea. But how? Bullets go off when they're hit on the back of the cartridge by a firing pin. Everyone knows that. The bullets have a little red dot in the middle of the cartridge base where they have to be struck. First, though, we'll have a bit of sport. Fire sets off bullet, doesn't it?

We find a fire. The *watu* always burn the *majani*, or grass, before planting. Distant smoke tells us where to go. It's up on the left side of Compound Hill, where the slope is gentle, and the *watu* grow *mahogo*, or cassava. We creep up on the burning slope, careful not to be spotted by the ragged fire-tenders, who surround and beat out errant flames with bundles of green twigs and leaves. They don't want to burn their compound.

From behind a big tree, George hurls a handful of live bullets into the flames. Nothing happens. Seconds tick by. Then suddenly, we're in the middle of a shooting gallery, bullets popping off and whizzing everywhere, including at us. One, George swears, parts his hair. We, in one direction, the fire-tenders in another, bolt for our lives. The poor *watu* must think they've awoken the *djinns* of the fire, if not *Shetani* himself.

At home, we decide we must use the ammunition more conventionally. We must make a gun.

'Let's start with a barrel,' I say.

'What'll weh use?'

'Water-pipe,' I say, remembering the pygmy *gabori*. 'We need one the same diameter.'

'Diam – a what?' Sometimes George seems a sniff short of a cold.

'Width,' I say. He nods.

'Whah'll wa get woon?' he asks.

'Engineering dump,' I say. That's where we find everything, even the steel helmets. All the scrap is there. I've seen a pile of off-cut water pipe.

We poke around the rusty pile.

'What 'boot this woon?' George asks, pulling out a piece of pipe with a two-inch diameter. The bullets are only quarter inch. Poor George. . . has he *any* idea at all?

'This one would be better,' I say, finding a thinner piece. Quarter inch. I drop a bullet in the end. The rim stops it falling through. Perfect.

Just then Jaswan Singh comes out from the workshop. A friendly old *Singa-Singa*, or Sikh, who always wears an immaculately wrapped maroon turban. Anand Singh's uncle. He's a fitter and turner in the workshop. He's helped me choose things from the scrap pile before.

'What you looking ?' he asks in Swahili. One thing about Geita *Singa-Singas* – they're all fluent. Unlike most Europeans.

*'Chuma,'* I say. Iron.

*'Hio?'* That one? He points at the pipe in my hand.

*'Ndio.'* Yes. I decide to press my luck. 'Please cut it for me.'

*'Wapi?'* he asks, taking the pipe. Where?

'What youse sayin'?' George asks.

'Shurrup,' I say.

*'Hapa,'* I tell Jaswan. Here. The pipe is three foot long. Needs a foot off.

*'Mimi itabidi ukate,'* Jaswan says, turning and going back into the workshop. I'll cut it. *'Kuja,'* he adds over his shoulder. Come. We follow. He puts the pipe in a vice, and saws it with practised ease. The unwanted end falls off.

*'Na sasa?'* Jaswan asks. And now?

'Please cut here too,' I ask, pressing my advantage. This is very labour saving. I show him where I want a slot, four inches from one end. For the chamber, where the bullet will go.

*'Je, ni wewe kufanya?'* Jaswan asks. You, what are you making? His smile is tinged with suspicion. *'Bunduki, labda?'* A gun, maybe?

*'Apana,'* I say. No. Lying is easy when there's a higher

purpose. Jaswan sets to cutting the slot with a jigsaw and a grin. This bit of cutting is complicated. Two parallel cuts halfway go through the pipe, then a longer cut joins them, and half the diameter is removed. We could never have done this without Jaswan.

'*Chukua hio,*' he says at last. Take it. He jokes that I shouldn't shoot anyone. He *knows* it's a gun. He is such a nice old man.

'*Asante sana,*' I say, taking the pipe. Thanks a lot. Jaswan has done the hardest part for us. We walk back to the camp.

'Ya spehk Uffricun real gud,' George says.

'And you don't,' I reply.

'Ah don' wanna spehk blurry Uffricun,' he spits, 'it's munkeh-talk!' I stop and grab his shirt collar. I pull his face close. He pales.

'Don't ever say that again,' I breathe.

'Okeh, keep yoor blurry hair on,' he stammers. I let go his collar. We walk in silence. Why do English people, even those new out from Yorkshire, think so badly of the *watu?* A constant problem for me. I'm between both. Neither European nor African. I don't want to hate either, though, in a way, both expect it.

'Come to my place tomorrow,' I growl when we come to where our paths fork, 'we can start work.'

'Yoor plehse?' He looks relieved we're still in business.

'Yup. I've got other things we need.'

'Okay. I'll cum t' yoor plehse,' he says.

At home Umali is curious about the piece of iron pipe. '*Je, Jimu, ni wewe kufanya?*' he asks. Jimu, what are you making?'

'We're just playing,' I reply. Last thing I want is Umali to twig.

'This is not for playing,' he says, clicking his tongue. 'You are building a gun!' He's holding the barrel up, squinting through it. There's nothing for it. I have to admit the truth, persuade him not to tell Mum.

'*Ndio,*' I say. 'Yes, yes, it's a gun. Please don't tell Mama.'

'*Wewe!*' Umali says, shaking his head. You! 'You are not afraid of the danger of a gun. You think bullets will just turn to water?'

*'Maji?'* I ask. Water? What's he talking about?

'The *Maji-Maji* 'water-water' rebellion against the Germans long ago.' I remember something about it. It was before the First World War. Between 1905 and 1907. I ask Umali to tell me.

A spirit medium called Kinjikitile Ngwale claimed he was possessed by a snake-spirit called Hongo. He changed his name to Bokero, and announced to the people that, by the use of *maji*, water, mixed with castor oil and millet seeds, the bullets of the German occupiers would be magically turned into water.

Confident it would happen, Bokero's followers, known as the *Maji-Maji*, hurled themselves at the Germans, who mowed them down in great numbers. Altogether, hundreds of Germans and close to three hundred thousand *watu* were killed, before the cry of *'Maji-Maji ni wongo!'* the *Maji-Maji* is a lie, spread through the country. The rebellion collapsed.

'No,' I say at last. 'I don't think this way.'

*'Pole pole,* Jimu,' he says, smiling wearily. Slowly-slowly, Jimu. This means be careful. 'I haven't forgotten your father's gun.' When I shot God. He'll never forget. But he's smiling. He won't snitch to Mum.

Next day George is there nice and early. I place our gun-barrel on the kitchen table.

'Hoo'll weh fire it?' George asks.

'With a nail,' I say.

'A nayle?' he asks, bewildered.

'Yup, but first we have to make a stock.'

'A fookin stock, whah's 'at?'

'The wooden bit,' I say. I've found a plank under the house. No clue how it got there. I put it beside the barrel, and draw the outline of rifle butt and stock. 'Here,' I say, giving him a saw. 'Cut out along the pencil mark.'

'Okeh,' he says, pleased to have 'summat' to do. I leave him to it, and go in search of hosepipe clamps. The ones used to hold a water hose on a tap. I've seen some rusty ones on the rubbish outside the mill. By the time I return, two clamps in hand, George has finished cutting. A reasonable job.

'Now,' I say, 'we make a groove for the barrel.' After two hours working with a small, rusty chisel and hammer, we've excavated a long hollow on the top of the stock. We sandpaper it smooth. With the hosepipe clips or clamps, we secure the barrel into the slot. It begins to look gun-like.

'What nayle we gonna use?' George asks.

'This one,' I say, producing my work of the previous evening. It's a six-inch nail, bent at ninety degrees two inches from the head. I've filed the end to a sharp point. Bolt and hammer in one piece. I slot the long pointed end into the back of our barrel. When it's in as far as it'll go, the point reaches where the back of the cartridge will be.

'How'd we mak it gaw?' George asks.

'With rubber,' I say, 'a strip of inner tube rubber, and a nail.'

'Anoother fookin nayle?' George exclaims.

'Like this,' I say, driving a two-inch nail into the front of the stock. I retrieve a rubber strip from my pocket. Leftover from catapult making. I attach one end to the hammer-nail, the other to the nail on the stock. I pull the hammer-nail back, then release. It springs smartly forward. It will strike the cartridge hard. I cut a groove in the stock, where the hammer-nail, under tension, can recess. This is our trigger. A flick of the thumb will fire the gun.

We're in the front garden, six yards from the big tree. I'm holding our gun, aiming at the broadest part of the trunk. This isn't an accuracy test, which can come later. Beside me, wildly excited, is George, who lost the coin-toss to be first shooter. On my other side is Sandy. Behind us, excited too, but filled with trepidation, are Becky, Gretchen, Dieti and Lutoli. Is our homemade gun going to work?

I prise the bent-nail bolt slowly upwards from its deep recess. Nothing happens. I increase the force. It moves a bit more. I apply more pressure, and suddenly it jerks forward on its stretched rubber spring. There's a sharp crack as the point strikes the back of the bullet, and smoke pours out the chamber and barrel. Sandy yelps and runs away. Everybody dashes to the tree to check the damage.

Our little *0.22* bullet has wobbled about in the ill-fitting, smooth-bored water pipe, and, on emerging, turned completely sideways. It's hit the tree horizontally, side-on, instead of with its point. All it's done is half-bury itself in the bark, and I easily dig it out with a penknife. The hard, white wood under the bark is unmarked. I feel crushing disappointment. All this effort, and we can't even penetrate a tree!

We try twice more, with the same result. It becomes apparent that our gun is also wildly inaccurate. Aiming at one tree from ten yards, I hit another two yards to the side. Our *bunduki*, or gun, project is a singular and humiliating failure. Disaster is complete when, hearing the shots, George's father, who happens to be in earshot, arrives and confiscates our invention, at the same time getting most of his bullets back. We've thrown eight in the fire and fired only three from our gun. He drags George away by the ear.

Umali is relieved. He hasn't told Mum what George and I were making, but he's been tormented with anxiety. *'Sikuweza kulala usiku,'* he says, beaming happily, despite my grumpiness. I didn't sleep at night. *'Risasi sio maji, Jimu!'* Bullets are not water, Jimu. May as well have been, I muse angrily, the way that stupid bullet turned side-on to the tree! In a curious way I am forever linked to Bokero and his *Maji-Maji* warriors.

# Twenty-six

Ninth of December 1961. *Uhuru*. At precisely midnight, Tanganyika Territory will gain independence and be just 'Tanganyika'.

Far away in Dar-es-Salaam Sir Richard Turnbull, the last British Governor, is preparing for a formal handover of power to the new Government under *TANU* and *Mwalimu* Julius Nyerere. The symbolic guard for the hauling down of the *Union Jack* will be provided by a contingent of sailors from *HMS Belfast*, World War 11 heavy cruiser of the Royal Navy. It'll be a brief ceremony, then Sir Richard, carrying the folded flag, will board *Belfast*, and sail away forever. The newest member of the United Nations will be born. In a dozen places across the huge country, smaller ceremonies are about to commence.

In Geita we assemble at eleven pm on the edge of the dusty parade ground at the *boma*. A detachment of two hundred King's African Rifles, complete with military band, marches up and down, rifles sloped and gleaming bayonets fixed. The *askaris* wear khaki shorts and shirts, brown leather belts and boots, tightly wound puttees and red fezzes. They look very smart, and they're perfectly in step.

Contrasting with the khaki uniforms of their men, the four white British officers are dressed in full-length regimental whites, complete with corded revolvers in holsters and glistening white pith helmets. The European expatriates look on glumly. The minute hand on the big clock moves inexorably towards that which they dread.

The *Union Jack* on the flagpole flutters tiredly in the light breeze. Does it know the empire-game is up? The marching band comes to a halt, while *askaris* wheel around at the far end of the parade ground, white officer strutting peacock-like in front. On the small wooden platform next to the flagpole another white officer stares fixedly at the flag. To his right is the retiring District Commissioner. To his left is a small African man with white hair. Not unlike Nyerere himself. New *DC*. Just behind these notables are wives and children, black and white, all dressed for the occasion. Standing at attention beside the flagpole are two immaculately turned out *askaris*.

The minute hand on the clock approaches its zenith. The bandmaster brandishes his stick, and the band begins to play *God Save The Queen*. Not *Gorde Sieve Our Greasious Quinn*. I still prefer Jackson's version. Suddenly there's a crackling sound, followed by ear-shattering bangs, as fireworks erupt in riotous colour into the sky. It is midnight.

The sky is lit by catherine wheels and rockets, trailing pink, orange and red light. The band breaks into a different tune. *Mungu Ibariki Afrika*. God Bless Africa. The two *askaris* by the flagpole are lowering the Union Jack. In its place they raise a new flag. It's got two broad green stripes at top and bottom. In the middle is a black stripe, separated from the green by two thin gold, or yellow, ones. Green represents land, black the people, and gold the country's mineral resources. The breeze blows stronger, and *this* flag flies with a flourish. *Mungu?* God?

The *askaris* fold the Union Jack into a tight triangular shape. They must have rehearsed this over and over. A very tall one takes it and marches stiffly to the podium. He continues up the three steps, comes to a halt in front of the white officer, stamps his foot mightily, and hands the triangle to the *Muzungu*. He takes it and salutes. The *askari* salutes back, about turns, and marches to stand beside the flagpole. It's over. Tanganyika is British no more.

Tribal dancers erupt onto the ground, the shrill ululating of women drowning out the second verse of the anthem, *Mungu Ibariki Tanganyika*. Several European women are weeping openly. On the podium the ex and new District Commissioners are shaking hands. From this minute the *askaris* and their officers are no longer King's African Rifles. Now they are in the Tanganyika army. They're standing at attention. The officer in front has his white pith helmet in his hand. He's raising it and shouting something, but we can't hear what. Must be 'Hip-Hip-Hooray!' The *askaris* take their fezzes off as one, and raise them in salute. They've practised *this* too.

How strange, I think. Tribal warriors, then *Schutztruppe* in the First World War, then *KAR*, fighting for Britain, far from their own country, now Tanganyika army. How many different things they've had to learn. I wonder how long the white officers will be allowed to stay.

This is it, then, I muse. I'm ten and a half, and I no longer live in a British colony. What is going to happen to us now? I look at the gleeful, whirling dancers, then at the sad faces of the *Wazungu*, my *Wazungu*, because I'm white like them. I've heard several say they won't stay. Can't live under 'them'. Am I the same? Do I want to go away too? I look at the dancing *watu*, the beaming faces of the smart *askaris*.

I think of Umali and Amina, who are not here. Lutoli, Kaiser, Tembo. No. I don't want to go. I belong here. These *watu* are my *watu*. I know them better than I know the *Wazungu*. I've had more kindness, more happiness with them. The *Wazungu* don't even speak their language. How can they expect to understand, or like, people if they don't know their language? I'll stay, I won't go.

It is strange how even momentous historical events come and go, leaving little trace. Like water closes over a thrown rock. For a few days there's nothing else than *uhuru* on everyone's mind. Then the reality of hot, sweltering days, the burning sun, the relief of evening coolness, and everything which was before, reinstates itself, is once again most important, and life moves on. Geita never felt governed by the British, and it doesn't suddenly feel governed by the new rulers in Dar.

Nothing has changed in the months since *uhuru*, except the sign outside Lone Cone Club. It used to say *'Whites Only'*. Now it says *'Members Only'*. I believe they've made the new black *DC* and his wife members. Where does that put Higgs's *bibi?* Nobody's saying.

We continue our efforts to escape boredom. When we don't feel like getting really dirty and 'running wild' with our African friends, we're stuck with each other, and there's nothing to do. At such times we have to use our imaginations. Of course, there's the big swimming pool at the club, and the weather is always hot. But there's a limit to how much you can swim, or play in a pool. There are reptiles and birds to tease, but even that has its limits.

New ideas are continually sought. Some end up as plans to do something, like building a go-cart out of an old pram, or making bows and arrows from small tree branches, and hunting anything that moves. Some ideas are just that, ideas, not acted upon. We think about things, discuss them, and develop new ideas.

The international collection of *jambas* is an example. It's one of those monsoon days when the rain comes down in drops the size of pomegranates and the corrugated-iron roof resounds to the torrential impact with deafening noise.

How many nationalities are there on the mine? Italians, Germans, English, French, Jewish, Cornish, Scots, Chinese, Indians, Africans of different tribes. . . All, we decide, must have something particular and related to race in the gas they emit from their backsides. We should, we decide, creep up behind individuals who look like they're going to emit, and 'catch' it in a paper bag. *'Jamba'* is Swahili for fart. The words 'international' and 'chase' speak for themselves.

We hypothesise on the subject at great length and in great detail. German *jambas*, we feel, will have something sharp, acrid and toxic about them, Germans being, by consent of Dieti and Gretchen, military people who can make explosives very well. Italians, being cowards to a man (or woman) will have softer, more fragrant, perhaps tomato-tinged, *jambas*. Scots *jambas* will be mean, short, sharp, and lacking in body. English ones must be honest, roast-beef flavoured, and loudly delivered. Indians' will smell of curry and chillies, and come out wailing, like their music. We aren't too sure about the others. However, careful catching, sniffing and comparison will shed light.

In the future, confusion, even anger, occurs among adult attendees of Lone Cone Club, when certain children invade their rear-body space, holding open paper bags pointedly close to their backsides.

It's 1962, and Geita is invaded by cowboys. There's a company based in Nairobi called *Airspray Limited*. They spray insecticide from specially adapted aeroplanes on crops all over East Africa. The gigantic cotton plantations to the west and south of Geita, some which measure their land in tens of square miles, have decided the future of pest-control in their fields is from the air. *Airspray* send out a team.

A ground crew with two long-wheelbase Land Rovers towing trailers, leaves Nairobi and heads for northwestern Tanganyika.

On board are support workers, including an engineer and pest-expert. There have a store of dry chemicals to be mixed with water for spraying. They also have spare parts for the plane and the Rovers, because there aren't any out here. It takes the ground crew three days to reach Geita. In the whole district there's only one club, or large group of *expats*, and that's Geita mine. Everyone's delighted when the travellers roar out of the bush and announce they'll be camping beside the club for a week. Visitors are scarce and very welcome.

Sven Edmündsen is engineer and crew-boss. A huge, powerfully built, red-haired, wild-bearded man in his forties, he's Sweden's answer to the great macho man of Africa. In Nairobi he has a grand house, a pretty Italian wife, two children in expensive private schools, and a white gull-wing 1955 *Mercedes-Benz 300SL* sports car. In the bush he's a heavy drinking, rabble-rousing, dictator over crew and pilot. Provided he's obeyed, he's got an uproarious sense of humour, and is a man others like to be around.

They set up camp on open ground near the club. They pitch a huge bell tent for stores and three smaller ones for quarters. Their two Kikuyu labourers share one, Sven has one, and the pilot and pest-*fundi* share the third. On his shortwave radio Sven contacts base in Nairobi and tells his pilot to come.

What took the terrestrial crew three days takes the pilot four hours. Suddenly overhead from out of the heat-shimmered sky is the reverberating throb of a 235 horsepower *Lycoming*, flat four, 0-540 six cylinder aerial engine. Until then I haven't encountered such raw aeroplane engine-power. The noise bounces off the surrounding hills and echoes down the valley, until there's nothing else in the world.

Everyone stops to stare at the bellowing midget in the sky. This is the *Piper Pawnee* the ground crew told us is coming from Nairobi. *Piper* name all their planes after North American Indian tribes. The pilot is Eric Butler, a young befreckled Rhodesian from 'Down South'. He's every bit as wild as his boss, Sven, but he's got the controls of the plane, and he's determined to show us.

'Get your fat arse down here!' Sven yells into the microphone.

'In due course,' Eric's voice crackles from Sven's speaker, as the *Pawnee* rockets past, just ten feet from the ground, before turning on its tail and shooting skywards, corkscrewing as it climbs. It's so powerful it stands on its tail, defying gravity. He levels out at five hundred feet, roars round the very edge of Compound hill, an angry insect with a deafening voice. Geita has been woken.

Eventually the *Pawnee* lands. By then we've run the half-mile to the landing strip. Sven and Eric have a good-humoured row, and everyone repairs to the bar of Lone Cone Club. There's serious business at hand. The business of drinking.

When the visitors and their hosts are quite merry, Eric decides the time has come to take the children for a ride in the *Pawnee*. He's a good flier when sober, he says, but better when 'oiled'. It's throttle *after* bottle for him. We're queuing up, and I'm at the front. Behind me are Dieti, Andrew, Antonio, Becky, Sophia and Gretchen. To no avail. Eric calls the big girls first. Gretchen, Becky and Sophia.

The *Pawnee* is a unique aircraft. It's small, but immensely strong, built to withstand rough treatment, collisions with small trees, bumpy landings, short runways, and any weather. Her cockpit is a little, upright, glass enclosure, halfway down the fuselage, designed to give the pilot all-round visibility in the air. The huge *Lycoming* engine gives the plane a power-to-weight ratio no other commercially built aircraft can match.

On the ground the *Pawnee* stands with her nose pointing skywards. The runway in front can't be seen from the cockpit until the tail comes up on the take-off run. 'Till then the pilot steers by looking out one side, staying parallel to the runway edge. There's only a single seat, so we have to go one at a time, half-standing, half-sitting on the radio beside Eric. This is particularly difficult for the big girls, but Eric doesn't mind. I do. I don't like Gretchen sitting so close to him, her legs bent over his knees. He starts the engine, and without ado opens the throttle.

The hugely powerful engine hurls the plane round in its own length, throwing up an impenetrable cloud of dust, to stand facing upwind. Then it's hurtling across the flattened scrubland, and seconds later shooting impossibly into the sky. I'm glad to see Gretchen still alive after they land.

Eventually it's my turn. The raw power of the plane is like riding on the back of a buffalo gone berserk, the g-force tugging at cheeks, neck and back. There's hardly time for fright. We're rocketing across the sky towards the hillside. Through the blur of the hurtling propeller I make out individual trees and rocks. Unless we turn, we're going in. At the last moment Eric tugs the stick to his left and stabs the opposite rudder. The Pawnee yaws, banks and turns, the hillside slipping past just inches from our wingtip.

Eric's laughing like a maniac. 'Like that?' he yells above the crescendo of the engine.

'Yes,' I lie. Will I ever get back on the ground alive is all I'm thinking. Soon, miraculously, I do. I watch as others take their joyride. There's a common factor. Each is paler after their flip with Eric. Even Lutoli. He's terrified, and it takes a lot of persuasion getting him into the cockpit. When he gets out, he is violently ill. *'Mimi si kwenda huko tena!'* he exclaims when he's stopped vomiting. I won't go up there again! Later he tells me that, whereas before he always believed hell and damnation was deep underground, he now realises it's in the sky, and *Shetani*, the Devil, is a freckled *Mzungu* pilot. He doesn't like him. He's *blurryfucken!*

I, on the other hand, have huge respect for Eric. He goes spraying cotton every day, after drinking all night. He flies out at sun-up to land on strips of dirt road where the crew have flattened grass and bush on the sides, fills up with chemicals, takes off, sprays cotton, lands, refills, takes off six or more times, before heading back to the airstrip just ahead of sunset. He constantly jokes about his job.

'Watch thine airspeed,' he laughs, 'for the earth shall rise up and smite thee!' It's an old saying from WWI Royal Flying Corps days, but he faces danger daily, and it never fazes him. Sometimes he spots *suckers* on the golf course, and, being Eric, 'buzzes' them. This includes charging straight at them at full throttle, six feet off the ground, turning through ninety degrees to pass between trees, levelling, causing the golfers to hurl themselves flat and pray. He roars overhead, in touching range, then rockets skyward, barrel rolling on the way.

When he lands, the crew extracts bits of cotton-plants from spray-pipes on the trailing edge of the wings. Spray-pilots in East Africa have died flying into concrete-hard anthills. The ants here build mounds four, even five, feet high. They can't be seen for vegetation. Meeting one at a hundred miles an hour is a hell of a way to find it. Eric lives a charmed life.

The *Selekali*, or police, Land Rover screams into the club drive and brakes in a shower of small stones and a cloud of red dust. The government police from the *boma* always arrive like that nowadays. They've become very confident. The Rover has hardly stopped when the passenger door flies open, and a tall young *askari* in khaki uniform and bright epaulettes jumps down. He stalks to where Kaizer and I sit on the low wall.

*'Ambapo ni Mzungu ya ndege?'* he commands, addressing Kaizer, who until then was enjoying an icy *Whitecap* while watching red ants carry potato-crisp fragments up a crack in the cement wall. How should he know where the *Mzungu* of the bird is? And he doesn't like the look, or tone, of this *askari*, three, even four, decades his junior. It's Sunday afternoon, and he's enjoying sitting here, not being harassed. Maybe the pilot from Kenya is in the bar. Probably is.

*'Ndani,'* he says laconically, and as disrespectfully as possible. Inside.The *askari* snorts derisively, then strides round the back of the Rover. He opens the door. Two very drunk and sheepish Kikuyus get out, looking scared. They are the Airspray Ltd labourers.

*'Ngoja!'* the *askari* shouts, before heading into the club. We don't have long to wait. Two minutes later he emerges with a bemused Sven Edmündsen and Eric in tow.

'These Kikuyus,' the *askari* announces in broken English, 'is your!' The Kikuyus look apprehensive. One has a big lump and a cut on his forehead.

'Yes. . .' says Sven.

'Drink *moshi* making by criminal!' says the *askari*.

'Solly *Bwana!'* the injured man whispers.

'This time, this time. . . they go. Not allow Kenya Kikuyus running here-wild!' admonishes the *askari*. Sven and Eric nod. They're getting off lightly. Through the side window of the Land Rover I see there's someone else in the back. I get up and walk around. The door's still open.

Sitting on the raised mudguard, with handcuffs on and a huge steel dustbin-still between his knees, is someone I recognise at once. It's Moses' brother, Iwe. He stares at me ruefully. *'Jambo* Iwe,' I say. He looks very sorry for himself. 'I didn't got the line-sense,' he explains.

There's another regular, and very dashing, visitor to the mine. Otto Müller has a good-looking, blue-eyed, blond son called Werner. Gretchen's cousin. In 1962 he's fifteen, and already six foot tall. He's at school in Mwanza, and goes there by boat from Lotanga every weekday morning. The hard-working ferryboat *Lotanga*, which Dad, Umali and Wait sailed from Kampala in Uganda all those years ago. On weekends Werner helps Otto with his farming business. One of the tasks Otto gives him is to drive to Geita mine and sell farm produce to the employees.

There was once an elderly Volkswagen Beetle on the farm, but Werner, learning to drive on a winding dirt road near Lotanga, rolled it down the side of a precipice. The body was trashed, but the chassis, engine, gearbox and wheels survived. Otto and Werner cut the bodywork away, in front leaving an exposed driver's seat, gear lever, clutch, accelerator and brake-pedal. Behind that they built a raised wooden-sided box to load goods.

Every Friday, early in the evening, Werner roars into town in his ramshackle vehicle. He goes straight to the club, where his arrival is heralded by his engine's noise, and everyone comes dashing out to seize a share of the fresh, high-quality produce of Lotanga. Legs of pork and lamb, home-cured bacon, cartons of fresh frozen milk, still cold after sixty miles of hot road, bunches of carrots, cabbages, runner-beans, onions in netting, and other things not otherwise seen in Geita. Lotanga is much more fertile, has more water, and is run by a proper farmer. The prices are high, but nobody cares.

When his load is sold, which only takes minutes, Werner goes in to the club with his customers. He's only fifteen, but this is Geita, Tanganyika. When a boy is big enough, he's big enough. Nobody minds, except perhaps his father, who is far away in Lotanga, that he drinks some of the profits in beer. Werner is popular and always surrounded by adult club members, who ask after his parents, Lotanga, and how things are going in Mwanza. After all, although everyone gets trips with Fritz, they don't see Mwanza more than once in three or four months.

There are two others who show great interest in the dashing young man-in-a-go-cart. Gretchen, his second cousin, and Becky, my sister, are both fourteen, and it's apparent they like him. To my relief, and proving his lack of taste, Werner prefers Becky to Gretchen, and I'm able to breathe again. But it isn't all rosy for me. Mum is protective of her daughter's virtue, and I'm given the task of shadowing Becky if she goes anywhere with Werner.

There follow boring hours of sitting outside the club, near the pool, watching them hold hands and sometimes kiss. Werner sleeps over at the Blüger's house, and Becky is forbidden to go there during those times. I see to it she doesn't sneak away when nobody's looking. I don't endear myself to the young sweethearts, but Mum is pleased with my surveillance work. I will have more of this to come.

Before Becky and Werner can get too serious, long leave to England beckons. I don't want to go because I want to be with Gretchen. I know I'm in love with her because I can't get her out of my mind, and when she's close I feel so full in my chest, like it's going to burst. At night in bed I've stopped imagining I'm in my little enclosed canoe on the wild ocean.

Inspired by movies where the hero dies slowly and in agony while a beautiful woman laments at his bedside, I nightly live and relive a tragic and drawn-out scene of my own death, after fighting bravely to save Gretchen and suffering a terrible wound. Gretchen, who too-late realises she loves only me, is weeping and sobbing by my side, but still looks ethereal and beautiful. Sometimes she wears a T-shirt and jeans, sometimes a dress, but she's always Gretchen, my one and only love. My love is pure, and I don't demean it by letting a kiss, let alone other things, enter the script.

'Please don't die,' she whispers in my ear, her hand gently brushing my forehead. But it's too late. There's nothing anyone can do. I feel the death rattle in my throat. Like those cowboys who wait till their lady is there before they expire.

'I love you,' I manage to gasp with my last breath.
'I know you do,' she says. 'I love you too. . !' Death has always been around me. Now I'm in love with dying, just so long as Gretchen is there. How easily Freud's *libido* turns to *Thanatos*.

# Twenty-seven

Six times there are man-eating lion scares. Lions don't normally prey on humans. Men and their weapons are far too dangerous. Like many wild, but sentient and intelligent creatures, lions avoid the noise, smoke, guns and artificial nighttime light of man. They have, however, an unforgiving social order, and when an elderly member of the pride, or one with an injury, is unable to play a full and active role, he is excluded and has to fend for himself. Lacking the speed and agility essential to the hunt, and the help of comrades, the outcast seeks out slower, easier prey than before. Hunger overcomes natural phobia, and the outcast is inevitably drawn to the vicinity of humankind.

Victims of a 'rogue' lion at Geita are the most vulnerable people, selected as least-risky choice. The compound has no electric light, and none of the *watu* have a gun. Even so, the lion is careful to choose someone who wanders away from the settlement. Being old, or injured, he relies more on stealth and concealment than speed.

The history of lion attacks on *watu* is the stuff of folklore. One man is pulled from his bicycle and dragged three hundred yards from the path in 1956. The remains of his body are found three days later, flattened, bloodied grass pointing the way. His lower belly and genitals, and soft neck-flesh, have been consumed. The lion is saving the rest for later. The remains are his grisly larder. Then, in '59 a woman walking from one of the latrines of *machula* fame is attacked. Her baby is torn from her arms and taken off into the bush. No part of it is ever found.

When a lion attack happens, Geita panics. Mr Snel orders everyone to stay indoors, especially at night. If you go somewhere it must be in a car. These are to be parked close to the front door. Outside lights are to be left on – lions don't like it. On leaving the house, you dash to the car and lock yourself in. Makes me think lions can open cars unless locked from inside.

During a 1960 scare Mum doesn't obey the rules. 'It's a man-eating lion,' she tells a chiding Mr Snel, 'not a *woman*-eating one!'

I'm eleven in 1962, and Geita is again under siege when we

return from Arusha. There have been four known lion killings of *watu* in three weeks. Some say there's more than a single rogue at large, because, while one victim is taken from a footpath near the mine, three are attacked inside the compound. The latter behaviour, seeking prey inside a human encampment, is unusual even for a rogue.

We've lived too many years with this on-off danger. After a week of obeying the rules, Dieti and I decide to ignore the curfew about walking in the bush. It's far too hot and boring to stay indoors. Besides, we've been away in Arusha three whole months, and there's fun out there in the scrub and jungle. We've never been attacked by a lion, and we're confident we won't be now.

'Let's go to Tarzan-Swings,' Dieti says. His German accent has almost disappeared, except when he's excited, which is sad because it used to be amusing. He's spent the night with us because he's not allowed to walk home in the dark. It's a dashing idea. The girls say we're crazy, and they don't want to end up as a lion's lunch. We say we're not scared of any lion, and, besides, we'll take big sticks.

'If you go, I'll tell Vati!' Gretchen warns her brother.

'Okay, we won't go,' Dieti says, but his foot nudges mine under the kitchen table.

'Let's read comics,' I say in my best 'defeated' voice.

'Okay,' Dieti says in his. And we shuffle off to my bedroom. We burst out laughing after we close the door. 'We better wait a bit,' Dieti cautions. Good idea. The girls will be suspicious a while. Maybe we gave in too quick. We read old *Classics*. Mine is falling apart, and even the sellotape has turned yellow and is peeling. After an age we hear the girls leave the house. In the circumstances they'll walk directly, and quickly, to the Blüger place. Good, we're on our own. There's only one person to elude now – Umali. That should be easy.

We're out the house, running helter-skelter downhill towards the club on Bottom Road. We've got *rungus*. They're inch-thick sticks, four foot long, with three-inch solid balls of wood at the end. Made by selecting the right small tree and digging it up. The ball is the root-bit. The *rungu* is cut to length, stripped of bark, and dried in the sun. A natural weapon. More than equal to a lion should we meet one.

Turning right on Bottom Road, we carry on to where the road curves to the left, and the settled area ends. Here the natural vegetation begins again. We plunge off the road onto a footpath, which winds into the bush. We know this area well. After three minutes we come to one of our favourite places. 'Tarzan-Swings' is what we call it. There's a natural clearing in the bush. In the middle is a gulley four yards wide, and at the bottom a fast-running stream.

On the banks are great weeping willows, their down-hanging branches and tendrils reaching tentacle-like towards the ground. Selecting and grasping one, we make Tarzan-like whoops, and swing over the gulley and stream. It's exhilarating. Sometimes in the past my 'rope' has broken and I've fallen into the water. I'm better at choosing ropes now.

We swing several times, and then decide to go home. We've proven our point – no man-eating lion can scare us! But even we know staying here too long is chancing our arm. We start on our way back. It's strangely quiet. Eerily so. Not even a *njiwa*-bird cooes.

We are just approaching where the path joins Bottom Road, when Dieti digs me painfully in the side. I turn instinctively to complain, and freeze. We're stopped, staring back up the path.

He's huge. Massive. Gargantuan. I've never seen a lion so close, and I didn't imagine they could be so big. He's close. I can smell his fetid, rotten breath. At eleven, I'm four foot tall. The lion's higher. He's got a great head and magnificent mane. His mouth is half-open, and we see his yellow fangs and hear rasping breath. One of his ears is shorter than the other, like the top's been bitten, or ripped, off. He's getting closer. We are stationary, staring at him. His eyes are cloudy yellow and bloodshot. He doesn't blink.

Dieti, several inches shorter and a lot thinner than me, is white as chalk. His lower lip trembles, his eyes are saucer-wide. I can't think what to do. What *should* you do? My heart beats hard and fast in my chest. I can even feel it in my neck. *'Huyu na ngoja ana potea'* comes to mind. Umali says it. He who waits (hesitates) is lost. Is that the advice we need? I've got to do something. Before I can decide, it's taken out of my hands.

The lion takes a step towards us. Instinctively, we take a step backwards. He takes another. So do we. He starts strolling, we turn and walk. He follows, his breathing loud and rattly. We turn onto Bottom Road. When we're eight yards from the path, the lion joins the road behind us. 'Don't run,' I whisper through clenched teeth.

Dieti's in a daze, like an automaton. He's just coming along, doing as I do. He's still very white. I count our steps. One, the lion takes one too. Two, three, four, he keeps in step. We've covered a hundred yards of Bottom Road. The lion is walking a bit quicker now. He's no longer in step. We walk faster, try not to run.

The gap is down to fifteen yards. My self discipline dissolves and I break into a run, pulling Dieti with me. Looking over my shoulder, I see the lion look confused. He isn't running. He's stopped now, just staring after us. We reach the bend in the road, then he's out of view. We keep running all the way home.

I tell Umali what happened. In minutes he's got a posse of *rungu*, panga and spear-wielding, excited *watu*, who head off to find our strolling lion. He must be *mzee*, old, Umali says, or sick. Otherwise he'd have had us. I think that's what gives Umali the courage to go after him. After nearly an hour they return, disappointed. They can't find the *simba*. At the club that night, Dieti and I are celebrities. For someone speechless with terror, Dieti has undergone a rebirth.

'I wanted to throw stones at him,' he says to Mr Snel, 'only Jimmy wouldn't let me!' I listen to this in amazement. 'I think we could have killed it, ' Dieti confides, his courage immense now the lion's not about.

The rogue-lion-hunt is redirected to south of Bottom Road. Next day two hundred spear-wielding tribesmen, plus six *selekali*, or police, *askaris* with rifles, sweep the bush. But it isn't them who get the credit this time.

Two miles further south, next to his *shamba*, a Gallua tribesman sets a lion-trap. He tethers a kid-goat to a stick in the ground. This is the bait. If a lion grabs the kid, that'll move the stick. Just six yards away, balanced on two tall forked sticks, is an ancient Arabian muzzle-loading *jazail* loaded with powder and ball. The flint-bearing hammer is cocked, the trigger connected by fishing line to the goat-stick. He checks his trap carefully, gives the kid a dish of water, and retires to bed in his hut.

He's woken by a loud retort, goat bleating and agonised lion roaring. He runs outside with a spear for protection. He doesn't need it. The *jazail*-ball has struck the lion in the chest, penetrated his heart. He's lying on the ground in the moonlight, his lifeblood gushing from his wound. The kid, unhurt, still bleats in terror .

Next day the *simba* is displayed outside the mine store. The tribesman has sold it to Marcello Barelli, who wants the skin. He's huge, seven foot long, plus a tail of four foot. It's the same lion that walked after Dieti and me. He's got the mane, and the half-torn or bitten-off ear. He's also got a septic foot and three claws missing.

'Thees,' says Mr Barelli, 'eesa why he no catcha you, Jeemy!' We've a lot to be grateful for. Even sepsis.

Meantime, the English language gains no favours from me, or those I know. Umali's 'come quigelly', my 'muttony on the bounty', Jackson's 'Greasious Quinn', Antonio's 'Inglish in the pinglish', Iwe's 'line-sense', Choudhry's 'ledger shits' and many *watu's* 'blurryfuckens' are just examples of how the King's English is murdered in Geita.

I grow up believing snakes are bad tempered, because Ursula Blüger, Gretchen and Dieti's mother, is always alluding to it being so. 'I voss cross like-a-snake!' she exclaims to anyone who cares to hear. 'Gretchen vos cheeky, und I vos like-a-snake-cross!'

Ursula continues to be cross like a snake, on and off for years. When Gretchen's twelve she 'vos kissing vis a boy', which made Ursula 'cross-like-vun-big-snake'. It made me cross like a bigger snake, though I never knew if it was true, or which boy it was.

Also abusing the language is the mine Seychellois motor mechanic, Spiro, of mixed Greek and African blood, and the strangest of accents. As a boy, I think cars are powered by a person under the bonnet, because it's always the 'injun' who's 'forked'. It seems unnecessarily cruel to me. The back of a car is clearly tiresome too, because projecting from there is the 'exhausting pipe'. I can never work out if 'rainwipers' are there to clean the air or the windscreen.

One day Antonio manages to 'borrow' a pair of walkie-talkie radios from his dad's Land Rover. They're ideal, he says, for planning and co-ordinating a *machula* attack. We decide to try them on a practice run. We'll pretend we're ambushing the *machula*, and use the walkie-talkies to communicate. There's no *machula* coming – he's already done his stinky work today. We'll pretend. Antonio will 'see' the *machula*, and radio the alert to me. We separate and crawl through the undergrowth. After a few yards I stop. The radio crackles into life.

'The *machula* is-a-coming,' it says, 'are-a-you-a-ready to attack-a-heem?'

'Roger!' I reply, pressing the 'send' button. That's how soldiers speak on radios.

'Eesa-not-a-Roger, ees-a-Antonio!' comes the furious reply. Walkie-talkies will never work in Geita. Not with Antonio!

I begin to take notice of the signposts in Geita. The signwriter's an elderly Sikh who, when not writing signs, works for Adrian Venter in the reduction works. *'Mane Rod'* says the sign at the top of the hill. Is a warning to carry a stick in case of lions? *'Mwanza-80 mils'*, says one where the road leaves the mine. *'Petrouelem-Dangres'*, says the big red and black sign at the filling station. *'Take Care – Croconiles'*, proclaims a red and black sign at Nungwe Bay. Are they sure they swim here from the Nile? Barrat Stores has a very special sign. It's neatly done in black, with paint on cardboard:

*NO AKS ME CREDITS - MABE YOU NO PAY.*
*ME GIV CREDIT, MABE ME CRY,*
*ME NO GIV, MABE YOU CRY . . . BETTER YOU CRY!*

The signs are beautifully painted, but nobody bothers with spelling. Makes it ridiculous to learn it at Arusha. What's the point of perfect spelling? We understand, don't we?

I'm so bored with other kids. Mum says I've been a little old man from when I could walk. One Sunday at the club I go outside looking for Kaizer, my old friend. The *Wazungu* in the bar are already well oiled on *Whitecap* and whisky. The kids are mindlessly eating crisps and drinking *Pepsis*.

Kaizer is much more interesting. I ask Ishmael, the barman, if he'll sell me a bottle of *Whitecap* for the *askari*, and he agrees, as long as he delivers it to him personally, because Mr Snel, the manager, has strong words about selling *pombe* to *watoto*. I resent that. I'm not a child!

'*Asante sana,*' Kaizer says when he gets the beer. Thanks a lot. '*Ni moto leyo.*' It's hot today. Ishmael leaves us.

'Tell me about the Japanese,' I say.

'*Hawa,*' he says, 'them'. He takes an appreciative swig from the bottle, wipes the back of his hand across his mouth. His stories of fighting in the jungles of Burma are the most entertaining tales in Geita. I can imagine myself crawling through the undergrowth, a Lee-Enfield rifle with fixed bayonet in one hand, my ears pricked for the sound of enemy movement, a twig breaking, the sudden flight of startled birds. When Kaizer speaks, I'm there.

'*Hawa,*' he says again, 'treacherous people. They fight like tigers, didn't mind if they die, but did worse than that.'

'How?' I ask, keen to hear how bad they were.

'One day in the great Kabaw valley, we come to a wooden Japanese fort on top of a hill. They've been under attack by an Indian division for three days. They've killed lots of Indians.' Just like John Wayne, I snigger. But these are not red-Indians. They are *Indian* Indians. I suppress my humour. 'There are dead Indians everywhere. But the Japanese have losses too.'

'Their commander decides to withdraw his remaining men because he can no longer defend the perimeter. He leaves six badly injured soldiers behind, with pistols and hand-grenades, and orders them to kill as many of the enemy as possible before dying.' Kaizer takes an exaggeratedly appreciative swig of *Whitecap*. It's very hot and close today. It'll rain later, I can tell.

'You like my stories, don't you?' he says.

'I do, *mzee*, old man, they are tales of a brave man,' I say.

'You, child, will charm the whole world, one day,' Kaizer laughs. He drinks more beer, then continues. 'We creep through the bushes towards the log fort. We know what the Japanese can do. They may be completely quiet one minute, and then suddenly the whole world may go mad with bullets and explosions. They are so sly, so prepared, so dangerous....'

Kaizer stares at me. Suddenly he looks very old. His hair, short and curly, has always been shot-through with grey, but now it's snow-white. He looks smaller, too, than the Kaizer I know.

'We come,' he says, 'in range. They must start shooting. Nothing. We wait, not to expose ourselves by leaving the undergrowth and bushes. Nothing. Then Samuel, an *askari* from Uganda, draws the pin on a hand grenade and throws it over the rampart. We lie low. There's an explosion. We wait for shooting, a machine-gun. Nothing.' Kaizer sits silent on the wall for half a minute. He shakes his head.

'The platoon commander, a *Bwana* called Lieutenant Harris, who none of us like, mainly because he speaks bad Swahili and looks down on Africans, gives the order to advance. He shouts, "Let's go boys!" We aren't his "boys", but this is the army, and we have Japanese to fight. Maybe when this war was over we'll fight the *Wazungu*. Who are they to rule us?' He smiles enigmatically. I'm a *Mzungu*, after all. He sips his beer, looks into the dark distance.

'We jump out of our hiding places, rifles with bayonets fixed, and make a dash over open ground to the fort. We run like madmen. We know these people are clever. They can wait, let you think you're safe, get you in the open, then shoot you with two, three, or more of those terrible machine-guns. I've seen men cut to pieces, just when they think they were safe.' He takes a deep breath.

'We get to the wooden poles. They are trunks of young trees, a foot wide, pointed on top, tied by rope in a stockade. One *askari* throws another grenade over, and it goes off. Then we're climbing, standing on other's shoulders to reach the top. As the *Mzungu* Harris puts his head over the parapet, he's hit between the eyes. He falls back, eyes wide open, brains hanging out the back of his neck. *Wazungu*, you see, can also be killed!' Kaizer pats me gently on the shoulder, 'even you, Jimu.'

'*Najua,*' I say. I know. Dad died, after all.

'Others get over. I'm fourth or fifth,' Kaiser says. 'We can't see where the shot comes from before there's another, and the Ugandan Samuel falls to the ground with a bullet through his throat, gurgling, blood pumping from a huge hole in his neck. We see who shot him. A Japanese soldier, perhaps eighteen years old, who looks only twelve, with no legs, tied to a small tree, his stumps stuck in the earth. I look at him, and he points a long pistol at me. His eyes are wild, like a cornered *fisi*. I bring my Lee-Enfield up and fire at the same time. My bullet hits him in the forehead, blows half his head away. He collapses against his ropes, brains dripping onto his lap. It's very close.' Kaizer puts down his empty *Whitecap*.

'Meantime the others find there was only one Japanese still alive. He's lost an eye and half his jaw. One of our Mills hand grenades. He's lying there, moaning. Bayonet thrust through the heart, and he's quiet. We've won the fort.'

'Very brave,' I say. I don't find it strange that, at age ten, I hear the most gruesome details of war. The Swahili, unlike the English, don't dress things up for children.

'What happens then,' says Kaizer, 'is terrible.'

'What?' I ask. What can be even more terrible than I've heard?

*'Makopo,'* Kaizer says, tins. 'Food, labelled in Japanese, with pictures of the contents on. They are among the kit of the dead Japanese soldiers, in small rucksacks. We haven't eaten fruit a long time. Our rations are bully beef and biscuits. Some *askaris* grab the tins, open them with pocketknives or bayonets, and start to eat. Within seconds the first one staggers, tries to scream, falls to the ground and is dead before he gets there!'

'Poison?' I ask.

'Cyanide,' Kaizer answers. 'Kills quicker than any other poison. Three men die in minutes. The others stop before they're poisoned too. The Japanese don't care how they kill us, even if they do it *after* they're dead.'

Suddenly this war-stuff feels ugly to me. I thought soldiers were men with *heshima*, honour. This is something else, alien. Cowardly, even. I shudder at the thought of being killed with poison by an enemy who is already dead. Such behaviour is not only without *heshima*, its downright *hovyo*, or completely without manners. *Majinga* behaviour, loutish and immoral.

Cyanide! That's what they use in the 'reduction works' on Top Road. Part of the process of refining gold. By the time they've got pure gold out, there's a grey mud-like residue called 'slime'. This is dumped to form a 'slimes-dam' a mile west of the mine.

Over the years they've made three slimes-dams. They're over a hundred yards long, forty wide, and thirty foot high. They've dried to a brick-like grey consistency, except on the top of the one still being used, where the surface remains runny. There's a noxious, acrid, sour, choking smell there, which never goes. We children are forbidden to approach the slimes-dams. Some of us, particularly Dieti, Lutoli and I, ignore that, and go there anyway.

It's strange, climbing the steep path up the sides, walking on the grey lunar surface, trying not to breathe deeply, feeling we're getting away with murder. It can't be *that* poison, or we'd be dead long ago. I should be. Last week Lutoli jumped in one of the stagnant pools on top of a dam and pungent grey water splashed in all directions. I got some in my mouth. It tasted like nothing I knew, horrid. Like biting a raw pawpaw, only worse. I spat it out, and spat some more. Couldn't get rid of the taste for hours.

*'Mina jua,'* Kaizer says, reading my thoughts. I know. *'Wena chesa huko.'* You play there. Are there no secrets at all in Geita?

Cyanide. . . I file away a thought for the future. If anything ever happens to Gretchen, I'll want to die. The cyanide is there. I wonder how much grey slime I'll have to eat to do the job.

301

# Twenty-eight

In June 1963 we go on long leave. Mum's contract is renewed every two years. Within that time there are two periods of leave. After one year, we have two weeks 'local' leave, spent anywhere within the East African Community of Tanganyika, Kenya and Uganda, all expenses paid by the company. After a further year, it's 'long' or 'overseas' leave for four whole months, fully paid, anywhere in the world. The generous leave allowance, and payment by the mine of boarding school fees, are the reason most expats stay so long in their jobs.

The day before we leave I pay a visit to Mlozi, the *mchawi*. He appraises me without expression, sitting cross-legged on his *mwamba*-rock. I tell him we're going far away across the sea.

'Further than Bagamoyo?' he asks. That's forty miles.

'Much further, and over a bigger lake than the great one at Nungwe.' He stoops and crawls into his crude hut, and emerges with a small piece of still-furry animal skin, tied with thong into a little bag. I think it's from a goat.

'This will bring you safely back,' he says, giving the golf ball- sized bag to me, 'only you must not open it, or look inside. It has strong *dawa*, but must stay closed.' I take it. This is the first time he is helping me. I tremble at the power of the medicine in my hand. I won't tell Mum, or she'll make me get rid of it.

I believe in the power of the *mchawi*, and the *hirizi*, or charm. I will take the *dawa* to England. Who knows, I might need it there. I'm staring at Mlozi. He gives me a very rare half-grin, before turning away and resuming his strange and incomprehensible monologue with the sky.

Our long journey begins with the drive to Mwanza. There we catch the gari-moshi to Dar. Two days and nights. Much excitement. Becky and I are able to appreciate the scenery, not being blinded by the misery of going back to Arusha. Even so, I'll miss Gretchen, whom I love from afar, though I pretend not to. Hot, dry plains, herds of grazing wildebeest, water holes, small groups of elephants, patches of verdant green, isolated villages, ramshackle stations, running, laughing *totos*, wizened hawkers of fruit, elephant-hair bangles, carved wooden rhinos, elephants, lions, tall red-gowned Masai cattle herders, replete with spears and beads.

Beyond Dodoma, where we're delighted not to alight, the locomotive struggles up into the ever-cooler heights of central Tanganyika.

A hand-rung bell calls us for meals in the dining car, a very splendid Victorian statement of art, craftsmanship and excess. In sumptuous luxury, several courses are brought on silver trays by waiters in white, badged *EAR & H* uniforms, and red fezzes. Between meals, we watch the country glide by, consume *EAR & H* chewy peppermint sweets, drink many ice-cold *Coca Cola*'s like the advertisements command us, and re-read *Illustrated Classics*.

The heat of the hinterland, having returned on the descent to the coastal plateau, begins to abate again as the train races towards the sea. The acacias, the flat-topped African trees, and stunted, thorny ones of the plains allow an occasional palm tree to share their space. The palms grow more numerous, until they're in the majority. Soon the red soil changes to a lighter, sandier colour, and only palms grow. At this part of the journey we begin to smell the sea.

The *Agip Motel* in Dar is a notable institution in more ways than one. It's in the middle of town, half a mile up a straight and potholed tarmac road from the beach. *Agip* is an Italian company whose main business is petroleum. Their premium petrol, advertised on huge billboards in Dar, is called *Super-Corte-magiori.* This has to be said with an Italian accent. Their other business is motels. The best I've seen.

The motel, which I can't distinguish from a hotel, is an oasis. The temperature outside far exceeds forty Celsius, and the air sweats with humidity. Stepping through the glass doors, we enter a refrigerated paradise. There's a lounge, with iced drinks in tall glasses, a dining room where cool, unbothered, smiling waiters in white uniforms and red fezzes bring platters of cold meats, bread and salads to our table. The manager, a jovial middle-aged Italian lady, stands nearby, checking fastidiously on our comfort and satisfaction.

We've had lunch, and checked into our room. It's even cooler here than downstairs. Mum and Becky are sharing a double bed.

303

I've got a single. We've got our own bathroom. The big window looks down the street to the beach, and the deep-blue sea beyond. Can't believe it's so hot outside. We couldn't have stood it much longer. We open the window and look out. It's like colliding with a heated sheet of corrugated iron. It's so hot it takes our breath away, and burns our cheeks. This is a crisis. We've got to get to the beach and swim in that blue water. But how, with that furnace outside, are we to get there?

Becky provides the answer. With the window hurriedly closed, she stares through the glass and makes a brilliant observation.

'Chemists!' she says.

'Chemists?' I say. What's she talking about?

'Chemist shops have air-conditioning,' she says. She's a genius. We can see two chemist's signs, equally spaced between here and the beach. Hurriedly we change into costumes and T-shirts.

'Mum, Becky and I exit the *Agip* into the dazzling furnace, and dash for the first sign. The string-pulled bell sounds as we enter the shop. We let the door close and stand just inside, savouring the 'coolth', as Becky calls it. The young Indian lady behind the long wooden counter smiles. She's used to heat-refugees coming in and not buying. After three minutes we're ready for the next hundred yards. We stand inside the door of the second chemist, bracing ourselves for the final dash to the sea. That'll be even better than air-conditioning.

Becky and I peel off our T-shirts on the run, and continue straight into the water. It's tepidly warm, but once we're in it's refreshing anyway. It's beautifully blue, like one of those holiday postcards on a stand in the last chemist. And smooth as a breathless pond. We turn and look back at the beach.

The sand shines brilliantly white in the sun. Every ten yards or so a coconut palm leans crazily over the water's edge. Pulled up on the beach between the trees are half a dozen *jahazis*, open sailing dhows with outriggers on one side, in the curious manner of the Tanganyika coast. White *kanzu*-clad *Warabu*, or Arab, fishermen, their faces deep mahogany-brown, sit in the shade of the palms. A few are mending nets, others playing a strange game. The objective is to flick a pebble with a thumb, so it strikes another and drives it into a small hole in the ground. I don't know what they call it, but it's causing excitement and laughter.

This is truly paradise. The beach runs along a narrow channel towards the harbour. It's sheltered from the Indian Ocean by the headland, which is why the water is so calm. A cargo ship comes down the channel, heading for port. As it passes, a hundred yards away, its wake spills rolling towards us. By the time they get here they're over six foot high. It's great fun diving over them.

Mum's more cautious than us. She can't swim. She's lying in six inches of water at the edge, being assaulted and rolled over by the wake-waves as they run up the beach. It's so nice to see her laughing.

Two more ships provide wave-entertainment. Then we spot another ship on the horizon. As she approaches, we see she's bigger than the others. She's tall and lavender-mauve in colour, and has a wide vermillion funnel. *'Union Castle!'* Mum shouts from the water's edge.

It's the Mail ship we're catching to England, the *MS Kenya Castle*. Our excitement and happiness can hardly be contained. What could there be better? The glorious beach, the warm sea, the *dhows*, palm trees, and there, steaming closer every minute is a great ship, which tonight will carry us over the waves to England. Sometimes good things overwhelm me.

*Kenya Castle* displaces seventeen thousand tons, and is 576 feet long. That's what it says under the big picture at the reception desk, where, having climbed the gangplank from the baking heat outside, we are, again, relieved by the coolness of air-conditioning. She takes up to five hundred and twenty-six passengers. She's a mail ship, and carries, in addition to passengers, mail and assorted cargo between South and East Africa, and England. Fore and aft are covered holds and cargo cranes.

She's a handsome ship. Our cabin has a porthole and three bunks, two on the floor, one above. I dabs the top bunk. The bathroom is along the passage, and has six toilets and four showers.

Becky and I run around exploring the ship. There's a lovely little swimming pool on the after deck, closed, emptied and netted over in harbour. There's a grand dance floor in one of the big rooms and a huge dining room too. There are bars in several places, and a library. Downstairs, along from reception, are several glass-fronted shops selling all kinds of things. Plus a ladies' hairdressers. Becky likes the look of that. My eyes fall immediately on very large yellow packets of cigarettes in a shop window. They're called *Matinee Filters*, and they're two bob for fifty. They come from Rhodesia, and are duty-free on the ship.

An hour after we board, the ship's speaker system announces we will be sailing in half an hour. 'All ashore that's going ashore,' the man says. Some people are kissing and hugging. Some are crying. Not us. We're just wildly excited.

The ship's horn bellows, a long deep sound, followed by three shorter, sharper blasts. Stragglers shuffle down the gangplank, and no sooner has the last one stepped onto the wharf, than the crew begin to wind the gangplank into the ship. Men are running up and down the quay, loosening great ropes from huge steel bollards set in concrete. There's vibration underfoot. The engines are coming alive. The horn sounds again. A narrow gap appears between us and the wharf.

The water boils as the propellers thrust it churning down the length of the ship. The gap widens. On the other side two tiny tugs are pulling us. The vibration changes and increases in strength, and *Kenya Castle* starts to glide forward. The tugs release their hawsers and back away. We gain speed, and now the wharf is drawing away on our right. A yellow and black boat bobs in our wake, waiting to collect the pilot.

Music blares out on the afterdeck by the pool. They're giving away cold drinks and ice cream in paper cups. Becky and I join the throng of children trying to get as many ice creams as possible. They're very generous, or stupid, because it's help-yourself, and there are boxes and boxes full.

We're gorging ice cream as the ship sails past the *Inn By The Sea*, and the beach where we swam just this afternoon. There are people in the water, jumping over the waves like we did. Mum finds us. It's six thirty, and the first sitting for dinner is at seven. There's just time, if we hurry, to shower and dress.

Supper is formal. We're shown to our table by a white-uniformed *maître d'*, who pulls a chair out for Mum and Becky, but not me. I don't care. Who wants his chair pulled out? The table is round, with six places. Two old ladies and an old man sit down. Mum makes polite conversation. Geita, now where on earth is that? Posh accents.

They come from Nairobi, in Kenya. The 'posh' *Mzungus* of East Africa. The old man is an engineer. His wife's a teacher, the other old lady her sister. The bread rolls are fresh, warm and delicious with melted butter. As good as Umali's *sconsies*, but I won't tell him. The soup is tomato, very good. I choose roast chicken as main course. Mum and Becky go for steak pie. We finish off with ice cream. Someone says the shops are open after supper. I check my money. I know what I'm buying.

Half an hour later I'm sitting on the deck in front of a covered hatch, smoking the first of my newly purchased *Matinee* cigarettes. This is bliss. No one can see me here, and I've got more cigarettes that I ever thought I'd have. I'll be spending lots of time here. It's getting dark. The sun looks like a big ripe orange on the horizon one minute, and then it's gone.

Sleeping in a bunk on a ship at sea is special. It's almost, but not quite, the same feeling when I imagine myself cocooned in my canoe. There's the gentle fore-to-aft pitch, the left-to-right roll, the constant vibration of the engines, the creaking of the whole ship as it weathers the sea. From the porthole, directed from an attached scoop, is a fresh stream of sea-air. This is as near as possible to paradise. In the neverland between waking and sleep, I imagine Gretchen comes to sit on my bunk. She's smiling. 'I love you,' she whispers in my ear. If only dreams came true!

Our course is north, first port of call Kilindini Harbour, Mombasa, where we dock next evening. There's loading and offloading of cargo, passengers leaving and others joining. Then we're back at sea, heading north in the Indian Ocean, towards the Red Sea. We have five days at sea. Hours of swimming and sunbathing, making friends who smoke with me in the hiding place behind the hatch, sleeping, or just staring in wonder at the ever-changing hue and colour of the sea.

At the neck of the Indian Ocean we enter the Red Sea. For a day we're close to the African shore, and see bleak red cliffs and rocky outcrops. An officer says we're five miles off, which I find hard to believe. It looks close enough to swim.

Aden is a very Arabian town. Mum's nervous about Becky. She remembers the trader in Benghazi who wanted to buy her for six camels, the one who said he'd 'look her good'. The ship doesn't dock here, but anchors outside the harbour. We're taken ashore in wooden motorboat-tenders which are not as well built as *Lotanga*. We have two hours in the bazaars, and Mum buys a camel saddle-seat, made of leather-covered wood. Soon we're back on board, sailing for Suez, Egypt. It's a day's voyage, then we're at the entrance to the Suez canal.

The canal is close to a hundred miles long. It heads due north from Suez to enter the *Little Bitter Lake*, which connects to the *Great Bitter Lake*. From there it runs a short way to Lake Timsah, then it's a ruler-straight northern course all the way to Port Said on the Mediterranean.

There's not much to see, except sand and desert, the occasional camel, and a very infrequent Arab on a camel. There is one thing I see which I'll never forget. Cleopatra's needle, an officer tells me. A tall, impressive stone monument in the desert, close to the canal. I particularly note this structure because we're gliding past it as I cut my twelfth birthday cake.

The ship's chef and confectioner is a proper Yorkshireman, who Mum talks to about my forthcoming birthday. He responds by making a huge light blue birthday cake, with the words 'Jimmy' and 'Twelve' written in white icing. I am surrounded by twenty children of different ages, singing 'Happy Birthday', as I make my first cut in the cake. That's when I spot Cleopatra's needle. I don't see anything else worth remembering. After sixteen hours we enter the Med at Port Said.

That night at dinner the old engineer from Nairobi drinks two whole bottles of South African wine, and becomes even more talkative than his usual raucous self. At the next table the steward, Dennis, is being very gracious to the ladies. One of them, whose name is Mrs Johnston, seems very happy to have his attention. She has a loud, irritating voice. The old engineer says she's flirting with the steward. Her husband, a grumpy man with a grey beard, doesn't seem to mind, or notice. The engineer says to his wife 'she's mutton dressed as lamb.' I ask Mum what that means. She tells me it's big-people's talk.

We stop at Genoa in Italy. Here Mum depresses Becky and me by dragging us to see a 'famous' cemetery, where they first bury people for a few years, then dig them up, collect the bones, put them in little boxes, and plant them in a 'memorial wall' with photographs of the dead person on the front. I manage to persuade Mum to buy me a very realistic toy cap gun. It fires special, very loud caps. It'll make me famous in Geita, because nobody's ever seen, or heard, a toy gun as real as this.

I've got more adventurous where I smoke, and taken to lighting up on the boat deck. It's ten at night, and the ship is chunneling along to the west into the teeth of a blustering, salty wind. The moon is full, and there's a broad, shimmering golden highway of moonlight on the sea. It stretches all the way to the horizon. Suddenly the lifeboat beside me comes to life. I nearly choke on my cigarette.

There's somebody, or something, in the boat! A corner of tarpaulin lifts and out pops a man's head. In the moonlight I recognise him. It's the dining-room steward, Dennis. He doesn't see me. I'm in the shadow of the boat. I hear him whisper something. There's more rumbling, then a lady's head joins his. Her voice is clear, as is her anxiety.

'Are you sure there's no one?' she says. Who could miss that raspy voice? It's the lady with the angry bearded husband at the next table. Mrs Johnston, that's it. The very irritating voice. She, labelled 'mutton dressed as lamb'.

What's she doing in a lifeboat, at night, with a steward? If they wanted to talk there'd be no need to climb in there. They've been up to something, and I know what it is. I wish Umali was here. I could tell him I've caught *Wazungu* doing secret *jigi-jigi* in a lifeboat. I stay in the shadows as they climb awkwardly down. He's first, then he turns to help her. She's standing with one foot in the boat, the other on his cupped hands. She slips, and they fall together on the deck. She cries out, but it's hushed. Her pain isn't enough to overcome her fear. They struggle to their feet, briefly kiss, and leave in opposite directions. He passes me by inches.

Marseilles, a brief stop. Then Barcelona. The *Rambla*, a long, wide boulevard crowded with shops and people. Not my scene. Far too busy. Gibraltar, now that's better. A slower pace, very

British. The passage is coming to an end. Leaving Gib, the ship turns north up the Atlantic, towards our destination. Thirty-one days after embarking in Dar es Salaam, we disembark in King George V Docks, London.

We travel by train to Plymouth in Devon. My eldest brother, Bertrand, who is still in the navy, has married, and he, his wife and two-year-old daughter, live in a large caravan in a park at Plymstock. My brother Fraser, also still in the navy, has rented a chalet in the park.

Becky and I are resentful of our brothers. They talk with Mum about things we don't know, and times we weren't there. There are other unpleasantnesses. Bertrand decides to discipline me and orders me around. I don't like the food they eat. It generally comes out of a tin, and it's usually things I've never seen before, like 'spam', a foul concoction of cooked tinned meat. They don't have fresh fruit.

Bertrand's got an old bicycle, which he grudgingly lets me ride. Cycling around a footpath in the park, I come across three older boys. I'm twelve, and they're at least thirteen or fourteen. I stop and talk with them. They ask me where I got my funny accent, and I tell them. They start calling me 'wog' and 'nigger'. Strange, I think. These *Wazungu* are just like those in Geita, though so far apart. In Geita they've always said 'Jimmy's run wild, like a native.' Here, in green and pleasant England, I'm being called wog and nigger. Do they have, *can* they have some extraordinary extrasensory communication with Geita bigots? I don't know. But I'm not going to let them get away with it.

I remember my vows to myself. I said, long ago, I am my own father. I meant there is no man to fight for me, so I must do my own fighting. Also, in my pocket I have Mlozi's little leather bag of *dawa*.

These fools know nothing of the power of a *mchawi*. I'll teach them to treat me like this. I dismount, take two steps towards the nearest boy, and punch him with all my strength on the earhole. The impact is so hard a harsh vibration travels all the way up my arm. He falls on the ground and rolls about in agony, crying like a lady opera singer. I take two steps towards the second boy, but he runs off. The third has retreated beyond range. I look down at the squirming one on the ground. There's

310

blood pouring out his ear.

'That's how we niggers fight!' I say, remounting my bike. At last Mlozi has given me the *hirizi*. With that I cannot fail. It's about time he helped me. He may be strange, and all, but he's my Swahili brother in the end. Later my big brothers have to placate the boy's father, who says I 'attacked for no reason.' His 'innocent' son has a burst eardrum and needs an operation.

'Apologise!' Bertrand says when he drags me to the caravan door.

'I won't!' I say through clenched teeth.

'You will!' he says, twisting my arm behind my back.

'Okay,' I say, seeing there's no way out, unless I attack my own brother, here in front of the boy's father.

'That'll do,' the man says, surprising me by his lenience. When I look where his eyes are focused, I realize why he's being so nice. Fraser has just stood up and is glowering. I find out they've met before. Two months ago this man drank more than he should have, and began to randomly abuse women in the King George. Fraser thrashed him and threw him out in the rain. This, he must think, is a violent family.

We travel down to Cornwall by train. It's half an hour to the Tamar River, which marks the border between England and Cornwall. The railway bridge was designed by a famous engineer called Isambard Brunel, in eighteen ninety or something. What kind of name is *Isambard?* Sounds like a Muslim singer. Was he like the Singa-Singas in Geita - name only, no songs? Who cares, anyway? It's a strange-looking thing, the bridge, like huge elongated oil-drum-sized pipes looping into the sky. I don't know why they think it's great.

Mum's got a special mission. We're going to St Day, to see Dad's sister, Natalie. The one Fraser told me about in Geita. She's the one who spent the family money. Why Dad died in Tanganyika. It's on the train Mum tells us the real agenda of our visit.

The mine has fallen on hard times. The government in Dar es Salaam is taxing it to death. They believe foreign-owned companies should pay the entire cost of developing the country. They're killing the goose that lays the golden egg. Geita Gold Mine's days are numbered. Mum hasn't told us before, because she didn't want to ruin our holiday.

Even more pressing than the state of the mine is our education. Becky has outgrown Arusha, and has to go to secondary school. I'll be in that position next year too. If the mine's going to close, it's best our education should continue in Britain. Next week Mum's going back to Tanganyika. We're not going with her. Becky and I look at each other and burst into tears. We didn't expect this.

Aunt Natalie lives in a terraced cottage in St Day, near Redruth. It's just like her, small, old, and seen better days. I don't like her, or her house. I remember what Fraser said. She spent all the family's money. She's why we're poor. Becky's going to live with her in a place called Elstree in Hertfordshire. That's near London. Aunt Natalie's got a job looking after a rich old woman there. How much older can that lady be than Aunt Natalie? *She* looks a hundred.

Natalie and Becky will live in the very old lady's house, and Becky will go to a local day school. As these plans are unveiled in the low ceilinged, damp-smelling cottage, Becky sits weeping silently, accepting her horrible fate. I'm still waiting to discover mine. Something tells me I won't respond passively like my sister.

'You, Jimboy, will be staying with your cousin Mabel in Redruth,' Mum says.

'No I won't!' I'm not even going to begin this discussion.

'You have to. You can't come back with me. . .' She's trying to be gently persuasive. Poor Mum. I know she means well, but I won't let her go back alone. If I do, I'm sure I'll never see her again. I've got to stand firm, regardless of what she says. It's for her own good.

'Remember Dodoma?' I ask. Where I jumped out the bus. I know this question will put her mind in the right way. It means I'm deadly serious.

'Why?' Mum asks, alarmed. I know she thinks I'm not only emotionally brittle but half-mad too. I've done enough to deserve that. Shooting God, killing Tembo's puppy, spying on Mr Valari's corpse, abusing Alice and Mrs Snel, swearing at adults, jumping through the back window of a moving bus. . . Add to that being stung by a scorpion, narrowly escaping a black *mamba*, being chased by a lion, throwing live bullets on a fire, manufacturing a firearm, and my latest coup, the near-killing of the English boy in Plymstock caravan park, and her concerns are clearly well founded.

It's a long, hard process wearing Mum down. I see a chink in her determination when she says I'll have to go to boarding school in Nairobi, Kenya, unless I stay here. I'm due to go to high school next year. I agree readily. At least Kenya's not so far. By the time we get to cousin Mabel's house, the odds are even. Her house is even smaller than Natalie's. She's enormous, and her husband is thin and short. Nothing fits. No way will I stay here, in this country, with these people.

I can't bear to be so far from Geita, or, I suddenly realise with a jolt, Gretchen. I've been missing her terribly. Am I in love? Must be, or I'd be able to stop thinking about her for a bit. I want to go back, marry her. I know I'm a young, but there must be exceptions. Some twelve year olds get hitched, surely? I wonder what she'll say. I make the most important speech of my life.

'I'm not staying here, no matter what you say,' I say to Mum and Mabel. 'If you try to force me, I'll run away. You can't watch me all the time, and I'll go as soon as you don't.' There are expressions of surprise and anger. Mabel plays right into my hands.

'I'll take you in hand,' she says in a strong Cornish accent, 'if I have to whip your behind till it's black and blue!' Thank you Mabel.

'You will not!' says Mum. The battle is won.

A week later Mum and I stand at the rail on the *British India Steam Navigation Company* ship, *BI Uganda*, as she eases away from the King George V docks in London. There's a waving crowd on the wharf. In it, at the front, are Becky and Aunt Natalie. Natalie's wearing a black fur coat. Becky's holding a small white Maltese Poodle. Mum bought it to cheer her up. Becky looks very sad. She cried when she had to go ashore. Natalie gruffly told her not to be so silly. I know Mum would change her mind about her too, if it wasn't too late.

We retrace our journey from Dar. Gibraltar, Barcelona, Marseilles, Genoa. I refuse to visit the wall-cemetery again, though Mum's keen. What is it with her and Italian burials?

Then it's Port Said and the canal. I see Cleopatra's needle again, from the starboard side. Last time it was port. Suez, and the Red Sea. I can't wait to get home. I'm missing everyone. Not just Gretchen, but Umali, Amina, Lutoli, Kaizer, even Higgs and Fritz. Not to leave out Sandy, Gooloogooloo, Snow-White, and several other *kukus*.

The two days on the *gari-moshi* are a forced delay. It can't pass quickly enough. At last we're at Mwanza station, and there is Fritz, teutonically erect and, as always, unsmiling and stern.

'Velkom beck,' he says, taking Mum's suitcase grimly. In the Land Rover he tells us the news. Dr Weiss telegrammed from Switzerland to say he was coming back early from leave. I hadn't realised he was away. Gretchen is at home with her family in Geita. I'll be seeing her soon. I've begun to forget what she looks like, and she's even stopped visiting me in my dreams. Fritz has no more news for us, lapses into his usual silence. I can almost hear the heat.

# Twenty-nine

At Lone Cone Club Mr Snel is perturbed by the sniggering behaviour of young Dieter Blüger. Mr Snel has had several *Whitecaps*, and, as usual, has become expansive to his sycophantic audience of Gordon Praze, assistant manager, Harold Norris, explosives storeman, Josef Weiss, doctor, Eugen Blüger, Dieti's father, and close personal friend, plus several mine wives.

As he sits on his barstool, he occasionally, and surreptitiously, shifts his backside slightly, to allow a small passage of flatus. Beer, in excess, does that. He continues his monologue about the pioneering days when there were no wooden houses at Geita and he and his colleagues lived in tents. His attention is interrupted. Dieti, standing on the bar rail, because he's small, is not only sniggering, but rattling something. What an annoyance kids can be, Mr Snel thinks. It's in his expression.

Gretchen, Sophia and I are watching Dieti from a table near the door on the verandah. He got the short straw, and he's on a mission for all of us. To catch Mr Snel's *jamba* in a paper bag. It's difficult keeping straight faces, not bursting into laughter. Poor Dieti. By losing the draw, he's not only got to catch it, but smell it too. That's the rules.

Mr Snel purposefully ignores Dieti. But his body language tells another story. We can tell he has a strong urge to fart again. To hell, he must think, shifting his bum, and letting go. This one is different to the previous ones, which were sly and surreptitious. Unexpectedly, there's a squeak and a loud roar from his backside. This is what Dieti's waiting for. He has the paper bag open and in position. Mr Snel is just turning to see what he's doing, when Dieti folds the bag closed, jumps down, and, forgetting himself, shouts 'I haff it!' The accent is back. Excitement.

Everyone is taken aback to see Dieti fleeing gleefully to the door onto the verandah, again shouting, 'I haff von, an Afrikaner von in ze bag!' We convulse, but try to pretend we're uninvolved.

Mr Snel is a fast thinker. He's sussed what's going on, but

decides to ignore it. Outside the club, in the shelter of the hibiscus plants, Dieti sniffs the contents of the bag.

'It smells uff beer!' he says. We fall about. Then it's our turn to take a sniff. I can say this about *Whitecap* – it can really brew up in the guts!

BL Thomas, Deputy Head and Sports-Master leads an 'assault' on Mount Meru annually. There's a big board on the wall in the assembly hall, and on it, in golden letters, are listed the years and names of pupils who 'conquered' the mountain. Becky's name is there under last year, nineteen sixty-two. This year it's my turn.

Anyone who has been to Arusha knows how the Mountain dominates the town which lies in its shadow. Every aspect of Arusha life is determined by Meru. The clear drinking water flows from its streams, the cool and temperate climate is due to its snow and ice-clad heights.

At some time or other, everyone who knows Arusha feels driven to climb Meru, whose Masai name means 'the one who does not make a noise', for the ancient volcano has slept since its last eruption in 1877. That one, or an earlier eruption, tore a huge chunk out of the crater's side, leaving a razor-edged ridge upwards to the summit. Meru is not an easy mountain to climb. Far more have climbed Kilimanjaro, which, although higher, has a gentler slope, and easier route to the top. That's why BL Thomas loves Meru. He's tough, and wants Arusha pupils to be tough too.

We go by bus to Momella Gate in the Arusha National Park. There are four teachers, including BL Thomas, and fourteen pupils. We begin hiking over a great expanse of open grassland, led by a *wa-Arusha* park ranger and ten porters. We see warthogs, several different types of buck, and a solitary, furious-looking, terrifyingly large, African buffalo. The worst tempered animal in Africa, they say.

Someone says we shouldn't worry, because the most dangerous animal in Africa is a monkey with a machine-gun. We laugh. The buffalo stares with renewed malevolence through dark, hooded eyes, his tail swishing like a pendulum. Even the ranger looks anxious. Schmedjie goes even paler than usual. Just

316

when we think it's all over for us, the beast backs away, making grunting noises, into a copse of small trees and bamboo. We go on up the slope, relieved.

Schmedjie's face is pink from exertion. There's a giant fig-tree arch, where we stop and eat lunch of bread and butter with hard-boiled eggs, washed down with sweet tea made on a primus. Then we continue upwards into a forest of alpine trees. White and black colobus monkeys stare languidly down at us, like they've seen it all before, while hornbills and other screeching birds of several kinds and colours erupt from the canopy in panic. I never thought I was scary before.

We emerge from the forest. There are tall cliffs ahead in the distance. Now we're in a grassy glade. The afternoon sun is hurtling in a ball of bright orange towards the western horizon. We can see plains far below, in gaps between the clouds. Clouds *below* us... I've never seen that before, except from the *Argonaut* on the way to England, and the air-sick-making *Dakota*.

Between here and big-sister-mountain Kilimanjaro is a seemingly endless plain of green, criss-crossed with shadows from the peaks of Meru and other mountains. Kili's peak is shrouded in mist. Somewhere between here and Kili, Schmedjie says, is his family home. I must come home with him soon, he says.

Here, now, in the middle of the glade, we reach Miriakamba Hut. We're 8100 feet above sea level, and it's getting cold. We've been walking six hours, and are glad to stop. We spend the night, eat hot tomato soup and bread, and talk excitedly about tomorrow until we fall asleep.

It's steeper next day. Since we left Miriakamba the slope's got worse with almost every step. We enter the dense Montane forest. It's lush with ferns, lilies and flowers, and criss-crossed by icy mountain streams. We take one tired step after another. This is getting difficult. There always seems to be a huge tree, a stream, or waterfall gushing over moss-covered rock, in our way, and our course, already treacherous through steepness and the slippery mulch underfoot, winds tortuously.

My foot slips in muddy water and my shoe comes right off. I'm not so sure this climb is such a good idea. Nor is Schmedjie.

'Shit,' he says, 'I wish we were on top.' So do I. I struggle back into my icy, wet shoe. An ordinary school-shoe. *Bata* lace-ups. Andrew Miller's castoffs. Someone said buy hiking boots, but where's the money? BL Thomas has stopped with the forward crew, and is waiting for us by a great fallen tree. We're the stragglers. After ten minute's respite, we continue.

After five hours we reach Saddle Hut, 11480 feet above sea level. The air is thin and cold. This is the last 'base-camp' before the 'assault' on the summit. We've been climbing up 'Elephant Ridge'. I never see an elephant, and doubt anyone ever does. 'Too bloomin' steep for such things,' Schmedjie says.

The 'hut' is not for sleeping in. Here the mountain slope is even steeper, and there are no longer trees. The ground is grey ash and volcanic stone. Left from ancient eruptions, BL says. My feet sink four inches deep with each step, and ash sucks at my wet shoes. The summit ridge is outlined against the darkening sky, with the lesser peak of 'Little Meru' in front of it.

The main peak, intermittently hidden by wafting cloud, is a tall, wide, grey cone, draped with snow, which glitters in the dying sunshine. Forbidding, lunar, otherworldly. Looks close, yet far. The porters light a fire against the biting cold, and burn big tree-branches they've found in the forest. We sit round the fire and sing hymns, lead by BL in a fine soprano voice. He's Welsh and loves to sing. *'We'll gather lilacs in the spring,'* he sings. Not here, you won't!

After two hours, and a meal of hot sausages in baked beans, we lay our sleeping bags on the ash slope. It's only eight o'clock, but we're getting up at one in the morning. Lying zipped up in my bag, I let my fingers dig in the ash. It's ice-cold. No wonder I feel cold under my body. I put my head into my bag and breathe inside to get warm.

'Not much fun here,' Schmedjie whispers.

'Nope,' I whisper back.

'I'm cold,' he says, and I hear his teeth chattering.

'Go to sleep, you two!' a lady teacher hisses from nearby. The cross one who teaches French.

We lie on our backs, heads up the slope, feet pointing down, staring at the sky, which is suddenly dark and pinpricked with a thousand winking stars. The Milky Way is up there. It's so cold

I'll never be able to sleep. My feet, in two pairs of socks, still in my shoes inside my sleeping bag, feel like solid lumps of ice. There's only one thing I can do to make me feel better.

Think about Gretchen. How should I think about her? I've died a hundred ways already, with her, beautiful but distraught, weeping inconsolably by my bedside, touching my brow, kissing me gently on the lips as I expire. Tonight, on the stark volcanic ash of Meru, I imagine her alone in a house. There's a war, and I've gone off bravely to fight for liberty. I've been killed. Yes. The Japanese. We live somewhere they invade.

Where did Kaizer, my *askari* friend, fight the Japs? Malaya, that's it. The Kabaw valley. An ambush. I've walked into it and died bravely fighting to protect my pinned down comrades. After a long battle they kill the treacherous Japs, then carry my body through the bush to Gretchen, who's waiting in the house. It's so darn sad when she sees my broken, bloodied corpse, I find myself sobbing into my sleeping bag. I've mastered the art of thinking myself into deep misery.

Somehow I must have slept, because I'm woken by BL Thomas bashing an empty bean tin with a rock. It's a 'wonk' sound, not at all like a bell.

'Rise and shine,' he's shouting as he beats the empty baked-beans *kopo*. Schmedjie groans and looks at his luminous *Oris* watch. It's one in the morning. The porters have already revived last night's fire, and one is making porridge in a huge *sufuria*. We roll up our sleeping bags. They're staying here. We're not taking anything we don't need for the final assault on the summit. We gobble our hot oats with lots of sugar.

We assemble for a final talk by BL. Nobody is to be alone between here and the summit. Watch your footing. Try to keep up. If you get left behind, and feel you can't continue, stay close to the route the others took, and wait for them on their way down. Time is important. The weather can change suddenly up here, bringing strong winds and icy conditions. When we reach the summit we'll stay only briefly, before coming back down the same way.

It's dark, and fiercely cold, as we set out on the last leg. It's almost two in the morning now, and even at this height the sun won't wink on us before four-thirty or five. For a while it's straight up, a blind ascent, one climber behind another. After ascending for two and a half calf-and-foot painful, hard-breathing, hours, the sun's first rays suddenly pierce the dark from behind a rocky escarpment. Within minutes the world is bright and sparkling with light.

We're negotiating an undulating ridge of rock and ash, which sweeps away in a curve to our right. It seems like forever, one foot threatening to slip over the edge, the other trying to maintain purchase. Ahead, the others draw away from us. Schmedjie's limping, and I don't feel that good either.

I don't know how, but suddenly we're at Cobra point, and the dreadful ash-ridge is below and behind us. The views are stunning. We can see the rim of Meru's crater. Away to the west, the bold grey rock and glittering snow of Kilimanjaro's peak floats above the clouds. Far, far below, in the direction where the pale blue sky is unbroken by cotton wool cloud, the great Rift Valley of East Africa is laid out like an artist's impression. Is this what artists call *inspiration*, I wonder, or is that breathing-in, which is getting more and more difficult?

Miss Moss, the cross French teacher, has attached herself to Schmedjie and me. Maybe it's because we're stragglers. Truth is, Schmedjie has blisters. Big, bloody ones, on both his ankles. His Mum bought him special climbing boots, and they're a worse disaster than my *Bata* shoes. Schmedjie stops and pulls his boots off. Then he tries to pull off his socks. The back ends don't want to come off because they're stuck with blood and stuff to his heels. He's in a lot of pain.

There's still an hour to go to Socialist Peak, the new name for Meru's summit. I persuade Schmedjie not to rip his socks off. He puts his boots back on and we carry on upwards, Schmedjie limping ever more painfully, Miss Moss wheezing almost as bad as Marais used to, and me just wishing all this could end.

Nearly an hour of agony. We reach a place where the rock is covered with slippery ice, and very steep. We can't see any of the others. Miss Moss finds a flat rock to sit on. It's right on the edge of the crater, and we can see a gigantic cone of ash at the bottom, like the remnants of a giant's barbecue.

Socialist Peak is just above. Just one more big boulder, can't be more than a hundred yards, and in a clear patch we briefly see some of the expedition going up a path on one side. It's unmistakably BL leading them. An icy wind is whistling, almost howling, through dark clefts in the rocks. Cloud and mist whirl about, and the view of Socialist Peak is whited out.

'Far enough,' Miss Moss wheezes, 'we've conquered the mountain, we don't need to go up on that rock.'

'That's right!' Schmedjie exclaims, tugging one of his boots off. I'm tired. I'm scared. I've never been in a place like this. All I want is the warm cosiness of the dorm at Arusha. Why did I come on this stupid thing anyway? I subside onto the rock beside Schmedjie. We've conquered the mountain.

The others start to stream down from Socialist Peak. We join them in the descent.

'No, you didn't conquer Meru,' Mr Houghton says. We're dumbfounded. 'You got to the crater-rim, but you didn't go up Socialist Peak and sign the book, so that's not a success, is it?'

Schmedjie and I are in tears. This isn't what Miss Moss said. She told us we didn't need to climb that little rock, that we'd already conquered Meru. One more failure to add to my list. How can I ever trust these cheating *Wazungu?* I wish I was home with my honest *watu* in Geita. They wouldn't deceive me like this. 'English sheets!' Schmedjie says. I agree. He's white, but he's a *mutu* too!

That night in bed Gretchen weeps beside my deathbed, as I lie dying. I'm a brave mountaineer who never made it to the top, but did his best and saved the lives of others. It's so sad. I fall asleep weeping for our lost love. My last thought is how pretty she looks when she cries. She's wearing the same sparkling white dress she wore that May Day at the club, when Becky was May Queen. That's when Gretchen suddenly scratched her bum.

Schmedjie invites me to spend the long weekend with his family, and I eagerly accept. Usually I watch the lucky ones whose families live within range leave on Friday afternoon, knowing I'll have nothing to do for four days, and have to sleep in an empty dorm, which is very spooky. I get so scared that I hide a thick two- foot stick under my mattress, and after lights-out move it under my pillow. If any spooks try to get me, I'll give them a go.

The Schmedjies arrive in a black *Citroen DX*, like the ones in films about French police. There's Mr and Mrs Schmedjie, and Ulla, Schmedjie's sister, who is twelve and pretty, in a pixie-way. The whole family are blonder even than Gretchen, and pale-skinned. They talk to each other in a language even more guttural than German. Finnish. Last week in a row Matwiga called him *Mulisha*, or finished. When did they start, I wonder.

The road to Moshi is untarred, stony and potholed, and the *Citroen* undulates on its hydraulic suspension like a boat on the sea. I get seasick. They have to stop twice and I vomit on the side of the road. Fortunately it's only forty miles to their house. I go to bed early, because the smell of stew in the kitchen makes me feel worse.

Early on Saturday morning everyone is up and ready for the day's adventure, a trip to *Kibo Hotel*, halfway up Mount Kilimanjaro. It's at the very end of the road up the mountain, the highest point accessed by car. From there on up it's walking and climbing. I still don't feel very well and don't want breakfast.

The car journey up the mountain is awful. I try to sleep, but the nausea won't let me. Nor will the popping in my ears. After two hours of winding round hairpin bends and precipitous passes, where the world is far below in miniature, seen in gaps in the clouds which waft by like shredded cotton wool, we emerge onto an alpine plain, and there, in a clearing, is the hotel. When we get out the car it's very cold, even though the sun is shining.

We're sitting in a large dining room and food is about to be served. I'm terribly cold. I excuse myself and go out into the sunshine. There's a bench in front of the hotel, and I sit down. It feels a bit warmer in the sun, but still my teeth chatter, and I'm shivering all over. After ten minutes Mr Schmedjie comes out to check on me.

'Are you okay?' he asks.

'Cold,' is all I manage to say. He puts his hand on my forehead, and looks surprised.

'But you are very hot, Jimmy,' he says.

'Cold,' I say.

'Have you had malaria before?' he asks.

'Yes,' I say.

'You've got it again.' Now I begin to feel nauseous and I vomit on the ground, my stomach heaving even though it's empty, and all that comes up is horrid, bitter yellow stuff. 'We'd better get you back to the school,' Mr Schmedjie says.

Their long weekend and visit to *Kibo* ruined, they drive me back to Arusha. I'm so ill, so cold, even though they wrap me in a blanket, that I don't even notice the journey. By the time we reach school I'm unconscious. I lie in my sickbay bed day after day.

There is something I can do to entertain myself. I feel that one of my top molar teeth is a hard green crystal. When I close my jaw firmly, the sharp point meets the lower molar. If I increase the pressure, the green crystal 'penetrates' the lower tooth. Strangely, it's a pleasant sensation, not easy to describe, like biting on hard liquorice, feeling it give way and divide at the force of the bite.

Why is it pleasant? The entire thing is false. I don't have a green crystal for a tooth. It cannot penetrate another tooth. But the sensation is real, and re-experienced at will. It banishes other things. I tell the doctor. He says there may be 'an organic cause'. Malaria can do that. Something about 'somatic hallucinations'. Whatever that means. Why teeth and the sensation of one tooth being penetrated by another made of crystal? The psyche, he says, is beyond analysis.

Sickbay is a haven of peace. Being there means no lessons, lying in a comfortable bed with good counterpanes and pillows, and sharing the room with only four others. The food is better than the muck we normally eat at school. Because we're sick we have perks, such as a never-ending supply of *Classic* comics to read. They're confiscated from the dorms for reading by torchlight after lights-out. There's a pretty nurse with red hair who walks around and checks on us by day and night. Everyone's in love with her. Except me. I'm only in love with Gretchen. I think about her every time the lights are out. One day I'll marry her. I wonder if she knows.

It's because it's so nice in sickbay that nobody wants to get better. We claim to feel worse than we are, because that's how to prolong paradise. Here we feel valued, important and privileged. The risk is the check-up by the visiting doctor. We live in fear and dread that he'll say we've recovered enough to go back. Tactics evolve.

Another boy in sickbay shares a secret. Eating toothpaste makes you vomit and gives you a temperature. The first part is true. I get violently sick. Temperature. . ? No, it doesn't do that. Old faithful is needed. Go to the bathroom when doctor's approaching. Run hot tap till very hot, drink as much as possible. Take a mouthful, hold, and limp as if very ill back to bed. Only swallow hot water when doctor produces thermometer. Reading is up by at least one and a half degrees. Doctor checks carefully, says you've got to stay another day. Yahoo, but don't show jubilation.

We constantly discuss how to stay longer. One chap decides to 'fall' off the garden wall and hurt himself. He's allowed out there because he's re-something. Re-suppurating, someone says. Re-coperating someone else says. Anyway, he falls, and breaks his leg. He's been told he's well enough to go back to his dorm next day and is determined not to. With a broken tibia, he's taken to the General Hospital, where a plaster cast is applied. Next day, despite his heroics, he's back on his dormitory, back to classes, with plastered leg and walking stick. Garden-wall-jumping just doesn't work.

# Thirty

Anand Singh is a fine figure of a man. He's a Sikh. There's a saying – 'all Sikhs are Singhs, but not all Singhs are Sikhs'. Anand is. He was Dad's second-in-command on Geita ropeway, and proved a loyal friend to Mum after Dad died. 'Anytings you are wanting,' he says, 'be telling me pliss, I am getting!'

He's a big man, with an impressive beard, and he always wears a neatly wound turban, crimson, blue or orange. He served with the Indian Brigade in Burma during the war, and distinguished himself against the enemy. Mentioned in dispatches, Higgs says. Knew his commanding officer in the Irrawaddy delta. I've seen Anand talking with Kaizer. Different battles, same war, same country – Burma. They like and respect each other.

'*Mahindi mzuri,*' Kaizer says. Good Indian.

'First-class fellow, you know!' Anand says.

Anand came to Tanganyika with a group of Sikh volunteers, all ex-Indian Brigade, who sought their fortunes in the African bush. He managed, a few years later, to bring his wife from Punjab, and soon they had three children. They're a happy family. Anand works hard, while his wife looks after the home and kids.

When Dad died in February '57, Anand was stricken. He loved Dad like an older brother. He sadly accepted the number one job on the ropeway, with loyal Wait as number two. He even took over MZ202, Dad's beloved Land Rover. It's a paradox. Here's this upstanding, trustworthy, respected and promotable man, who is faithful to his wife, and widely respected, but, because he's an Indian, he can't join the Club. Still, it matters little to Anand. He's teetotal and wouldn't enjoy the drunken talk of the *Mzungus*.

Then Anand gains fame for something else. Ridge-Eight, known as 'Rijate', is where the ropeway to Geita mine starts it's seventeen mile run over hill, valley and bush. The history of gold digging at Rijate involves tragedy, failure and bancruptcy before the ropeway came. Its advent brought success by reducing costs, and, at last, made the low-grade Rijate ore profitable. Rijate is a subsidiary gold-bearing-ore-source to Geita mine.

The tunnels dug into the hillside by the early nineteen-twenties miners are crude. Narrow, shored up with logs hewn from the hillside, and only five foot high, they lead into darkness, and curve where the old diggers followed the yellow seam. The gold-bearing seam is only sixty to a hundred feet deep, and its zigzags makes it tedious to follow in a tunnel. Much easier to blast the top of the hill to kingdom come, or *blurryfucken* as the workers say, collect the ore, and shovel it into ropeway buckets.

The disused tunnels provide the sweating, labouring men with something they value, even in the bush at forty degrees, with midges biting, and real snakes in the grass. Privacy for intimate bodily functions. They have become bush toilets.

In 1963, working at Rijate, trying to fix a problem on a suspended bucket which is stuck and holding things up, Anand feels an urge to relieve himself. He enters an abandoned tunnel, shining his torch ahead. He comes to a fork and finds a convenient spot. He undoes his belt and the buttons on his trousers, and squats down. When he hears the growl, he thinks he's got here just in time. Then he sees the eyes. Bright yellow eyes, big as teacups, staring at him from the dark just yards away. The next growl is louder, and the eyes advance.

Anand runs, without waiting to pull up his trousers. He's constrained at the ankles to short steps, and just five yards ahead of the growling beast. He erupts into bright sunlight, 'and am exposing my secrets!'

Wait hears the leopard before he sees it. On the back of the Land Rover is Dad's old Czech *Brno* twelve-bore over-and-under double-barrel shotgun, which Mum gave to Anand. It's loaded with two rounds of buckshot. Wait grabs it and whirls, just as Anand reaches the car and the leopard erupts from the tunnel. He pulls both triggers and the beast collects the impact from two barrels. It slides to a halt, dead, its blood-spattered nose against the back wheel. How strange. Dad loved Anand, and, though he's dead, it's his old shotgun which saved Anand today!

I'm twelve when I see the dead leopard. Anand drives MZ202 to the mine store, as part of a tour to show the beast to everyone. The bush telegraph has already done its work. *'Chui anajaribu kula Singa-Singa!'* Leopard tries to eat Sikh. That's around the mine-store workers long before triumphant Anand and Wait roll into the compound.

The *chui* lies on the back of the short-wheelbase Land Rover. His neck is bent, his head against the cab's back window. His tail extends four feet beyond the tailgate, its tip brushing the ground. He's six foot long if he's an inch. His nose and eyes are peppered with shot, and the side of his throat raggedly torn and bloody.

Wait stands atop his kill, waving Anand's shotgun. There's applause from the *wanaume*, or men, and a very grateful Anand. Embarrassed, but smiling, he knows he's escaped by a whisker and owes his life to Wait. And, he tells Mum, to 'your velly gracious late husband.'

At Lone Cone Club there's a peril more dangerous than Anand's, or any other, leopard. Harold Norris. He's a Sussex man, who always seems sixty years old. His chin juts out so far that his bottom teeth protrude. This, and a nasal twang, give him a distinctive, very odd voice. He has a general-factotum type of job, nobody knows exactly what, including Harold. He loves to stand at the bar and tell long-winded stories of reminiscence about 'early days' in Geita. They lived in tents then, and lions sauntered in at night. His stories always start by defining precisely which year he's talking about. But a subject hasn't come up yet. There's a detailed analysis of daughter Carol's age, and what wife Hilda was doing at the time.

'It was in 1949. . . Carol was three. Yup.' Pause. 'Carol was three, and Hilda was learning to drive. . . No, it was in 1948. Carol was two, and Hilda first came to Geita.' Pause, scratching of prominent chin. 'No, it was in 1947. . . , Carol was one, and, and. . . ...and then again, maybe it was in 1949. . .' Big accentuation on word 'then'. Thoughtful expression. More chin scratching.

'No, it was 1946!' Harold looks pleased, takes a mouthful of beer. Now, his victim thinks, after several minutes of trying, Harold's finally pinned down the year, and can get on with his story. Harold looks thoughtful again. His chin gets even juttier. 'Now let me see. . , it was in 1947. Carol was one, and Hilda. . .' The victim despairs and looks desperately for rescue. Nobody has ever heard a whole story from Harold. He's never sorted out when it was. There was only one person bold enough to say what he thought.

It's 1956, and Dad is having a quiet beer. Harold sidles up and stands beside him. 'Hello Dick,' he says, bottom teeth glinting.

'Harold,' Dad says, many times exasperated by endless stories which don't start, 'why don't you go where you're wanted?' Harold is taken aback, and never collars Dad again. Mum says Dad is cruel. Dad says it's either that, or shoot the bugger.

In '63 Harold's still at the bar most nights, waiting Venus-Fly-Trap-like for another victim to regale with how old Carol was and what Hilda was doing. Sometimes, not able to trap an adult, he comes out from the bar to bore us kids with his never-starting stories. We dash for cover when we see him.

My relationship with Mrs Snel has been fatally jaundiced, at best, since that long-ago day I told her to 'Speak Swahili, dammit!', then continued decapitating her precious flowers. And what I said about her private parts, of which she got the gist if not the words. To me she's the epitome of *Mzungu* oppression. To her, I'm the devil. *Shetani* himself! It's not on purpose that I add fuel to the incinerator. I know I must keep on the right side of the dreaded *Wazungu*. If I can, I avoid the old harridan. But fate steps in.

It has its origin in a small, dense wood in a narrow valley near a caravan park at Plympton, Devon. It's 1962, and we're here on holiday. Fraser says I have lived too long with 'two women'. It's about time I become a man. I must kill something to 'become a man'. He has a small four-ten gauge shotgun and a box of cartridges. He takes me into the wood, points at a little brown bird in a tree, and orders me to shoot it. I point the gun, determined not to be 'soft', and pull the trigger. The gun barks, the little bird disintegrates. Fraser pats me on the back. 'Well done!' he says.

I'm bewildered. I've killed again. Like Tembo's puppy. But was it fair? Did the bird have any chance? When she hears it, Mum says there's a bird-widow somewhere, and poor little baby birds with no father. I'm sad and tearful, which Fraser says proves what a *sissie* I've become.

In Geita I wrestle with confusion. Am I really a softie, a 'mummy's boy', like Fraser says? If not, why was I so upset about the bird? Maybe you have to get used to killing, in order to toughen up. It says so in war comics.

Just then Charlie Praze gets the first pellet-gun in Geita. Soon he boasts about shooting lots of birds. He feels nothing at all, he says. I nag Mum 'till she gives in and buys me a used *Gekado 1.77* airgun from a shop in Mwanza. It's made in Germany, like the old Mauser rifles. I take target practice, shooting empty cans and poisonous blue-headed lizards high on tree-trunks. Charlie says pigeons are good to eat. I shoot a couple. Umali roasts them. They taste rancid and there's hardly any meat. Is this God's punishment? Maybe he doesn't like me having any kind of gun.

It's an ordinary, boring afternoon. I've had the gun a month and don't know what to shoot any more. The sun is scorching the bush. I'm walking up the narrow footpath from our house to Top Road. It's very still, quiet as the graves at Samina. The air shimmers in the heat, and there's no breath of a breeze. I wonder where the *njiwa*-birds are today. Just to hear a friendly *ooh-oor-oor* would make me feel less lonely. Have they fled because they think I'll shoot them? I won't do that. They're my *rafikis*, friends.

There isn't even a *Mwewe* bird soaring high on the thermals from the burning land. Are they, too, departed? I approach a tall acacia tree through the elephant-grass beside the path. Suddenly the silence is broken by a loud, almost human, and very eery sound. *'Haa-daa-daa',* it goes, *'haaa-daa-daa'.* There's a drumming sound of big wings beating the air, and a most curious creature alights on a branch high in the tree.

The *hadeda ibis* is a very strange bird. It's a guinea-fowl-sized, long-legged wader, with a scimitar shaped, downward curved beak, half again as long as its body. With this it fishes the shallows. Its light-grey body is relieved by a bright orange flash on its bill, and blue-green on its tail and wingtips. It has staring yellow buttons for eyes.

I've seen a *hadedas* before, but from a distance. This one is ranging far from its Lake Victoria home. I remember, long ago, Umali talked about this bird. Witchcraft, like the *fisi*, and long life, were involved. *Kagogo* is their Swahili name. *Wazee*, or old people, are often called *kagogo*.

Perching high in the acacia, oblivious to danger, the strange bird contemplates me beadily. It's more than spooky. After loudly announcing its arrival, it's quietly analysing me with those evil buttons. No surprise ancient Egyptians mummified ibises, and entombed them with their dead. Not just *watu* are superstitious. I feel dread run up my spine.

I'm being challenged by God. He hasn't forgotten me, and now he is here in the guise of a bird. Something else. I've only seen *hadedas* in the air or on the ground. Why is this one perching in a tree? It proves that this is a challenge. I bring the airgun to my shoulder and take aim.

As puzzled as me, scientifically, but not superstitiously, is Mrs Snel, who, unseen and unsuspected by me, is also watching the *hadeda* from the other side of the tree. She's known for her interest in ornithology and this *hadeda* has been intriguing her for weeks. Today she's lucky. She's just arrived when he makes his loud call and perches. She focuses her Zeiss camera.

My pellet hits him square in the head. There's a brief flurry of wing and tail, and the heavy bird plunges, stone dead, at Mrs Snel's feet. She's dumbstruck. Then she yells in fury. 'Who did that, who shot the bird?' I can't see her, but I recognise her voice. The grass rustles as she stalks round the tree.

Only one escape. Oblivious to scratches and pokes of thorn and twig, I plunge into deep elephant grass and throw myself flat. Mrs Snel goes round and round the tree, ever more breathless. She passes me by feet, while I hold my breath and try to still my pounding heart. She returns to the *hadeda*-corpse, then, at long last, goes away.

Next day is a Sunday. At the club Mrs Snel strides purposefully my way. She stops feet away and my heart pounds again. 'Did you shoot the ibis bird?' she asks.

'Me?' I say without expression, 'what ibis bird?'


It's Saturday the twenty third of November '63. It's ten in the morning. Gretchen, Sophia, Antonio, Stefano and I are playing near the weighbridge on top road. We like watching the trucks full of wood drive onto the metal platform to be weighed. We hear Dieti shouting from far off. He's running our way. 'Kilt,' we hear him shout, but the other words are indistinct. He runs up, out of breath, and stops.

'President Kennedy,' he wheezes, 'kilt in Dallas!'

'What?' I ask. The president of America?

'*Vati* heard it on hiss shortwave radio. Kennedy vos shot, in Dallas, yesterday!' The girls start crying. I don't understand them. They don't even know the president. Or America. Antonio and Stefano agree it's silly. We go off to play our own, boys-only game. Who's Kennedy anyway? Where's Dallas? But Gretchen looks so pretty, even when she's crying. I wish I could hug her.

For Christmas '63 Mum gives me a second hand bicycle. It's red, and a girl's one, but I neither know nor care. It's my first bike and I discover the freedom of the road, or, at least, the dirt tracks and footpaths of Geita. My bike has a cable-driven speedometer on the handlebar and that spurs me to reach speeds which astound me. Downhill, pedalling furiously, I go more than fifty miles an hour. This, on sandy surfaces strewn with stone, wearing no helmet, nor any protective gear.

Charlie Praze, the assistant manager's son, has always had a bike. It's another thing that separates and divides us. Just like I have no father, and he does, I have no bike, and he does. Now I have one, he cycles to my house often, and we ride off somewhere together.

Charlie is a year older than me and has always been taller and stronger. From when he was nine, his parents, who can afford it, have sent him to boarding school 'at home' in England. Where Becky is now. To us in the colonies, that's the height of posh. School 'at home' is a 'good thing', because it stops children 'going native'. That's what Charlie's mother tells Mum, knowing she can't afford to send Becky and me to a private boarding school in England.

One day Charlie arrives at my house and asks me to ride with him to a village ten miles away. On the way we come across three ragged *totos* aged between six and seven. They're very frightened of us, which I don't understand. Charlie jumps off his bike and leans it against a tree. Then he breaks off a twig, holds it like a gun, and points it at the terrified *totos*. In Swahili he snarls 'Give me all your money!'

The *totos* burst into tears and plead, saying they have no money, but please don't kill them. I watch in horror. The poor kids think the stick in Charlie's hand is a gun. White people, or *Wazungu*, have strong magic. Even though they've watched him break the twig from a tree, they believe he can shoot them with it. When the smallest of the three, a little girl, produces two ten-cent coins and offers them to Charlie, who is laughing delightedly, I break my silence.

'Stop it,' I say.

'What?' Charlie says, turning to me, surprised.

'Stop making them cry,' I say.

'Why should I?'

'Cos it's cruel,' I answer.

'You're a girl,' he says. Seeing their chance, the three *totos* disappear into the undergrowth beside the path. Charlie looks around.

'You've let them go,' he snarls.

'I'm going home,' I say, turning my bicycle.

'I don't like you anyway,' Charlie shouts. I don't care. I have already decided I don't like him either.

'Oh yeah,' he shouts, 'and I'm going to have your little Gretchen!' He makes the horrible sign with an index finger through the loop two others. I stop and let my bicycle clatter on the road.

'You what?' I say, my hands balling into fists, my throat constricting. I take two steps towards him, but he laughs and rides off.

'I'll get you!' he shouts as he pedals away. I have exactly the same thought, only it's *me* who'll get *him!*

I'm pedalling uphill towards our house when I have my first attack. It starts with an urge to cough, then cough again, harder. It gets worse and worse, until, after dropping the bike onto the ground, and kneeling on all fours in the dirt, I vomit. Then the coughing starts again and leaves me fighting for breath. After a long time I recover, but I'm not strong enough to pedal my bike. I push it the rest of the way. I don't know why I've had the coughing fit and don't mention it to anybody.

At home I tell Umali about Charlie. He says he's a bad *Mzungu*, and I did right to confront him.

Two days later, lying on my bed reading a comic, I have another attack. This time it's so severe that, trying to dash to the bathroom to vomit, I faint. I strike the side of my face on the big brass doorknob. When I come to, my face is burning and there's a pool of blood on the floor. From a nasty graze on my cheek. Sandy is whimpering and licking me desperately. Umali hears the thump, and comes to investigate. He hoists me to my feet. He's amazingly strong for someone with pin-legs.

'What is it?' he asks in Swahili, 'what is making you fall, Jimu, are you sick?' He looks anxious. His eyes are wide and there's sweat on his brow.

'*Nine kohoa,*' I begin. I was coughing. I can't continue because the coughing starts again. Umali helps me to my bed, but I cough so hard I vomit all over the counterpane before I can lie down.

'Jimu, Jimu, you are *really* sick,' he says. He uses the word *ugonjwa*, which conveys seriousness. Dad was *ngonjwa* just before he died. I regain my breath at last, but now I feel a new emotion. Panic. *Watu* who are *ngonjwa* always die. I'm going to die. I tell Umali.

'You won't die Jimu,' Umali says soothingly, *'pole'*, peace, but his words belie his expression. I'm sweating profusely and feel exhausted. Umali fetches a damp cloth and wipes my face. He rolls up the counterpane and pulls it out from under me.

'*Lala* Jimu.' Sleep. I'll tell Mama you are *ngonjwa*, and she'll call *Bwana Muganga*.' The doctor. He draws the curtains on the bright sunlight. I'm so sleepy. Umali gently wipes the graze on my cheek with a cool damp cloth. Then he leaves, closing the door behind him. I notice a large *sufuria* on the floor. Just in case. I didn't see him bring it in.

I awake to find Mum and Josef Weiss standing beside my bed. 'Vot iss wrong?' he asks.

I start to speak, but coughing stops me. I think my lungs will burst, and I vomit on the floor, missing Umali's *sufuria* by a foot.

'Is serious,' I dimly hear Josef say to Mum. I notice Umali's worried face behind them. 'He plays viss the *totos*, so vot you expect?' Josef says to Mum.

'What do you mean, Doctor?' Mum asks.

'He hass Tuberculosis, *TB*, is vot I mean,' Josef replies. 'Bring him to hospital in der the morning, und I do der chest X-ray.'

Next morning Mum drives me to the hospital. In Geita there's really only one hospital, if wards, operating theatre, dispensary and doctor's office make a hospital. I have another coughing fit on the way, which makes Mum drive poor Maisie far too fast for the dirt road.

The hospital is known as the 'African hospital', because only Africans are admitted there. If *Wazungu* need to be in hospital, they're admitted to that little bungalow known as the 'European Hospital'. Where Dad died, and the murderer Stroessner blew his brains out. If a *Mzungu* needs surgery or an x-ray, it has to be done at the African Hospital.

Maisie skids to a halt with locked wheels in a cloud of dust on the stony ground. We walk past the big mango tree out front. It's one of the places Lutoli and I often sneak at sunset, when nobody can see us, to throw big sticks and knock down mangoes. Soon they'll be ripe again. At this time of day the tree is the hospital waiting room. Sitting on the ground at its base are twenty *watu*, all waiting to be seen by a nurse or the doctor. They'll wait for hours and hours, sheltering from the fierce sun in the tree's shade.

'Jimu!' I'm hailed as we go past. It's Lutoli. I stop. He looks thin.

*'Nini unafanya hapa?'* I ask him in surprise. What you doing here?

*'Nina kohowa,'* he answers. I am coughing. He gives a short cough to demonstrate.

*'Mimi vile-vile,'* I say. Me too.

'Come on,' Mum says, waiting.

'I won't go unless Lutoli comes too,' I say defiantly. Mum stares at Lutoli, at me. Her face breaks into a smile. She's known Lutoli from infancy.

'Come, Lutoli,' she says, 'I don't care what the doctor says!' We walk into the hospital. Josef is waiting.

'Vot iss ziss?' he exclaims when he sees us, 'der United

Nations, *TANU*, or vott?'

'He's my friend,' I say.

'Your friend, eh?' he says, cocking his head.

'*Mna ugonjwa?*' he asks Lutoli, who's trying to hide behind Mum. Are you ill?

'*Ndio, Bwana Mukubwa,*' Lutoli whispers, his voice hoarse with terror. Yes, Big Master.

'*Mna kohoa?*' Josef asks. Are you coughing?

'*Ndio,*' Lutoli manages. Yes.

'Dass ist ein plague,' Josef retorts to Mum. 'Der *TB* iss all arount!'

'Can you see both boys?' Mum asks.

'Vell, vot a mudder you are,' Josef mutters, grinning despite himself. 'Der mudder to der naughtiest boy uff Geita, und now also to hiss black freund!' If it was up to Josef, he wouldn't separate the races anyway. Saw enough racial hatred in Germany. But unwritten colonial rules have to be obeyed. Not now. 'Come in, all uff you!' he says, his gruff voice breaking into a laugh. 'Vott can zey do to me, *eh?*'

X-rays show we both have 'spots on der lungs', which means tuberculosis. We are lucky to live in our time, Josef says, because just twenty years ago there was no effective drug treatment. Josef starts us on Streptomycin. It's the antibiotic which kills the TB bug, which he says is *mycobacterium tuberculosis*.

Streptomycin is given by injection into the bum. The syringe is made of glass, and very big. The needle is thick, because the preparation is viscous, or is that *vicious?* The pain when Josef plunges the needle into the upper outer part of my buttock is bad. When he presses the plunger it's unbearable. After the injection my whole cheek is numb and achey. We have to have another injection, twice a week, for six weeks.

Walking to the hospital for my third torture I think I can't go through with it. Mum's persuaded me I must because I'll die if I don't. My feet carry me unwillingly closer to the hospital. I'm in two minds. My heart's pounding with two kinds of fear: death-fear and vicious-injection fear. My mouth is dry, and I feel sick. I'm terrified. There's a debate in my head. I can't face this injection. My bum still aches from the last one. I'll refuse to have it. I'll go in to the hospital, then refuse. That's manlier than just not going. That's stating my case.

Lutoli and I are truly *wadugu*, brothers. He's waiting for me under the mango tree, and he's made the identical decision to me.

'*Sitaki!*' he exclaims. I don't want.

'*Mimi vile-vile!*' I reply, relieved I'm not alone.

'*Kuja!*' shouts the male orderly in white shorts and shirt, standing in the open doorway. Come! Josef only gave the first injection, and then the orderlies did it. Lutoli and I look at each other. Should we run for it? There's a wordless conversation between us. It's ridiculous. If we didn't want the injection, why have we come? We've got this blurry *ugonjwa*, sickness, and we'll die without treatment.

Lutoli's eyes say he's beaten. Reluctantly, he walks into the torture chamber. I'm just behind. He undoes the top of his shorts and lies facedown on the couch. A grinning orderly appears, holding the huge glass syringe needle-upwards. He's actually enjoying this. It's the last straw. Even as the needle pierces Lutoli's skin, I'm turning to run.

Too late, there are two more beefy orderlies between the door and me. There's no escape. How have they anticipated me like this? Later, Josef tells me, 'I know you, Jimmy, I know you vill try to run vun day, so I tell zem votch you, und zey do.' It's a choice. Impossible wrestling match and injection, or injection only. I submit in terror and futility.

For six weeks I have to rest at home. Sandy is with me all the time. Finally I'm allowed to ride my bike again, and hang around with Lutoli and my friends. The TB is cured, Josef says, looking at the latest X-ray. Certainly I'm feeling better, and that horrible cough has gone. Lutoli says he's better too, and it was all worth it. I'm still cross about the injections. You should be grateful, Mum says. I am, but why did it have to hurt so much? Something to do with a saying I heard. What was it? Oh yes – 'gaining pain', or is it 'paining gain' – sounds stupid either way.

# Thirty-one

I'm enchanted by Red Indian kayaks from cowboy films. They're so cleverly made, of sticks bound with rawhide, and animal skins stretched tight over the frame, to make a robust, waterproof and portable vessels. What a thing, I think.

With one of those, I can go out on Lake Victoria at Nungwe Bay. It's only fifteen miles from the camp. My own boat! Maybe I can even fit a sail. I have images of my canoe gliding along on open water, leaving a long straight wake behind. Perhaps, even, it'll turn into the long-range canoe of my imaginings.

Three times in the last two years I've gone into the bush with Umali's panga and cut long sticks from trees. I've laboured long to bend and tie them into canoe-shape with self-made sisal string. I've stretched and nailed old bed-sheets over the outside, and painted them with leftover house-paint for waterproofing. Three unmitigated disasters. Everything wrong. Paint not waterproof, comes off in the rain. The twigs of the frame change shape with drying out, and my canoes end up like bent sausages. Tembo mercifully notices my humiliation and burns the evidence on the fire outside his hut. I'm grateful.

One day I have a *Eureka* moment. If you can't do it, I think, find someone who can. Jaswan Singh, the old Sikh who helped with the gun, is the obvious choice. Sure, he's a fitter and turner, not a carpenter, but wood, steel, what's the difference?

I need a plan for my canoe, something I can show the old man. I sit with a pencil and paper and draw my very first boat-plan. It's got two long, bent side-poles of wood, joined to a single bottom, or keelson, by a dozen ribs. After rubbing out and re-drawing several times, and labeling it *Jimu's Plan*, I take to the engineering works.

'Dis vun vill be capsizing,' Jaswan says, scratching his luxuriant plaited beard. He met Dad many times in the early days, in the company of his cousin Anand. He told Mum, just like Anand, that he would always be there to help us. I know he meant it. It doesn't strike me that I'm taking advantage of the old man's promise. He's staring from under his big glasses. 'Dis boat, Jimu, cannot be staying up on thin bottom like dis,' he says. He takes a pencil from behind his ear and draws next to my plan.

'Now,' he says, pointing out the differences with his pencil, 'wit wider bottom, there is chance.' He smiles. 'If you wanting building, I help. But you do working, yes?'

'Yes,' I say eagerly, 'thank you.'

'Vell, first you must be deciding what woods you are using. For top-pieces, I t'ink two inch by one. We are having plenty.' He points to a pile of cut timber on the floor. 'How big you are wanting boat?'

'Dunno,' I say.

'Vel, say nine feet longs, then you are needing eleven foot for allow bending, yes?'

'Yes,' I say. Jaswan is very clever.

'So, you are selecting two pieces, and cutting eleven foot. You know how use saw?'

'Yes, I know.' He smiles.

'Be using this vun,' he says, handing me a roll-tape measure, 'marking eleven feet. Then you are needing two short vuns, ten feet, for go lower, under top vuns, yes?'

'Yes,' I say, completely out of depth.

'Vell, starting now. I am having work to do. When you have cutting these woods, calling me.'

'Thank you, *asante,*' I say. He smiles.

'You are reminding me much your fader,' he says, and leaves me to it. I pick up his tape measure and walk over to the pile of timber. It's the beginning of my first real construction project.

It's the day after I start my boat building when Dieti comes to my house just after I've returned from the engineering works. He's found a remarkable thing on Top Road. He's never seen anything like it before.

'Look at zis,' he says excitedly when he arrives. Excitement still brings back his German accent. I've also never seen anything like it. It's a glossy magazine. On the front cover is a photograph of a topless lady. She's got big tits, very pale in comparison to the rest of her, which is deeply tanned. She's smiling. Doesn't look ashamed at all. The magazine is called *Playboy.* Odd, what's a playboy, or any kind of boy, got to do with tits? What does *play* mean?

'Gretchen hass titses like dese,' he says, 'I haff seen zem!'

'Really?' I say, suddenly more interested.

'Zere's more inside,' Dieti says, 'look!' He turns a page, and there's a completely naked lady lying on a beach. Her breasts are huge and only a raised knee hides her privates.

'Where did this come from?' I ask.

'On der road, somevun must haff dropped it,' he says. He turns more pages. More naked ladies. It makes me feel strange all over.

'What you going to do with it?' I ask.

'You keep it,' he says.

'Thanks,' I say. 'That'll be nice.' But where will I hide it? Just then footsteps sound in the passage, and Dieti shoves the magazine under my pillow. It's Umali. He wants to know if we want *chai*, tea. No thanks we say. He leaves, and out comes the magazine. It needs serious study.

The boat building is slow. I select bits of wood, measure them, mark the desired length with a pencil, and saw off the excess. Jaswan sets up a trestle table, and begins to assemble the pieces. The two eleven foot lengths are screwed together at the ends, and then separated in the middle by a two-foot-six plank. This, Jaswan says, will be a 'thwarting' or 'seating'. The two ten-foot lengths are also attached at the ends, but separated in the middle by a shorter plank of twenty inches. Thus the bottom, though flat, will be narrower than the top of the canoe.

Next Jaswan sets me cutting sixteen two-foot lengths of one-by-one inch timber, for 'ribbings' to join the top and bottom. When they're cut, Jaswan marks each end, and gives me a jigsaw to cut out notches. These will help attach them. When it's done, he drills them with a big drill, and screws them in place. It's been three days work, and the frame is beginning to look like a canoe.

'I am having canvas you can be using for outer-skin,' Jaswan announces. He holds up a thick roll. It looks perfect. 'You can be using small nail only,' he says, producing a jam-jar full. One inch, with big flat heads. I spend the day cutting and nailing canvas to  cover the ribs. Jaswan intercedes often, to help me pull the fabric tighter. By evening, there's a very definite canoe on the trestle table.

'Tomorrow,' Jaswan says, 'you can be painting. I am having

339

tin thick oil paint not needing – green.'

'Thank you, green's great,' I say. What a kind man!

One afternoon when I'm at home, because I have to wait two days for the first coat of green oil paint to dry before applying a second, Dieti arrives in again an excited state. When he's like this he blinks furiously and his head nods repeatedly. Charlie Praze called him 'Noddy' once, but the title never stuck. He *is* a funny little chap, but he doesn't need a nickname from Charlie. At twelve Dieti's still the size of a nine year old, and his mother often laments that 'Dieter vill chust not grow!'

Dieti is so excited he has difficulty telling me why. Between the violent blinking and nodding, and his other habit of stammering, it's almost impossible to understand him.'Come,' he says 'qvick, she is. . . zere. . . in ze bass, nakkit!'

'Who?' I ask.

'Gretchen. . .*und*...,'

'*Und?*' I say, despite myself.

'*Und, und,*' he nods, whether in agreement or in habit I cannot tell. I think it's habit because there's nothing to agree with.

'*Und* Gretchen, in ze bass, und, und. . . she iss nakkit!'

'Ze bass?' I ask incredulously, wondering how Gretchen could be in a fish, naked.

'In *mein haus,*' Dieti adds, nodding and blinking together. A fish in the house, with Gretchen, naked, in it. Suddenly I understand. She's in the bath, at Dieti's house. He sees my comprehension. Gretchen. At fifteen she's blossomed into a beauty. So perfect, so poised, so fragrant, so. . . *artistically* created. How can the same God who invented scorpions, killed Dad and sent me to Arusha, make someone like Gretchen? When I'm near her I feel I'm with an angel. She knows how I feel, and she's amused. I'd love to see more of her. Her body, that is.

'Ve go, yes, ve spy from der upstairs. . ?'

'Yes,' I shout, his excitement mine now, 've go now!' His accent is catchy. Ve, I mean we, run the winding footpath to Dieti's place, arriving there breathless, but wildly motivated. We dash past the framed old picture of Eugen Blüger with *Generalveldmarschall* Erwin Rommel in the lounge, me avoiding Rommel's steely gaze. He wouldn't approve of this.

'Up zere,' he gasps as we approach the bathroom door. There's a hatch in the ceiling. Dieti holds a finger to his lips. Splashing sounds come from the bathroom. 'Bring zat,' Dieti whispers, pointing at a corner-table. I take a glass vase off and place it on the floor. Then I lift the table and carry it to over. Dieti stands on it and pushes the hatch-door open. It's very dark up there. He pulls himself up and his short legs disappear.

'Are you komink?' he whispers from the void. I climb on the table and grab the edge of the opening. I haul myself up. It really is dark up here. After a while my eyes grow accustomed and I can make out Dieti's silhouette. A few paper-thin slivers of light show where the joins are in the corrugated iron sheets of the roof. The overlaps between the sheets may be waterproof, but light has a way of getting through.

I look and feel my way. The ceiling is built of raw sections of sawn timbers, which threaten to splinter my fingers at every touch. The planks make squares 4 foot across. Between is only ceiling board. Three quarters of an inch thick, made of compressed wood fibre, sawdust and glue. It's soft, and not very strong.

'Zat vay,' Dieti whispers, trying to control his breathing. I look and see a small round hole, half an inch wide, five yards away. Through it a yellow beam shines, illuminating a patch of corrugated iron roof.

'You first,' I say, suddenly seeing something very funny in this. It reminds me of the name of a mythical book called 'Jumping Off Mountains,' by Yugo First. I fight to suppress a giggle.

'Okay,' Dieti whispers, and he starts crawling towards the light. I stifle my ill-timed chortle and follow. It's very difficult feeling my way along the supports, and I already have splinters in both hands and knees.

Dieti reaches the light. I feel a surge of jealousy. He's going to get the first look. Gretchen. . . I want to be first to peep through the hole. I wish Dieti would, well, I wish he wasn't up here with me. God has a strange way of giving you what you wish for.

I'm just behind Dieti, his foot no more than six inches from my nose, when he makes a fatal error. He puts his weight on the weak board between the wooden supports. With a tearing sound it gives way, and Dieti plummets, with a loud crash, into the bathroom below.

The rent in the ceiling is three foot by two. In the brief millisecond before hell breaks loose, I see the top half of Gretchen, wet blonde hair hanging limply, at one end of the bath, and a stunned Dieti half-kneeling in front of her, one arm at a crazy angle over the side of the bath. Gretchen's arms are just coming up to cover her chest.

Dieti was right. In that briefest glimpse I see they're just like the ones on the lady in Playboy. Only better. Gretchen's mouth is opening to scream, and she's jumping up, covering her groin with a facecloth. I've seen enough, though in better times I'd like to see more.

I furiously retrace my crawl back to the hatch. The screams burst about me. Gretchen, shocked, indignant, angry. Dieti in agony.

I reach the hatch and climb down. No point closing it. The game's up. I flee down the corridor. As I near the kitchen I collide with Dieti's mum. Mrs Blüger was in the garden. She's hurrying to investigate the commotion.

'Vot is it?' she shouts, grabbing me by the arm and pulling me down the corridor. The sound from the bathroom has changed. Gretchen has stopped screaming, but Dieti is howling like a hyena.

As we reach the bathroom the door flies open. Gretchen has a towel around her. Dieti is still in the bath, his arm over the side. His face is contorted in agony and he's sobbing. There's blood on his lips. He hit his mouth on something.

'They were spying on me!' Gretchen yells furiously. She throws the door open and points at the devastated ceiling. Of all the Blüger family, only Gretchen has no trace of a German accent.

'You fell from zere?' Mrs Blüger asks Dieti. He subdues his anguished sounds to a whimper.

*'Mein arm, mein schulter!'* he gasps, trying to hold his arm and shoulder at once, spittle and blood coming from the corner of his mouth.

'Vot you sink you are doink?' Mrs Blüger demands. 'Vait

ven *Vati* hears about zis!' She turns to me. 'You too, Jimmy!' she spits. 'Your mudder vill know abowt zis!'

'Sorry,' I say lamely.

'You *vill* be,' says Mrs Blüger, letting go my arm and going to examine Dieter. I'm free. I run, pursued by all the *jinnis* and *djinns*.

At home I lock my bedroom door, get into bed, and cover my head with the blanket.

I get off very lightly for my part in the botched venture. Not so, Dieti. He hits the side of the bath with his left arm, breaks both radius and ulna, and dislocates his shoulder. His mouth-bleed is from catching his lip on the broken ceiling-board. He has to wear a plaster cast on his arm for two months. Fortunately, after the shock of what happened, Mr and Mrs Blüger, and even Mum, see a funny side. 'Boys vill be boys,' Eugen says to Mum. Gretchen decides it was quite funny, really. . !

How am I going to face her? It's obvious I wanted to see her naked. But it was Dieti's idea. If she was amused by me doting on her before, she'll be laughing to *tapika* now. Vomit. But Gretchen is a strange girl.

I'm lying on my bed reading a comic. It's a hot afternoon, just for a change. Gretchen doesn't come round often now Becky's in England. I could go over to the Blüger's house, but I don't know if I can face her. My shame is too keen. It's only three days since our disgrace.

'Hello.' A melodic female voice. Gretchen, standing by my bedroom door. She's come over, even though Becky's not here. She's wearing blue dungarees and a bright yellow shirt. Her blonde hair is cut short. She looks radiant.

'Hi,' I say, sitting up on my bed, trying to keep my voice even. 'May I come in?' A half-smile plays at her lips. What's she up to?

'Sure,' I grunt, my voice squeaky, my heart racing. She comes in. She has something in her hand. A rolled-up magazine. My heart pounds. I know what it is. Dieti took it back two days ago.

'Can I sit?' she asks. There is nowhere except my bed. This would be so great, if I hadn't spied on her. She doesn't wait for my answer. She's sitting on the edge of my bed, smelling of wild flowers, looking like a Nordic goddess. She unrolls the magazine. It's the Playboy Dieti found on Top Road. How did she get it?

'Do you think my tits are like these?' she says.

'Dunno,' I say, my thoughts reeling. Is she here to tease me? There's a smile tugging at the corner of her mouth. I decide to play her game.

'Maybe they are,' I say, trying to sound nonchalant.

'You had a *good* look, didn't you?' she says.

'Maybe, maybe not. . .'

'Come on, I saw you up there, staring at me.'

'Yes,' I reply truthfully. Why isn't she angry? Why does she think this is funny?

'You like me, Jim?' she asks, looking serious.

'Yup.' What else can I say?

'I know,' she says. 'Do you think I'm as pretty as the girls in this magazine?' She's watching me closely, her face only inches from mine.

'Of course you are,' I say. 'Prettier!'

'Was it you or Dieter's idea to spy on me?' She's using her brother's formal name. What does it mean? Now here's a conundrum. If I say it was *me,* I'll be a filthy beast. If I say *him,* I'm selling out on Dieti.

'It was me,' I say.

'No it wasn't. Dieter told me it was his idea. You know, I wish you were older. You're a brave little man.' I like the man bit, not the 'little'. She's getting up to go. There's something I need to know.

'Where did you get the Playboy?' I ask.

'Under Dieti's bed, when I helped Mum turn his mattress.' Now I see...and thank goodness she's saying *Dieti*, not Dieter. Must be softening. 'As soon as I saw it,' she continues, 'I knew it was connected to you boys spying on me.' I remain silent.

'Bye,' she says sweetly as she leaves my room. I lie there, my senses reeling.


My canoe is built, painted, and ready for launching on Lake

Victoria. I've named her *HMS Geita*. She really looks the business. Everyone's jealous. Jaswan is delighted with the result. He's even made me two laminated wooden oars, and fashioned and fitted swivelling iron rowlocks. All from scrap on the dump. Then the bomb strikes. I am not allowed to launch it on the lake. Mum's spoken to Mr Snel, who says I'll be eaten by a crocodile, or drown. So no lake. The club swimming pool is as far as *HMS Geita* will ever go!

I decide to bide my time, do sea-trials on the pool, and work on Mum and Mr Snel later. *HMS Geita* is launched on the pool, and soon becomes a source of great fun to all the *Wazungu* children. Now there's more than just swimming to be had.

The pool is huge, Olympic size, which makes it fifty metres long. Kids crowd into the canoe, as many as six at a time, paddle about, rock and capsize her, squealing and falling in the water. They turn her upright, clamber back in and carry on. The green oil paint never dries, and I don't know why. It leaves green streaks all over the sides of the pool from scraping by.

I take lots of passengers for rides in my canoe. Principal among these is Sandy, who stands in the prow like an old sea dog, and won't get off even when I put the bow up against the side. When nobody's there *HMS Geita* floats forlornly, upright or capsized, at one end of the pool or the other, depending on the breeze. My canoe has become a fixture in Lone Cone Club pool.

Becky has been writing heart-rending letters about how unhappy she is in England. Aunt Natalie's a real witch to her, she says. She begs Mum to bring her back home to Geita. She can continue her studies through a correspondence course. I can tell Mum's weakening. I'd love to have Becky back, so I add my powers of persuasion to hers.

Meantime light entertainment comes again to Lone Cone Club. Dieti and I are walking past the half-open door to the room behind the bar, the one where glasses and ashtrays are washed, and crates of beer and cold drinks stored. Mrs Snel's in there with the cleaning maids and a hullabaloo is going on. The maids are screaming in laughter, and she's shouting at them.

'What,' she yells in broken and nasal Swahili, 'has got into you?' This ignites fresh paroxysms of laughter. 'I only wanted a Swahili *kisimi*. . !' Fresh gales of uncontrolled mirth. Dieti and I fall about. Mrs Snel is asking one of the maids to give her a Swahili lesson, but saying *kisimi* instead of *kisimo*. The 'i' in place of the 'o' is critical. She's asking for a Swahili clitoris!

# Thirty-two

On the twelfth of January 1964 African rebels led by a Ugandan revolutionary, self-styled 'Field Marshal' John Okello, seize power from the Arabs in Zanzibar. The Sultan, Jamshid-bin-Adbullah, scion of the ancient Albusaid dynasty, whose influence once stretched from Muscat in Oman in the north, to the coasts of Tanganyika and Kenya, the islands of Zanzibar and Lamu, and across the Indian Ocean to the shores of India and modern Pakistan, is deposed. He and his family are plucked from certain doom by the Royal Marines, and taken to England on the carrier *HMS Centaur*.

In a frenzy of hate-driven killing, seventeen thousand Arab men, women and children are killed, some driven into the sea and shot in the water, others force-marched inland to hastily dug mass-graves, where they are shot and thrown in.

For many days the straits of Zanzibar, between the island and the little Tanganyikan port of Bagamoyo, is littered with bloated corpses. Sharks in feeding-frenzy consume many. Some float up onto beaches north and south of Bagamoyo, where hyenas feast on the bounty.

On holiday with relatives in Bagamoyo is Amil Mistree, a clerk who works with Mum at the mine store. Amil is a small, trim man, with very thick glasses. He's nervous, and reminds me, perhaps because of the magnification of his eyes by his spectacle lenses, of a rabbit caught in torchlight. He panics if his 'legder shit' doesn't add up, and asks Mum to 'be helping me pleeze.'

At Bagamoyo, Amil and his relatives are woken in the small hours by the distant sound of explosions and gunfire. Zanzibar is only four miles away. They'e alarmed. Later that morning, towards noon, bodies begin to float up onto the beach below his cousin's house. Many have chunks bitten off by sharks. Flies carpet the rest. Panic-stricken, Amil takes his wife and children and flees the coast. Three days later, exhausted, dusty and terrified, he arrives back at the mine, after travelling without sleep on a bus. He goes straight to see Mum at the mine store.

His is the first news of the massacre to reach Geita. Until then all that's known is that the 'corrupt' sultan has been overthrown by 'valiant freedom forces' on Zanzibar.

'I am shaking,' says Amil, 'it is terrible. They are keeling everybody. I want to go to Kenya!' Suddenly all the Indian clerks want to go to Kenya. Aziz declares he cannot live in a country with '*blurryfucken* murder going on.'

'*What* kind of murder?' Mum asks.

'Any fucken kind!' he says.

There are many eyewitnesses to what happened, Mistree being just one, for the government to keep it secret long. All over Tanganyika, and outside, for many have fled, witnesses describe the horrors they saw.

After a week, the government-run news agency admits there have been 'limited' casualties during the coup. It will be years before the figure of seventeen thousand will be admitted. The offspring of former slaves, or 'silavs' as the *Warabu* say, have exacted awful vengeance from their overlords.

The leader of the Afro-Shirazi party, the revolutionary regime on Zanzibar, is Sheik Abeid Karume. Soon he sees John Okello, the coup leader, as a threat, and Okello flees the island. Within days *Mwalimu* Julius Nyerere, president of Tanganyika, meets Karume in Dar-es-Salaam. On the twenty-sixth of April 1964 they announce to a waiting public, and hastily assembled international media, that Tanganyika and Zanzibar are merging forthwith into a single republic, to be called *Tanzania.*

I'm in Arusha when Tanzania is born. The president of the new state is Julius Nyerere, the vice president Abeid Karume. We are in class when the local *TANU* leader goes from one classroom to another, giving each group of children a talk about how corrupt the ex-sultan of Zanzibar was, and the courage and wisdom of President Nyerere and Vice-President Karume.

We get detailed instruction on how 'Tanzania' is to be pronounced. It is *TUN-ZUN-EE-AH,* not to be said the way of the 'English Colonists', rhyming with 'Tasmania'. After the dignitary has departed, Matwiga is jubilant. 'Our country is powerful,' he says, 'even more powerful than Kenya, or England!'

'Kenya is more powerful,' growls Dobson Muwengi, a Kenyan who came to Arusha School the previous year. He's fifteen, the rest of us only twelve or thirteen. He's a foot taller than us, and twice as strong. He's been made prefect by Mr Houghton, and loves to throw his considerable weight around. There's murmured discussion at what he says, and we agree, without reservation, that Kenya is the most powerful. It's amazing how we switch from the pronunciation of 'Tanzania' to the power of Kenya.

Dobson Muwengi is proving a blight on our collective happiness. Not only does he push us around, but he also snitches to Miss Baxter, or the teachers, when we do anything that's not allowed. He needs a lesson, but how?

'We could ambush him and beat him up,' Matwiga suggests. Schmedjie, Allen and I are not so sure. Muwengi's very strong. Anyway, even if we do, he'll just tell on us, like always.

'Let's think of something more subtle,' Schmedjie says.

'Don't know what you mean,' I say.

'Secret, more secret,' Schmedjie says.

'Why you don't say so, instead of that sub-tull stuff?' Matwiga snorts.

'Well, we're only twelve,' I say, 'and Muwengi's fifteen.'

'So?' Matwiga asks.

'We have to be careful. . .'

'Subtle,' says Schmedjie.

'Oh no!' snorts Matwiga.

'No, look,' says Schmedjie, I have a plan.

'What?' Matwiga and I ask together.

We hate Dobson Muwengi and ought to do something about it. Trouble is his size. We decide discretion is called for and valour can wait for another day.'

'Dis-kre-shun, val-oor, sub-tull?' Matwiga says, 'you mean we be sneaky?' That's a word he understands. Me too. Anyway, Schmedjie is our thinker, so we turn to him for a plan. Without hesitation, he suggests a stink bomb, which he thinks will 'stink the bugger out'. It sounds brilliant and we eagerly agree. Only none of us know anything about chemistry and we haven't a clue how to proceed.

'Listen,' says Schmedjie, 'we can make a very easy stink-bomb!'

'How?' asks Matwiga.

'Hydrogen Sulphide,' says Schmedjie.

'Hide-my-what?' Matwiga says, crossing his eyes. It makes him look really curious.

'Fool!' says Schmedjie. 'It's a chemical, stinks very bad.'

'Like what?' says Matwiga, more interested.

'Like a very bad fart.'

'That's what we need,' pipes up Allen, left out till now.

'But,' intercedes Matwiga, 'where we get this *hide beside?*'

'Eggs,' says Schmedjie, 'rotten eggs.'

'Why you not say so? Why this fancy stuff?' Matwiga exclaims.

Schmedje ignores him. 'All we do is get a couple of raw eggs. We make a little hole in the shells, then leave them in a sunny place a few days. Boof – hydrogen sulphide!'

'And?' I ask, feeling even further out of the discussion than Allen.

'Put them in a Marmite jar which we can seal, then unseal and put under Dobson's bed when he's sleeping.' Schmedjie has an evil grin.

We can only speculate on the nightmares of Dobson Muwengi over the next weeks. Every night after lights out, we wait for him to snore. Then the Marmite bottle comes out, the top comes off, and the bottle goes under his bed. Soon his snore changes, and he begins to toss and turn. He never wakes, but his sleep is inhabited by unimaginable demons. There's collateral damage too, because his closest cronies have their beds next to his, and they too sleep restlessly.

In the early hours, before the first light creeps through the dormitory windows, one of us holds our breath, retrieves the bomb, shuts the top, and replaces it in the locker. In the mornings Dobson looks tired and confused. We love it. This we call 'Secret Revenge, Codename: Stink-You-Out'. Whether it's caused by our hydrogen-sulphide bomb or not, Dobson Muwengi mellows towards us, and the problem is solved. The Marmite bottle is ceremonially buried.

In July 1964 Becky wins the battle and comes home to Geita. It's fabulous seeing her. She's fifteen, and quite the young lady. She's got a woman's shape and talks with an English accent. She's even forgotten much of her Swahili. She's brought the first part of her correspondence coursework with her. Mrs Day, the accountant's wife and ex-teacher, is going to supervise her two hours a day.

The gang re-unites – Gretchen and Becky, Sophia Fortuna, Antonio, Dieti and me. I haven't seen Lutoli in months. He's gone off somewhere with his fat aunt. Anyway, it's a joyous time, and we eagerly listen to Becky's English adventures. Then, like everything, we adapt to Becky being home, and go back to normal.

One afternoon about four pm I'm alone down by Tarzan-Swings, where the creepers hang from the trees over the stream, and where we were chased by the old lion with the septic paw. Suddenly there's a sharp retort from somewhere off to the left, invisible through the dense bush. It's still echoing from the treetops as I run to investigate. Through bush and bramble, tearing reaching creepers from arms and face, I find the source.

Bending over the still quivering body of a Thomson's gazelle is a black man in smart, pressed khaki shirt and shorts. He turns at my approach. It's Fritz, our stern driver with the German accent, the former *schutztruppe askari* with von Lettow Vorbeck in the First World War.

'Hallo,' he says, clearly uncomfortable like I've never seen him before, 'I vos chust shooting.' My eyes go to the gun he's holding. He sees my stare. 'Zis iss *mein* old gun, from der vore.'

'You kept it all these years?' I say, impressed. It's 1963. That war ended in 1918. Forty-five years. Suddenly I realise Fritz is very old. He must be seventy, at least. I notice for the first time his short hair is completely white. Like Kaizer.

'You vonte tell zem?' he says, for the first time I've seen him not scowling. 'Zey don't like der blacks haffink ein gun. . .' This man, despite his gruffness, is an old soldier and a distinguished elder, and he's having to plead with me, a mere child, not to tell on him. In independent Tanzania!

'Of course not!' I say. No point speaking Swahili to Fritz, he doesn't like it.

'You *vonte?*'

'I won't. Can I see your gun?'

'Here, der iss no bullets in.' He hands it to me. It's a beautifully made thing. The wooden stock is smooth with age and polish. The barrel and metal parts are jet-black. This gun has been lovingly kept. It's got a bolt, like Dad's *Wesley Richards 375 Magnum,* the gun I shot God with. Engraved on the side of the chamber is *'Gew.98 Mauser'.* Gew is short for *gewehr,* or gun, in German. Under that, in small letters it says 7.92. Fritz sees where I'm looking.

'Vos design 1898,' he says, 'und der bullets iss 7.92 millimetre.' He smiles shallowly. 'Vos replacing der *Mauser* model '71, vot vos smoking too much, und giff avay der position.'

It's beautiful. What a treasure! 'You keep it at home?' I ask.

'Yes, but iss hided. You vonte tell zem?'

'I vonte, *nein,*' I say, despite myself, 'your secret is safe with me.'

'Sanks,' he says, slinging his lovely old rifle, and turning to the dead Tommy. He's drawn a big knife. He'll butcher it here. Lots of meat for his family. His gun is a great asset to him.

I'm walking away between the thornbushes when my attention is caught by a mound on the ground with rocks arranged round it. At one end is a two-foot high stone. It's a *ziara,* someone's grave, out here in the bush. It looks like its been tended, because there's no elephant grass growing on it. I turn back to Fritz.

*'Nani hi?'* I ask. I want to know who was buried here. He stands up from his task.

*'Mein bruder*, Hans,' he says. His brother Hans? I didn't know he had a brother. He stares at me speculatively, trying to decide something. Then he says it.

'Your fadder iss buried at Samina, yes?'

'Yes.' What's Dad got to do with this grave?

'Next to hiss grave iss ein odder grave, von a vite voman, vun Mrs Villiams,' he says.

'Yes,' I say. I know that. But what's the connection.

'Mrs Villiams vos shot und kilt by Mr Stroessner in 1951,' Fritz says. I know that too. Dad read about it in a newspaper in Johannesburg. Mum never stopped telling us about that, or how strange it was he ended up buried beside her.

'Vell der driver vos also kilt by Mr Stroessner. . .'

'Yes, I know,

'Hans, *mein bruder*, he vos der driver.' Suddenly it makes sense. Here in this patch of forsaken ground is buried the other victim of that night's awful work by the madman Stroessner. A few miles out, off a fork in the *Boma* road, Dad lies dead beside poor Mrs Williams. Here lies the poor driver who was taking her so trustingly to Mwanza that fateful morning.

'You look after his grave,' I say.

'He vos goot man. Vos by me ven ve fought vid *Obersti* von Lettow Vorbeck in der *schutztruppe*, in der forst vore.' He's finished speaking, returns to his butchering.

Fritz is a strange old man. He never says much about himself, which is why I'm so surprised to hear about him from Kaizer.

It turns out that in this year, 1964, the legendary Paul von Lettow Vorbeck has died, more than half a century after he first took up his post in *Deutsch Ost Afrika.* In the national commemoration of his life, the West German *Bundestag* votes to fund back pay for any of his still-living *askaris* from the World War I *Schutztruppe.*

A temporary cashier's office is set up in Mwanza, and 350 old men gather to make their claims. That's all, out of a total of thousands of *askaris* in the *schutztruppe* during the war. Very few produce the certificates given them by Vorbeck in 1918. Some offer fragments of their old uniforms as proof of service. Suddenly the German banker in Mwanza, who's got the money, comes up with a brilliant idea.

Led into a room one at a time, each claimant is given a broom, and ordered in German to perform the manual of arms. Not one man fails the test. Not a single one was 'trying it on'. Among the old men is Fritz. But he's a quiet person.

Coincidence can be a strange thing. I've just been enamoured by Fritz's old *Gew.98,* German-built *Mauser* rifle, when I become aware of another *Mauser* rifle. This one's a .22 Mauser bolt-action rifle of much more recent vintage. It's one of the assistants at the mine store who finds the box. A *baruti*, or dynamite box, which has been put on a deep shelf years ago, then lost to memory when other things are put in front of it. It contains the 'personal effects' of Stroessner, the German who shot Mrs Thomas and Fritz's brother that early morning in 1951.

When he's told about the discovery, Mr Snel decides to open

the box and dispose of the contents. There, among several mouldy shirts, shoes and trousers, is the rifle. Why it wasn't destroyed after the murders, nobody knows. The pistol he used to shoot himself was thrown in the lake.

'Can I have it, Mum?' I ask when she tells me about it.

'No, Jimboy, you can't. 'Who'd want a murderer's gun, anyway?'

'I do,' I say, 'it's not the gun's fault.'

'No,' she says with finality. 'Mr Snel is handing it in to the police, and they'll destroy it.' It's final. No *Mauser* .22 for me. I never understand this thing about destroying guns, which have killed someone. They're made to do that, aren't they? 'I'll have to destroy this fridge,' someone might say, 'it made its contents cold you see...'

'Anyway,' Mum says, 'you're dangerous enough with that airgun!'

Mlozi's hut has long settled into the corner of Top Road and Compound Hill, and the banana-thatch roof is completely overgrown with thornbush. Useful, keeps lots of animals at bay. There are other plants growing around the hut. Some I recognise, some I don't. Chillies, wild garlic, a spiky dark-green leafed plant. *Bhangi*, Lutoli says. Cannabis.

In just six or seven years Mlozi's gone from a fresh-faced, if dirty and oddly attired teenager, to a fat man who looks forty. His long braids are brown and streaked with gray, and have more coloured ribbons than ever. He's lost all his front teeth. There are long raised scars on his forehead and cheeks, where he's scratched himself with a shard of glass. There are hundreds of small bones tied to his ankles.

It's a long time since I first saw him. Or since he was saved from stoning by the *n'gombe*-rich *mzee*. I tried telling him his *dawa* worked for me in my fight with the boys in England, but he just spoke to the sky. Anyway, the *watu* have finally accepted his presence, and as the years pass some begin to doubt he's mad, or possessed by *djinn* or *jinni*. The numbers of doubters grows. There are those who believe he is *mchawi*, witch, who has powers which can heal their illnesses, or relieve their poverty. They bring him *ugali* and fish, *mboga* and flying ants.

354

He doesn't always acknowledge the gifts.

The *wasikini* consider Mlozi more than just *mchawi*, but indeed a prophet. They come to him for advice, and forecasts of their futures. In return, they share the spoils of their begging with him. He's particularly keen on brightly coloured cloth, which he tears into ribbons. Mlozi doesn't talk. He mumbles in a high-pitched voice. It takes practice to understand what he says.

'Go to the tall *Mzungu* woman in the house of the water tank, and you will be rewarded,' Mlozi tells a squatting one-eyed *masikini*. He's talking about Mrs Barelli. Two hours later the masikini is back. He's been given an old ball-dress. It has lots of coloured ribbons. Mlozi's eyes widen with excitement. Two prizes in one – the *masikini*, though male, has a dress to wear, and Mzlozi has more ribbons. His reputation as *mchawi* is enhanced.

# Thirty-three

Heath Fotherington is a middle-aged, Home Counties, Oxbridge-sounding man. He came to Geita, people say, as a 'remittance man' from Hampshire. Remittance men are common in Tanganyika, and probably everywhere where the sun never set on the old British Empire. They are, it is said, from powerful and wealthy origins, but so disgraced their families that they were paid annual stipends to go abroad and stay there. A condition was that, if they ever returned to England, they would be cut off from further emoluments, and, in all likelihood, end up in the gutter.

If Fotherington is an aristocrat, he doesn't say so. But he speaks and acts like one. He was appointed as mine store manager in Geita by 'friends' at the *Rhodesia-Katanga Mining Company* head office in Chelsea, which, it's rumoured, was arranged by the Colonial office. Talk about smoke and fires – he's a remittance man.

He arrived in 1955, to take command at the mine store. He had a military past, everyone thought, because of his bearing and speech, and the way he stuck his rolled-up newspaper under his arm, like a baton. He also marched everywhere. He never said anything about that, which spawned speculation that he disgraced himself, or worse, in the service of *HM* forces, and left under a cloud. We never know for certain. But he does look like a comic version of a pale-skinned, plump, desk-bound military type.

Fotherington has no doubts about himself. He's 'happily single', and has brought with him his only companion, a Maltese poodle, given to him as a parting gift by his aged mother. He and the poodle become a common sight on the footpath between his house and the mine store. He dresses in brilliant white safari suits and a cream Panama hat, 'to keep the sun off'. There's something very Noel Coward and 'Mad Dogs and Englishmen' about him.

Of the business of the mine store, Fotherington never claims to have any knowledge. That, he says, is the 'province of Number Two', to know, and to do. He, he says, is 'Number One', which means he doesn't need to 'get his hands dirty', or 'bother with detail'.

'Number Two' is Mum. She left school at fourteen, not because she wanted to, and despite achieving the highest marks in her class. She had to work with her mother and sister to bring up four younger siblings. They did sewing for a factory, and delivered the finished items miles away on foot.

After 23 years of marriage, the hardships of the war, poverty and having a handicapped daughter, Mum also suffered Dad's illnesses and injuries after the war, and his early death. Despite her early departure from school, Mum is an intelligent and able person. She has handwriting, which everyone really admires. She calls it *'copperplate'* and explains it was taught by nuns at Marist Brothers boarding school in Natal, where she spent six years.

When she starts at the mine store in '52, her appointment is a favour by Mr Snel to Dad. She proves not only an invaluable worker, but also a guide and mentor to other staff. They value her precision, her handwriting, and her organisational skills. The mine store, previously chaotic, becomes a beacon of efficiency.

Apart from Mum, the clerical staff comprises six Indian men and an Italian woman. In one corner of the room, cut off, not by a wall, but by his reclusive character, is bald Mr Hessler. No one ever understands his job, but it's something to do with ordering special machinery for the ore mill. He keeps his own files and counsel. Between his desk and Mum's is Mr Fotherington's. When, infrequently, he's in the office, he reads old English newspapers, and leaves 'Number Two', and lesser numbers, to do the work.

Mum is a chameleon with an incredible ability to adapt according to whom she's with. She doesn't talk down to anyone, no matter how incompetent or foolish. It makes people comfortable with her. Though she sets high standards for herself, she never complains if others don't meet them.

Among the staff are diverse characters. Aziz is an effeminate, slim, fair-skinned young man from Pakistan, which recently split from India. The *watu* say he's *mfeba*, or homosexual. Chavda is a dark Bengali, forty-something, solidly built, short and bearded, with very formal, strongly accented, Victorian English. He's perpetually on the verge of leaving his wife because she's 'not playing game.' Nehru, who the others joke is a son of India's President, is a round faced, smiling, retreating young man, whose parents are from Bangalore and have a tailoring business in Mwanza. Amil Mistree, who brings news of the Zanzibar massacre, has two significant roles – nervous wreck and thick spectacle wearer. His anxiety prevents him doing much, and he's constantly blinking. The *watu* call him *bundi ogopa*, or frightened owl.

Rosanna Barucci, the Italian lady, is the only European assistant. Her English is atrocious and difficult to understand, and her writing worse. But she's young and pretty, and has an infectious sense of humour. Sometimes this gets her into trouble, such as when Mum tells her we're stopping in Italy en-route to England.

'Be careful,' she says conspiratorily, 'when-a-you-go-a-my-country.'

'Why?' Mum asks.

'You are-a-weedow, no?' Rosanna says, hands on hips.

'I'm a widow, yes. . .'

'Well-a, we throwa stones ata weedows eena Italy!' It doesn't go down well. Mum recounts Rosanna's warning many times over succeeding years. It badly affects her opinion of Italy. For years she says Italians are 'so cruel, they stone widows, you know?'

Mum's desk is in the centre of the office. There's always a queue waiting to consult her. Aziz stands waiting patiently while she completes an entry in a thick black ledger. When she looks up he grimaces and says 'thees ledger shit is sheet!'

'Let me see the sheet,' she says.

'The shit is wrong, all figures wrong, I am wanting balance, but I am not getting..'

'Calm yourself Mister Aziz,' Mum says, taking the document from him. 'This problem is not so bad. . . what you have done is add the last two figures, when you should have subtracted them.'

'Oh, thank you Mrs Penhaligon!' He shuffles away, relieved. Nehru is next.

'Thees ledger shit is completely wrong, and I am not getting what I am wanting. .'

After Nehru is Chavda. Then Rosanna. Waiting behind her,

twitching and blinking furiously, clutching a huge ledger to his chest, is Mistree.

'I canta unerstan theesa theeng,' says Rosanna. All morning Mum deals with her own work and that of the other clerks.

Mum entertains her colleagues. Swahili, Indian and European are always asking her to perform 'cabaret', as soon as the onerous presences of Hessler and Fotherington are out of the office. Hessler is most feared, and nicknamed *'Kiwanja ya ndege'.* Landing place of the bird, or aerodrome. Some call him *Embakasi,* the airport in Nairobi.

*'Fanya Bwana* Norris,' an Indian clerk says. Do Mr Norris. Him of the jutting jaw, nasal accent and never-ending search for *when* he wants to talk about. A circle of clerks quickly forms round Mum. African workers from the warehouse join. Bush telegraph, or is it mine store telegraph? Everyone's grinning in anticipation. Mum puts down her pen, and strikes a Harold Norris pose. She can jut her jaw just like him. She assumes his faraway look.

'It was in 1959,' she intones nasally. The chuckles begin. Her audience is spellbound. 'Carol was two, and Hilda was pregnant, no, Hilda was two and Carol was pregnant. Now let me see. . . no, it was 1854. Hilda wasn't born, and Carol was nowhere...' Roars of laughter. People are clutching their sides. Mum should have been an actress.

'And then again. . .' Mum intones, jaw sticking out ridiculously. There's shuffling and stifling of giggles. Mum goes on. 'No, it was 1525, and Hilda. . .' Something is wrong. The audience is trying to look busy, reaching for files, putting on serious expressions.

'Very nice!' says Embakasi, who's come back early from lunch. 'I vish zer vos so much enthusiasm für der verk!'

When he goes out again, it's *'Fanya Embakasi!'* Do Embakasi.

'Vell,' says Mum, putting a book on her head to create a smooth landing-strip, and assuming an angry expression, 'der verk iss nussink für you, you only play der fool!' There's a riot. One time Embakasi sneaks back and sees himself portrayed. Instead of being furious, he laughs as loudly as everyone. Mum has a way about her.

'You are vasted here,' Embakasi says, 'you shood be on der stage.'

Mum is a joker and entertainer. It's her personality, and I know its source. It's because she doesn't want anyone to be sad. She's had more than her fair share of that in her life, seen enough. She wants to cheer people up, make fun and laughter. She's a polished comedian. People who don't know would never imagine the tragedies she's endured. She's a natural choice in amateur plays, especially comedies. In Geita she becomes a central player in the stage performances at Lone Cone Club.

In 1964 the performance committee, of which Mum is secretary, meets over cocktails to discuss staging a play. Someone has suggested *Aladdin and his Magic Lamp*. Mum thinks that a bit stilted, and suggests it be set it in China instead of Arabia, and called *Aluvadin* (for 'hell-of-a-din') *and his Magical Gamp*. It's agreed. Here begins the saga of the *Untoward Fake Chinese Writings*.

The play has reached the stage of final dress rehearsals, the costumes have been designed, cut and stitched by volunteers. Mum looks hysterical in her long black cloak, pointy scarlet collar, black mascara makeup and false beard, and she evokes a convincing and sinister wicked uncle to Aluvadin, played by Rosanna Barucci, of widows-will-be-stoned fame. There are only four days till the performance.

Mum decorates the edge of the stage with Chinese-looking inscriptions, painted in black on pieces of hardboard. Geita's Chinese carpenters have been recruited to construct the stage props, so they're witness to the new signs. Ah Wong, the Chinese boss-man, objects vociferously. 'Why-ah-you a-wite-ah-dis?' he enquires of Mum. She doesn't know what he means. He turns to his countrymen and gives a short, high-pitched speech. As one, they look outraged, lay down tools and march off to the Chinese quarters.

It takes Mr Snel hours of diplomacy to intercede and make peace. Mum's accidental writings have allegedly 'foully and wickedly' abused the Chinese carpenters, with vulgar sexual suggestions, and terrible aspersions on their parentage. In the peace deal, the signs are turned round and rewritten on the back by the Chinese. We discover the meaning of the new signs after the play is over. 'Wide-eyed white people are illiterate monkeys', they proclaim. For all that, the pantomime is a resounding success, and popular demand results in three performances.

Late in '64 Heath Fotherington goes to England on long leave. After he's been gone a month, Mr Snel asks Mum to see him at his office on Top Road.

'Any problems at the mine store?' he asks.

'Nothing I can't deal with,' Mum replies.

'Good. Then I'll send a message to Mr Fotherington, saying we don't require his services any more!' Thus, from long distance, Heath is fired. His salary was sixty-five pounds a month, compared to Mum's thirty pounds. Mum takes over his duties, and they give her a five pound raise. It isn't much, she said, but he never did anything anyway.


By mid 1964 Charlie, with whom I'm struggling after the stick-gun threats to the *watoto* and his abuse about Gretchen, Dieti, Antonio and I, all thirteen, are keenly interested in female anatomy. The problem is there are only four *Wazungu* girls on the mine. The culture in Geita, and all Tanzania, precludes even the notion of thinking about tribal girls.

One only has to see what happened to Higginson. It's two-way too. Young *wanawake* aren't remotely interested in *Wazungu* boys. The *Wazungu* girls are Gretchen, who I've loved for years, Becky, Sophia Fortuna, and a newcomer, a Cornish girl called Megan Hewlett. Her family came to Geita last year. Her dad's an engineer, and both her mum and dad are keen Lone Cone clubbers. Megan's also fourteen, like Gretchen and Sophia. She's slim, and prettier than Sophia, who we think is fat, but she's not a patch on Gretchen. Becky is pretty, everyone thinks, except me. These girls will be the focus of our study of female anatomy.

It's Dieti, as always, who comes up with a plan. He overheard Gretchen talking to Sophia and Megan, and gained the impression they were discussing nude swimming. There's only one place on the mine they can do that – the swimming pool at the club. Suddenly a lot of things make sense. We already know the girls like to go swimming on their own.

We've often wondered about their giggling and secrecy. This is why. They're swimming nude in the pool. All we have to do is find a way to spy on them, without them knowing. We consider the possibilities. The main problem is there are no plants or bushes close enough to the pool to afford good spying positions.

It's Charlie who suggests the upside-down boat idea. He's been friendlier lately, and hasn't talked ugly about Gretchen again. My wood and canvas canoe has remained floating on the pool for many months. It's become an accepted fixture. People play with it. They row it around, dive off it, and don't mind it being there at all. It's often capsized, left floating upside down on the surface.

Sadly, the design is better suited to upside-down-ness than right-way-up. So much for old Jaswan Singh's careful drawing. Perhaps *HMS Geita* should have been a submarine. There's a foot of air inside when it's upside down. . . an ideal place to hide if we know the girls are coming.

The boat is unlikely to attract attention because it's always there. With goggles and flippers, we can skulk underneath. When we hear the girls splashing we can swim out on underwater sorties, and feast our eyes on close-up naked female bodies. We can swim back under the boat for more air, then venture out again. It's a cunning plot, we agree unanimously.

Three days after we confirm our plan, an opportunity arises. It's nine in the morning, another cloudless day with an already blazing sun. The big people are at work.

Dieti comes running through the bush, along the path through eight-foot elephant grass and thornbush, to our garden. He's wearing his swimming costume, and has flippers and goggles clutched in his hands. Excitement still brings back his stammer and German accent.

'Zey are goink,' he shouts breathlessly, 'zey are on ze vay!' Charlie and I are sitting outside with our catapults, taking target practice at a blue-headed lizard high on a gum tree. We leap into action. We dash through the grass to the club. We can't afford to be seen or the game will be up.

When we reach the pool there's nobody there. Dieti stands on the bench in the men's changing room to keep watch. For once the boat is upright. Charlie and I swim out and capsize it. We check the air pocket underneath. There's at least a foot. Suddenly Dieti dives into the pool, shouting 'zey are komink!' We submerge together, and come up under the canoe. Our breathing is so amplified in here, I fear we'll be heard.

After an eternity we hear girly laughter and splashing. D-Day! This is what we're waiting for.

How does love begin? What is it that lights the fire of emotion in a young boy's heart? How does what was ordinary yesterday suddenly become everything? What drives young boys to want to die, let alone live, for the sake of their beloved? I don't know.

At fourteen, Gretchen is a beauty. She's tall and lithe, blonde and blue eyed. She has a pretty face, charmingly freckled, she's shapely but slim, inquisitive and mischievous, all at the same time. Her figure is of an older girl. Thin waist, long legs, and prominent breasts. And she's exceptionally intelligent and humorous.

They're out there somewhere, not far from where we cling to the thwarts of the capsized canoe. Our goggles and flippers are on. All we have to do is hold our breath and swim out, and wonders and mysteries will be revealed, magnified by goggles and water.

Antonio and Charlie waste no time. They're off. Dieti inhales hugely, and plunges. He wants to study Megan. I don't blame him, but she's not a patch on his sister. That's who I want to examine. Strangely, I hope she'll be different, all over, including down *there*, to other girls. She has to be. She *is* different, in *all* ways!

I can hardly contemplate Gretchen having the same bits as other girls. Surely an angel like her doesn't pee? Other biological functions don't enter the equation. She's too perfect, too beautiful, too ethereal and angelic, to indulge in basic human functions. But there's that paradoxical and fervent hope she *is* like other girls, that she *does* pee and other things, so she'll be human, not an angel, after all, so I'll have a chance with her. I'll forgive her all these things, and love, protect and cherish her all my life.

Her breasts I've seen before, scantily covered in a bikini top, leaving little to speculate on, and without even that when I got an aerial view that day in the ceiling. But down there, under the water, it's going to be different. I've always averted my gaze, for fear of discovery by those sky-blue, mocking eyes. This time she won't know of my presence.

Transparent green water, dulled girlish laughter, splashing, bubbles ascending to the surface, a shiny film three feet above. Clear view for ten feet, then the green of pumped lake water closes off further vision. Holding breath, swim towards the yelps and giggles and wanton splashing. Kicking flippers, heading forward, where are they? Breath running out. Have to breathe. Won't make it. *Have* to breathe. Breath bursting to come out. Turn, swim, back, stay deep, kick, kick, kick. Hands out. Where's that darned boat?

Suddenly the side looms, under, come up in the foot of trapped air. Exhale explosively. Take deep breaths. Heart pounding. Where are they? Must be somewhere else. Get breath first, let pounding in chest and ears subside. Breathe. Regain composure. Ready to try again. This time different direction. I'm about to swim out when Dieti comes back. He says he blew his first sortie because his goggles were full of water.

'But I've seen zem,' he gasps, drawing air into his lungs. 'Zey are nakkit, *oochi!'*

'Where?' I whisper breathlessly.

'Becky's over zere,' he says, pointing to one side. I'm not interested in my sister.

'Gretchen?' I ask, cutting him off.

'Next to her.' I'm off again, deep breath, mouth closed, head down, kicking, going deep. . . back into the green opacity, dull girly shrieks and splashing reverberating in my head. Then I see a foot. A female foot. As soon as I see it, it convulses in a kick and disappears in an explosion of bubbles. My breath is getting short again. Time to retreat.

I turn and kick out for the boat. And don't find it. I swim and swim and swim. Right into the concrete side of the swimming pool. I don't see it coming, because the only thing that matters is getting away out of sight before letting go my breath. The impact knocks my goggles off.

I surface involuntarily. It's funny what guilt and fear can do. I'm convinced every living person and thing is on to me, watching and waiting. As my face meets air I know the game's up. Nobody notices.

Sophia, Becky, Megan and Gretchen are ten yards away, in the middle of the pool, so taken up with their own antics they don't spot the surfaced spy. They're oblivious to other pale shapes gliding beneath them. Antonio, Charlie and Dieti, moving shark-like through the shallows.

I become brazen. I breathe easily, let oxygen revive me. Then, with the patience of the unnoticed, I check out the range and direction of my target. Gretchen's long blonde hair marks her out. She's a little away from the others. Her laughter really does sound like breaking crystal, pure and melodious. My breath comes harder when I see, just an inch under the water, the soft whiteness of her breasts.

I take a huge breath and submerge. I kick off from the side in the direction of Gretchen. Slim, moving legs, hard to see for bubbles. I can't get too close, or I may get kicked, leading to instant discovery. What to do? Suddenly the question is redundant.

Gretchen, on reaching the other side, turns and stops swimming. Now she treads water, her legs moving only gently. She's looking in the direction of the other girls. If she looks nearer, just below her, I'm there, a stationary white whale. This isn't right, this is someone I love! What am I doing here, spying on her? She's only five feet away.

I close my eyes inside my goggles. It can't be like this. When, if ever, I see this, it'll be because she wants me to, not a sordid, stolen thing. It's all out there, on the other hand, just feet away through the water. All I have to do is open my eyes, and feast. No, that's disgusting, wrong, beastly, because anything hurtful to Gretchen is hateful to me. I don't want her humiliated, or sad. I have an urge to produce a magical towel and reach out to her with it, eyes closed, so she can cover her nakedness.

Reluctantly I force myself deeper and head back in the direction of the canoe. My breath comes out in an explosion, and it takes me a minute to breathe normally. The air under here is warm and stagnant. Charlie has come back. He's breathing like a locomotive. 'I saw Sophia's fanny!' he gasps. It's crude. I won't be talking about Gretchen or what I've seen. 'I'll look at

Gretchen now,' Charlie says.

'Too late,' I exclaim, determined he will not, 'they've spotted us. . .' I have never forgiven him for what he said he was going to do to Gretchen that day on our bicycle ride.

'Have they?' he says, surprised.

'They have now!' I say, using both arms to flip the canoe over into its upright position. The girls scream in unison. The game is up. But they don't know we were spying. No, we just happened to be doing one of our crazy experiments under the canoe, when they decided to go skinny-dipping. They've reached the side and pulled their costumes on underwater. At that range there's nothing to see.

'What you doing down here?' Becky shouts.

'Swimming,' I shout back, 'you?'

That night in bed I think only of Gretchen. She's unmistakable. Becky is shorter and has darker hair. Sophia is dumpy, with black hair. Gretchen is the sun-kissed blonde, with golden skin, long golden hair, and legs and arms of a swimmer or ballerina. In my dreams I'm back in the water, and there's no one else in the pool except Gretchen and me. She swims breaststroke, just two feet above me. She knows I'm watching and doesn't mind. Her arms and legs flex and straighten in breaststroke. My interest is all of her.

Her flat, golden stomach, punctuated by her belly button, meets her rib cage, and higher up her breasts thrust forward with each stroke. Her flat belly ripples with muscle as the ship of her lithe body powers through the water. She rolls onto her back and continues swimming. Now I see the taut shape of her buttocks. If I could surface I'd love to see the view up there. It's my first erotic dream. In the morning I'm ashamed. I've let myself, and Gretchen, down. I pray to God to return me to the way I used to think about her. This carnal stuff is dishonest and scary, and what will Gretchen think if she ever knows my thoughts?

# Thirty-four

In late '64, aged thirteen, I come home from Arusha for the last time. Primary school is over. There's a quota for non-African children at the two respected high schools in Tanzania, at Mbeya and Iringa. Only twenty of the brightest are allowed, which rules me out. My grades, and those of my friends, are shocking.

Mr Houghton is interviewed in the East African Standard about why so few of his pupils make the grade. 'If you start with poor material,' he says, 'what do you expect?' He goes on to say half the children at Arusha School couldn't even speak English when they started. Describes me well. Schmedjie, Allen and Matwiga also feel well portrayed, and we're all rather proud of ourselves. We say goodbye with the casualness of young people who don't stop to think this is the end of friendships.

Now, at last, surely Mum will relent. I've singularly, or as part of a plurality, if I count the others, failed at school. She'll accept it, and arrange an underground job for me on the mine. I know I failed as *tunnyboy*, but that was the sun. There's no sun in the tunnels or *stopes*, so I can be a miner. Can't be that much to it.

'No,' she says in a tone, which brooks no argument, 'you are not going underground!'

'Well, what am I going to do then?' I'm exhausted by her persistence. Can't she see school and I don't get on well?

'You are going to St Mary's in Nairobi.' Nairobi's in Kenya. I've never been there. St Mary's doesn't sound too good.

'What's that?' I ask.

'A Catholic boarding school. You're very lucky, because Mr Snel has arranged for the mine to pay your fees, and it's very expensive.'

'But I don't want to go,' I say, despair seizing me again.

'I'm going with you,' she says.

'What?'

'You've got three weeks holiday, then I'm taking you to Nairobi, and we'll have a nice time there. We'll stay in a hotel and visit your new school. Please, Jimboy, don't make this any harder than it has to be.'

I try to argue, but it doesn't have any effect. I decide to play for time, await developments. Surely, life being what it is, something will come up. Perhaps a full-frontal assault on the idea of Nairobi is ill thought out. Maybe an opportunity to change my destiny will arise. Unfortunately, something dreadful happens, which puts my little problem into terrible perspective.

It's Amina who breaks it to me. It's the middle of the day, and I'm bored reading the same old books. I'll have to get another good book from Higgs, or Mr Hessler. Hammond Innes, Desmond Bagley or Alistair MacLean. Good adventures, those. I must be the best-read *Mzungu* kid in Geita, and it's all due to Higgs and Hessler. It's improved my English no-end. I've caught up with boys my age at school. I learnt more here, in the bush, than in any school.

I get off my bed, where I've been lying for an hour, intermittently reading and trying to think of a way to avoid Nairobi. Sandy jumps down and follows me into the yard. It's awfully hot and bright, and I have to shade my eyes.

Something's going on. Umali and Amina are sitting outside their quarters. Tembo's with them. Nothing odd about that. But I *know* something's wrong, badly wrong. You don't grow up with people without becoming sensitive to everything about them. They aren't just sitting there, they're sharing bad news, awful news. Terror grips me, and I almost fight my footsteps towards them. My heart is pounding, my mouth dry. What is it? What can be so bad? As I reach them and look down, Amina turns her head to me, and I see she's crying. Tears are streaming down her cheeks and her face is contorted in anguish. Umali looks up. He's also weeping.

'Jimu,' Amina croaks, swallowing hard, *'kaa, mtoto, kaa.'* Sit, child, sit. She pats the log beside her.

*'Nini kilitokea?'* I gasp. What's happened?

'Lutoli,' she says in a whisper, 'Lutoli *amefariki!'* My head spins. No, I've mis-heard, Lutoli can't be dead! I feel a thump in my chest. I sink onto the seat beside her.

*'Nini?'* I say.

'He was killed, Jimu, by the cotton-lorry, it fell on him when it rolled in the road.' I can't believe what I'm hearing. I play for time. The conversation can't end, because then it will be true. . .

'*Wapi?*' I say. Where?

'Between the cotton-gin and Mwanza,' she sobs, 'last night.' She sniffs loudly, wiping her eyes on the back of her hand.

'*Alakini. . .*' I interject. But. . . . Amina puts her scrawny arm around me.

'*Pole toto, pole!*' she murmurs. Peace, child, peace!

'*Sababu?*' Why?

'We don't know, child, it's a matter of God. . .'

'*Alakini. . ?*' I whimper. But..? My eyes fill with tears, masking my vision. 'Why did the lorry fall on him?'

This time Umali speaks. His voice is strangled, and he's weeping shamelessly. He looks very thin, very old. 'Lutoli was travelling to Mwanza on top of the lorry.'

'*Sababu?*' I ask. Why?

'His mother sent him to buy medicine, medicine for her back.' Amina whispers, 'he was on top of the lorry when it overturned.' She sobs loudly. 'The poor boy was crushed!' I can't believe I'm hearing this. Not Lutoli, not my oldest, best friend in the world! But why are they saying this if it isn't true? It's this detail which does it. It's this that brings it home. Something so trivial, so normal. Going to buy medicine for your mother. Then, out of nowhere, sudden, violent death. It isn't expected. Not in the script.

I see Lutoli standing there, smiling his big smile, his eyes twinkling with mischief. Only he's not there. He's dead! I'm never going to see him again. Never hear his voice, never share a joke, we're never going to lie in the sun together at *Kichoncho* again, and plan the future of the world.

The first dreadful, hopeless, painful sob erupts from deep inside and I can hardly breathe. Amina wraps her arms round me. Umali stands and puts his hand on my head. Our little family has been shattered, and grief has flown to us on dark wings.

How do I deal with this bereavement? Do I know how to? I don't know. All I know is God is, yet again, targetting me. He won't let me be happy. That's why he took Dad, sent me to boarding school, ensured I was always in trouble, and now, finding me still resilient, he's taken my best friend.

Lutoli, *Lutoli!* I can't believe he's dead. A *mzoga*. A corpse. Like Tembo's puppy, and Mr Valari (senior). How can someone so young and handsome and alive suddenly turn into a *mzoga?* 'Lutoli is only thirteen!' I say to the sky, to God. 'Why can't you leave him alone?' There is no answer. There never is. I recall how I felt when I dragged Dad's gun out and tried to shoot God all those years ago. If there's no answers, you have to shake things up. Maybe shooting God doesn't work, but what else *is* there? If God made us, if he exists, then he needs to look in my heart. He'll find hate - pure, black, hate, like I'm sure he never intended. Hate for him being unkind. For being a torturer. For being unfair. And, most of all, for not caring! So much for religion, for God, and for all the things the priests say. Even while they do so, there's murder afoot, and 'God' is the perpetrator.

Lutoli's *maziko*, or funeral, is on his mother's *shamba*. There's no road there, just a footpath winding six miles through the bush. Mum has no choice but to let me go with Umali and Amina. One of the Chinese carpenters kindly makes up a crude coffin. It has four rope handles. Umali and Amina collect it from the carpentry works and take it to Lutoli's aunt's hut, where Lutoli's *mzoga* is lying. The *selekali*, or police, brought it there from Mwanza mortuary. It's sewn up in a canvas bag, and Umali tells me it's soaked with blood, which has clotted and dried.

Umali won't let me go when they deliver the body. I know what he thinks. I'll want to see the *mzoga*. I won't, really. That phase of my life is past. I don't want to see Lutoli's crushed, bloodied *mzoga*.

The *watu* transport Lutoli's coffin on a low cart made from plywood and two pairs of pram wheels. They pull it with a rope, others holding the back to prevent it going sideways, through six miles of tortuous jungle path. Leading the procession are two weeping, wailing women, his mother and his fat aunt, who, to my mind, was more like a mother. His mother hadn't had that much to do with him of late. Yet she it was who sent him on his errand of death.

We reach the *shamba* after more than two hot, sweaty hours, itching and burning from insect bites, thornscratches, perspiration and plain old heat. The fresh pile of red earth directs us to the grave. More than a hundred *watu* have come, only a few I recognise. Most are wearing tribal gowns and *kanzus*.

*'Tunahuzunika!'* wails an old woman with red clay marks on her face. She's even fatter than Lutoli's aunt, who's too overcome to speak. 'We are grieved!'

*'Ghamu!'* chorus a hundred voices. A word for collective sadness and grief. The surrounding forest resounds with crying.

The fat woman wails loudly. 'Our child Lutoli, he who we loved, travelled only thirteen years.' She opens her ample arms to the sky, then she continues, 'The day before yesterday, he was crushed by a lorry. . .' Standing beside me, Amina grips my arm. She's crying shamelessly. Right now, I don't know what's wrong with me. My eyes are dry. I can't cry.

'This is not the meaning of his life,' the preacher-lady says. *'Apana!'* No! *'Mungu...'* There's that word again, God! *'Mungu alimwita nyumbani.'* God called him home. Yes, I think. God does that. It's his style. Only it's not 'home' at all. It's just a hole in the ground. Just before they start filling the grave, Amina asks me to say something.

'Lutoli and I walked together all the years we had on earth,' I say in a strangled voice. 'He was my friend, my brother. . .' Then the tears come. I can say no more. Umali and Amina both reach for me, and pull me to them. Our bitter tears flow.

I reach into my *kikapu*. It contains just two things. A goodbye *barua*, or letter I've written to Lutoli, wrapped in a piece of leather I cured myself. The hide of a mole I caught, skinned, salted, soaked, dried and scraped, like Lutoli and I did together so many, many times.

The letter says, in Swahili, that even though you are gone, you will be with me all my life, and we shall meet again, wherever it is that people meet. I didn't know what else to write. The other thing is my beloved Chevrolet steering wheel, the one Lutoli and I cherished all those ten years, ever since I found it on the beach at the Inn By The Sea in Dar-es-Salaam.

I'm standing, trembling with grief, blinded by tears, holding the wheel in one hand, the leather-parcelled *barua* in the other. Amina takes pity on me. Gently, she takes them from me, and hands them to Umali, who lies down beside the grave, and carefully drops them onto Lutoli's coffin. The two *wanaume* with the shovels start putting soil into the grave.

Three young women and an old man are standing a little apart from the others. They're better dressed than the other *watu*. Amina tells me they come from the Lutheran mission near Biharlomoulo. The old man makes a signal, and they begin a hymn I've heard many, many times. It's a Swahili version of an old German hymn – *Gott ist die liebe*, God is love. Taught to the *watu* in the time of *Deutsch Ost Afrika*, the establishment of Lutheran missions, and von Lettow Vorbeck's brave *schutztruppe*.

You just can't escape that history. I've even heard old Kaizer humming the same tune outside the club. Told me they used to sing it in the Burma bush when they buried their dead. One of the young women sings very high, the other two a little lower. The old man harmonises in a deep base. Without backing, they sound like the very angels.

It's exactly the same hymn the *wanaume* sang when they filled in Dad's grave all those years ago. I know, because Mum talked about their beautiful voices for years, and never forgot the tune. Can it be fate? Dad, Lutoli, both so loved by me, the same hymn, the same language, so many years apart?

> *Mungu ni pendo, apenda watu.*
> *Mungu ni pendo, anipenda.*
> *Sikilizeni furaha yangu,*
> *Mungu ni penda, anipenda.*

> God is Love, loves his people.
> God is love, he loves.
> Listen my friends,
> God is Love, he loves you.

There is no doubting the serene beauty of the voices, nor the emotion or sincerity of the singing, but I've just about had enough of God. If he loves us, why does he keep killing us? Why is Lutoli now lying broken in a hole in the ground? Grave – pah! It's just a posh word for a hole. And me, I never got that thing right, how to bring back dead people! *'Iko ko mbinguni,'* Amina says, pulling me to her. Can she be right? Is he really in heaven?

Next day my feet carry me up the steep rocky hillside to the site of Lutoli's and my country, Kichoncho. I sit on a *mwamba*, or flat rock, in the clearing where we made our declaration of independence all those years ago. It's midday. I haven't eaten breakfast, felt too sick.

The sun is high in the shimmering pale blue sky. A lonely *njiwa*-bird coo-cooes, a haunting, mournful sound. Does he know what has happened? That Lutoli is dead? There are no *mwewes*, or hawks navigating the high airwaves today. Is that out of respect for my departed friend?

I can see Lutoli standing here, beside this rock, smiling. We're making up our list of constitutional rules for our republic. I've just suggested 'no bad *Mzungus*'. He counters, laughing, half his face hidden by a rusty army helmet, his brilliant white teeth flashing, with 'no bad anybodys'. The image is strong. I can almost reach out and touch him. Hot tears run down my cheeks. I weep inconsolably for the loss of my best friend. Then I weep for Dad, poor Jan Marais, Mr Valari (senior), and even Tembo's puppy. Then for life itself.

# Thirty-five

It's only a week after Lutoli's funeral when I reluctantly travel with Mum to Kenya. If there's anything positive about going to Nairobi, it's that Gretchen is at school there, in Loreto convent, the girl-equivalent of St Mary's. I don't know if I'll get to see her, though. We fly direct, but bumpily, from Mwanza to Nairobi in an aged East African Airways DC3, or *Dakota.* As always, I'm airsick.

*Brunner's* hotel is less salubrious than the *New Stanley,* which is famed throughout East Africa. There, even film stars on location in Kenya or Tanzania are photographed sipping pink gins in the *Thorntree* bar. Old *Brunner's* is old-fashioned, respectable and affordable. Mum and I book in and are shown to our room. A bit strange, at thirteen, to share with Mum, but there it is. We're famished, and go down for lunch as soon as we've freshened up. There are only three other diners, all at different tables, when we sit down. We're next to the window. We order, then talk about the school. I still hope I can wear Mum down.

'St Mary's is a very good school,' she says, 'I'm sure you'll like it.'

'I won't!' I say.

'Someone mention St Mary's?' says an old gentleman who was sitting at the next table, but's now standing by ours.

'Yes,' Mum says, 'my son, James,' she smiles at me, 'is going to be a boarder there.'

'Really?' says the old man, pulling a chair and sitting down stiffly. One leg sticks straight out, like there's no knee. What a cheek, I think, scowling. 'And where are you from?' He's got an accent. I've heard it somewhere. London. Cockney, that's it. Those war films, the London blitz. The firefighters talk like that. Flames everywhere, men in tin helmets trying to put them out. *'Stawn va crauws, might, vis is a bloomin shau, innit?'*

'Tanzania, near Mwanza,' Mum says. No point saying Geita, no one's heard of it.

'Tanganyika, eh?' he says, shaking his head as if he doesn't believe it. 'Name's Lopey Perkins, 'cos I lope 'stead of walk. Got the 'Lopey' name in Tanganyika, only when it was German East Africa, or *Deutsch Ost Afrika!*' He laughs. 'Mind if I join you?' he belatedly asks.

'Not at all,' Mum says, to my annoyance. Lopey. How sad to be called that. He's had his meal and orders coffee. It's obvious he wants company, is keen to have a chat .

Lopey is seventy-four. He first came to Kenya from London, to manage a farm in the northern highlands. That was in 1910, when he was twenty. The job wasn't to his liking, so he went to Nairobi to seek his fortune. He did 'vis and vat', before joining another Londoner in a newsagency-cum-tobacconist-cum-gambling-shop-cum-illegal-liquor-outlet and clandestine pub, which thrived in the happy-go-lucky pre-war settler town.

'Mind if I smoke?' he asks, lighting his pipe with a match before he gets an answer. We don't mind. The tobacco smells like Dad's. He rests his stiff leg on the other one. It looks funny, one leg sticking out like a pikestaff. He puffs his pipe contentedly, and continues. *One leg off, and a stick stuck on?* Becky would love this!

In August 1914, *Oberstleutnant*, or Lieutenant Colonel, Paul von Lettow Vorbeck, acting against the express orders of hapless *Deutsch Ost Afrika* Governor von Schnee, forbidding offensive operations, brings the First World War dramatically to East Africa. Realising he's outnumbered and outgunned many times by the British, he launches an audacious pre-emptive attack against the railway over the *Deutsch Ost Afrika*-Kenya border. It was down that line the British will bring an invading army, and Vorbeck knows it.

The attack, though only causing minor damage and little loss of life, galvanises this sleepy outpost of British empire, until now obsessed by fears of the looming European battles to be fought by their kith and kin against the rampant Germans under the terrifying plan of their nefarious war strategist, *Feldmarschall* Graf Alfred von Schlieffen.

The slaughter at Passchendaele, Verdun and many other battles will exceed their worst fears. Now bellicose farmers and white hunters, bearing motley arms, flood into Nairobi, demanding uniforms and a mission. Some form their own units with made-up names. Lopey, on a rush of patriotism, sells out to his partner, buys an antique *Lee-Metford* rifle, and joins a rabble calling themselves the *'Kenya Avengers'*. They run around a field to get fit, and practise shooting at crows. Then they're ordered to grow up, join a proper unit, or go back to their farms.

Seventeen companies of King's African Rifles are hastily augmented by settlers and two brigades of Indian and British troops fresh from India. Recruited as lieutenant into the *KAR*, Lopey takes part in the disastrous amphibious assault against Tanga on the second of November 1914. Some say General Aitken is more suited in appearance and style to colonial campaigns of the eighteen hundreds, than fighting a quality foe like Vorbeck. Aitken's ineptness is exceeded only by that of his polyglot army.

Vorbeck allows the landing by withdrawing his *schutztruppe* inland. The allied forces follow, thinking this is a pushover. They run into a murderous machine-gun and rifle-fire ambush. Three hundred are killed in minutes, mostly officers and NCOs. There's a lull. From the German positions the *Schutztruppe askaris* hurl abuse at the terrified Rajput and Punjabi soldiers lying prone on the ground. *'Wahindi ni madudu!'* – Indians are insects. A Punjabi's rifle goes off by accident, and a hundred Rajputs flee all the way back to the beach and into the water.

Lopey leads a *KAR* platoon across a field where hollow logs contain hives of ferocious African bees. Roused by the noise of battle, the bees attack. One man is stung three hundred times. Hundreds of Indian and *KAR* troops flee towards the safety of the sea, pursued by dive-bombing bees.

High in the leaves of a palm tree a *Schutztruppe askari* sniper spots a *KAR* officer trying to stem the retreat. It's easy to tell an officer – he's white, and wears a pith helmet. The *askari* has one of the best rifles ever to come out of Germany. The *Mauser Gew 98* (*Gewehr*, or rifle, 1898) has largely replaced the old, smoky, model 71, and it has never been bettered. A bolt-action carbine, it fired a 7.92 calibre round, of which it holds five in a box-magazine.

This is amazing. Lopey's describing the same gun that Geita's driver, Fritz, has in his hut. I tell Lopey I've seen one. Not who's got it, 'cos that was a promise. Yes, those guns must still be around, he says. There were thousands, and, provided they were cleaned and oiled, there's no reason they shouldn't last forever.

The *askari* is a crack shot, and his *Schutztruppe* officer has issued him with this state-of-the-art rifle, fitted with a *Zeiss* telescopic sight. He has modern *spitzer* bullets, with pointed tips, and superior long range ballistics. He works the bolt, ejecting a spent cartridge, and inserting another *spitzer* into the chamber. Leaning with his back against the high Baobab trunk, he takes careful aim. It's a long shot, just over four hundred yards. He presses his cheek firmly against the oiled stock, inhales deeply, holds his breath, like he's been trained by Vorbeck himself, slowly steadies the wavering of the sight across the target, and gently squeezes the trigger.

'If it 'adn't 'it bone,' Lopey says, 'it would have gone straight frew, and I wouldn't be called Lopey.' The pointed bullet strikes the top of his right tibia, just below the kneecap, and shatters the bone. How he gets off the battlefield, later famed for the 'Battle of the Bees', is a saga of agony and crawling, and rolling into a ditch where he lies 'till the shooting stopped.

It's a rout. The British side suffers eight hundred dead, five hundred wounded, two hundred and fifty missing, against the Germans who lose fifteen Europeans, and fifty-four *askaris* dead or wounded. Vorbeck, ever a gentleman, is magnanimous in victory, allowing the British to collect their dead, and retreat in orderly fashion to the beach. He orders the enemy wounded to be treated in Tanga hospital, alongside his own men.

Outnumbered eight to one, Vorbeck has bloodied the British Bulldog's nose. He's also captured sixteen machine-guns, hundreds of rifles, and six hundred thousand rounds of ammunition. It will supply his *schutztruppe* for a year.

'I 'eard vem singin', the German *askaris*,' Lopey says. 'Got ter give it to vem, vey've got good voices! It was while I wuz beein' carried off on a stretcher, dauwn to va beach. Vey must've been five 'undred yards away, but we 'eard em. Vey was singin ver marchin song. It went like vis. . .' And the old man actually begins to sing. In perfect Swahili!

*Tuna-kwenda, tuna-shinda,*
*Tuna-fuata Bwano Obersti,*
*Askari wana-endesha,*
*Askari wana-endesha,*

*Tuna-kwenda, tuna shinda.*

We go, we win,
We follow *Bwana Obersti,*
The *askaris* drive on,
The *askaris* drive on,
We go, we win.

Incensed at the ignominious defeat of his massively superior force, Aitken orders a bombardment of Tanga town by *HMS Fox* and two other warships. The first naval shells hit the hospital, crammed with British and Indian casualties. Others hit the retreating allied lines. In ten minutes the British losses are doubled. The bombardment ceases. Aitken goes to pieces. His career is over, his reputation destroyed.

'It were only va shelling wot stopped vem singing,' Lopey says.

Lopey is taken on board the cruiser *HMS Fox*, part of the navy's Tanga blockade. The ship's surgeon removes the bullet. It's he who tells Lopey it was a *spitzer*. He's extracted many, and is an expert on bullet wounds. He gives Lopey two choices. 'Wired straight, or off,' he says. Lopey choose swire. His knee never bends again. His nickname is born.

I wonder if Fritz, our surly German-African driver, shot him. Could it have been with that same old *Mauser gewehr* he showed me down by Tarzan-Swings? In deference to my oath to Fritz, I'm not saying anything. But I never seem to be able to get away from the old war in Tanganyika, do I?

'Vat Vorbeck,' Lopey muses, 'hell of a soldier. Know what 'e said when he was asked why the bloomin' bees attacked us, and not his men?' He's asking me.

'No.'

'*Gott mitt uns, und die bienen auch.*'

'What's that mean?' I say.

'God wif us, and the bees too.' Lopey smiles in reminiscence. 'Cheeky devil, but 'ad a point, he did. As if 'e didn't capture enough guns and ammo from us at Tanga, just a few months later, in April 1915, *Gott* was wif 'im again.'

'What happened?' I ask. I love talking about the *Schutztruppe* and von Lettow Vorbeck. It's connected to Geita. There's Fritz, the driver, who was in the *Schutztruppe*, as were several old askaris. Though Kaizer himself wasn't, his father was.

'A ship called *SS Rubens,*' he says, knocking tobacco out of his pipe by hitting it in his palm. 'British ship, captured by va Germans in va North Sea, re-named wif a neutral Norwegian name. Vey loaded her in Emden, wif munitions and supplies for Vorbeck, ven sent 'er round the Cape of Good Hope to run va British blockade. When she got off Tanga, she made a run for it, chased by a whole bleedin' flotilla of Royal Navy ships. *HMS Hyacinth* shelled her, set her ablaze, but her Captain steered for va beach, ran her aground. She didn't sink. Next day va fire was out, and the supplies were fine. Va Germans and ver *askaris* waded out and retrieved the cargo, 'appy as Larry!

And,' Lopey says, tamping dark tobacco into his pipe bowl, 'there was nuffink ve could do to stop it.'

'Guns?'

'Hundreds, half a million bullets, *Spandau* machine-guns, small field-guns, shells, new uniforms, boots, cases of whisky, cigarettes. . .' Lopey shakes his head. 'Vorbeck was a good soldier, also lucky. Vat's what yer've got to be in life, young man, lucky.'

What an interesting man Lopey Perkins is. I know a lot about the East Africa campaign, but always like to hear more. It's funny, living where the *Schutztruppe* fought, being British myself, and then meeting someone who fought on our side. But *is* it my side? I don't know which side I'm on. I like Germans, and I like the Swahili people. I think I'd have been in the *Schutztruppe* myself, though not during the *Maji-Maji* revolt. That was murder.

Lopey is lonely. His wife died long ago. Typhoid, he says, an epidemic, which killed indiscriminately. His two grownup sons are no longer in East Africa. They only write when they want money, he says. He insists on showing Mum and I Nairobi, drives us all over the town in his two-tone brown and beige Ford Prefect. Everywhere we go people recognise and wave at Lopey. He's very well known.

After the first war, with his wired-up leg, he decided to make money, and started his own match factory in the Ngong Hills near Nairobi. They were called *Lopey's Matches* and sold all over Kenya. In five years he was a millionaire. 'Lived the life of Riley,' he says, grinning with his pipe clenched in his teeth. Then he lost his money. Unfair competition, he says. He worked as a letting agent and debt-collector from then until he retired, a year ago, at the age of seventy- three.

Lopey takes us out to Westlands, the Nairobi suburb where St Mary's school is. It's six miles out of town and has lush, leafy roads and great mansions. The school is on a huge piece of land. There are manicured lawns, cricket pitches, rugby and football fields, and an eighteen hole golf course, of professional standard, Lopey says.

The school building is a huge double-storey horseshoe. On one side, both floors are given over to classrooms. On the other it's dormitories. The joining bit of the U is dining room and kitchen downstairs, and bedrooms for the Catholic Fathers upstairs. The open part of the U leads down a broad flight of stone steps to an Olympic-size swimming pool.

There's not much time to look, because Mum and I have an appointment with the Headmaster. Mum's made me dress up in beige trousers and a white shirt, and she's bought me new brown shoes. I think it's my first pair of *new* shoes ever. Lopey waits on a bench looking out over the quadrangle in the middle of the horseshoe.

Father O'Leary is a big and very old man. His study is huge and panelled in wood. There are thousands of books on the floor-to-ceiling bookcases. In one corner there's a tall, wide earthenware vase, and protruding from it are several long thin canes. I don't like the look of them.

'Pleased to meet you,' he says with an Irish accent, rising from behind his desk. He shakes hands with Mum, not with me. He motions us to sit. 'So this,' he says, staring at me over the top of his half-spectacles, 'is young Francis.' Here we go again. Just like Miss Baxter in Arusha. Enemies call me that. Unless they call me Jimu, or at least Jim, I know times are going to be hard.

'We're a proud school,' he says, and Mum nods to show she appreciates that. 'There is strict discipline, a strong work ethic, and the highest grades of any school in Kenya.' Mum's nodding again. 'Our boys excel in all the sports, so they do. Did you see the playing fields, golf course, the swimming pool? Yes? We have other sports. For example, all boys do boxing, and there are no exceptions.' He's staring fixedly at me from under hedge-like eyebrows.

'What think you of sports, Francis?' he asks. His eyes are icy-blue and bore unblinkingly into mine.

'I like games,' I say weakly.

'Games? Here you will learn to play *sports*, become good at them, like all the boys.'

'Do I *have* to box?' I ask in a small voice. His face breaks into a grin.

'To be sure, here are no exceptions. You'll be learning to love it. It'll toughen you up, build character.' Mum's looking strained now, and I know her smile is forced. Father O'Leary changes the subject. 'We need to talk about the subjects you'll study.'

Mum and Lopey leave me at St Mary's, and he drives her to *Embakasi* airport for her return flight to Geita. I'm shown to my dormitory by a particularly sullen senior who doesn't even address me by my name, calling me only 'you'. It's upstairs from the classrooms, and leads off from an outside passage overlooking the quadrangle. The unsmiling lout hands me unceremoniously to the dorm prefect. 'He's for you,' he says, then leaves.

'I'm dormitory prefect,' the red-haired boy announces, 'but *God* to you. Do I make myself clear?' He's got dandruff in his red hair and his teeth are yellow. There's a sniggering knot of six boys round him, here for the entertainment. If this is God, I finally understand why he does such cruel things…he's a *jerk!*

'What's your name?' I ask, perhaps foolishly.

'Clever, eh?' says the prefect in an exaggerated nasal tone, taking my forelock in his fingers and beginning to twist.

'Stop dat!' comes a barking, oriental-accented voice from behind the others. The prefect lets go my hair. A short, broad-faced Asian boy with very wide shoulders steps forward. He faces up to the redhead.

'You wan' tlouble, Loper, you come Kim!' he spits. Must be Roper. So that's the prefect's name, not *God* after all. He looks far too shaken and pale to be God. In fact he's positively quaking.

'Look, Kim. . .' he begins, but Kim cuts him off.

'No *you* look,' he says. 'You bully, that all!' He turns to the other five. One's already gone. 'Wan tlouble with Kim?' he asks. As a body they turn and find sudden interest elsewhere. When they're all gone, including Roper, who scuttles away in the distraction, he turns to me.

'Me name Kim Dong. Jus' like ding-dong. I come Kolea. My fadder, he deputy ambassador. We be flen, yes?' He smiles, transforming his face. 'Dey all lubbish.'

'I'd like to be your friend,' I say, feeling intense gratitude to my benefactor.

'I have plesent for you,' he says, 'come with me.' He walks to the row of steel lockers against the far wall of the dormitory. I realise there's no one else in the dorm. They've scuppered. Kim's got quite an effect. He opens his locker and takes out something wrapped in a cloth. 'Dis for you,' he says, handing it to me.

I take it pensively. It's heavy. What can this strange little chap be giving me, so soon after meeting? He's watching me intently. I unwrap the package. Inside is the most beautiful hand-axe. It's got a handle like a sheath knife, and a shiny, razor-sharp three-inch-wide axe-head in place of a knife-blade. I don't know what to say.

'If me not lound, you chop-chop bastas, yes?' I smile weakly. 'By way, what name?' Kim says.

'Jim,' I say. 'Jim and Kim, dat sound good,' he says. 'Loper give you tlouble, you call Kim. Or use axe. Unastan?' And before I can answer, or thank him for the gift, he's gone. I cradle the axe in my hand. Will I chop-chop the other boys if they 'give me trouble'? What will Father O'Leary say?

It isn't long before it's apparent that St Mary's and Loreto Convent have little interaction. I'm unlikely to see much, or any, of Gretchen. I miss her so much! All I can look forward to is seeing her in my dreams. Will she, just in a dream, kiss me with her perfect lips?

# Thirty-six

The 'new boys' are weighed on a Saturday morning. Father Cox, Dean of Studies, operates the scales. Strange thing for a 'studies' dean to do. It's decided by weight who will box who in the preliminary bouts of the *All-Kenya High School Boxing Championships*. There's no choice. Everyone boxes, at least till they're 'eliminated'. I don't like the sound of that.

I'm a pragmatist. I'll fight if I have to, but running away seems wiser. Maybe it's growing up with the lions and *fisis* in Geita. Doesn't pay to go toe-to-toe with them. 'When you see one, run like the dusty-wind,' Umali says. I agree. Now, willingly, and for no possible benefit, I have to stand and fight someone who, just for pleasure, wants to kill me. It's crazy.

On Monday the fight-lists are posted on the noticeboard. I can't believe what's there. Penhaligon–Roper. Right at the top of the list. Bantamweight. Bryan Roper. Prefect. Redhead bully, who's only left me alone because of my Kung-Fu bodyguard, Kim Dong. It hasn't stopped him sneering from a distance, or whispering that 'he won't be here always, then I'm gonna eat you!'

Worst of all, Roper is last year's all-Kenya schools bantamweight boxing champion. He may have red hair and freckles, but he's built like a weight lifter. I've seen him in the showers, and I know he's going to smash me in the ring. I'm walking back to my dining table, feeling nauseous, when Roper sidles past, grinning. 'Can't bring Kim into the ring, Jimbo,' he whispers, 'I'll have you to myself.' He swaggers off, arms and leg-calves as thick as treetrunks, and bulging with muscle.

'Wat dat one say?' asks Kim, who's become my shadow. He's even swapped places with another boy to sit next to me for meals

'He's gonna get me,' I say miserably, 'in the ring.'

'You fight Loper?' Kim asks.

'That's what it says.'

'You know box?'

'Nope.'

'No wolly, I teach you Kung-Fu!'

'No time, it's next week,' I say.

'Ah, so, I teach you one-punch. Special punch. All you need.'

'Thanks Kim,' I say, 'but I think I need more than that.'

'You win, sure you win, Jim.' My little companion is beaming. His confidence in me is flattering, but misplaced. Compared to Roper, I'm a gawky no-hoper. He's a ruddy tiger, and I'm for it, big-time. In Geita I could go off, get my catapult, and shoot him in the forehead with a good pebble. Or I could make a bow and shoot him in the chest with a bamboo arrow tipped with a five-inch nail, its point flattened with a hammer and filed to razor-sharpness on granite. Not, alas, here.

'You're very good to me,' I tell Kim. 'I had a friend before, a very good friend. .'

'You *had* good flen?' he asks.

'He died,' I say. I tell him about how Lutoli and I grew up together, learnt to talk under the big baobab tree. I tell about the Republic of Kichoncho on Compound Hill, the tuberculosis we had together, the trust we shared. And how he died under a ginnery-lorry. By the time I'm done we're both crying.

'You good fella,' Kim says, wiping his eyes with a handkerchief. 'I know when I see you.'

There's talk round the school. Roper's going to smash up Penhaligon. What good luck, having me to himself in the ring, where my 'yellow friend' can't save me. I should have known better than to 'cheek' Roper. After all, his family is famous sugar farmers, very rich and respected in Kenya. Who am I, from the bush in Tanzania, who doesn't even have a father, to insult Roper? He's last year's champ, and he's going to give me a pasting. They're all going for the show.

Lopey Perkins comes to visit in his two-tone *Ford Prefect*. He promised Mum he would, and is as good as his word. He finds me sitting on a bench in the quadrangle. As always, he's dressed in grey flannels and a tweed sports-jacket. He sits down beside me, his knee-less leg projecting like he's going to hang clothes on it.

'Why so glum?' he asks, tamping tobacco into his curved *Meerschaum* pipe.

'I've got to box a boy called Roper on Saturday,' I say miserably. He strikes a match on the side on the bench, holds it to his pipe, and draws deeply. He lets the fragrant smoke curl from his nose. The smell reminds me of Dad.

'Bryan Roper?' he asks, 'last year's champ?'

'Yup.' How does Lopey know?

'Nairobi's a small place,' he says, reading my thoughts.

'What am I going to do?' I ask. He takes a deep puff from his pipe and looks thoughtful.

'Only fing you can do, Jim, is win, vat's what!' he says at length.

'How can I beat Roper?' I ask. 'He's stronger than me.'

'First fing you do is stop saying vat,' Lopey says. 'You can beat 'im if you want.'

'How?'

'Well, I'm no boxing *fundi*, but I've been in a fight or two, and I know a few fings,' he says.

'What?'

'Well, he'll be dancing round, being fancy, trying to hit you wif his left and right hand.'

'And?'

'You 'aven't time to train as a boxer, like him, so you just go in vere as a fighter.'

'How do I do that?' I ask. Just then Kim comes along.

'Hello,' he greets Lopey, 'you Jim flen?'

'I am,' Lopey smiles, 'you too?'

'Me him *good* flen,' Kim agrees.

'He says I mustn't try to box Roper, but *fight* him,' I say.

'One-punch, hard one face, dat all,' Kim says. 'I teach!'

'Now, Jim, see, you 'ave more friends van you fought,' Lopey says. 'Tell you what, you let vis friend of yours shauw you 'ow to frow one big punch. Vat's all you'll need. No fancy footwork, nuffink, just vat punch, and you'll end it vere and ven.' He turns to Kim. 'Kung-Fu, aye?'

'Flom velly small,' Kim says. 'Only five.' How does Lopey know these things?

'You teach 'im va punch,' Lopey says. He stands, tapping his pipe on his hand. 'I'll be 'ere to watch va fight, Jim. You learn vat punch from your friend.' He turns to leave, then turns back again. In his hand is a five shilling note. 'For you,' he says, 'buy some sweets and colas.' He vaults away on his straight leg.

'You come with me,' Kim says. 'We go plivate place, me

teach you one-punch. Den ve have smoke, yes?'

Saturday afternoon, it's half-past four. I should be down at the gymnasium, getting ready for my fight with Roper. Three rounds of two minutes. How am I going to even walk there, let alone survive? I'm terrified and feel queasy. I've practised Kim's punch as best I can.

The trick is making a tight fist, holding the elbow close to the body, and turning the fist as far outwards as it'll go, till the bent fingers are facing up. Then, after taking in a deep breath, begin to slowly exhale, at the same time bringing the bunched fist arcing up from low down, rotating inwards, so the bent fingers will face exactly downwards at impact. It has to be done at short range, so not to waste energy before hitting the target. Even more important, you have to drive away every other thought, every other impulse, every ambition, and every emotion. It needs purity, no pollution by anything to weaken the effect. I'm doubtful I'll have a chance to use 'one-punch'. Not with Roper dancing around like a marionette, poking his fists out with lightning speed.

'We go now,' Kim says. There's sympathy in his voice, but insistence too. I feel ridiculous. I'm sitting on my bed. I've got *PT* shorts and a T-shirt on, and plimsoles with short white socks. I don't look like a boxer. I've seen Roper and partners going to the gym. For 'sparring', or something. They wear fancy stuff, black shorts and singlets, red shoes with deep treads. And they look confident. Especially Roper. He ripples the muscles on his shoulders, and grins at me like a *fisi*. He mouths 'gonna getcha!' I'm sure he will. I've had it. The old priest in Arusha said 'A time to live. . . a time for something-to-do-with-stones, and a time to die.' My time is up.

'Betta go now!' Kim repeats.

'Okay,' I sigh, standing up.

'Old man, you flen, he waiting,' Kim says. Lopey. How does Kim know he's here? We leave the dormitory and start the long walk to the gym. Dead man walking! It seems the whole school has turned out to watch. I scan the faces for Gretchen, but she isn't here. If she was, and I got killed, at least she'd hear my last whisper that I love her. Meantime a boy in red shorts is being pounded mercilessly by a bigger boy in black. I don't trust this fight-by-weight thing. Those two can't weigh the same.

I see Lopey. He's sitting by the ringside, and his straight leg is sticking out sideways. His *Meerschaum* pipe is firmly clenched in his teeth. Next to him is Father O'Sullivan, dean of discipline. They're talking and laughing like old friends. How do they know each other? He sees me and waves. Father O'Sullivan nods my way and smiles. It's an evil and knowing smile.

Suddenly the smaller boy in red shorts lands a huge blow on the forehead of the bigger one in black, who falls straight on his back with a loud wallop. The referee, Father O'Donaghue, stands over him, counting. . . 'Seven, eight, nine, ten!' He waves his arms, fight over by knockout. The fallen boy sits up, looking confused. He's led from the ring. Father O'Donaghue walks to a corner and looks at a list. 'Next bout,' he shouts, 'Penhaligon versus Roper.' Bryan Roper, standing by the ropes, pulls two apart and jumps into the ring. He dances around, flicking punches into thin air. A blast of applause rises from his acolytes.

'Get him!' one yells.

'King Roper!' shouts another. Yet another makes loud chicken-noises. For me. Saying I'm frightened. Laughter ripples through the crowd of more than two hundred.

Kim helps with the gloves. They're old school ones, brown and cracked, not like Roper's, which are his own, red and shiny-new. Kim does up the long laces. He punches me affectionately on the shoulder

'Lememba,' he whispers, 'one-punch. Loper, he fall down!' I climb warily into the ring. Father O'Donaghue points to a corner, where there's a stool. Lopey's left his seat and is standing just outside the ring. I put him down as my 'second'. Kim joins him. When I sit down, Lopey leans forward and talks in my ear. He almost has to shout because of the noise.

'Vis is your chance,' he says, 'vis is vere you shauw vat lout wot you're made of. Do' ya hear me?' He grabs my chin and turns my face to his. There's a determined glint in his eye.

'Yes,' I say softly. Doesn't seem to be anything else to say. My heart is pounding so hard – it feels like it's going to exit my chest. There's a bitter, burning sensation in my throat. Like bile after vomiting.

'Good. Daun't worry if 'e 'its you.' Is he stark-raving mad?

That's exactly what I'm worried about. Kim winks, smiles encouragement. Okay for him too. 'Do it for your lovely muva,' Lopey says. My mother? Yes, well. Maybe….I can try.

'Seconds out, round one,' Ref O'Donaghue shouts. Lopey doesn't have to get out. He already is. A bearded man with red hair climbs down from Roper's corner. His father. They look alike. The ref motions to approach and touch gloves. The look in Roper's pale blue eyes is murderous. Like a wild animal. He said he'll knock me out in round one. After he's 'played with me a bit'. His chest muscles ripple. We go back to our corners. A uniformed boy rings the bell, and Roper leaps across the canvas at me.

The first jab stings the side of my face. I didn't see it coming. Nor do I see the second, which is straight on the nose, and makes my eyes water. Everything swims. There's a fast moving, blurred image of Roper dancing about, then darting in, and pain follows. I put up my gloves to shield my face.

He hits me in the stomach, winding me. I feel like vomiting. I put my gloves lower, he hits me in the mouth. Funny, the blows don't hurt as much. I'm aware of them, but they sting less. I try punching when he gets close, but he ducks aside and wallops me on the temple. I'm dizzy, then the bell rings. I've never had two minutes so slow. Or so horrible. Why do they do this? Why make people fight? The audience are hyenas, baying for blood.

I'm sitting on my stool. Lopey's wiping my face with a wet cloth. Blood pours from my nose. He produces a thick tissue, tells me to blow. I try, but it hurts too much. I'm breathing through my mouth.

'You did well,' Lopey shouts. ''E's using up energy. 'E 'asn't knocked you dauwn. . .' That's comforting, I think. Not yet, he hasn't. There's all the time in the world for that, and meantime he'll torture me. The wet cloth makes my face sting again.

'Seconds out, Round Two,' the ref shouts, and the uniformed boy rings the bell. Roper's out from his corner like he's jet-propelled.

'One-punch!' Kim shouts as I get to my feet. Roper hits me twice on the nose in rapid succession, then on my cheek. My head rocks. Suddenly I feel different. I can't explain how. I'm not frightened anymore. I'm angry. Furious. He hits me again, knocking my head back.

It's rage like I've never known. It bursts in my chest and pounds in my temples. Life isn't everything. One-punch, I think, one-punch! Might as well try. My right arm moves down, bending at the elbow, my fist clamps iron-hard inside my glove, my wrist strains as it rotates outwards.

Roper hits me on the nose. I hardly feel it, though blood spurts onto the canvas. I don't care. He can hit me if he wants, but I'm going to unload a punch like never before. It's for Mum, for Dad, for Lutoli, for Umali, for Becky, for Gretchen, for Sandy, for Geita, for me, for life, for death, for everything.

I breathe in as deep as my lungs can draw, bend my left knee, begin to exhale, rotate to my right, and uncoil my loaded fist. It's this or nothing. Remember England. I need one shot like that. Then I had Mlozi's leather pouch with its *hirizi*, or magic. Not now. Anger will have to do.

My fist comes up in an arc, twisting through ninety degrees, my every muscle convulsed in one supreme effort. It smashes into Roper's face just as he darts forward. I hear a bark like a dog from my own throat, and feel an impact judder down the length of my arm, through shoulder, into my spine. There's a harsh crunch on my knuckles. Like ice breaking.

Roper stops. Completely. For a moment he stands, shock and incredulity on his face. Then he topples and falls backwards. He hits the canvas like a bundle of logs. Silence breaks out. The shrieking applause from his acolytes chokes off.

The referee bends to inspect Roper, who's stretched out in the middle of the ring. His red-bearded father jumps in frantically. The ref counts, and Roper doesn't move. He's out. I've won. Kim jumps into the ring and raises my hand. So ends the unbroken wins of the Kenya-Bloody-champ.

I climb down. My face is a mess. Lopey and Kim put my dressing gown on me. Then they lead me out. Lopey's brought cakes and a flask of hot, sweet tea. We sit on a bench. 'You done it!' Lopey says.

'Did I?' I say. I still can't see straight.

'You did,' Lopey says.

'One-punch, see, it work, Loper, he KO'd!' Kim laughs. We eat cake and drink tea. There's never a sweeter tea break.

'You fix him good,' Kim says.

'Did I?'

'Bryan Roper's got a broken jaw,' Lopey says. Suddenly I feel satisfied. Maybe, even, this has all been worthwhile. Does this make me Kenya champion? I ask Lopey. No, that'll take more fights. No thanks, I say.

'What's you surname, young man?' Lopey asks Kim.

'Dong,' Kim replies.

'Is Ling Dong, the deputy Korean ambassador in Nairobi related to you?' Lopey asks.

'Dat,' says Kim, grinning widely, 'am my fadder!'

'Like I told ya, Jim,' Lopey laughs, 'Nairobi is a small place!'

It takes weeks before the bruises fade, my nose is back in shape, and I can breathe properly. Roper's away for two weeks, then comes back with a wired-up jaw. He doesn't tease me now. Nor do his friends. He doesn't look half as cocky. I strut around school as equal partner to my good friend Kim. Some boys come to us for advice, even protection. We never turn them away.

# Thirty-seven

Kim and I are seasoned smokers. We discover we started at the same age, five. This gets us into big trouble at St Mary's. There's a dense copse of bushes next to one of the playing fields. Kim and I find a way into a thicket with a tiny clearing in the middle. This becomes our den and smoking-place.

Kim's got a source of cigarettes on the 'outside', and we're never short of Sportsman filters and matches. We keep them here, in our den, protected by a biscuit tin. We come once a day, more if we can, and light up in safety. Then one day we're spied on by one of Roper's gang. Lacking the courage to face us, the coward waits till we're gone. He finds our haul and takes it to Father O'Sullivan, dean of discipline.

It's Friday night. I'm half asleep in my dormitory bed. Suddenly there's a sharp pain in the back of my neck. I'm physically pulled up into a sitting position. In the darkness, I see Father O'Sullivan at the foot of my bed. He's wearing a white cassock, and holding the end of a shepherd's crook. The handle is round my neck.

'Up, boy,' he growls. I get up. I'm aware of other boys watching in terror from the darkness. O'Sullivan makes night-raids frequently, and we live in dread.

'To my office,' he orders. I follow him lamely. The door's open, the light on. He sits behind his desk. The clock on the wall says ten o'clock. There's our biscuit tin on the desk. It's open. There's a packet of *Sportsman* cigarettes and matches in it. It isn't secret anymore. I blink in the bright light, feet together, hands at sides. This is how you stand when seeing the dean of discipline. One boy got flogged for shifting from foot to foot.

'Well, boy,' he says, pushing the tin at me, 'what do you say?'

'Nothing,' I mumble. No point. He's got the evidence. I can't deny it. Smoking is prohibited. If I say anything, he'll want to know more. If he doesn't know about Kim, I'm not going to tell him. If he knows, it won't be through me.

'Nothing?' he asks in a deceptively soft voice, 'did you say *nothing?*'

'Yes,' I whisper, my throat dry.

'Well then, we'll be needing to jog your memory, won't we?' I know what that means. He stands and walks round the desk. In the corner is the three-foot high earthenware vase, and sticking out of it are several long Malacca canes. He selects one and takes it out.

'Bend, boy, hands on desk,' he says. I bend forward, splay my fingers on the smooth wood. He flexes the cane in two hands, feeling its springiness. 'Three of the best,' he says, 'just to help your memory.' He steps back and raises the cane in the air, up almost to the ceiling. Then it flashes down.

The pain is indescribable. It's worse than anything I've ever felt. It's almost beyond endurance. The top of my buttocks explode in agony. We're not allowed to straighten up when the blow lands. My fingers ball into fists, I involuntarily bite my lip, but don't move. The second blow hits. If anything, it's worse. It's on the same place. I almost jerk upright, but manage not to. Third. It's beyond belief. Nothing can describe it. Somehow I remain bent over. He's putting the cane back now, walking round behind his desk. He sits.

'You may stand up,' he intones softly. How can someone who causes such pain talk so gently? I straighten up. He's staring at me with a look that's almost compassionate. 'Now,' he says, 'I hope you've recovered your memory. I ask you again, what have you to say?' He taps the side of the smoking-tin with an index finger.

I want to blurt out it's a tin with cigarettes and matches, and belongs to Kim and me, that we've been smoking in the bushes, and we're very sorry. . . But I know I can't. I mustn't say anything. If I do, he'll flog Kim too. He knows what he knows. I've started by saying nothing. I've got to continue, no matter what. I stare back, hands at sides, feet together.

'Well?'

'Nothing,' I say, though it comes out as a sob. I'm disgusted with myself. But my bum's on fire. It's burning, and it feels like there's a lion gnashing it.

'Recalcitrant?' he asks, almost sweetly. 'Brave?' He shakes his head. 'Not brave,' he says, 'foolish.'

'I know nothing,' I say.

'Have you taken leave of your senses?' he asks in a silky

voice, 'do you know what trouble you're in?' He's standing again, walking to the canes. He reaches for a different one. It's longer.

'Bend,' he intones like in communion. I lean over the desk again and splay my fingers. Somehow I don't scream or jerk upright. It's over again. Another three. I don't think the last one hurt as much. He's sitting again. I'm standing upright. Have to.

'Memory better?' he asks solicitously. 'Regained your senses?'

'No,' I whisper. He stares at me a long time. I stare back.

'A hero, eh?' he asks, 'suffering to protect your friends?' I'm vindicated. Friends, not friend. He's just fishing. He doesn't know about Kim, or he wouldn't use the plural. Also, if he already knew about Kim, he wouldn't be trying to find out from me. He knows I'm guilty, that's why I'm here. But he doesn't know about Kim. The coward who's told on me hasn't said anything about him. Either he doesn't know, or he's frightened Kim will find and get him. And, for a different reason, I haven't told. The dean can give me a thousand of his 'best', and I still won't tell.

'Not going to talk, are you?' he says, shaking his head and looking sad. 'A pity you aren't as single-minded with your studies.' He stares, trying to decide what to do. His eyes go briefly to the pot of canes. Then he seem to change his mind. 'This unpleasant matter is not closed,' he says, 'but you may return in shame to your bed.' I turn and leave with as much dignity as I can muster. What *shame*, you nasty old bigot?

'What happen?' Kim whispers from his bed.

'He's got our tin,' I whisper back.

'I hear, he flog you,' Kim says.

'Yup.'

'What he ask?'

'Who else.'

'You tell?'

'No.'

'He flog thlee-time, two-time!'

'I know.'

'You no tell him me smoke?'

'No.'

393

'You velly good flen!'

'Thanks.' There's silence for a minute. Then he talks again.

'How he find tin?'

'Someone told him.'

'Who you think?'

'Dunno.'

'Tomollow me fine out. Den fix him.'

'Good, Kim,' I say. If he can find out, Kim will definitely fix him. But how can he find out? Cowards are very careful. Cover their tracks. The burning on my bum has been replaced by a dull throb. It takes a long time to subside.

We rise at six every morning, shower, dress, and assemble in the school church for mass. It's cold in Nairobi at that time, and there's never enough hot water for everyone. So, freezing after a cold shower, we shiver in the unheated stone church, and say over and over: 'Hail Mary, full of grace. The Lord is with thee. Blessed art thou amongst women, and blessed is the fruit of thy womb, Jesus. Holy Mary, Mother of God, pray for us sinners, now and in the hour of our death. Amen.'

Our version is different: 'Hail St Mary's, full of crap. The fathers are with thee. Cursed art thou amongst everyone, and painful the bruises on our bums, by Jesus. Bloody St Mary's, Mother of pain, do us a favour, piss off now and forever. Amen.'

To avoid the cold and drudge of morning mass, we take turns locking each other into our tall wall-lockers. When it's our turn, we sit it out in the dark, cramped space, but it's preferable to going to church. We've got tiny spy-holes in the doors of our lockers, so, holding our breath, we can watch Father O'Sullivan do his dormitory inspection. Sometimes it's difficult not to laugh.

In the showers I see my backside in the big mirror. There are horizontal bruises across the top of my buttocks. They're deep purple, with bright red edges. Nearly all the boys have welts on their bums. Bright purple and red new ones, brown and yellowing old ones. Many have both. It's a uniform under the clothes.

It isn't only the dean of discipline who flogs us. There's also the dean of studies. Father Cox is a short, stout man with a monk's haircut, bald on top, ringed with a thick roll of hair. He's got a points-system. There are 'plus' and 'minus' points in the classrooms. If you pass a test, you get a plus. If you fail, it's a minus. If you talk in class, or are caught reading a comic, or chewing gum, or a hundred other things, you may be given one, two or even three minus points, in one go, at the discretion of the teacher or a power-crazed 'prefect'.

Just before lunch on Mondays, Father Cox makes a tour of the classrooms. The class prefect gives him a list of all the plus and minus points. Anyone with plus five is given a 'big plus', which goes towards his term report. That means he won't carry any plus points forward, and will begin the next week with zero. Anyone with minus-five has to leave the class and queue up outside Father Cox's office. They wait for ages, until he completes his classroom tour. Then he comes and flogs each boy in turn, in the order he sent them. The others, waiting terrified in the queue, hear the loud whacks, and shuffle forward, as, one by one, their jet-propelled classmates hurtle past, faces contorted, hands caressing buttocks.

The psychological pain of the points system is even worse than the physical. On Fridays the best and cleverest score you can ever have is plus four. Too few to have them taken away on Monday, enough to ensure you won't be flogged. It's rare to be in that position. More usually it's minus four. Too few for flogging, but dangerously close. When it's like that, it's rare you get through Monday morning without gaining the fateful extra minus. Or two, if you're at minus three. The prefects just can't help themselves.

There are other developments. Someone wants to curry favour with Kim. He knows who told Father O'Sullivan about our smoking. Kim's a strange chap. He won't tell me who the informant is. Something to do with honour, an agreement he made. But the traitor is someone we both know. Roper. He was seen going into O'Sullivan's office, our smoking-tin in his hand! I actually feel sorry for him. Unable to beat me in the boxing ring, he's resorted to filching on me to the dean.

'What me do?' Kim asks. 'You wan keel?'

'No,' I say, 'leave him. I'd hate to be him.'

'Okay, but I talk him. I know he scare.'

'Okay,' I say. After that Roper's even more retiring than

before. I wonder if he knows it's only me preventing Kim from knocking him into next week. There are few distractions, apart from treachery and floggings. Many boys are convinced there's a tunnel between St Mary's and nearby Loreto convent. For the fathers to get to the nuns. They do a lot of *jigi-jigi.*

Sven Edmündsen, the airspray engineer, comes to take me to his home for the day. He arrives in his 1955 white gull-wing-door *Mercedes Benz* sports car, and we hurtle through Nairobi with the wind blasting our hair. Sven's on leave, but his crew, including mad Eric, the Rhodesian pilot, are spraying crops somewhere near Geita. This makes me homesick. We arrive at Sven's sprawling house. His wife and two young sons are waiting for us. What's it like growing up in the bush, they ask. I tell them it's nice. We eat Norwegian food. Tasteless.

# Thirty-eight

My maddest escapade begins mundanely, if starting in the bush, travelling over untamed territory by Land Rover, then catching a steamer on Lake Victoria is mundane. Normal for me.

I've been travelling to St Mary's boarding school this way for over a year. It's 1965 and I'm fourteen. I've always hated boarding school, and spent much energy pondering how to avoid it. Trouble is, and always has been, what on earth will I do, and where will I go if I succeed in running away? The question has nagged me since I was seven, and answers aren't forthcoming.

In my imagination I build a primitive mud hut on the shore of Lake Victoria. I plunder ideas from Robinson Crusoe and Swiss Family Robinson. After all, I'll never be able to show myself to a *Mzungu* again, or I'll be caught and returned whence I flew.

My daydreams and nighttime imaginings lead me into mental anguish. Perhaps I'll succeed in establishing a bush hideaway and manage to survive. But won't I be lonely? Can I persuade another boy to run away with me? Oh, how I miss Lutoli! There are no other boys I'll get on with. There's Kim, but I know he won't run away. Worse, will I ever see Mum again? If I do, I'll be caught. If I don't, why run away? After all, it's missing *her* I hate most about boarding school.

And how will I protect myself from lions, leopards, and snakes. . ? I'm good at making and shooting a catapult, but what will that do against a charging rhino? Can I steal a real gun somewhere? The airgun's too weak. My wish to escape is purely emotional. Logic? None, not a trace.

But the thoughts won't go. What if I build that proper canoe? A watertight one, covered with animal skins, unsinkable? I can put food in, and store water in kalabashes, then seal myself in. If it's on the sea, the wind and tide will carry me wherever, while I'm safe and snug inside. How will I see out, know where I am? A periscope, perhaps. No, it'll never work. And, again, I'll not see Mum. Nor Gretchen. Self-defeating. But the canoe's a nice, cosy idea to fall asleep on, knowing I'm not committed because it's only thought.

How many nights I have lain in my dormitory bed at Arusha and Nairobi, exploring such ideas and notions I cannot say, except that they were many thousands, probably every night for over eight years. It was worse when the holidays were drawing to an end. I needed the distraction from the horrible truth.

In the last few days of every holiday at home in Geita I stayed in bed, avoiding contact with anyone. My daydreams about escape, my hapless scheming and plotting about a hut by the lake or a sealed-in canoe, were better than seeing people and places I'd soon be missing. Paradoxical, avoiding what I didn't want to leave?

My mind has been playing these games since I was six, when I first arrived in Arusha. Now I'm fourteen, have been at St Mary's a year. The Easter holiday has galloped to an end. I've done my usual, and withdrawn to bed and musing. The dreaded morning comes. Five am, and the Land Rover blows its horn in the drive.

We travel to Mwanza, arrive at eleven. The sun's already high, searing white. We're dropped off at *Mwanza Hotel*. Fritz is going to the bank on mine business. Then he'll find a shady alleyway between the adobe buildings by the lake to eat lunch, cool down and pass time. Later he'll collect us and drive down to the docks. *MV Victoria* is scheduled to dock at five, and sail at six.

Mum has befriended the first officer on *Victoria*. Jack's a nice man. He's bearded, pipe smoking, middle-aged and suntanned, and cuts a dashing figure in his white tropical uniform. His wife and children live in Port Bell, Kampala, from where he sails on *Victoria*. After each tour he has a fortnight at home. He's a former *Peninsula & Oriental Steam Navigation Company* officer, and sailed on 'real ships and real oceans' for years. Now he's satisfied to live in the sun, for good pay, and never be more than two weeks away from home.

Jack meets us on the gangplank. 'Back to torture?' he asks sympathetically. He smiles wryly. Unknown to Mum, the minute the boat sails from Mwanza he'll give me a cold bottle of *Whitecap* and a whole packet of *Crownbird* cigarettes. That's what I love about Jack. A gent.

Sometimes I have a loosely formed idea that something different, significant, even exciting, is going to happen, but I can't say what. It happens many times. Now I feel it again. I've endured a whole year at St Mary's. For the whole holiday I've tried, like in previous years, to persuade Mum not to send me back.

My efforts are futile, and my pleas, pestering, threats and blackmail fail. Yet pride, and hatred of boarding school, makes it impossible not to join the losing battle with all the energy and cunning I can muster. Deep down, at the beginning of the first term in 1965, I have a vague, delicious, anticipatory feeling, that this time I will have more than just tearful pleas, threats to change love for hate, bribes of undying devotion, or even promises, despite my tender years, to don a miner's helmet and lamp and go down the mine to wrestle a living from the gold-bearing quartz and granite. Something else will happen.

Mum is unmoveable. She, poor lady, pleads, cajoles and bribes in turn, pointing out I need an education, can't grow up 'wild' like my little black friends, who, despite their cunning, knowledge of nature and ability to survive, and even thrive, on very little, can't read or write, do arithmetic, or quote the date of any historical event, apart from recounting fireside stories handed down from equally 'illiterate and innumerate' elders and ancestors.

Mum and I both know, as always, that our arguments, tears and remonstrations are screenplays we've written for ourselves, and nothing will come of them. The last day of the holiday will arrive, my cases will be packed, and early next morning, while the sky is still black and cool, Fritz will pull into the driveway, his tyres squeaking on the gravel. There's a grim inevitability about it that no amount of scheming or arguing can change.

This time, despite the well-rehearsed drama, I have that feeling of something different. There's going to be a difference. Something will present itself. An opportunity unthought and unexpected. It will declare itself suddenly and dramatically. And if it means not going back to school, I'll seize the chance. Is it a product of wishful thinking, or desperation? Is it a remnant of child-like magical thinking?

It's anticipation, knowledge. A point of change is coming. I'll show them that Jimu doesn't accept boarding school. The opportunity, when it shows itself, will be seized. It's only this, which lets me carry on with the fruitless, hopeless, pleading charade. I go through the motions, inch by inch 'giving in' to the inevitable, but excitement is mixed in with my sadness.

Ten minutes after parting from Mum, I watch her fade into the amorphous shapes of receding people on Mwanza quay. Shortly afterwards, while I still taste the salt of tears, and feel a choking lump in my throat, I take my first sip of ice-cold *Whitecap* from a clucking Uncle Jack. Off the port side, just fifty yards away, bucking like a wild colt on the white wash and waves of our wake is an unmistakable shape.

*Lotanga!* Her paintwork is faded. She's loaded to the gunwales with laughing *watu* and cargo. Bunches of bananas, live chickens hanging upside-down on string, black goats, brown sheep. Grey smoke curls from her thin funnel. She's going to Mwanza, perhaps for the tenth time today. The half-naked skipper smiles and waves. Big white teeth. I wave back. Strange to think Dad, Umali and Wait brought her all the way from Uganda.

Lake Victoria is an enormous body of water. The indomitable explorer John Speke, in his tireless quest for the source of the Nile, found himself on the shore of Lake Victoria late in 1858. Staring at the vast body of water from a high vantage point, he declared it to be 'the great blue pearl of Africa'. He wasn't wrong. It's roughly rectangular, aligned North to South.

Between the most southern point at Mwanza in Tanzania, and the northern shore at Jinja in Uganda, is 400 miles of open water. From Bukoba on the Tanzanian west shore to Kisumu on the eastern shore in Kenya is three hundred miles. The total area covered by the lake is sixty thousand square miles. By comparison England covers less than forty thousand, and the whole British Isles only slightly exceeds the size of Lake Victoria.

There are ports on all sides of the lake, and vessels ranging from sailing canoes with outriggers, to large *dhows* of ancient Arabian design and traditional build, ply the waters as in centuries past. They carry goods and human cargoes, legitimate and smuggled, in the time-honoured tradition of an ancient water-highway connecting three huge countries, which, between them, cover an area as big as all Europe. In the shallows by the lake's edge, fishermen cast out nets like those of their forefathers, and pull in rich harvests of fish for sale in village markets.

For me the greatest spectacle on that beautiful inland sea is the passage of a steamer. The first steam-powered vessels were introduced at the beginning of the century by the Germans in *Deutsch Ost Africa*. When World War One ended, Britain, already the colonial power in Kenya colony and the Uganda Protectorate, took power in Tanganyika Territory, their name for *Deutsch Ost Africa*. Then they controlled every port on the great lake. A few German steamers not sunk in action by the British were recruited into service, and others were added.

I don't know the number, nor the names, of all the steamships carrying commerce on the lake in the nineteen sixties, but there are at least ten. Most are rusting hulks, conveying produce from one lake port to another, plus a few fee-paying tribesmen travelling *al fresco* on deck, some with goats, sheep and chickens, some with only personal possessions tied up in cloth or bundled into broken suitcases, and yet others with nothing at all.

Some steamers and *dhows* with similar cargoes can be smelt for miles downwind. But even the rusting hulks, seen underway from a distance, with foaming bow-waves in front, set against the crimson of a rising or setting sun, are things of extraordinary beauty.

There are two special steamers on the lake, princesses of the water. The older is *SS Usoga*. She is, I know, a very old ship of between two and three thousand tonnes. Built more than half a century ago, she has gracious lines, a tall black funnel, and a row of solid brass portholes along the sides. On board, the decks are laid in teak, and the guardrails are mahogany. She has twenty double cabins, immaculately fitted out in teak and brass, a sumptuous dining room for fifty, a bar, and a magnificent Victorian lounge overlooking the stern. She's a gracious old lady.

The other special ship is newer, built on the Clyde in Scotland in the late nineteen fifties in a *'CKD'*, or Completely-Knocked-Down form, transported to Mombasa on the Indian Ocean coast of Kenya, railed to Port Bell, Kampala, in Uganda, welded together, and launched as the flagship of *EAR&H*, or East African Railways and Harbours, fleet. She isn't built as solidly as the *Usoga*, but at three and a half thousand tonnes is bigger, lighter, faster, more airy and more reliable than poor old *Usoga*, whose coal-fed steam engines have seen better days. *Victoria*'s not a steamship like *Usoga*, but a diesel-turbine powered vessel, hence she's called *MV*, for Motor Vessel, *Victoria*.

I've sailed to school before on both *Usoga* and *Victoria*. I love them both. Particularly on the homeward run.

*Victoria* has a cruising speed of ten knots, so she could make passage from Mwanza in Tanzania, on the southern shore, to Kisumu in Kenya, in fifteen or sixteen hours, if not for the time wasted loading and offloading passengers and freight at the small Tanzanian port of Musoma, thirty-five miles south of the Kenya border on the north-east shore.

*Victoria* departs Mwanza dock at six on Sunday evening. She makes her way effortlessly through the calm lake waters. There's a spectacular sunset over the lake, and a cool, relieving breeze borne of evening and movement. Underfoot is the comforting deep throb of the great diesel engine. I've had a whole bottle of *Whitecap*, and smoked two *Crownbird* cigarettes, and I feel less bereft and homesick now.

I still have the sense of anticipation. It's occurred before at times like this, but never so powerfully. I *know* something's going to happen. It will be because I'm fed-up with it not happening.

It's slavery, I think, when where you are, what you do, who you do it with, is decided by others, without consultation. I've begged Mum to arrange home tuition for me. Why do I have to go away? The impossibility of arranging, or affording, a home tutor deep in the African bush never occurs to me. Grown-ups are all powerful, omnipotent. It's they who make me go to boarding school, isn't it? They're the only ones with money, cars, and power. If they wanted me to have a home tutor, it would happen. I've made an alternative offer too. I'll give up this 'education' thing. I don't need it. I'll work on the mine. Why can't they accept a fourteen-year-old? Too small? That's an excuse. They're just against me. They punish me by sending me away. I'll show them!

It's cosy in my cabin. Almost as nice as my imaginary canoe. I'm in my bunk and half-asleep when we dock in Musoma at ten.

I hear rattling and banging as the crew go about their business. It's strangely comforting. I'm fast asleep before *Victoria* returns to the open water on the last leg north to Kisumu, Kenya, a hundred and twenty miles away.

I wake at six in the morning. The ship is powering its way through flat, calm water. There's no land anywhere. The freshness of the breeze is invigorating and strangely exciting. Today's the day. An outline of a plan is forming in my head. I knew it would. I go for breakfast in the dining room at the stern. It's a feast. Bacon, eggs, tomatoes, toast and marmalade, coffee. And a cigarette.

Standing on the deck, leaning on the taffrail, watching the ship's wake, savouring the pungent smoke from a Crownbird, I feel a sense of well-being and optimism. Jack is beside me, smoking his pipe. What a nice man. I wonder if he suspects.

The morning draws on, Victoria chugs northwards, and by eight we're in sight of three Kenyan islands. The sun is a vicious white circle of unbearable brightness and heat, and shade on deck is difficult to find. The water reflects the sunlight like molten metal. Small *mtumbwis*, dug-out canoes paddled by half-naked tribesmen, appear, the occupants vigorously wielding oars towards destinations only they know, their bodies and canoes shimmering in the wavering, light-bending, heat. In the distance a larger vessel, a *mashua*, with a dirty yellow patch of sail fluttering in the breeze, makes its way somewhere else. Lake birds soar and dive after invisible fish.

At ten we see land-proper. The Kenya coast of Lake Victoria. The ship closes with the torpid town of Kisumu surprisingly soon. The rusting cranes and barges moored to the shore drift into view. So do the glinting, unpainted corrugated iron roofs of town buildings. Some are, blissfully, painted. They're red, green, and a kaleidoscope of colours, mostly weathered and rust tinged. But raw steel roofs among them mirror the blazing sun, bedazzle the view, and send laser-like, blinding, rays straight to the eye, causing screwing up of eyelids and shielding with a hand.

The engine groans in reverse. The water boils astern, and the ship slows as if tugged back by a giant hand. She glides slowly, gracefully, alongside the berth of concrete piles, wood and iron. Ropes fly, yells resound in Swahili, men in tattered clothes run to secure mooring ropes. It's midday, and we've arrived.

I've done this trip many times. I know the routine. The train to Nairobi leaves at six this evening and arrives early tomorrow morning in the Kenyan capital. There, a Father from St Mary's will be waiting on the platform to take me to the school in his car.

I have six hours to kill, in the hottest, worst town on lake Victoria. I call it the 'blinding headache town'. It's the sun reflecting from those iron roofs which blinds me, and I have to walk around with my head bent, looking at my feet. I get the fiercest headaches, like the top of my skull is going to explode and leave my brain exposed to be fried by the sun.

Six hours, supposedly, with nowhere to go, except hang around. I'm a lone European boy, with a huge suitcase to lug about, a hundred shillings to last as three months' pocket money, never enough, and a train ticket to Nairobi in the top pocket of my jacket. The jacket is equally gruesome to carry or to wear in this over-heated hellhole.

Things won't go according to the plans of others today. I've had enough of that, my life dictated by strangers. Mum colludes with them, but it isn't what she really wants. How can she really want me so far away? Dad's been dead nine years. She lives alone. She's always frightened alone. I know, because she says so. Sometimes a misled but well-meaning mother needs positive action to make a proper decision.

To hell with Mr Snel, the manager, to hell with the bosses, to hell with those who make laws about children going to school, to hell with Father Cox, Father O'Sullivan, and all the fathers. They're misguided, stupid, evil, or all of those. They'll learn today that, Jim can, will, outsmart them. They'll be amazed and awed by my courage, vision and resourcefulness. They'll have no choice but to meet at a table of negotiation. This will be my future with big people. Negotiation as equals, not *diktat!*

When you're going to do something unexpected or illegal, or contrary to instructions, you need an alibi, an excuse, or a damn good explanation. I'm not out to be an overt rebel, palpably ignoring rules and expectations. No, I'm going to craftily manipulate events, with every angle, every argument, and every question, addressed by cogent, intelligent and reasonable argument. I'm the victim of circumstance, not the author. I will occupy the moral high ground.

Last night it happened: walking on deck, I met a sailor of mixed Arab-African race. He stood beside me, staring at the moon rising above the horizon as Victoria thunders northward. Behind us was a phosphorescent wake. We spoke, and I recall every word.

'*Una enda wapi?*' he asks. Where you going?

'Nairobi,' I answer, though I'm determined not to.

'*Gari moshi?*' he asks.

'Yes, the train. How else?'

'What time does it go?'

'*Sa kumi na mbili,*' I say, twelve hours. In East Africa the day is measured from when the sun comes up. So seven in the morning to Europeans is one o'clock to the *watu*. Twelve hours means six pm.

'*Apana,*' he says,

'No, you say, what do you mean?'

'They've changed it. It goes every day at seven am now.' This is exactly what I want to hear. It turns out not to be true, but who cares about truth? Here's my excuse, legitimate and not self invented. I've been told to catch the six o'clock train. There isn't one, so I can't catch it. I can't be blamed for that!

I am now, I convince myself, abandoned in a hellhole, and my clear and irrefutable duty is to go home. I can't do that by simply staying on the Victoria for the return trip to Mwanza. Jack will find a 'solution', and make it possible for me to continue to Nairobi. He'll use contacts, find a lorry driver going that way, or insist I stay overnight at his house, and catch the train tomorrow. He's dangerously sensible, too resourceful, too kind. I can't risk him.

First thing is to get away from Europeans. They're too nosy, too interested, too interfering, to let me execute my plan. I carry my case from the harbour, down a side road leading from the European type buildings and shops at the waterfront, out towards shantytown Kisumu.

When I get there, with aching arms from my heavy bundle, which I've changed from hand to hand several times, there are no white faces. Instead, the dusty streets, bounded by wood and iron shacks in stages of decay and rust, are thronged with black people of several tribes, laughing, yelling and talking at once in Swahili. It's not only my first language, but also the common tongue of the lake.

I walk among these bustling people, safe and relaxed. They, I know, will understand and sympathise with my plan. Just like me, they can't comprehend the workings of white men's minds.

A fat mama is selling *karanga*, peanuts, on an upturned tea chest, measuring them out with a small tin which once contained baked beans. I like the look of her. She has a kind face, and I think she'll help. I approach, my case pulling painfully at my aching arm. *'Jambo Mama,'* I say, using the polite greeting for an older woman.

*'Jambo Mzungu ndogo,'* she replies, beaming. Hello small white person.

'I want to catch a bus to Tanzania,' I say. Her smile fades and she cocks her head to one side.

'Tanzania, child, why Tanzania?'

'My home, my mother,' I manage to say, suddenly overcome with emotion and longing. Some for Mum and Becky, some for Gretchen. Some just to be home in Geita. Tears pour down my cheeks in a totally unplanned, but genuine, display of sadness. She's around her makeshift table of upturned tea chests in a second, putting her great fat arms around me, and hugging me to her breast so tightly I can hardly breathe.

*'Pole, ndogo, pole, usi lia. . .,'* she croons, stroking the top of my head with one hand and forcing my face between her huge breasts with the other. *'Pole.'* Pronounced *pohl-eh*. It's the most comforting word. It means 'peace', 'be calm' and 'I sympathise', all in one word. 'Quiet small one, peace, don't cry,' She says, 'God will help, God will help.' In my dejected misery a little flame is lit. I have found an ally. Even if God doesn't help.

'Come home with me,' she says. 'We will talk, and if you want to go to your mother, we will make it so.'

She orders a young female assistant to continue selling *karanga*, takes my heavy case in one hand, my hand in her other, and leads me down a succession of more and more confusing alleyways, until we come to the hovel which is her home.

*'Mimi ni* Ngina,' she says. I am Ngina. She places a rough-

hewn wooden stool on the ground outside for me to sit on, then fetches another for herself. 'Now tell me everything, white-man-small. Does your mother send you away, and know you are not happy?'

'She is forced by *Mzungu* bosses.'

'But you are a *Mzungu*, little one, she chuckles,' her great belly wobbling.

'Yes, but not like them!'

'I see that,' she says, shaking her head and smiling. 'You are a *Mzungu Ki-Afrika-kabisa*!' A proper African *Mzungu.*

*'Asante sana,'* I say. Thanks very much.

'You must home-go at once, tell your *Mama* you can, together, stand against the bad *Mzungus* who separate you. They are evil, unkind, and you, my small African *Mzungu*, will win.' She smiles again, and squeezes my shoulder.

'My brother Kalebu is *lori-busi* driver. He leaves tonight, not to Tanzania, but a place call Narok, a hundred and ten miles from here. You get off there. You will find another *busi* to take you Narok to Ikoma, from there another to Mwanza. With God's help you will come, at last, to your home and your *Mama*.' I relax. This is what I was praying for. 'Kalebu will be here in an hour. Meantime, rest. There is a *kitanda* inside you can lie on. Leave your case, it will be safe. Sleep a while, small *Mzungu*. Everything will come to pass. You will be back with your *Mama*, and she will rejoice.'

# Thirty-nine

The bed is of crude wooden planks, and its legs are placed in *kopos*, or cans of water. That's to stop the *kijitu*, or evil dwarfs, from climbing up. They're repelled by water. I lie on the hard grass mattress. I'm exhausted and soon fall asleep.

I dream of Gretchen. She's wearing a white dress, and grinning over her shoulder at me, while hugging another boy. He's got his arms round her narrow waist. They're muscular and hairy, and pull her so close he bends her body. I don't know who he is, but murder rears in my breast. Gretchen winks prettily, and disappears, leaving me in a long, dark tunnel, like a hill-shaft at Geita mine.

Ngina's brother arrives at four pm. They leave me till quarter to seven. They discuss their visitor, who's so desperate to go to his *Mama*. By the time I awake, they've decided he'll take me to Ikoma in his bus.

We'll drive forty miles to Kericho, forty more to Sotik, thirty to Narok. There we'll cross the Tanzania border, go through the village of Lambayala, and continue a hundred miles to Ikoma. He'll introduce me to a Tanzanian driver there. This man will take me on, south and east, past a village called Manyanya, which means tomatoes, and another hundred and twenty miles to Mwanza. There's three hundred and thirty miles of dirt road, untamed bush and ancient bus ahead.

I've had long *busi* trips before. But there are seven or eight stops this time, which take an hour each, Kalebu says. The *watu* have to relieve themselves, eat, drink, load and unload heavy *mzigo*, or luggage. The roads are bad, and we won't average more than thirty miles an hour. Add seven or eight hours for stops, and the journey will take eighteen to nineteen hours. If we don't break down. From Mwanza, Kalebu says, I'm be on my own.

We leave from a bus stop, the only evidence of which is the existence of a hand-painted, fading yellow and black sign nailed to a very unhappy-looking tree. It's seven in the evening. Early twilight. Kalebu is wearing a rakish but tatty red cap, on which 'KTTC' is just discernible in yellow letters. Kenya -Tanzania - Transport Company. On the bus, in large red letters, is the legend

*'Lands-Rokett'.* The bus makes the Dodoma-Arusha *Duma Upesi,* or Fast Cheetah, look modern.

It's what's left of a *Bedford.* At least thirty years old, if not more, and wearing poorly. It's blue and red, or was once. It's covered with art everywhere a brush can reach. There's a few stencilled, fading advertisements. *'Drink Coca Cola, ice cold.'* Difficult if you've got no fridge, and no *watu* have. *'Smoke Sportsman, Kenya's favourite filter cigarette.'* Red packet. *'Crownbird gives you smoking satisfaction.'* No filters, yellow packet. What's best, filter or no filter, favourite or satisfaction? Hardly anyone speaks English, let alone reads it. The driver's door is missing. No matter, who needs one? The bonnet is bent and rusty. Old accident, never repaired.

If it was tight on the Dodoma bus, this is *squeeze.* The bus has seats for forty. Seventy are hell-bound to board. There's no queue, just a crowd. *Watu* of all ages, tribes, sexes and sizes. Some in groups, some alone, all with *mzigo,* or luggage, as big as themselves. Several *mzigos* are alive.

Squawking, bleating. *Kukus* hang upside-down, legs bound. Goats bleat, small ones carried, big ones tugged on ropes. A *batamzinga,* or turkey, Gooloogooloo's cousin. A calf. Pretty and confused. A *karamu,* or feast, is planned in a village somewhere between here and someone-knows-where. A wedding, perhaps.

There's a pungent odour of dung, urine, frightened animal, and unwashed humanity. Kalebu supervises boarding. It is chaos. His assistant is no older than me, but thinner. He looks sick. Belying his size and appearance, he hefts non-living *mzigo,* plus *kukus* in grass cages, onto the rusty roof rack. When they're parted from their *mzigo,* or not if it's *too* alive, the *watu* surge forward to jam the doorway, their *mzigo* reaching new heights of squawk and bleat.

*'Kuja, Mzungu,'* Kalebu says, grabbing my elbow and pulling me through the knot of struggling *watu.* He tugs me up the aisle, to three seats. In one is a grey-bearded *mzee,* or elder, in worn out trousers and a shirt of indiscriminate colour. The other two are occupied by an enormously fat *mwanamuke,* or woman, in a floral *kanzu* or loincloth, with Kikuyu tribal scars on her cheeks. She has huge breasts. Though covered by her *kanzu,* I can see

409

they're as big as pressure-cookers.

'*Malaika, hi ni rafiki yangu,* Jimu,' Kalebu says. Malaika, this is my friend, Jimu. 'Jimu, Malaika will care for you.' The huge woman's face creases in a smile, showing she has only bottom teeth. On her lap is a young billy goat. There are at least six chickens in the woven basket at her feet. She clenches herself, and manages to move her buttock a foot one side. She's still occupying a seat and two thirds. I have no choice. I subside into the sliver of space, and find myself hard against the bony *mzee* on one side, enveloped in pungent soft flesh on the other. The kid on Malaika's lap puts his head on my knee. I stroke his neck. The *mzee*, luckily, has only one piece of *mzigo*. A very small, battered cardboard suitcase. I wonder where he's going.

'*Jambo Mzungu ndogo,*' she says. Hello *Mzungu*-small. She's very friendly. 'Ngina told me your business.' She smiles broadly. 'Don't be afraid, I look-you always.' Staring into her eyes, I know it's true. She will. That's how it is. *Watu* tell the truth. They love children. I've never been let down. Different with *Wazungus*. With the *watu*, even dishonesty is somehow honest. I understand them. I feel instant warmth for fat Malaika. How did she get the name? The love song wasn't about someone as fat. Or *was* it? *Malaika, ninakupenda Malaika.* Malaika, I love you Malaika.

The diesel engine rattles into life, shaking the bus in a metallic jingle. The floor vibrates unrhythmically. Engine out of tune. I hope it will make the trip. Here I go again. Worry, worry and worry more. Mum took me to Dr Weiss last year. Told him I worry too much, make 'mountains out of molehills'. Josef says she's lucky I didn't die at five of cerebral malaria.

'I haff niffer heard uff a young vun vot didn't die in a coma like zat. So vat, he iss a leetle emotional und obsessive, *ja?* Ve can't know vot brain-damages he iss having.' He smiles. 'Jimmy iss vun devil, *ja?* But iss not his fault.' I look at Mum to see if she's clocked this. Not my fault. He removes his glasses, uncaps a fountain pen. He draws the outline of a brain in a continuous stroke.

'Here,' he says, pointing with the nib at an area near the bottom, 'iss der temporal lobe. It hass poor supply uff blood. Vid der high fever, it needs more oxygen, but can't get. So, some uff it dies.' Mum is visibly shaken. 'Ve call zis *medial temporal sclerosis*,' Josef continues, 'und der problem is zis area controls der emotions.' He puts his glasses on and grins. 'I sink zat iss vy Jimmy iss der handful!'

'Will you give me a letter to say I can't box at school?' I ask.

'Vy not?' he laughs. That's how I avoid a second fight.

Fat Malaika laughs too. *'Busi ni mzee, namna huyu!'* She indicates the old man on my side. The bus is old, like him! The *mzee* chuckles. Her laughter is infectious. There's a teeth-rattling grind of gears, and we jerk onto the road. Without warning, the twilight is replaced by a cloak of black, penetrated by the conical yellow beams of our headlights. The bus stop's on the outskirts of Kisumu, so it isn't long before the Land-Rocket is in open country. Soon the tar road ends, then we're onto bone-shaking dirt and stone.

I'm very tired, even though I slept this afternoon. It's anxiety about what I'm doing. I yawn. The ancient *Bedford* heads south, around the eastern edge of the Kavirondo Gulf. The moon comes out and lights up the glass-smooth water. After twenty miles we head away from the lake, into the hinterland of Southern Kenya. The road grows ever bumpier.

Fat Malaika's readjusting herself. She pulls a huge arm out from between us, and puts it round me. I don't resist when she pulls me to her. Her well-cushioned chest makes a soft pillow. I hear her heartbeat. It's a good heart. *'Lala mtoto,'* she says. Sleep child.

I shift between deep and fitful sleep on the jerky ride. We stop to pick up more passengers, who board noisily. I'm too tired to care. I wake and am surprised that two hours have passed. Many times I drift off for only minutes. There are longer naps, when I dream of a storm and a sea-canoe. Gretchen is with me. I ask who was the hairy boy hugging her, but she just laughs.

The bus groans and grinds to a stop. I open one eye. Nowhere. Nothing. In the moonlight I see palely illuminated, flat country running to the horizon. There's a thin, dark line where sky meets earth. I rub my eyes. On one side there's an interruption to the sweep of land. A long, low mud building, open on the sides, roofed with grass thatch. There's flickering light coming from it. A fire. Malaika stirs.

*'Wapi?'* I ask her. Where?

*'Sijui, lakini katika aw si-mbari* Sotik.' I don't know, but it's near, or not far from, Sotik. If I remember, that's only forty miles past Kericho, which is forty more from Kisumu. I look at my Oris. It's eleven at night. Eighty miles in four hours. 'Land Snail' would be a better name.

*'Kuamka Mzungu,'* comes the voice of Malaika. Wake up *Mzungu.*

*'Ku fanyaje?'* I ask sleepily. To do what? The open-sided hut has more lights now. Six. In the still night air I hear the low growl of hurricane lamps.

*'Chai, mtoto, na makate!'* Tea, child, and bread! *'Njaa?'* Are you hungry? Suddenly I realise I am. Ravenous. The *watu* are getting off the bus. We join them.

The floor is of pounded, swept mud, and there are three long tables of rough planks supported on logs stuck into the ground. The tired passengers sit on low benches, waiting for the proprietor and his wife to bring food. They expected the bus from Kisumu, and the wood-fire is burning with bright yellow flames. There's an arrangement of what looks like old metal ammunition trunks around it. An *mzee*, or old man, in a *kanzu* stokes the fire, and his wife mutters as she looks into the trunks.

*'Tiari?'* he asks. Ready?

*'Karibu,'* she says. Nearly. The wait is forever. It's cold after the heat of day. Finally the *mzee*'s wife pronounces satisfaction. The *makate*, pronounced mak-ah-teh, is placed on the tables. It's bread rolls, huge ones, in blocks of twelve. It's made of coarsely ground, unrefined wheat.

Bread never tasted as delicious, even without butter or jam. It's hot, yeasty, coarse and chewy, and just what we need. *Chai* is brought in huge teapots, which have been boiling on the fire. It's got everything in, tea, milk, and lots of sugar. Hot, stewed, sweet *chai*. Swahili-style. Poured into old baked-beans tins, or *kopos*. It's perfect. I drink a big *kopo*-full, and ask for more. There isn't better sustenance anywhere. Malaika is sitting beside me, eating hungrily, slurping and chewing with her mouth open. Just like the others and me. Malaika grins.

*'Mu-Africa!'* she laughs. An African! I nod. I am, I am.

*'Je, umeridhika?'* Kalebu asks, coming over to check on me.

Are you satisfied (full)?

'*Karibu alikuwa kutosha*,' I say through a mouthful of *makate*. I've nearly had enough. He pats me on the back and laughs.

'*Wewe ni mSwahili kabisa!*' he says. You are a complete Swahili! He heads back to his bus, still laughing. That's a compliment I value.

# Forty

The journey south continues. We can't see much, because there's no moonlight. The headlights are weak and jaundiced. Kalebu must have the eyes of a *fisi*, Malaika says. Only they can see in the dark. It's witchcraft. *Mchawi* things. She talks like Amina. We roar along the edge of a dark plain, and then slow to walking pace.

The road from Sotik to Narok is only thirty miles long, but parts were washed away in last year's monsoon. In low-lying areas it's gone completely, along with dozens of villages. Elsewhere the surface is broken by deep gulleys or *dongas*. The *PWD*, or Public Works Department, are doing their best to repair the road, but it's taking time.

We jolt and shake as the *Lands-Rocket* slows and descends obliquely into a wide washaway, crosses the rocky bottom and struggles up the other side. For a few minutes we're on the road again, then at another washaway. It's incredible how this ancient bus manages to climb out the holes. A Land Rover would struggle.

We begin to ascend the far side of a deep gulley. Halfway up the back wheels spin, we slew round, and the bus slides backwards. Kalebu reverses and tries again. Same result. Three more failed attempts, then he orders everyone off.

Pushing a bus up an incline of one in five at two in the morning, in total darkness, on the side of a muddy slope, in the company of *watu* of both sexes and all ages, is a unique experience. The *watu* sing as they labour. Not a song, more a rhythm made up in the harmony of numbers. It can only ever be like this in the heart of Africa. *'Moja, mbili, tatu!'* One, two, three! At three everyone heaves. Kalebu releases the clutch and floors the accelerator. The exhaust bellows and coughs black smoke, the back wheels spin, spattering us with mud and small stones, and we push. Ever so slowly, we inch her upwards. As we relax to draw breath, Kalebu pulls up the squeaking handbrake. Even so, we lose some of the gain by backsliding. What the dean of studies warns against.

The passengers are determined. No amount of failure dents their enthusiasm. With conviction like this, the bus *has* to move.

In slow, painful, steps it does. Bit by bit, we reach a point where, suddenly, on the dozenth attempt, the wheels find purchase, and the monster roars and gains the lip of the gulley. It's back on the road, or bit of road. A ragged cheer rises from the exhausted passengers. Kalebu stops. Covered in mud, we clamber on board. Our rest is brief. Fifteen minutes later we're stuck again. Off, on again. Washaways every mile. Mostly Kalebu manages without passenger-power, but there are five pushes in two hours.

I'm exhausted, filthy and itchy. I recognise the itch. Mosquito-bites. I've been eaten alive while pushing the lorry, or last evening waiting for the bus in Kisumu. It's hard to scratch through a layer of caked mud. Even fat Malaika is scratching. I feel sorry for her. Of all the passengers, she pushed hardest. There's muscle under those enormous breasts. She's exhausted, itchy and restless, like me.

The *dongas* or washaways are less frequent, and shallower. Kalebu treats them with disrespect, roaring and jolting down one side and up the other at full throttle. It's five in the morning, and the eastern horizon is just beginning to suffuse itself with a suggestion of soft light, when we reach a wooden pole with a fading stencilled sign:

**YOU AR LE VING KEN A      OP  OU  NJO ED  YOU**
**ISIT**
**'KWA ERI'**

A hundred yards further are two tall posts with a huge sign between them:

**W LCOM  TO TA ZAN A  ENJOY  OU  VIS T**

Thank heavens the signs are so clear! I'm in my home country now. Shortly we trundle into the mud-hut village of Narok. It's taken five hours to do thirty miles from Sotik, where we feasted so hungrily on bread and tea. This is as far as Kalebu and his bus take me. Here he turns left, towards a village a hundred miles west.

I'm standing under a gnarled tree with a bus stop sign nailed to it. The horizon is lighting up as the rising sun lips the far side of a jagged, rocky hillock. Kalebu brings my suitcase.

'*Ngoja hapa,*' he says. Wait here. 'At two hours a bus will come from Ikoma. It will take you there, then you get another to Mwanza.' Two hours is eight AM Swahili-time. Three hours to wait. Malaika is continuing her journey. It's her village they're headed for. She gives me a sweaty hug, then clambers back on board. The old bus roars off. It needs a new exhaust. I'm the only one who got off.

I sit on my case to wait. There's a cluster of silent mud huts down the road, and nearby a solitary *jogoo* greets the rose-coloured dawn. It's hauntingly beautiful. The itching is less, but I'm exhausted and sore all over.

I've never fallen asleep sitting up, without even a backrest. I do now. It's a strange sleep, because I'm dimly aware of rocking slowly forward, until I'm about to fall on my face, then rocking back. But I sleep, and even dream for two hours, because it's seven when I sit up look at my watch. I'm stiff and sore, but that's not what woke me. I look round and see six semi-naked *totos*, aged three to twelve, appraising me. They're laughing and giggling. 'Look,' one says, 'the *Mzungu* is awake!' Hello Rip van Winkle, or is it Gulliver? At least I'm not tied up with tiny ropes.

'*Jambo,*' I say, '*habari?*' Hello, how are you? There's a look of delighted surprise on their faces. They didn't expect me to speak Swahili. They burst out laughing. This is sport, a young *Mzungu* sitting on a suitcase on the side of the road in the early morning, speaking Swahili! Nothing as exciting as this ever happens.

'*Nina njaa,*' I say, I have hunger. The biggest *toto* steps forward tentatively. He's wearing a *kanzu*, round his waist, and nothing else. He reminds me painfully of Lutoli, only he's thinner.

'*Njaa?*' he asks.

'*Ndio,*' I say, yes.

'*Jina lako?*' he asks. Your name?

'Jimu,' I say, '*lako?*' Yours?

'Steveni,' he replies, grinning. '*Njoo na mimi, Jimu,*' he says, come with me. He turns and walks towards the huts. I pick up my case and follow, and the others skip along behind. It's seven thirty, and the sun is already high and dazzling. I feel I've been sleeping forever.

I really am like Rip van Winkle, waking to find the world changed. It's that over-tired, detached and dreamy state I've known before. When I had malaria half-way up Kilimanjaro. But this is just tiredness. I don't feel cold, I'm not nauseous, nor shivering. We walk into a large swept-earth compound connecting three mud and thatch huts.

'*Mzungu!*' Steveni announces excitedly to an old woman bent over a fire. It's a large one, of burning logs between three rocks. Just like Amina cooks. Balanced on top is an enormous blackened *sufuria*, and I know the smell of the bubbling contents. It's *ugali*, or maize-meal porridge. This one's thin and runny. It's drinking- porridge, or *uji*.

The woman straightens and examines me with one eye. The other's missing, and the eyelid's closed over a hollow place where it should be. She's very old, thin like a stick. I have met another *masikini*. She smiles, revealing she has no teeth.

'*Karibu Mzungu,*' she sputters. Welcome *Mzungu*.

'*Mzungu ana njaa,*' Steveni says. The *Mzungu*'s hungry.

'*Je, yeye kuelewa?*' she asks. Does he understand?

'*Yeye anaongea Swahili,*' Steveni affirms, smiling at me. He speaks Swahili. It's as if Lutoli is back. I knows he isn't, but there's something about Steveni, like I've known him for years. It's strange, yet comforting at the same time. Maybe Lutoli will never really be dead to me.

'*Kuwakaribisha sana!*' the old lady says, smiling more widely. Very welcome!

'*Asante,*' I say. She puts a long wooden spoon into the pot, withdraws it and tastes the porridge. '*Ni tiari,*' she says. It's ready. Steveni has plucked two lemons from a gnarled little tree. He gives them to her, and she cuts them with a knife-blade without a handle. She squeezes the juice into the pot, and stirs. She's got an old tin with sugar. She shakes some into the mix. One of Steveni's friends hands out the tin *kopos*, and the old lady fills them, using another on a long stick as a ladle.

The *uji* is hot, sour and sweet. It's the favourite breakfast for East African children or *totos*. I drink mine as fast as I can without scorching my mouth. Steveni, his friends and the old lady watch in fascination. They don't see *Wazungu* often, and probably never saw such a hungry one. I drain my *kopo*, and it's refilled.

After my second helping I'm satisfied. My hunger was extreme. Must be all that bus-pushing last night. The village is coming to life. An *Mzee* comes out of a hut, and sits on a wooden stool. Her husband, I presume. He looks a hundred. A yawning young woman with pendulant breasts appears, carrying a naked baby on her hip. *Kukus* scratch at the dry ground.

I feel very tired. I glance at my watch. It's nearly eight o'clock, or two-hours. That's when Kalebu said the bus would come from Ikoma. I thank my hosts, and give the old lady a five-shilling note from my pocket-money. She's overwhelmed, and claps her hands in gratitude. Even the old man claps. Steveni and the *totos* accompany me back to the bus stop under the gnarled tree.

In Tanzania eight o'clock means anything from nine to twelve. Time hasn't got urgency. I chat with Steveni until we run out of things to say. It's so much like talking to Lutoli. Then I can't help myself. The sleepiness starts again. There's something else.

I've got a headache. It's all over my head, a sharp, lancing pain. The headache I once described to Mum as two men sword-fighting in my head. The sun's high in the sky, blasting heat at the baked earth. I should be feeling hot, but I'm not. I feel cold. My teeth begin to chatter, and shivers run through my body. Oh no, I think, not malaria again!

I drift into a strange sleep. Images come and go. Gretchen, Mum, Becky, Umali. They all seem to be trying to warn me about something, but I can't hear. I've got some kind of strange-shaped helmet on my head, covering my ears. Is it an army helmet, or the *machula's* bucket, I wonder.

It's almost twelve when Steveni jumps to his feet and shouts that a *busi* is coming. I've nodded off, and I jolt awake. When I open my eyes it's on a world, which is blurred and painfully bright. And freezing. My head is exploding. I can hardly stop my jaw from quaking and my teeth from chattering. The muscles of my legs and arms twitch uncontrollably, and my knees knock together. I shade my eyes and look down the road. There's a cloud of dust approaching. I close my eyes as pain shoots through my head.

The bus squeaks to a halt. I don't know or care what kind of bus. I manage to ask the driver if he's going to Ikoma, and he says he is. Two other passengers saunter up from the village. Unlike me, they don't wait here for hours. I get on and pay my two-shilling fare. Then I collapse into a seat behind the driver. Steveni is waving goodbye. I feel so close to him, so sad to leave.

The bus turns and goes back the way it came. I lick my lips. They're very dry and sore. It must be the dust and the heat, even though I feel so cold.

I fall into a fitful sleep, and dream I'm being chased by the rotting *mzoga*, of Mr Valari (senior), who has two ferocious black *fisis*, with blood dripping from their teeth, as assistants. High in a branch of an acacia tree, Gretchen, wearing jeans and a T-shirt, and looking gorgeous, waves cheerily at me. What does it mean? I'm relieved to wake and find I'm only on a bus.

We stop at the village of Lambayala, but I'm only dimly aware of it. I'm very ill. The shivering shakes my whole body. Even my head rocks as my neck muscles declare independence. My lips are on fire. I lick them and taste salty blood. We continue our journey. I sleep.

The bus stops, and everyone gets off, except me. I'm unable to stand. The driver comes to look at me. *'Je, wewe ni mgonjwa, Mzungu?'* he asks. Are you ill, Mzungu?

*'Ndio,'* I manage to say. Yes.

*'Unakwenda wapi?'*

'Mwanza,' I say between shivers. That's where I'm going.

*'Ni mbali,'* he says. It's far.

*'Hapa?'* I ask. Here?

'Ikoma,' he says. It's another hundred and twenty miles to Mwanza. I look at my watch. It's seven in the evening. I've been sleeping for ages, almost all the way from Narok. We left there at midday, so it's taken seven hours to do a hundred miles. I don't know how I can continue.

*'Busi ya Mwanza,'* he says, pointing. The bus for Mwanza is there. The engine is running. It's about to leave and I'm going to miss it. The driver sees the panic in my eyes. He jumps out his

bus and waves frantically. The other bus has just started to move. He brakes in a cloud of red dust.

'*Mzungu!*' my driver shouts. Next thing, with help from this kind man, I'm seated again, and on the road south once more, towards Manyanya, and finally Mwanza. I realise I haven't given any thought to what I'll do there. Obviously, I'll have to get someone to contact Geita. But what will I say? How will I explain being back in Mwanza? It's difficult to think. My headache's bad enough without the effort. When I think, it gets worse.

This bus is almost empty. I'm so cold, my bones are in ice. My body's too tired to shiver. I feel my lips with my fingers. They're thick, like a steak. And throbbing. When I grimace the skin cracks, and warm blood oozes into my mouth. I don't know how, but I fall asleep. It's thirty-six hours since *MV Victoria* arrived in Kisumu, and twenty-six since I boarded the first bus. There's still a hundred miles to Mwanza.

Now I'm being buried in a grave, although I'm not dead. I can't move, or speak. I'm paralysed, but awake. I can't do anything to let them know I'm alive. Mum, Becky and Gretchen are there, crying. I don't know how I know, because the coffin's nailed down. We're in the little church in Geita one minute, then at Samina. I'm being lowered into a freshly dug grave. It's between Dad and Mrs Williams, even though there's no space for another grave.

My eyes are cameras outside my coffin. I can see everyone. At the back of the burial party are Umali and Amina. They're crying. Odd, Lutoli's with them. He's laughing. Then I see someone else. Behind everyone, shaking a bony finger at me, is the rotting corpse of Mr Valari. As I watch, a scorpion scampers out of his eye socket and down his disintegrating cheek.

I fall into deeper, non-dreaming sleep. It's like being dead. A few times I'm aware of distant voices, of stops and starts, cold and pain, but I drift back into soft cottonwool sleep. The hours and miles pass. I dream of Gretchen. She's very beautiful in white. The boy who hugged her is nowhere to be seen. We pass through the dusty village of Mananya.

The bus reaches Mwanza. I don't know time anymore. I also don't know how I get to Mwanza Hotel. Next thing I'm in a bed, in a coma. I find out later how I get there. The driver carries me to the hotel. He's the last in a series of good Samaritans I've met on the road. It's early morning, forty-eight hours after *Victoria* docked in Kisumu, thirty-six since I caught the bus in Kisumu, and twenty-four since I should have arrived in Nairobi. I don't realise I'm famous throughout East Africa.

When I don't get off the train from Kisumu yesterday morning, Father O'Sullivan goes back to St Mary's and telephones Geita via the radiophone. Mr Snel answers, and sends for Mum.

'Jimmy's missing,' he says. Mum feels a cold hand seize her heart.

'What do you mean?' she asks.

'He didn't arrive in Nairobi. Nobody knows where he is!' Mum faints. Mr Snel just catches her in time. When she comes to, he has taken command of the situation.

'I've sent out messages to everyone,' he says, 'first, to the steamer *Victoria*. Maybe the little bugger's hiding on the boat. She's on her way back to Mwanza, and East African Railways and Harbours are contacting her by radio. I've told the police in Kenya, Uganda and Tanzania to look out for him. Maybe he got off the Nairobi train somewhere, and forgot to get back on.' He gives Mum a cup of hot, sweet tea for shock. 'I've also contacted the *East African Standard*. Maybe someone will recognise him.'

Mum and Becky have a day and night of hell. If I'd known I'd cause such distress, I wouldn't have done it.

The radiophone jangles in the head office. Mr Snel picks up the receiver. It's the manager of the Mwanza Hotel. 'Read the *Standard* this morning,' he says, 'and I've got the boy.'

Mum and Mr Snel are driven to Mwanza by Fritz, who complains he can't go as fast as they ask. When they arrive at Mwanza Hotel, it's six hours since I arrived. They're let into my room by the manager. I'm there, but they can't rouse me. I'm in a high fever. I'm bundled up and taken to Geita, where Josef Weiss is waiting. He confirms the diagnosis. It's malaria. And total exhaustion.

I don't know much about the next few days. Then I'm better. They allow me a week to convalesce. At the end of that time, I'm taken by Fritz and Mr Snel himself to Mwanza, and put on a direct flight to *Embakasi* airport, Nairobi. They're taking no chances. There will be no mistake, no escape, this time. Father O'Sullivan will be waiting on the landing strip.

# Forty-one

It's May 1966. I'm fifteen, and the gold mine is closing. The government in Dar-es-Salaam has taxed it to death. Not satisfied with doubling company tax, they've invented other ways to wring money out of foreign-owned enterprises. The latest is 'Roof Tax". The *Wazungu* will, in addition to income tax, already trebled since Uhuru, pay a hefty new tax to fund corrugated-iron roofs for all the tribal people in Tanzania. The mine closes three months later.

Things move fast. People are leaving each day, heading home to England, South Africa, Italy, the Seychelles, Australia, Germany, and other places. There are very few foreigners left. It's strange – all the *Wazungu* who've ever came here leave in the end. Like Vorbeck himself, my great hero, we're finally going too. I hoped it would never really happen.

I've been home from St Mary's for a month. I'm never going there again. Only one person I'll miss. Kim. It was a tearful goodbye, though I've given him an address, and he said he'll come and see me. But we're leaving home in three days. Leaving Geita forever, leaving East Africa. I'm heartbroken. So are Becky and Mum.

There's even more heartache for me. Antonio says Gretchen has been seeing Arnoldo Bachelli, a swish Italian bachelor who came to Geita last year. Was he the hairy one hugging her in my dream? She and Dieti have been sleeping over at his house.

It's too painful to think about. What has he done to her? Dieti won't say when I ask. While I've never even let myself think about her that way, even closed my eyes to protect her nakedness underwater, along comes this interloper, and ruthlessly grabs that which was always only meant for me. Gretchen's eighteen, and Mum and Becky say it's natural she should have a boyfriend, and I'm far too young for her. Don't I know that? There'll be a girl for me one day. This does nothing for me. I hate her now, with all my heart. How can she do this to me? I've loved her so long, dreamt about her so many, many times.

Is there *no* justice, was she never able to see the value of pure, unselfish love and devotion? Then there's the other feeling. We're leaving, I may never see her again. Good! I don't want to!

Or *do* I? Pain nags, like a hard lump deep in my throat, and under my ribs.

There's more agony. We're leaving Umali and Amina. Their love has always been certain, not just hoped for. Tembo too. Poor old chap, he's only ever been good to me. Sandy's going to stay with Umali and Amina. Mum's done something awful. She had no choice but to give our *kukus* to Umali, who removed them to his *shamba*. He doesn't want old Gooloogooloo, our infamous *batamzinga*, because Amina is too afraid of him. So Mum donates him to the club.

She feels very guilty telling me it took three strong men to hold him down and cut his throat. What was the alternative, she asks. The alternative to the murder of my friend? If we just left him, the *fisis* and other wild things would tear him to pieces, and it would be a much crueller death. Anyway, she says, they said he made a great curry. Mum and Becky didn't eat any. I wonder if Gretchen did.

I haven't spoken to her since I heard about Arnoldo Bachelli. Hid in the grass when I saw her on Top Road. Becky says I'm silly, and she's sure Gretchen and Arnoldo didn't 'do anything'. Gretchen's upset that I think she did. It's so soon we go away, and maybe we'll never meet again.

It's our second-last night. I'm crying in bed. The silence of the night is shattered by a soul-piercing, unearthly, inhuman scream, and loud, excited hyena giggles. It's coming from up the hill, the direction of Top Road. Becky and I are jolted awake, and run to Mum's room, where she collides with us coming out.

'What is it?' Becky asks, her voice strangled with fear. The screaming has stopped, but the *fisis* haven't. They sound very close. They're making yapping, growling and maniacal giggling sounds, all at the same time. There are lots of them. Mum calls us to her room and locks the door. Even Sandy's come in. We pull the curtain aside, and try to see where the noise is coming from. The insane giggling continues, with loud growling too.

Suddenly there's an ear-splitting bang. It's a shot from a big rifle; I'd know the sound anywhere. The giggling ceases. There's a blood-curdling scream of a creature in agony. Then silence. We wait a long time. Nothing. Finally we get into bed together. Even Sandy. It's two in the morning. Someone has dealt with the problem.

When Umali comes to work at seven, for his very last time, he's got terrible news. Did we hear the commotion last night? Yes? Well, a friend of his was coming down to the mine from Compound Hill an hour ago, when he discovered a most terrible thing. Did we notice the racket came from up there? Yes? Well, who do we know lives on the corner of Top Road and Compound Hill, in a small hut next to a big flat rock, or *mwamba?*

'Mlozi, the *mchawi,*' I say.

'*Ndio,*' says Umali. 'There isn't much left of him.' In ten minutes I'm dressed and heading for Top Road. I reach Mlozi's place to find my old askari friend, Kaiser. Like me, he's come to see what's happened. He's lost his *askari*-job, and it's the first time I see him out of uniform.

'*Tukio la kutisha,*' he says gravely. A terrible happening.

'Mlozi?' I ask. He nods, and points at something on the ground. It's a piece of *kanzu,* or loincloth, and I recognise the zigzag black and yellow pattern. It's Mlozi's. It's heavily bloodstained. Lying on the ground next to it is part of a severed human foot. Two toes and a piece of skin. Nothing else, except a foot wide streak of blood on the rock, going in the direction of the tree-clad hillside.

'*Wakamkamata,*' Kaizer says. They caught him.

'*Fisi?*' I ask.

'*Fisi wengi, labda sita au saba.*' Lots of *fisis,* maybe six or seven.

'Who fired a gun?' I ask him.

'Bwana Higgs, he shot from his window to frighten them away.' Higgs, Kaizer's brother-in-law, has lost his job as *askari*-boss, but he's being retained to salvage material from the mine. They're demolishing his house last.

'Drunk?' I ask.

'*Lazima,*' he says. Of course. 'But he hit one. Did you hear it scream?' 'I did,' I say. When I get home Umali is waiting. I tell him what I've seen. He shakes his head.

'Everyone knew Mlozi was a mad *mchawi,*' he says, 'but it is horrible to be eaten by a pack of *blurryfucken fisis!*' True, I think. And we always thought Mlozi himself changed into a *fisi* at night. Now *fisis* have eaten *him*. . . That couldn't have been in his plan.

I look at my old friend and mentor. Even this terrible thing about Mlozi doesn't change the awful fact we're about to leave Geita forever. There's a deep sadness in Umali. He looks ancient now, a broken little old man.

I haven't noticed it quite so much before, although he was always old to me. He's even thinner, and his old eyes are misty. His devilish sense of humour has all but abandoned him. He's avoided the subject of us going. His irascible, jocular self is no more. It's like it won't be true if it isn't confirmed by talking. I know how he feels. I'm the same. It's our last day. I don't know how we'll get through it.

I sleep very little that night. Our garden is a dead place now. The *kuku*-run is empty, there's no gentle clucking from the little houses. No *jogoo* will greet the dawn with a raucous 'cock-a-doodle-doo'. There will never be another 'Gooloo-gooloo-gooloo-gooloo!'

Even the surrounding bush is saying goodbye. Where is my old friend the *bundi-msitu* bird? How can he know we're going? Call to me, spook me, just one more time, I implore. He doesn't. Faraway a hyena giggles, some crickets creak, throaty frogs croak from their bushy water-places. The bush can't be completely quiet, no matter how hard it tries. At about three I hear a farewell roar from an old lion. I'm going to miss you, I think miserably, as I try to get to sleep. There's a long journey tomorrow's hateful morning.

One day a fellow East African, though from Kenya, will write a song called 'Morning please don't come'. It isn't written yet, but it's what I'm praying. A line goes ...., *'for you will take my love away from me'*. Please, morning, *don't* come!

I'm sitting on my suitcase. All our furniture, except the beds, was taken away yesterday. They could have left it one more day. Sandy is lying on the floor beside me. Does she know what's happening? Does she know we're going, and she'll never see us again? I look at her. She's very subdued. Of course she knows. At least Umali will look after her. He's always liked her.

It's going on for five o'clock. I hear Umali clanging about in the kitchen. Packing up pots and pans for collection by someone.

He's just got to keep busy. I know him so well. If he stops, he might fall apart. Bustling about is his only way of dealing with pain and anguish. Mum and Becky have finished stuffing last minute things into their cases.

They're doing final checks in different rooms. In case they've forgotten something. There's a bright flash of moving light on the trees down the road. Headlights. Shortly it's in our drive, and there's a crunch of gravel and tyre. The Land Rover hooter shatters the silence. Fritz has arrived. Gretchen is with him. It's time to go.

Amina is controlling her feelings. She isn't crying. She hugs us in turn, taking particular time with Becky. They were always close. She hugs me briefly, and gives me a mock-*finya* on the arm, for old times. I know she's worried about Umali. He's still dawdling in the kitchen.

'*Kuja,* Umali!' she shouts at last, commanding him to come.

Umali shuffles reluctantly out of the kitchen at the last moment. It's as if clattering about in there was shielding him from the truth. He's standing in front of me. I haven't realised I've grown so much bigger than him. When did it happen? His expression is fixed, as if that way he can control his feelings. His shirt, as always, is torn and full of holes, and his ribs stick out on his chest. His thin arms reach out to give me a hug.

I put my arms around him, and it's like caressing a bag of articulated bones. In my arms I'm holding the dearest friend I ever had, more dear even than poor Lutoli, and now I have to let him go, get in the car, and drive away forever. Umali breaks away and pushes me towards the open Land Rover.

I get in beside Gretchen. She told Becky she wants to sit next to me. She wants to 'sort things out'. She doesn't want fifteen years of growing up together to end badly. Becky gets in the other side. Mum climbs in the front passenger seat next to Fritz.

The doors are closed. Umali and Amina are standing together at the bottom of the steps. His hair is as white as the snow on Meru. Amina's crying openly now, intermittently pulling her open hand across her face. Umali looks wooden. There's no expression at all, just a fixed stare.

I want to jump out again, give him another, very last, hug, but Fritz has started the engine, and we begin to roll down the gravel drive. Suddenly Umali turns and runs around the side of the house, out of sight. I notice Tembo standing at the entrance to the drive. He's holding up a hand in farewell. Probably the most demonstrative thing I've seen him do. My vision is obscured by tears, and the lump in my throat threatens to choke me.

'You know, Mrs Penhaligon,' Gretchen says in a mature and adult voice, 'we children had the best upbringing in the world, here in Geita!' Even in this desperate state, I can't disagree. I wouldn't have wanted to grow up anywhere else. The sun's coming up now, illuminating the familiar bush beyond Compound Hill.

Not very far from here runs the little road to Samina, where Dad has rested in his granite grave these ten years, all alone, except for Mrs Williams and Mr Valari (senior). Even nearer is the lonely grave of Fritz's brother, Mrs Williams' driver, killed that fateful morning on the Mwanza road. Lutoli's grave isn't far. And poor old Mlozi? If he was eaten up by the *fisis*, which seems certain, what has become of his physical body? Worse than an *mzoga* in its own ground. He'll be *fisi*-droppings, like those Lutoli and I collected and threw into Becky and Gretchen's independent country of Chola, near our republic of Kichoncho on Compound Hill. It's so long ago. Sad for anyone to end that way. Cycle of life, something we should just accept?

Now I think of it, I don't want to take all this with me. There's got to be another life for us somewhere. I'm leaving Geita, but Geita's leaving me too. The place, the people, dead and alive. Even pretty, sweet Gretchen, sitting right next to me, smiling with those sky-blue eyes, is not part of my future. This is the last time I'll see her. She'll be someone else's wife. Can it be that unrequited love ever endured so long in one boy's life? I turn my face to the window.

I remember something said by a Father at St Mary's. 'The past,' he said, 'is a foreign country.' I know my past will forever be that, a foreign country.

The comforting growl of the old Land Rover's engine is all that will be left once we go down the other side of Compound Hill. In Mwanza, I'll lose that too.

Will I come back as a man one day in the far future? If so, what will I find? Will the ghosts of my childhood be waiting here? And if they aren't? If on that future day I stare out from Compound Hill, to Rijate and Lone Cone, with a great Black *mwewe*-bird circling high above, will I find it impossible to believe anything important ever happened here at all?

END

The sequel to **'Speak Swahili, Dammit!'**, to be called **'A Swahili Mzungu Let Loose'** is due to be published in 2014.

Made in the USA
San Bernardino, CA
08 October 2013